Advances in Computer Vision and Pattern Recognition

More information about this series at http://www.springer.com/series/4205

Ling Shao · Jungong Han
Pushmeet Kohli · Zhengyou Zhang
Editors

Computer Vision and Machine Learning with RGB-D Sensors

Editors
Ling Shao
University of Sheffield
Sheffield
UK

Jungong Han
Civolution Technology
Eindhoven
The Netherlands

Pushmeet Kohli
Microsoft Research
Cambridge
UK

Zhengyou Zhang
Microsoft Research
Redmond, WA
USA

Founding editor
Sameer Singh
Rail Vision Europe Ltd.
Castle Donington, Leicestershire
UK

Series editor
Sing Bing Kang
Interactive Visual Media Group
Microsoft Research
Redmond, WA
USA

ISSN 2191-6586　　　　　　　　ISSN 2191-6594　(electronic)
ISBN 978-3-319-08650-7　　　　ISBN 978-3-319-08651-4　(eBook)
DOI 10.1007/978-3-319-08651-4

Library of Congress Control Number: 2014943409

Springer Cham Heidelberg New York Dordrecht London

© Springer International Publishing Switzerland 2014

This work is subject to copyright. All rights are reserved by the Publisher, whether the whole or part of the material is concerned, specifically the rights of translation, reprinting, reuse of illustrations, recitation, broadcasting, reproduction on microfilms or in any other physical way, and transmission or information storage and retrieval, electronic adaptation, computer software, or by similar or dissimilar methodology now known or hereafter developed. Exempted from this legal reservation are brief excerpts in connection with reviews or scholarly analysis or material supplied specifically for the purpose of being entered and executed on a computer system, for exclusive use by the purchaser of the work. Duplication of this publication or parts thereof is permitted only under the provisions of the Copyright Law of the Publisher's location, in its current version, and permission for use must always be obtained from Springer. Permissions for use may be obtained through RightsLink at the Copyright Clearance Center. Violations are liable to prosecution under the respective Copyright Law.
The use of general descriptive names, registered names, trademarks, service marks, etc. in this publication does not imply, even in the absence of a specific statement, that such names are exempt from the relevant protective laws and regulations and therefore free for general use.
While the advice and information in this book are believed to be true and accurate at the date of publication, neither the authors nor the editors nor the publisher can accept any legal responsibility for any errors or omissions that may be made. The publisher makes no warranty, express or implied, with respect to the material contained herein.

Printed on acid-free paper

Springer is part of Springer Science+Business Media (www.springer.com)

Preface

Depth cameras have been exploited in computer vision for several years, but the high price and poor quality of such devices have limited their applicability. With the invention of the low-cost depth sensors such as Kinect and Time-of-Flight (TOF) cameras, high-resolution depth and visual (RGB) sensing have become available for widespread use as an off-the-shelf technology. The complementary nature of the synchronized depth and RGB information opens up new opportunities to solve fundamental problems in computer vision, including human pose estimation, activity recognition, object and people tracking, 3D mapping and localization, etc. Furthermore, the robustness gained with depth cameras allow us to take computer vision out of the lab and into real environments (e.g., people's homes).

While it is beneficial to use RGB-D sensors in many vision applications such as object/scene recognition, human pose estimation, and gesture/activity recognition, machine learning plays an important role in bridging the gap between feature representations and decision making. For instance, the human pose recognition algorithm associated with Kinect adapts a well-known learning technique into a real-world task, where body parts are inferred using a randomized decision forest, learned from over 1 million training examples. The success of this algorithm bootstraps the investigation of applying intelligent machine learning techniques to this new type of sensor representation. Many systems have already demonstrated the possibility of making a better decision by learning useful information from a large set of RGB-D data.

This book brings together high-quality and recent research advances on RGB-D based computer vision. The targeted readers are researchers and practitioners working in the areas of computer vision, human–computer interaction and machine learning from both academia and industry. It can also be used as a reference book for graduate students studying computer vision, pattern recognition or multimedia.

We generally divide the chapters into four parts. In the first part, we have included two survey chapters, which overview the prior arts in this filed. In the second part, six chapters dedicate to the research of RGB-D based 3D reconstruction, mapping, and synthesis. In the third part, there are two chapters describing novel techniques that employ depth data for object detection, segmentation, and tracking. The last part consists of four chapters, demonstrating accurate interpretations of human actions with the aid of the depth information. In the following we summarize all the chapters.

In Chap. 1, Kadambi et al. explain the theoretical difference between the first generation Kinect and the recent delivered second generation Kinect from depth creation perspective. This chapter also investigates the methods that can correct artifacts on depth maps.

In Chap. 2, Berger summarizes the developments that include two or more RGB-D sensors in one scene. The chapter focus on discussing effective means of mitigating interference errors between multiple sensors in different applications. In addition, the chapter lists the most prominent datasets, which are publicly available.

In Chap. 3, Zhang et al. deal with the problem of calibrating the color and the depth cameras. The algorithm is designed to enhance the traditional checkerboard based calibration scheme because it does not work properly in the particular application. The new algorithm proposes a maximum likelihood solution for the joint depth and color calibration based on the assumption that points on the checkerboard shall lie on a common plane.

In Chap. 4, Koschan and Abidi present a new method to reduce the noise on depth map. Here, a joint bilateral filter is carried out in order to enhance depth information with the aid of color information. The novelty lies in the fact that the joint bilateral filter is applied to a common distance transform map, which represents the degree of pixel-modal similarity between a depth pixel and its corresponding color pixel.

In Chap. 5, Liu et al. aim at capturing real performances of human actors, in which the core problem is to reconstruct 3D human performance. To do so, the algorithm automatically tracks the motion of the handheld cameras and aligns the surface and skeleton of each tracked performer to the captured RGB-D data. In order to solve more practical problems, like occlusions and human body orientation changes, the system synchronize the signals from three handheld Kinects.

In Chap. 6, Liu et al. introduce three interesting applications where analyzing the depth signal plays important roles. In the first application, fusing depth and RGB information helps to accurately reconstruct a real human and provide personalized avatars for users. In the second application, depth-based human skeleton tracking is used to evaluate energy consumption of users during a game playing. In the last application, authors show the possibility of obtaining more accurate human action classification by interpreting the depth map.

In Chap. 7, Feinen and Grzegorzekpresent a novel approach that is able to facilitate the RGB-D object retrieval application. The main idea is to match the curves derived by object contours. However, the traditional 2D curve matching is incapable of handling viewpoint changes. To overcome this problem, this chapter comes up with new ideas that match 3D curve configurations.

In Chap. 8, Berger et al. deal with the application of reconstructing the gas flow from three Kinect cameras. In this chapter, a new subpixel accurate flow detection algorithm is proposed, facilitating the sparse image data such as the Kinect spot pattern. Afterwards, they exploit the sparse spot detection algorithm to provide masks for a GPU-based visual hull reconstruction.

In Chap. 9, Tian develops a RGB-D based computer vision system to assist blind and visually impaired persons. The core technique contributed by the chapter is a stairs and pedestrian crosswalks detection algorithm based on RGB-D images. The system serves as a navigation aid that can help blind users to gain improved perception and better understanding of the environment changes.

In Chap. 10, Han et al. utilize Kinect in a smart environment, where sensing the location and identity of the users is essential. In this chapter, viewpoint invariant features are extracted from the object shape and used for detecting human. Moreover, human re-entry is identified by a boosting-based classification algorithm, in which depth information helps to select suitable positive samples.

In Chap. 11, Dominio et al. discuss the effective features that characterize static hand poses. Several depth-based descriptors have been presented and examined in the chapter. The final conclusion is that some features, such as curvatures, distance, and correlation features, have better performances. The combination of multiple features allows to obtain much better performance.

In Chap. 12, Liang and Yuan present a unified framework to enforce both the temporal and spatial constraints for hand parsing. In this work, a superpixel Markov Random Field is leveraged to efficiently remove the misclassified regions produced by per-pixel classification. Finally, a rotation-invariant hand gesture recognition algorithm is designed to recognize digit number gestures.

In Chap. 13, Krupka et al. describe a novel classifier architecture based on discriminative ferns ensemble. This classifier architecture optimizes both classification speed and accuracy, given a large training set. To speed up the algorithm, simple binary features and direct indexing are employed. In addition, a large capacity model and careful discriminative optimization help to gain the algorithm accuracy.

In Chap. 14, Yao et al. propose a new hand segmentation and gesture recognition system. The contribution is a 3D contour model from the classified pixels. Instead of matching between images, this 3D contour model can be coded into strings. Therefore, the correspondence sample gesture can be found by a fast nearest neighbor searching method.

Sheffield, UK	Ling Shao
Eindhoven, The Netherlands	Jungong Han
Cambridge, UK	Pushmeet Kohli
Redmond, USA	Zhengyou Zhang

Contents

Part I Surveys

1 **3D Depth Cameras in Vision: Benefits and Limitations of the Hardware** 3
Achuta Kadambi, Ayush Bhandari and Ramesh Raskar

2 **A State of the Art Report on Multiple RGB-D Sensor Research and on Publicly Available RGB-D Datasets** 27
Kai Berger

Part II Reconstruction, Mapping and Synthesis

3 **Calibration Between Depth and Color Sensors for Commodity Depth Cameras** 47
Cha Zhang and Zhengyou Zhang

4 **Depth Map Denoising via CDT-Based Joint Bilateral Filter** 65
Andreas Koschan and Mongi Abidi

5 **Human Performance Capture Using Multiple Handheld Kinects** 91
Yebin Liu, Genzhi Ye, Yangang Wang, Qionghai Dai and Christian Theobalt

6 **Human-Centered 3D Home Applications via Low-Cost RGBD Cameras** 109
Zhenbao Liu, Shuhui Bu and Junwei Han

7	**Matching of 3D Objects Based on 3D Curves** .... Christian Feinen, Joanna Czajkowska, Marcin Grzegorzek and Longin Jan Latecki	137
8	**Using Sparse Optical Flow for Two-Phase Gas Flow Capturing with Multiple Kinect** .... Kai Berger, Marc Kastner, Yannic Schroeder and Stefan Guthe	157

Part III Detection, Segmentation and Tracking

9	**RGB-D Sensor-Based Computer Vision Assistive Technology for Visually Impaired Persons.** .... Yingli Tian	173
10	**RGB-D Human Identification and Tracking in a Smart Environment** .... Jungong Han and Junwei Han	195

Part IV Learning-Based Recognition

11	**Feature Descriptors for Depth-Based Hand Gesture Recognition** .... Fabio Dominio, Giulio Marin, Mauro Piazza and Pietro Zanuttigh	215
12	**Hand Parsing and Gesture Recognition with a Commodity Depth Camera** .... Hui Liang and Junsong Yuan	239
13	**Learning Fast Hand Pose Recognition.** .... Eyal Krupka, Alon Vinnikov, Ben Klein, Aharon Bar-Hillel, Daniel Freedman, Simon Stachniak and Cem Keskin	267
14	**Real-Time Hand Gesture Recognition Using RGB-D Sensor.** .... Yuan Yao, Fan Zhang and Yun Fu	289

Index 315

Part I
Surveys

Chapter 1
3D Depth Cameras in Vision: Benefits and Limitations of the Hardware

With an Emphasis on the First- and Second-Generation Kinect Models

Achuta Kadambi, Ayush Bhandari and Ramesh Raskar

Abstract The second-generation Microsoft Kinect uses time-of-flight technology, while the first-generation Kinect uses structured light technology. This raises the question whether one of these technologies is "better" than the other. In this chapter, readers will find an overview of 3D camera technology and the artifacts that occur in depth maps.

1.1 Introduction

The physical world is three-dimensional. It is surprising then that conventional cameras perceive the world in two dimensions, while even primitive animals perceive the world in its richer three-dimensional form. Today, using technology such as Microsoft Kinect, it is possible to collect 3D data with the ease and cost of point-and-shoot photography.

In today's consumer landscape, there are two primary 3D camera technologies: **structured light** and **time of flight**. A structured light camera projects an active pattern and obtains depth by analyzing the deformation of the pattern. The **first-generation Kinect** (2010) is a structured light camera. In contrast, a time-of-flight

---

We thank the following people at the Massachusetts Institute of Technology for their contributions to the chapter: Nikhil Naik, Boxin Shi, Ameya Joshi, Genzhi Ye, Amol Mahurkar, Julio Estrada, Hisham Bedri, and Rohan Puri.

A. Kadambi (✉) · A. Bhandari · R. Raskar
Massachusetts Institute of Technology, Cambridge, MA, USA
e-mail: achoo@mit.edu

A. Bhandari
e-mail: ayush@mit.edu

R. Raskar
e-mail: raskar@mit.edu

© Springer International Publishing Switzerland 2014
L. Shao et al. (eds.), *Computer Vision and Machine Learning with RGB-D Sensors*,
Advances in Computer Vision and Pattern Recognition,
DOI: 10.1007/978-3-319-08651-4_1

camera measures the time that light has been in flight to estimate distance. The **second-generation Kinect** (2013) is a time-of-flight camera. Microsoft's strategy for moving to time of flight for their second Kinect raises the question whether one of these technologies is "better" than the other.

By the end of this chapter, we expect that the reader will have a better understanding of the benefits and limitations of different 3D camera technologies. More importantly, readers will learn the underlying cause behind depth artifacts and the accepted strategies to fix them.

1.2 3D Data Storage

1.2.1 3D Point Clouds

A **point cloud** is set of data points defined in a coordinate system. Using M to refer to the number of points and N for the dimensionality of the space, the point cloud is written as follows:

$$P = \{p_1, \ldots, p_M\} \quad p^T \in \mathrm{R}^N. \tag{1.1}$$

A common technique to store point clouds in memory is to form an by array denoted as P where each row vector in corresponds to a point. We require two conditions to define an N-dimensional point cloud:

1. $p_i^T \in \mathrm{R}^N \quad i = 1, \ldots, M$.
2. The object of interest is in the convex hull of the points.

The first condition is satisfied with any camera that acquires depth. The second condition is more restrictive and is discussed in detail in the 3D scanning section (Sect. 1.9). In this chapter, we are particularly interested in 3D point clouds, i.e., the set of points defined by real-world coordinates X, Y, and Z.

Often we are provided additional information for each point in the cloud. Suppose we are provided a K-tuple of "information" for each point in the cloud. This is described as the following set:

$$F = \{f_1, \ldots, f_M\} \quad f^T \in \mathrm{R}^K. \tag{1.2}$$

which is stored in memory as an M by K array. Taken together, the feature array F and the corresponding point cloud array P represent the space of data we consider in this chapter. As a concrete example, if we are provided the 3-tuple of the color reflectance at each point in R^3, we have color and depth. This is known as **RGB-D acquisition**. For simplicity, we refer to the point set as the "depth data" and the feature set as the "RGB data."

1.2.1.1 A Note on Organized Point Clouds

Point clouds from depth cameras, such as Microsoft Kinect, can be further classified into **organized point clouds**. In such point clouds, it is possible to index the spatial X and Y coordinates in a logical manner, e.g., by rows and columns. In contrast, unorganized point clouds have no structure in the spatial coordinates. Organized point clouds are a much more powerful data format that greatly facilitates registration and other types of vision algorithms.

1.2.2 Registering Color and Depth Data

We must have correspondence between the depth and color data. This would be a simple task if the depth and color maps were acquired with the same camera. In practice, when the cameras are separate, the additional step of registration must be performed on the depth and color maps. Depth registration error is a practical phenomenon that can occur spatially, when shadows or occlusions are present, or temporally, when camera frame rates are not synchronized.

For many computer vision researchers, the registration error may not be significant. However, this may not be true when specific correspondences between depth and color edges are required. To ensure proper calibration between depth and color calibration, note that classic checkerboard calibration [35] is imperfect for depth maps (there are no edges). Zhang and Zhang propose a maximum-likelihood solution that is able to take into account uncertainty in depth values (Fig. 1.1).

1.2.2.1 Sparse Versus Dense Depth Maps

In many modalities, we obtain a point cloud that is **sparse**. In such a case, depth values are provided for only a small subset of coordinates. This commonly occurs

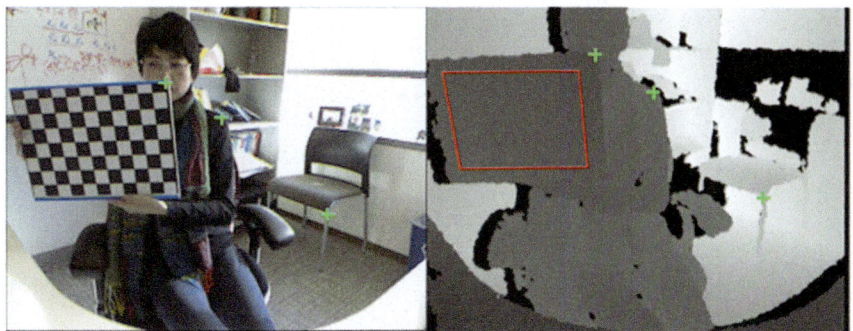

Fig. 1.1 Registering RGB and depth images for commodity depth cameras using a checkerboard. At left is the color image and at right is the depth image [34]

in the case of stereo computer vision where it is challenging to find matches for all points in typical scenes. It can also occur in other modalities to suppress noise, i.e., when many points with a low confidence are redacted. In contrast, a **dense** point cloud has depth for almost every real-world coordinate within the scope of the imaging device. For many applications, it may be desirable to have a few high-confidence 3D coordinates. As a case in point, many finger-tracking algorithms use a sparse depth map to associate hand positions with gestures.

1.3 Universal Artifacts

In this section, we discuss some example artifacts that are present in the depth maps. These artifacts are somewhat universal as they exist in many classes of consumer 3D camera technology (e.g., structured light, time of flight, and stereo). In Sect. 1.3, we discuss artifacts that are relevant to specific computer vision tasks.

1.3.1 Holes

Depth maps can be generated using various methods, including structured light, stereo correspondence, and time of flight. Regardless of the technique, it is common to find **holes** in the depth map, where depth data are missing. An example of this is presented in Fig. 1.2. Observe that the ground truth depth map has no holes, but the recovered depth (with a stereo camera) has many holes.

1.3.1.1 Fixing Holes in Depth Maps

Fixing holes is an important preprocessing step that, if performed correctly, can improve the quality of the depth map. The typical recipe for hole filling is as follows:

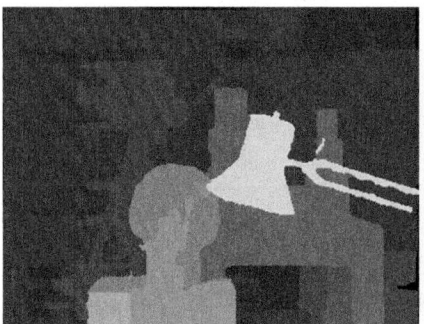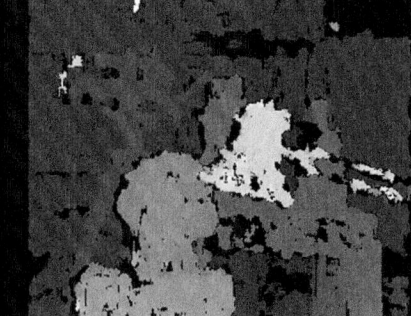

Fig. 1.2 *Left* Ground truth depth map from the Tsukuba dataset. *Right* Measured depth image with a stereo camera. The *black* values are "holes"

1 3D Depth Cameras in Vision: Benefits and Limitations of the Hardware

Fig. 1.3 Bilateral filtering. At *left*, the input is noisy but has a clear edge discontinuity. At *right* is the filtered output. Figure from [6]

Fill the holes by exploring correlations between neighboring depth pixels, subject to the constraint that sharp depth edges are preserved.

A reasonable starting point might involve using a median filter with an adaptive window size to correct for the holes. Unfortunately, this method violates the constraint of keeping the depth edges sharp. The accepted techniques can be broadly divided into **filtering methods** or **classification methods**.

1.3.2 Filtering Methods

A popular hole-filling method is to use a modified **bilateral filter**. Readers may be familiar with the bilateral filter from computer graphics [6]. The basic idea is to smooth noise, while preserving sharp edge discontinuities (Fig. 1.3). A bilateral filter can be transposed to operate on 3D point clouds and is often a standard processing step in the API of camera manufacturers.

One extension is to combine a temporal approach with bilateral filtering to achieve the dual goal of preserving edge discontinuities and filling holes [4]. In particular, a joint bilateral filter is used:

$$D_f^p = \frac{H(C_{\text{map}}, \Omega^p)}{k^p} \sum_{q \in \Omega^p} \hat{D}^q f(p, q) h(\|I^p - I^q\|) \qquad (1.3)$$

where $H(C_{\text{map}}, \Omega^p)$ is a function that evaluates the reliability of the depth values in the neighborhood Ω^p. This additional function allows the filter weights to be selected by discriminating between pixels that belong to different objects. Figure 1.4 shows the published results of the technique.

Another hole-filling technique combines belief propagation with the additional step of cross-checking two input images to identify the confidence level of a pixel [1]. The depth map is then smoothed by using color information and the confidence labels. In the final step, the authors utilize an anisotropic diffusion technique for disparity map refinement. A key point to note is that in anisotropic diffusion, depth edges are not smoothed. This adaptive smoothing method is called *directed anisotropic diffusion*. Figure 1.5 shows a few of the published results.

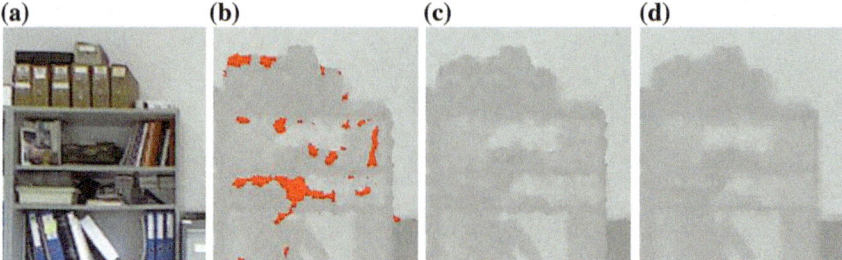

Fig. 1.4 a A cluttered scene. **b** Holes in the depth map; observe the co-occurrence of shadows. **c** Intermediate filtering. **d** Filled holes using neighborhood information. Figure from [4]

Fig. 1.5 Anisotropic filtering from [1]. The first row consists of reference images, the second row the smoothed depths, and the last row the ground truth

1.3.3 Segmentation/Classification Methods

An alternate strategy to fill holes is to exploit classification information. If two pixels belong to the same object, it is possible that the depth values can be robustly interpolated. As such, color-based segmentation and clustering is an extremely popular hole-filling technique [19, 33]. In [18], a color-based clustering method is combined with change detection to find coherent pixels (Fig. 1.6). The key addition is change detection that allows static objects to be classified together. This result is shown in Fig. 1.7.

1.4 Causes for Holes

Why do holes occur in depth images? The most common reason for holes is **occlusions**. Many 3D cameras require different views of an object to obtain depth. When an occlusion occurs, the object is present in only one view and it is not possible to obtain depth. In a more general sense, any time there is a **matching ambiguity**, holes can be found. Such ambiguities occur in ill-posed matching problems, i.e., when point correspondences cannot be found. Note that because time-of-flight sensors use a single viewpoint to obtain depth, occlusions and matching ambiguities are non-factors. Another source of error occurs at **depth discontinuities** where windowing effects smear the foreground and background depths together. Windowing is a rather broad term and encompasses both hardware-level windowing, e.g., by "flying pixels" in time-of-flight range imaging, and software-level windowing, e.g., by patch-based correspondence.

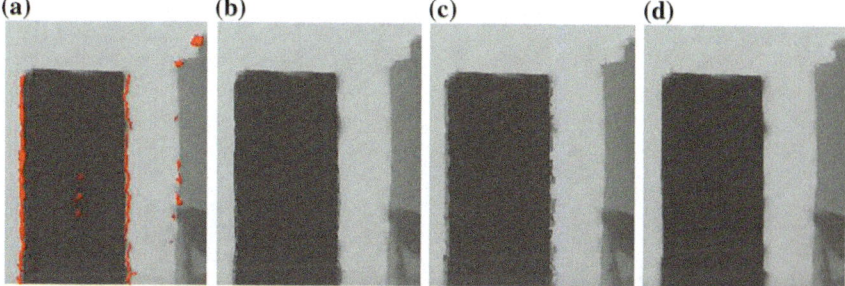

Fig. 1.6 Filling holes on the 2010 Kinect for Xbox 360. **a** Kinect depth map; observe the holes in *red*. **b** A simple median filter. **c** Inpainting algorithms. **d** Strategy from [4]

Fig. 1.7 Intensity-based segmentation. *Left* Depth map with many holes. *Right* Processed depth map with the spatiotemporal technique of [18]

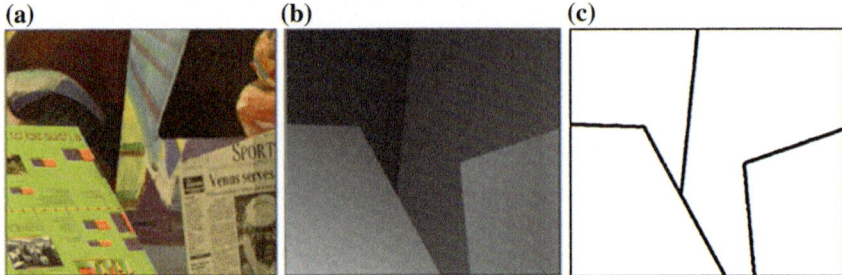

Fig. 1.8 **a** Photograph of a scene. **b** Depth map. **c** Depth edges

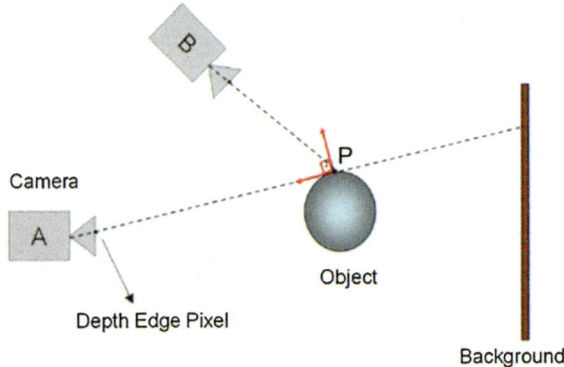

Fig. 1.9 Depth edges are view dependent. The surface point *P* corresponds to an edge in camera *A* but not in camera *B*

1.4.1 Morphological Edge Erosion

Another important artifact in depth images is the lack of sharp edges. Depth discontinuities, also known as depth edges or occluding contours, correspond to sharp changes in a depth map of the scene. An example of a depth map and its depth edges is illustrated in Fig. 1.8. Depth edges, such as intensity edges, form the backbone of several vision algorithms. Thus, it is very desirable to preserve sharp depth edges that correctly map to the scene.

The first thing to note about depth edges is that they are view dependent. As illustrated in Fig. 1.9, depending on the camera viewpoint, surface points may or may not correspond to edges [3]. Parallax-based methods, such as structured light and stereo, use different viewpoints and can therefore lead to smoothing of depth edges. In particular, the tendency of parallax-based methods to use window-based correspondence exacerbates the problem, and recovered edges are often smoothed to an intolerable degree.

Sharpening edges in stereo range images is not new task; we refer to the following classic papers for extensive discussion on the topic: [7, 22, 25]. A reasonable solution is to reduce the patch size (for correspondence) in a carefully chosen manner. For instance, in [14] and [17], the window size is reduced based on the amount of disparity variation. While the edges are indeed sharper, the technique is considered computationally expensive. Another alternative is to rectify the edges in *post-processing* of the depth map. One option is to employ bilateral filtering in a similar fashion to the hole-filling algorithms discussed in Sect. 1.3.1.1. For example, in [5], they combine color data with joint bilateral filtering in the depth images to preserve edges. They demonstrate results on the first-generation Kinect that uses structured light. The idea is as follows: First, using the RGB image, pixels with the wrong depth values are detected and removed with a region growing method. This creates holes, which are now filled with a joint bilateral filter that is carefully chosen in context of the noise properties of Kinect [5].

In short, the basic idea for any type of edge rectification for parallax-based 3D cameras is very similar to the techniques used in hole-filling algorithms. Some key priors include edge correspondence between the color and depth images [5] and color- or motion-based segmentation [18, 33].

In time-of-flight cameras, the situation is a bit different. Since only one viewpoint is used to obtain depth, the edges are often much sharper. We must remark that current generations of ToF sensors have low spatial resolution and this can lead to optical mixing of foreground and background objects [16]. Despite this, depth edges are still better preserved in time-of-flight sensors and the depth edges do not need to be post-processed to the degree of structured light systems. Of course, post-processing can still be applied to improve the acquired depth map. For example, in [31], an algorithm is proposed to find straight edges in the depth image. In [20], a denoising algorithm that implements the total variation image prior is used. The total variation prior minimizes the Manhattan (L1) norm of the gradient and has been shown to promote piecewise smooth functions. The result from [20] is shown in Fig. 1.10.

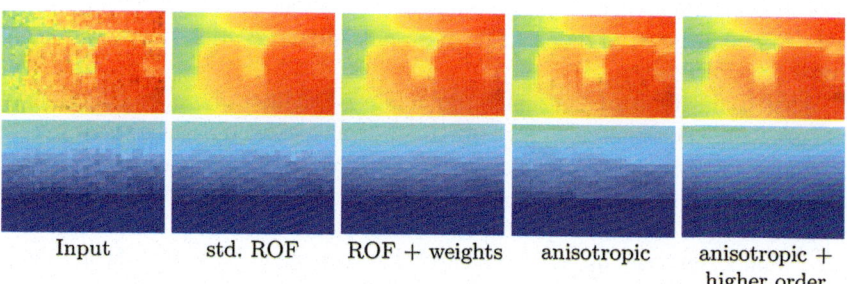

Fig. 1.10 Enhancing edges in time-of-flight imaging. At *left* is the input and at *right* is the anisotropic total variation method from [20]

1.5 Ambient Lighting

Ambient lighting can be a problem for some 3D cameras that use active illumination, such as stereo or structured light sensors. Creating cameras that can operate in ambient lighting fills a practical need. One such example occurs in outdoor robotics, where 3D cameras are trusted to work in sunlight.

Each 3D technology is affected by ambient lighting in different ways. Computer stereovision does not rely upon active illumination and is therefore robust to ambient lighting. In contrast, structured light relies upon a projected intensity pattern to obtain depth. The pattern can become corrupted by ambient light and ambient shadows. We may therefore state that structured light cameras are, in general, not robust to ambient light. Infrared structured light systems, such as the first-generation Kinect, use an optical filter to reject wavelengths that are not in the active illumination, but this helps only marginally (sunlight contains a significant amount of near-infrared light).

The new Kinect uses time of flight to obtain depth. This technique is resistant to ambient light, allowing the new Kinect to be used outdoors. However, when the scene is too bright, the imaging sensor saturates and all information is lost. In outdoor experiments, the time-of-flight Kinect outperforms the old structured light Kinect. For details on why the new Kinect is resistant to ambient light, please refer to Sect. 1.11.

1.6 Motion

The 3D cameras that we consider are all designed to operate on **dynamic scenes** where there is motion. That this capability exists is a testament to strong hardware design and development: Many of the 3D sensors are inherently multishot techniques. Concretely, this means that multiple photographs of the scene (these are called subframes) are required to obtain a single depth frame. If there is substantial motion between the subframes, severe artifacts will be seen in the depth frame.

What is the limit of consumer technology? Qualitatively, a speeding car at 60 mph cannot be captured with an active 3D depth camera (consumer grade), but a person performing an exercise activity can be captured. A separate issue is in synchronization of the optical and imaging elements. In the standard computer vision practice, motion blur has not been, to the best of our knowledge a key issue. For less common applications, such as using 3D time-of-flight sensors for heart motion detection, it is necessary to preprocess the subframes using an algorithm like optical flow [26]. A similar "flowlike" preprocessing step is also described in [11].

1 3D Depth Cameras in Vision: Benefits and Limitations of the Hardware

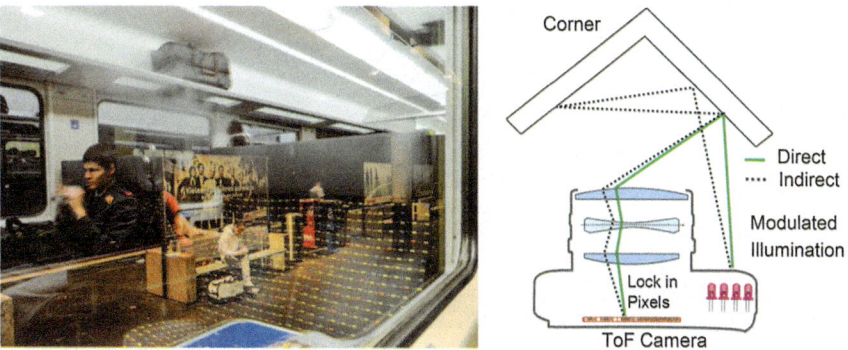

Fig. 1.11 *Left* Example scene with multiple reflections. Photograph courtesy Ayush Bhandari. Shot in a train station in Switzerland. *Right* Multiple interreflections smear together at a corner and provide incorrect depth readings

1.6.1 Multiple Reflections

When multiple reflections return to the camera, it is challenging for 3D cameras to obtain the correct depth. As an example scenario, consider a translucent object like a glass cup which contributes reflections from the glass and the background behind. As a real-world scene, consider Fig. 1.11, where the glass window of the train exhibits multiple reflections. Another realistic scene occurs at a corner, where multiple interreflections smear together (Fig. 1.11).

Handling multiple reflections is a very active problem in 3D camera design. However, the solutions are specific to the type of 3D technology. We discuss these problems in more detail in the specific sections on time of flight and structured light (Sects. 2.4 and 2.5, respectively).

1.7 Depth Artifacts for Specific Vision Tasks

1.7.1 Scene Understanding

Scene understanding is a core problem of high-level computer vision. In recent years, RGB-D data are being widely adapted for object recognition and scene-understanding applications in computer vision, due to availability of affordable depth cameras such as Microsoft Kinect. RGB-D systems provide both 3D information and an ambient illumination-independent channel, increasing the accuracy and robustness of these applications as compared to just RGB image data. However, these methods need to deal with inaccuracies and noise introduced in depth capture process. In this section, we summarize the commonly observed artifacts in depth maps. We focus on indoor scenes, which feature predominantly in these research problems (Fig. 1.12).

Fig. 1.12 Artifacts commonly occur in depth capture of natural scenes using commercial 3D cameras. *Left* RGB image. *Right* Depth map captured by the first-generation Kinect of the same scene. Pixels in *white* are holes in the depth map which arise due to specularities occlusion or clutter. Image courtesy [9]

The artifacts in depth maps that are introduced by the scene being observed are mainly related to ambient illumination, reflectance properties of objects in the scene, and their spatial configuration. Bright ambient illumination can affect the contrast of infrared images in active light sensors, resulting in outliers or holes in the depth map. A cluttered spatial configuration of objects can create occlusions and shadows, which also produces holes in the depth image. Moreover, smooth and specular surfaces appear overexposed in the infrared image, generating holes in the depth map. Currently, computer vision algorithms deal with holes in depth maps using simple inpainting methods [9, 28] (PrimeSense). Applying some of the more sophisticated filtering techniques may improve accuracy for scene-understanding tasks.[1,2]

1.7.2 3D Indoor Mapping

Obtaining a full 3D map of an indoor scene is a classic use case of 3D cameras. We now describe in specific detail the artifacts that occur when obtaining a full 3D map of an indoor environment.

1.8 The Drift Problem

The drift problem usually occurs when the depth camera is facing a scene with poor geometric variation, such as a planar wall. These scenes lack constraints on the degrees of freedom, and thus, estimating the camera pose is challenging. As a

---

[1] This is an open question.
[2] A related question: what impact will the new Kinect have on the accuracy of current scene-understanding techniques?

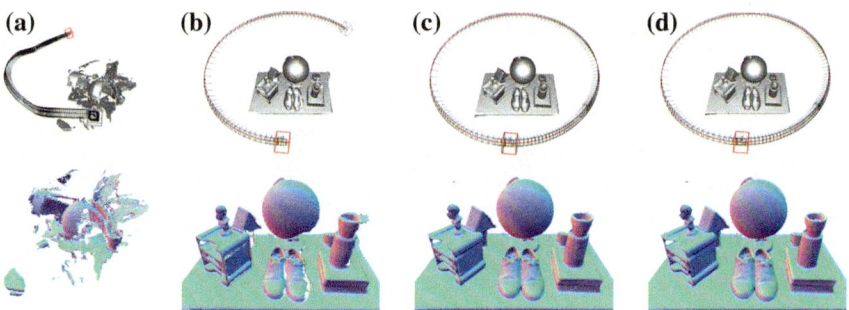

Fig. 1.13 Comparison between frame-to-frame alignment and Kinect fusion [13]. **a** Frame to frame tracking. **b** Partial loop. **c** Full loop. **d** M times duplicated loop

result, the camera trajectory undergoes an uncontrolled drift in front of the scene. To overcome this issue, data from the color camera are necessary to constrain the problem. Since the features extracted in the RGB image will provide a strong localization cue, one can design a combined RGB-D camera system for localization and mapping [10]. By fusing data from the RGB camera and contour information from the depth camera, it is possible to mitigate the drift problem.

1.8.1 Accumulation Error

Due to memory constraints, most localization methods operate on a frame-to-frame basis. This is a sort of Markovian property: To recover the camera parameters for the current frame, we only consider shape alignment for the previous frame. Unfortunately, errors accumulate during the alignment process which can increase into significant artifacts over time. This is known as **accumulation error**, and the severity of artifacts is depicted in Fig. 1.13a. To resolve this problem, [24] and [13] propose a **global alignment** framework to eliminate the accumulation error. Instead of aligning the current frame only to previous frame, Kinect Fusion will align to all the frames which are already aligned. Here, the error introduced by each alignment step is not added together. The improvement in indoor mapping and camera localization is quite dramatic: Compare Fig. 1.13a with Fig. 1.13b–d.

1.8.1.1 Non-rigid Effects

A **rigid** alignment is one where a single transformation operates on each point. In contrast, in a **non-rigid** alignment, the transformation varies for different points. When performing indoor mapping, a typical assumption is that the scene is static. When this is not true a part of the scene is moving. Therefore, the transformation should be different for the moving portions: This is an example of non-rigidity in the mapping

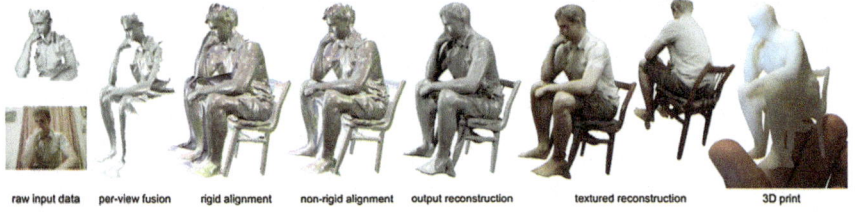

Fig. 1.14 3D scanning pipeline using the first-generation Kinect. The end result is a high-quality fabrication that can be 3D printed. Figure from [21]

process. In [32], a dynamic model of the scene is used as a template. By explicitly factorizing motion using such models and priors, it is possible to mitigate non-rigid artifacts.

1.9 3D Scanning for Fabrication

The previous section discussed indoor mapping of rooms. In this section, we discuss a related problem: high-quality 3D scanning of an object using consumer 3D cameras. Three-dimensional cameras are often described as "**2.5-dimensional**" cameras. Concretely, when using a Kinect to scan a human being, the camera is unable to obtain point coordinates for the backside of the human. In practice, the object of interest is rotated and the resulting point clouds are aligned.

The same artifacts that are present in Sect. 1.7.2 are also germane to 3D scanning. In particular, in Fig. 1.14, a high-quality 3D scan of a person is obtained by using a non-rigid alignment (this mitigates the motion of the person during and between scans). An additional design constraint is in the quality. Since 3D scanning often leads to 3D fabrication, high accuracy and detail are required. In [21], watertight algorithms are used to close up holes.

1.9.1 Finger Tracking

Another common application is finger tracking. Not surprisingly, 3D imaging of fingers is a challenging task due to the small scale of the scene (a finger is approximately 1 cm thick). The list of artifacts is long. Motion artifacts persist, especially when multipattern structured light techniques are used. Lack of clean depth edges due to parallax effects is also prevalent. In addition, line-of-sight obstruction, holes, and poor behavior in sunlight are further sources of artifacts.

With the advent of the new time-of-flight Kinect, several of these problems may be fixed. For the computer vision practitioner, we suggest using a time-of-flight 3D camera for finger tracking as occlusions, ambient light, and motion artifacts are mitigated (Fig. 1.15).

1 3D Depth Cameras in Vision: Benefits and Limitations of the Hardware

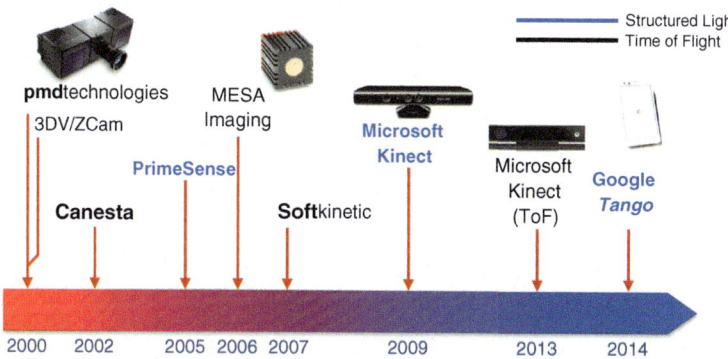

Fig. 1.15 Time line of structured light (*blue*) and time-of-flight sensors (*black*)

1.10 Time-of-Flight Depth Sensors

Time-of-flight cameras are a recent development that offer an interesting alternative to other ranging methods. As the name suggests, this optical instrument operates on the **time-of-flight principle**, where the depth of the object corresponds to the time that the light has been in flight. If the time delay is known, elementary kinematic equations are used to obtain the distance to the object. Consumer quality time-of-flight cameras are developed by a number of firms including MESA imaging system, SoftKinetic, PMD Technologies, and Microsoft, to name a few. One notable example of a consumer-grade sensor based on time-of-flight principle is Microsoft Kinect for Xbox One (2013).

In principle, we must mention that the time-of-flight principle is not a new technology. It has been used for decades in SONAR, spectrometry, spectroscopy and velocimetry, to name a few. However, recent advances in hardware have facilitated the inclusion of **time-of-flight cameras** into the consumer arena. To illustrate the rigor placed on the hardware, consider the following: Light travels one foot in a nanosecond. Thus, to obtain depth to centimeter accuracy, the hardware must be able to detect electronic delays on the order of 100 picoseconds, with the additional constraint that this must be done for each pixel in the array. The data that are obtained from time-of-flight cameras include an intensity image or amplitude image and an image of the time delays, which we refer to as the depth image.

1.10.1 Second-Generation Kinect

Although there are many flavors of "time of flight," we discuss only the operating principle that forms the technological core of the Kinect One. The basic idea is as follows. The Kinect contains a **reference signal** that modulates at a modulation frequency ω (the typical range of ω is between 50 and 150 MHz). The reference signal

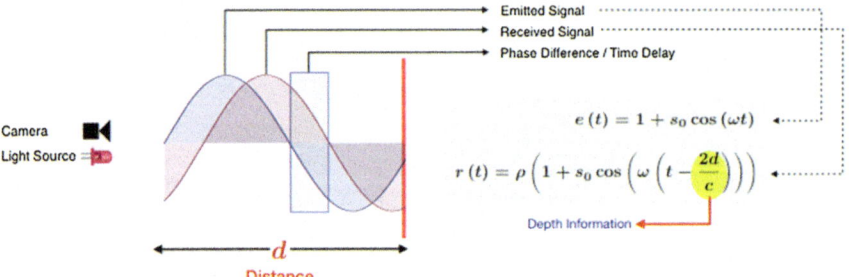

Fig. 1.16 Operating principle of the Kinect One. A phase difference between emitted and received signals encodes the distance

also drives a synchronized solid-state light source to strobe at a sinusoidal pattern. When the optical signal hits an object and returns to the camera, the waveform is offset in phase from the reference signal (Fig. 1.16). The phase offset encodes the depth of the object, and the intensity of the reflection encodes the albedo.

In particular, the light source emits a continuous-wave, periodic signal of form, $e(t) = 1 + s_0 \cos(\omega t)$ Upon reflection from an object at some given distance, the received signal assumes the form of

$$r(t) = \rho \left(1 + s_0 \cos \left(\omega \left(t - \frac{2d}{c}\right)\right)\right) \quad (1.4)$$

Each pixel in the time-of-flight camera samples the cross-correlation function between the transmitted signal and the received signal:

$$\underbrace{C_{e,r}(\tau\kappa)}_{\text{Cross-Correlation}} = \rho \left(1 + \frac{s_0^2}{2} \cos(\omega\tau + \phi)\right), \tau\kappa = \frac{k\pi}{2\omega}, k = 0, \ldots, 3 \quad (1.5)$$

where the phase of the fundamental frequency bin of the cross-correlation function encodes the depth. In principle, note that the fundamental frequency bin includes contributions only from optical sources that are modulated at frequency ω.

1.11 Benefits and Limitations of Time of Flight

A key advantage of time-of-flight cameras is that only a single viewpoint is used to compute depth. This allows robustness to occlusions and shadows and preservation of sharp depth edges. Recall that the existence of holes was largely due to occlusions, and as such, the single viewpoint of a ToF depth sensor is a very significant benefit. Another advantage is that ambient light is rejected (since it does not modulate at frequency ω) (Fig. 1.17).

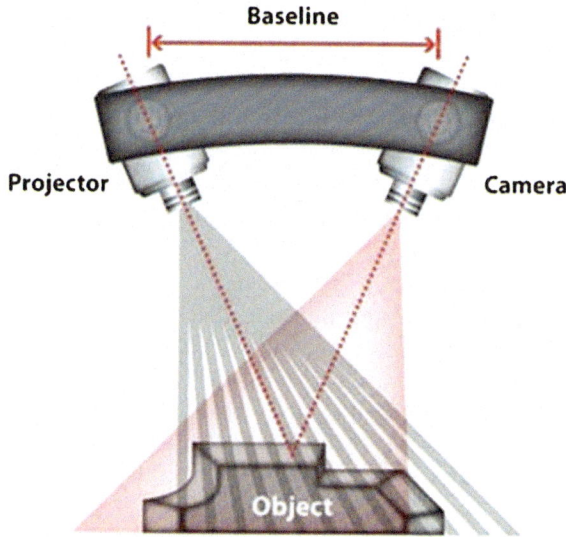

Fig. 1.17 Structured light system. Instead of using two cameras, the vision system uses one projector and one camera

Currently, time-of-flight cameras suffer from a low spatial resolution due to the extra processing that happens at the sensor level. Ambient light can still saturate the sensor, in which case the depth values are meaningless. Like multipattern structured light systems, time-of-flight cameras also require multiple shots. Therefore, the technique is susceptible to motion artifacts.

1.12 Structured Light Depth Sensors

Structured light-based depth estimation can be viewed as a specific case of stereo-vision system where a projector replaces one of the two cameras (Fig. 1.2). In this setting, structured light works by projecting a known pattern onto the subject of interest and the distortion in the project pattern encodes the depth information of the scene.

1.13 First-Generation Kinect (2010)

The first-generation Microsoft Kinect-based sensors use structured light for depth estimation. The system involves a colored camera, an infrared camera, and an infrared laser. The infrared laser emits a beam of light that in turn is split into multiple beams of light through the diffraction grating mechanism. This assembly mimics the operation of a projector. The projected pattern is captured by the infrared camera and is compared against the known reference code. The disparity between the projected code and the observed code accounts for the depth information of the scene.

1.14 Structured Light Benefits and Limitations

A major advantage of structured light is that it can achieve very high spatial resolution since it uses a conventional imaging device. Structured light systems do not require any special treatment at the sensor level. These systems are simple enough to construct at home using a projector and camera. One of the major advantages of the structured light-based imaging systems is that it circumvents the correspondence problem of stereovision-based systems. This is because any disparity in the setup can be calibrated from the knowledge of distortions in the projected pattern.

For comparable accuracy to a ToF camera, sequential projection of coded or phase-shifted patterns is often required to extract a single depth frame, which leads to *lower frame rate*. This is a restriction in that the subject is required to be relatively still during the projection phase. If the subject moves during the time when the pattern is projected, then the measurements will be characterized by motion artifacts. Another limitation is that the reflected pattern is sensitive to optical interference from the environment. As a result, structured light-based methods tend to be more suited for indoor applications where the environment is controlled. Because structured light systems still rely on optical disparity, the technique is sensitive to occlusions and, by extension, to holes.

1.15 Comparison of First- and Second-Generation Kinect Models

The first-generation Kinect is a structured light vision system, while the second-generation Kinect is a time-of-flight system. Figure 1.18 illustrates the time line of the Kinect projects. Notable landmarks include the development of the first-generation Kinect in 2010, the Kinect Fusion algorithm in 2013 (Sect. 1.7.2), and the second-generation Kinect in 2013. In summer of 2014, an API for the second-generation Kinect is scheduled for release.

1.15.1 Hardware Specifications

Figure 1.19 tabulates the hardware specifications of the Kinect models. Note that despite the low spatial resolution that usually plagues ToF cameras, both sensors have similar spatial resolutions. The second-generation Kinect has a larger field of view, and therefore, it does not require a tilt motor. Beyond the inherent advantages

1 3D Depth Cameras in Vision: Benefits and Limitations of the Hardware

Fig. 1.18 Time line of the Kinect projects. The structured light Kinect was released in 2010, while the time-of-flight Kinect was released in 2013. Graphic courtesy John Elsbree

Comparing the Different Kinect Generations	1st Generation Kinect	2nd Generation Kinect
Color resolution/rate	1280x960 @ 12 Hz *or* 640x480 @ 30 Hz	1920x1080 @ 30 Hz
Infrared resolution/rate	640x480 @ 30 Hz	512x424 @ 30 Hz
Depth resolution/rate	320x240 @ 30 Hz	512x424 @ 30 Hz
Depth range*	0.4 m – 3.0 m *or* 0.8 m – 4.0 m	0.5 m – 4.5 m
Depth sensing technology	Structured light	Time-of-flight
Field of view (horizontal)	58°	71°
Mic array	4 elements	4 elements
Tilt motor	±27°	none

Reliable range; additional range possible, depending on conditions

Fig. 1.19 Hardware specifications of the first- and second-generation Kinect models

of time-of-flight technology, the second-generation Kinect also boasts a higher depth resolution, though this has not yet been verified.

1.16 3D Cameras of the Future

Kinect-style 3D cameras represent only a small part of 3D camera technology. In this section, we cover some technologies that may be of interest for applications outside the living room.

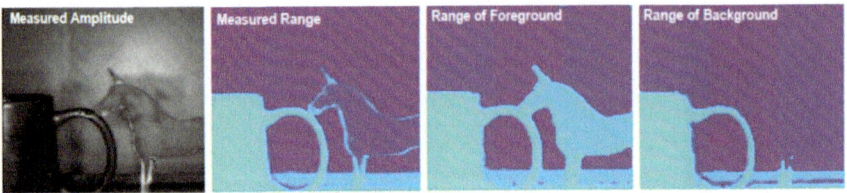

Fig. 1.20 A modified time-of-flight camera is able to recover the depth of the translucent unicorn. This is an example of emerging multidepth cameras. Figure from [16]

1.16.1 Multidepth 3D Cameras

Figure 1.11 provided brief insight into the problem of multiple reflections. Recently, several papers extend the time-of-flight camera paradigm to handle multiple depths that arise in a variety of scenarios. One such scenario is shown in Fig. 1.20, where a modified time-of-flight camera is able to recover the range of a translucent horse [16]. Other related papers include [2, 8, 23] and [29].

In Sect. 1.2.2, the registration of color and depth data was discussed. An interesting topic is whether it is possible to acquire both color images and depth maps with a single camera. In [15], a real-time implementation was proposed that extends time-of-flight technology to multiplex active light sources to provide color and range simultaneously.

1.16.2 Photometric Approaches

In addition to the depth sensor based on geometric approach, photometric cues play an important role in estimating the 3D information. The intuition here is that the object appearance viewed from a fixed position will be different, depending on the various lighting conditions. For example, given a white sphere illuminated by a point source which is far away, the surface points whose normal orientations have smaller angles with the lighting direction look brighter and vice versa. The shape estimation methods relying on the photometric information mainly include two types: (1) shape-from-shading [12], which uses only one image and can only recover the shape up to some ambiguities, and (2) photometric stereo [30], which uses at least three images from fixed viewpoint and different lighting directions to uniquely determine the shape. Note that the direct output of photometric approaches is surface normal, which is the derivative of surface. In order to reconstruct the 3D points or depth, integration has to be applied on surface normal.

Compared to a geometric approach, the main advantage of the photometric approach lies in its ability to recover delicate surface structures. Since the photometric approach relies on the analysis of how light interacts with surface reflectance, the quality of shape estimation depends heavily on the reflectance of target object.

Fig. 1.21 The photometric stereo 3D camera—GelSight (Johnson 2011) and its reconstruction of human skin

A comprehensive evaluation on surface normal estimation accuracy versus real-world reflectances can be found in [27].

If the surface reflectance can be carefully calibrated, the photometric-based 3D camera can be applied to sense microscopic surface structure (Johnson 2011). As shown in Fig. 1.21, the GelSight camera demonstrates a depth resolution of 2 microns, which is superior to geometric-based approaches (and of course Kinect-style cameras).

1.17 Mobile 3D Cameras

As the cost and size of mobile cameras and 3D sensors continue to decrease, consumer electronic manufacturers are finding it increasingly more feasible to incorporate 3D cameras into the next generation of mobile devices. In particular, industry trends show an intensified focus on applications within the context of augmented reality, image refocusing, and real-time key point tracking.

The LG Thrill was one of the first consumer mobile 3D devices (2010). This Android-powered smartphone featured two 5-megapixel cameras that used the stereoscopic effect to capturing 3D pictures and video. Even though the device was equipped with a glasses-free 3D display to match, it ultimately failed to take hold in the market because of its excessive weight and size and relatively poor photograph quality. In 2012, Pelican Imaging released a small 3-mm-thick light field camera array that can be embedded into mobile platforms. To calculate depth, Pelican uses integrated parallax detection and super-resolution (Fig. 1.22).

Fig. 1.22 *Left* Pelican's mobile light field camera. *Right* Google's Project Tango is an integrated mobile phone and 3D camera that projects an active pattern

In early 2014, Google's "Project Tango" smartphone, designed to calculate its orientation and location in three-dimensional space, was announced. This device is capable of collecting 3D data using structured IR and near-IR light. Alongside the device are two dedicated computer vision processors and a wide-angle motion-tracking camera that allow it to collect 250,000 3D measurements per second (Fig. 1.22). Most recently, HTC's One M8, released in early 2014, uses high-resolution stereoscopic cameras for refocus and background manipulation.

1.18 Conclusion

Three-dimensional cameras are primed to change computer vision in a meaningful way. However, 3D data must be used with caution. Rather than simply plugging in a depth map into an application, it is important to ensure that the depth map is a meaningful 3D representation of the scene; this usually requires correction of artifacts (the two main artifacts in depth maps are holes and edge erosion).

Let us return to the query that was posed in the initial stages of this chapter: Is time of flight "better" than structured light? We can now provide the following answer: *It depends on the task*. Concretely, Sect. 1.9.1 mentioned that finger tracking with a structured light camera is prone to holes caused by line-of-sight obstruction. Therefore, we can recommend using a comparable time-of-flight sensor for this application.

A final question that is raised is whether the technology used to capture the 3D data has any impact on the higher-level algorithms that are used. As a concrete example, if a scene-understanding researcher is collecting a dataset, does she need to discriminate between data that is collected with the first-generation Kinect or the second-generation Kinect? Will she see a significant improvement in performance? This is an open question.

References

1. Banno A, Ikeuchi K (2011) Disparity map refinement and 3d surface smoothing via directed anisotropic diffusion. Comput Vis Image Underst 115(5):611–619
2. Bhandari A, Kadambi A, Whyte R, Barsi C, Feigin M, Dorrington A, Raskar R (2014) Resolving multipath interference in time-of-flight imaging via modulation frequency diversity and sparse regularization. Opt Lett 39(6):1705–1708
3. Birchfield S, Tomasi C (1999) Depth discontinuities by pixel-to-pixel stereo. Int J Comput Vis 35(3):269–293
4. Camplani M, Salgado L (2012) Efficient spatio-temporal hole filling strategy for kinect depth maps. In: Proceedings of SPIE, vol 8920
5. Chen L, Lin H, Li S (2012) Depth image enhancement for kinect using region growing and bilateral filter. In: 21st international conference on pattern recognition (ICPR), 2012, pp 3070–3073. IEEE
6. Durand F, Dorsey J (2002) Fast bilateral filtering for the display of high-dynamic-range images. In: ACM transactions on graphics (TOG), vol 21, pp 257–66. ACM
7. Grimson WEL (1985) Computational experiments with a feature based stereo algorithm. IEEE Trans Pattern Anal Mach Intell 1:17–34
8. Heide F, Hullin MB, Gregson J, Heidrich W (2013) Low-budget transient imaging using photonic mixer devices. ACM Trans Graph (TOG) 32(4):45
9. Henry P, Krainin M, Herbst E, Ren X, Fox D (2014) RGB-D mapping: using depth cameras for dense 3D modeling of indoor environments. In: Experimental robotics, pp 477–491. Springer, Berlin
10. Henry P, Krainin M, Herbst E, Ren X, Fox D (2012) RGB-D mapping: using kinect-style depth cameras for dense 3D modeling of indoor environments. Int J Robot Res 31(5):647–63
11. Hoegg T, Lefloch D, Kolb A (2013) Real-time motion artifact compensation for PMD-ToF images. In: Time-of-flight and depth imaging. Sensors, algorithms, and applications, pp 273–288. Springer, Berlin
12. Horn BKP (1970) Shape from shading: a method for obtaining the shape of a smooth opaque object from one view
13. Izadi S, Kim D, Hilliges O, Molyneaux D, Newcombe R, Kohli P, Shotton J, et al (2011) KinectFusion: real-time 3D reconstruction and interaction using a moving depth camera. In: Proceedings of the 24th annual ACM symposium on user interface software and technology, pp 559–568. ACM
14. Jones DG, Malik J (1992) Computational framework for determining stereo correspondence from a set of linear spatial filters. Image Vis Comput 10(10):699–708
15. Kadambi A, Bhandari A, Whyte R, Dorrington A, Raskar R (2014) Demultiplexing illumination via low cost sensing and nanosecond coding. In: 2014 IEEE international conference on computational photography (ICCP). IEEE
16. Kadambi A, Whyte R, Bhandari A, Streeter L, Barsi C, Dorrington A, Raskar R (2013) Coded time of flight cameras: sparse deconvolution to address multipath interference and recover time profiles. ACM Trans Graph (TOG) 32(6):167
17. Kanade T, Okutomi M (1994) A stereo matching algorithm with an adaptive window: theory and experiment. IEEE Trans Pattern Anal Mach Intell 16(9):920–932
18. Kauff P, Atzpadin N, Fehn C, Müller M, Schreer O, Smolic A, Tanger R (2007) Depth map creation and image-based rendering for advanced 3DTV services providing interoperability and scalability. Sig Process Image Commun 22(2):217–234
19. Klaus A, Sormann M, Karner K (2006) Segment-based stereo matching using belief propagation and a self-adapting dissimilarity measure. In: 18th international conference on pattern recognition, 2006. ICPR 2006, vol 3, pp 15–18. IEEE
20. Lenzen F, Schäfer H, Garbe C (2011) Denoising time-of-flight data with adaptive total variation. In: Advances in visual computing, pp 337–346. Springer, Berlin
21. Li H, Vouga E, Gudym A, Luo L, Barron JT, Gusev G (2013) 3D self-portraits. ACM Trans Graph (TOG) 32(6):187

22. Marr D, Poggio T (1976) Cooperative computation of stereo disparity. Science 194(4262):283–287
23. Naik N, Zhao S, Velten A, Raskar R, Bala K (2011) Single view reflectance capture using multiplexed scattering and time-of-flight imaging. In: ACM Transactions on Graphics (TOG), vol 30, p 171. ACM
24. Newcombe RA, Davison AJ, Izadi S, Kohli P, Hilliges O, Shotton J, Molyneaux D, Hodges S, Kim D, Fitzgibbon A (2011) KinectFusion: real-time dense surface mapping and tracking. In: 2011 10th IEEE international symposium on mixed and augmented reality (ISMAR), pp 127–136. IEEE
25. Ohta Y, Kanade T (1985) Stereo by intra-and inter-scanline search using dynamic programming. IEEE Trans Pattern Anal Mach Intell 2:139–154
26. Penne J, Schaller C, Hornegger J, Kuwert T (2008) Robust real-time 3D respiratory motion detection using time-of-flight cameras. Int J Comput Assist Radiol Surg 3(5):427–431
27. Shi B, Tan P, Matsushita Y, Ikeuchi K (2014) Bi-polynomial modeling of low-frequency reflectances. IEEE Trans Pattern Anal Mach Intell 36(6):1078–1091
28. Silberman N, Hoiem D, Kohli P, Fergus R (2012) Indoor segmentation and support inference from RGBD images. In: Computer vision-ECCV 2012, pp 746–760. Springer, Berlin
29. Velten A, Wu D, Jarabo A, Masia B, Barsi C, Joshi C, Lawson E, Bawendi M, Gutierrez D, Raskar R (2013) Femto-photography: capturing and visualizing the propagation of light. ACM Trans Graph (TOG) 32(4):44
30. Woodham RJ (1980) Photometric method for determining surface orientation from multiple images. Opt Eng 19(1):191139
31. Ye C, Hegde GPM (2009) Robust edge extraction for SwissRanger SR-3000 range images. In: IEEE international conference on robotics and automation, 2009. ICRA'09, pp 2437–2442. IEEE
32. Ye G, Liu Y, Hasler N, Ji X, Dai Q, Theobalt C (2012) Performance capture of interacting characters with handheld kinects. In: Computer vision-ECCV 2012, pp 828–841. Springer, Berlin
33. Yoon K-J, Kweon IS (2006) Adaptive support-weight approach for correspondence search. IEEE Trans Pattern Anal Mach Intell 28(4):650–656
34. Zhang C, Zhang Z (2011) Calibration between depth and color sensors for commodity depth cameras. In: 2011 IEEE international conference on multimedia and expo (ICME), pp 1–6. IEEE
35. Zhang Z (2000) A flexible new technique for camera calibration. IEEE Trans Pattern Anal Mach Intell 22(11):1330–1334

Chapter 2
A State of the Art Report on Multiple RGB-D Sensor Research and on Publicly Available RGB-D Datasets

Kai Berger

Abstract That the Microsoft Kinect, an RGB-D sensor, transformed the gaming and end consumer sector has been anticipated by the developers. That it also impacted in rigorous computer vision research has probably been a surprise to the whole community. Shortly before the commercial deployment of its successor, Kinect One, the research literature fills with resumees and state-of-the art papers to summarize the development over the past 3 years. This chapter describes significant research projects which have built on sensoring setups that include two or more RGB-D sensors in one scene and on RGB-D datasets captured with them which were made publicly available.

2.1 Introduction

With the release of the Microsoft Kinect in November 2010, Microsoft predicted a significant change in the use of gaming devices in the end consumer market. After a preview at the E3 game convention in the Windows Media Centre Environment, the selling in North America started at November 4, 2010 and up to today more than 24 million units have been sold. With the release of an open-source SDK named *libfreenect* by Hèctor Martìn that enables streaming both the depth and the RGB or the raw infrared images via USB the attention of young researchers to use the Microsoft Kinect sensor for their imaging and reconstruction applications has gained. It was possible to stream $1,200 \times 960$ RGB and IR images at a frame rate of 30 Hz alongside computed depth estimates of the scene at a lower resolution. The IR image featured the projected infrared pattern generated with an 830 nm laser diode, which is distinctive and the same for each device. Shortly thereafter the proceedings

K. Berger (✉)
INRIA Rennes, Bretagne Atlantique, Campus Universitaire de Beaulieu, 35042 Rennes Cedex, France
e-mail: kai.berger@inria.fr

© Springer International Publishing Switzerland 2014
L. Shao et al. (eds.), *Computer Vision and Machine Learning with RGB-D Sensors*, Advances in Computer Vision and Pattern Recognition,
DOI: 10.1007/978-3-319-08651-4_2

and journals in the community included papers describing a broad range of setups addressing well-known problems in computer vision in which the Microsoft RGB-D sensor was employed. The projects ranged from simultaneous localization and mapping (SLAM) over 3D reconstruction over realtime face and hand tracking to motion capturing and gait analysis. Counter-intuitively researchers became soon interested in addressing the question if it is possible to employ several Microsoft Kinects, i.e. RGB-D sensors, in one setup—and if so, how to mitigate interference errors in order to enhance the signal. This idea is mainly counter-intuitive due to the fact, the each device projects the same pattern at the same wavelength into the scene. Thus, one would expect that the confusion in processing the raw IR-data rises quickly with the amount of sensors installed in a scene, Fig. 2.1. In the following sections I give an overview over several research projects published in the proceedings and journals of the computer vision community that successfully overcome this preconception and highlight their challenges as well as the benefit of each multiple RGB-D sensor setup. In the second half I list the most prominent datasets, that are publicly available, which were generated with RGB-D sensor setups. A tabular overview about addressed papers is found in Table 2.1. This overview over the state-of-the-art differs from other Kinect-realted overview reports in that it does neither include an in-depth evaluation of Time-Of-Flight sensors [20] nor a detailed introduction into the functionality of the sensor algorithm itself [14] nor does it focus on work capturing faces and gestures only [56]. Instead it provides an overview over multiple Kinect setups (Sects. 2.2–2.6) and publicly available databases generated with one or multiple Kinects (Sects. 2.7–2.11).

2.2 Multiple Kinect-Setups: Method of Comparison

As this chapter is a state-of-the art report it explicitly provides no new research contribution. Instead it shall be read as an overview and introduction to the work that has been conducted in the subfield of multiple Kinect research. I want to provide

Fig. 2.1 A simple scene (*left*) captured with the depth camera of one (*middle*) and multiple concurrently projecting kinects (*right*). The interference of more than one Kinect pattern results in degradations in the captured depth image (*white* pixels denote invalid depth values). This state of the art report lists significant papers that implemented setups albeit interference issues or to specifically address and overcome these issues. Reproduced from Schroeder et al. [44]

Table 2.1 An overview over different publications including multiple RGB-D sensors

Authors	Context	Number of RGB-D sensors in setup	Accuracy	Calibrated
Asteriadis et al. [4]	Motion estimation	3	Not specified	Yes
Berger et al. [8]	Motion estimation	4	Reprojection error of 1.7 px	Yes
Fuhrmann et al. [12]	Motion estimation	3	Deviation of 2–3 cm	Yes
Hossny et al. [15]	Motion estimation	2	Not specified	Yes (the authors provide a new autocalibration algorithm)
Santhanam et al. [40]	Motion estimation	4	Deviation of 3 mm	Yes
Wilson [53]	Motion estimation	3	Not specified	Yes
Ye et al. [54]	Motion estimation	3	Not specified	No
Zhang et al. [55]	Motion estimation	2	Deviation of 20 cm	Yes
Alexiadis et al. [2]	Mesh reconstruction	4	Reprojection error of 0.8 px	Yes
Berger et al. [7] and Berger et al. [6]	Mesh reconstruction	3	Not specified	Yes
Macknojia et al. [28]	Mesh reconstruction	5	Deviation of 2.5 cm at 3 m distance	Yes
Lo et al. [24]	Mesh reconstruction	2	Not specified	Yes
Nakamura [32]	Mesh reconstruction	2	Deviation of 3 % at 90° spacing	No
Nakazawa et al. [33]	Mesh reconstruction	4	Not specified	Yes
Ahmed [1]	Mesh reconstruction	6	Not specified	Yes
Olesen et al. [36]	Mesh reconstruction	3	60 % inlier at 8 px texlet spacing	Yes

(continued)

Table 2.1 (continued)

Authors	Context	Number of RGB-D sensors in setup	Accuracy	Calibrated
Pancham et al. [38]	Mesh reconstruction	2+	Not specified	No
Rafibakhsh et al. [39]	Mesh reconstruction	2	Deviation of 3.49 cm	Yes
Sumar et al. [47]	Mesh reconstruction	2	Reprojection error of 5 px	No
Tong et al. [51]	Mesh reconstruction	3	Biometrical measure deviation 1.6–6.2 cm	Yes
Wang et al. [52]	Mesh reconstruction	2	Not specified	Yes
Caon et al. [10]	Recognition	3	Not specified	Yes
Satta et al. [42]	Recognition	2	Not specified	No
Satyavolu et al. [43]	Recognition	5	Deviation of 3 cm	Yes
Saputra et al. [41]	Recognition	2	Deviation of 10 cm	Yes
Susanto et al. [49]	Recognition	5	Deviation of 13 cm	Yes
Butler et al. [9]	Interference	2 and 3	Deviation of up to 3 cm	Yes
Faion et al. [11]	Interference	4	Deviation of 21 mm	Yes
Kainz et al. [19]	Interference	8	Not specified	Yes
Maimone and Fuchs [29]	Interference	6	Deviation of 2 mm	No
Schroeder et al. [44] and Berger et al. [8]	Interference	4	Reprojection error of 1.7 px	Yes

The table lists for each publication the amount of employed sensors, the context pof application, the accuracy and whether the sensors where calibrated to a common world space. Note, that the specification of accuracy varies with the context of application between the mean deviation of a reconstructed 3D position from the original position in meters and the reprojection error in pixels or percentage into the camera a comparative table, Table 2.2 for the reader to have a quick overview of examined papers and their properties. The table is sorted alphabetically for each research field, i.e. *Multiple RGB-D sensor Setups for Motion Estimation*, Sect. 2.3, *Multiple RGB-D sensor Setups for Reconstruction*, Sect. 2.4, *Multiple RGB-D sensor Setups for Recognition and Tracking*, Sect. 2.5, and *Interference in Multiple RGB-D sensor Setups*, Sect. 2.6. I compared the amount of Kinects installed in each capturing environment (third column), and stated where the sources were available the measured accuracy of the capturings. As the statements were not unified, I have to provide them in different units to adhere to the source text. A slightly more detailed description is given at the table caption. Finally I state if the capturing setup was externally calibrated to a common worldspace, usually performed with a checkerboard or moving a marker around the scene.

2.3 Multiple RGB-D Sensor Setups for Motion Estimation

Santhanam et al. [40] describe a system to track neck and head movements with four calibrated Kinects. Three Kinects are tracking the patient's anatomy contour in depth and RGB streams while the fourth camera detects the face of the patient. The detected face region is used to guide the contour detection in the other three views. The detected contours are then finally merged to to a 3D estimate of the pose of the anatomy. The authors claim a precision of 3 mm at the expected 30 Hz. Wilson and Benko [53] use three PrimeSense depth cameras which stream at 320×240 px resolution and 30 Hz for human interaction with an augmented reality table. They compare input depth image streams against background depth images for each depth camera captured when the room is empty to segment out the human user. While the authors do not specify the accuracy, e.g. between the projected area and the captured area comprised by a hand, they claim to robustly track all user actions in 10 cm volume above the table. The depth cameras were placed next to each other and slanted such that each camera captures a different angle in the room. However their viewing cones may have overlapped. Fuhrmann et al. [12] have employed a stage setup with three Kinects for musical performances. They calibrated the cameras, which were observing the same $3 \times 3 \times 3$ m^3 interaction volume from different angles, for each stage performance. The tracking via *OpenNI* suffered only from latency between interframe capturing times. The sensors were employed such that they did not interfere destructively. Berger et al. [8] employ four Kinect sensors in a small $3 \times 3 \times 3$ m^3 room to mitigate shortcomings in the motion capturing capabilities of a single Kinect, Fig. 2.2 (left). To overcome depth map degradation through interfering patterns they introduced external hardware shutters. The idea was further evaluated by Zhang et al. [55] who basically performed the same capturing only with two Kinect cameras. Interference issues were circumvented by placing them opposite each other and assuming that the human actor acts as a separation surface between both projection cones. The authors claim a tracking accuracy of 20 cm. Their processing algorithm limits the original capturing framerate of 30–15 Hz. Asteriadis et al. [4] included a treadmill to

Table 2.2 Overview table for the benchmark datasets that are publicly available

Authors	Intended application	Datasize	Accelerometer data	Annotated	Link
Glocker et al. [13]	SLAM	151 MB	No	Camera path generated with kinectfusion [17]	http://research.microsoft.com/en-us/projects/7-scenes/
Lieberknecht et al. [22]	SLAM	≈100 kB	No	No	http://www.dropbox.com/sh/1kyhns6s1xpbmzw/RQKaYqdp7B/videos
Sturm et al. [46]	SLAM	50 GB	Yes	Ground truth pose via external markers tracked with motion capturing system	http://cvpr.in.tum.de/research/datasets/rgbd-dataset
Anand et al. [3]	Object recognition	≈7.6 GB	Yes	Annotated depth images	http://pr.cs.cornell.edu/sceneunderstanding/data/data.php
Barbosa et al. [5]	Object recognition	456 MB	No	Skeleton and meshes	http://www.iit.it/en/datasets/rgbdid.html
Huynh et al. [16]	Object recognition	No information	No	Faces labeled in input data	http://rgb-d.eurecom.fr/
Janoch et al. [18]	Object recognition	793 MB	No	Objects labeled in input data	http://www.eecs.berkeley.edu/~allie/VOCB3DO.zip
Lai et al. [21]	Object recognition	84 GB	No	Objects labeled in input data	http://www.cs.washington.edu/rgbd-dataset
Liu and Shao [23]	Object recognition	≈1 GB	No	Hand gestures labeled in input data	http://lshao.staff.shef.ac.uk/data/SheffieldKinectGesture.htm

(continued)

Table 2.2 (continued)

Authors	Intended application	Datasize	Accelerometer data	Annotated	Link
Luber et al. [25]	Object recognition	2 GB	No	Pedestrians labeled in input data	http://www.informatik.uni-freiburg.de/~spinello/sw/rgbd_people_unihall.tar.gz
Machado and Ferreira [27]	Object recognition	24.5 MB	No	Objects labeled	http://dl.dropbox.com/u/4151663/OR/Dataset/test%20set.zip
Negin et al. [35]	Object recognition	142 GB	No	Motion files containing the tracked joints	http://vpa.sabanciuniv.edu/databases/WorkoutSU-10/MinimalDataset.rar
Silberman et al. [34]	Object recognition	428 GB	Yes	Labeled depth dataset	http://cs.nyu.edu/~silberman/datasets/nyu_depth_v2.html
Sung et al. [48]	Object recognition	≈13.8 GB	No	Skeleton and activity/reachability lables	http://pr.cs.cornell.edu/humanactivities/data.php

I compared properties like data size (third row), the availability of the accelerometric data (fourth row) and the amount of annotation for ground truth (fifth row). For all datasets I listed the link under which they are publicly available. However, some datasets may require the request for login data simulate partially occluded motion for three calibrated Kinect sensors placed evenly in a quarter arc around the treadmill. Using a Fuzzy Inference system they were able to robustly map the human motion. Although they do neither state reprojection errors nor deviations from a reconstructed mesh they provide figures that the human motion could be fitted by a skeleton in up to 95 % of the recorded frames. An approach to analyse facial motion with two Kinects is presented by Hossny et al. [15]. They also provide a smart algorithm to automatically calibrate one Kinect to another based one rotation to zero angular positions. The processing of the depth maps to the face is done with geometric features that outperform conventional Haar features. They propose to overcome interference difficulties with mutually rotated polarization filters but do not state figures about the reprojection error. Very recently, Ye et al. [54] provided a solution for capturing human motion with multiple moving Kinects. In their setup, three Kinects were employed.

2.4 Multiple RGB-D Sensor Setups for Reconstruction

Alexiadis et al. [2] use four Kinect devices to reconstruct a single, full 3D textured mesh of a human body from their depth data in realtime. The authors claim that the re-projection error is less than 0.8 pixels. In a merging step redundant triangles are clipped. Object boundary noise is removed with a distance-to-background map. Rafibakhsh et al. [39] analyse construction site scenarios with two Kinects and exhaustively search for optimal placement an angles, concluding that the two sensors should not directly face each other. In their calibrated sensor setup they found a scene accuracy of 3.49 cm. Sumar et al. [47] test the sensor interference for two uncalibrated Kinect sensors in an indoor environment. They found, that in a marker tracking task, where the markers are less than 3 m from the Kinect the error follows a Gaussian distribution and does not deviate more than 5 pixels from the true centre of the marker. In ongoing work Pancham et al. [38] mount Kinects atop mobile robots which move in an overcast outdoor environment in order to segment out moving objects from static scenery. In that context the Kinect is used for differentiation between moving and stationary objects, and for map construction of the environment. They however do not state the accuracy of the reconstructed scene in relation to the amount of Kinects employed. In a very interesting approach to enable HDR scene capturing Lo et al. [24] place two Kinects atop each other and equip one with a polarized neutral density filter. This results in accurate depth values for regions that would have been overexposed in an unaltered Kinect capturing (The exposure difference between both IR images is roughly 1 EV apart). They recognise the fact that interference might occur but did not quantitatively evaluate that for their setup. However, the reconstructed scenes bear more complete meshes under headlight than with a single LDR capturing. Berger et al. [7] show in their paper the feasibility to use three Kinects concurrently in a convergent setup for capturing non-opaque surfaces like the interface between flowing propane gas in air. It is noteworthy that, although the projectors are masked such that they project on mutually disjoint surface areas, the projection patterns do not interfere destructively with each other while passing through the gas volume. Their approach has been altered such that an evaluation based only on the high resolution IR stream is possible as well [6]. Olesen et al. [36] show a system that involves up to three calibrated Kinects for texlet reconstruction. They evaluate different angular settings for the multiple sensors but interestingly conclude that the orientation does not significantly improve the capturing quality. In industrial applications Macknojia et al. [28] place three Kinects on a straight line next to each other while a fourth and a fifth Kinect are placed to the left and right respectively in a convergent manner to provide a calibrated capturing volume with a side length of 7 m in total, Fig. 2.2 (middle). Small projecting volumes overlap while objects like cars are captured. The authors state a depth error of about 2.5 cm at 3 m distance. Wang et al. [52] present work where two calibrated Kinects' depth maps are fused to reconstruct arbitrary scene content. The cameras are spaced 30 cm apart and the viewing axes converge towards the scene centre. Inaccuracies due to interference are handled in software by applying a his work Ahmed [1] provides a scene reconstruction mainly of human bodies captured from 6 calibrated Kinects. He deliberately excludes interference analysis from the discussion but mentioned temporal drift if software synchronization is omitted. Interference issues are also neglected by Nakazawa et al. [33] who placed four calibrated Kinects at the four corners of a capturing room, but rotated them by 90° such that they would capture a greater vertical range and a smaller horizontal range each. They concentrate on aligning depth data captured asynchronously by applying a temporal calibration by providing depth data at certain time instants. Tong et al. [51] reconstruct the human body from a setup consisting of three Kinects mounted on two poles at different heights. The subject is placed on a spinning turntable in the center of the poles. The deviation in different biometrical measures is stated to be in 1.6–6.2 cm. In their work Nakamura [32] place two Kinects in different angles between 10° and 180° from each other around the scene. The Kinects are not calibrated to a common world space but placed at a fixed distance to the scene centre. In an evaluation of the mean reprojection error for the varying angles they find that a spacing of 180° between each Kinect results in the smallest error while a a spacing of 120° results in the largest error, Fig. 2.2 (right). The Kinects do not project into each others sensor due to the scene content.

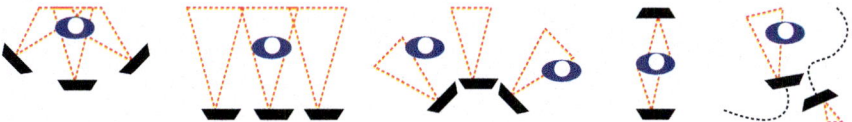

Fig. 2.2 Five typical capturing setups featuring multiple kinects. Multiple kinects are evenly placed in a virtual *circle* around the scene centre (*first*), e.g. [7, 8, 19, 33, 36, 43, 52], multiple kinects are in line to capture a volume with a large side length (*second*), e.g. [10, 24, 28, 29, 41], multiple kinects juxtaposed and facing away from each other (*third*), e.g. [53], and two kinects face each other, but are occluded by the scene content (*fourth*), e.g. [32]. Very recently work has been conducted with multiple uncalibrated moving kinects (*fifth*), e.g. [38, 54]

2.5 Multiple RGB-D Sensor Setups for Recognition and Tracking

Satta et al. [42] present research to recognize and track people in an indoor environment surveyed by two Kinects relying on a combination of RGB texture and depth information. It has to be noted, though, that the Kinects were installed facing away from each other. Hence, they did not directly project into each other's viewing frustra. Interference is not discussed further. Satyavolu et al. [43] describe an experimental setup that consists of 5 Kinects. One camera was used for tracking IR markers attached to a box, 4 others (evenly distributed around the scene centre) simulated interference/noise. The authors report that the Kinect deviated by 3 cm on an average from the actual position. Caon et al. [10] present an approach for tracking gestures based on three calibrated Kinects placed in a 45° angle. They varied different configurations between the three Kameras and although they did not state figures about the depth or tracking accuracy they do list the amount of invalid depth pixels for each configuration. Susanto et al. [49] present an approach to detect objects from their shape and depth profile generated when captured from several calibrated Kinects and state that there is no degrading interference noticeable due to the fact the the Kinects are placed at wide angles from each other. Although the paper focus on the success rate of the recognition they briefly state that the setup might show depth discrepancies of up to 13 cm. The tracking of humans in a room has been shown by Saputra et al. [41] who placed two calibrated Kinects at 5 m distance next to each other. Although the projection cones do not interfere with each other, the authors provide a detection error of human position of 10 cm.

2.6 Interference in Multiple RGB-D Sensor Setups

Following the work of Berger et al. [8], where external hardware shutters are used for mitigating interference between concurrently projecting sensors as described in detail by Schroeder et al. [44], Maimone and Fuchs [29] introduce motion platforms that pitch each Kinect with the Kinect that the own structured light pattern remains crisp in the IR stream while the other patterns appear blurred due to the angular motion of the camera. The depth map is realigned with the recorded egomotion from the inertial sensors included in the Kinect. It is noteworthy that they also managed to deblur the RGB-image using the Lucy-Richardson method. In a more generic approach Butler et al. [9] vibrate the camera arbitrarily. In a rather invasive approach Faion et al. [11] manage to toggle the projector subsystem to perform measurements similar to Schroeder et al. [44]. They use Bayesian state estimator to intelligently schedule which sensor is to be selected for the next time frame. Their maximal reconstruction error denotes 21 mm. Kainz et al. [19] describe an elaborate setup for eight Kinects mounted on vibrating rods and one freely moving Kinect suitable for various applications, such as motion capturing and reconstruction. All vibrating rods

2 A State of the Art Report... 37

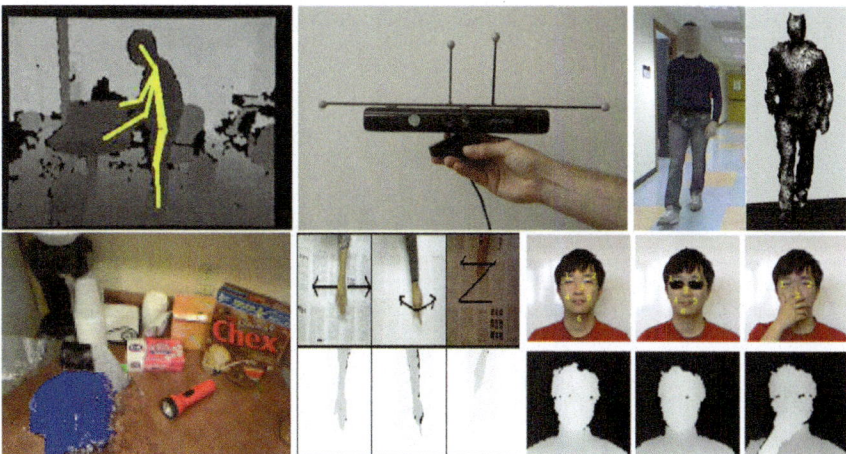

Fig. 2.3 A collage of the variety of benchmark datasets that are currently publicly available. *Top left* depth images with annotated motion (reproduced from [48]), *top middle* external tracking of kinect pose with markers (reproduced from [46]), *top right* tight mesh and skeleton alongside RGB-data (reproduced from Barbosa et al. [5]). *Bottom left* depth images with objects annotated (reproduced from [21]), *bottom middle* depth data with annotated hand movements (reproduced from [23]), *bottom right* face capturings in RGB-D stream anotated (reproduced from Huynh et al. [16])

were administered by a parallel circuit at slightly different frequencies. They do not give a quantitative analysis of the reconstruction error but provide qualitative figures of the reconstructed mesh (Fig. 2.3).

2.7 RGB-D Datasets: Method of Comparison

In this part of the chapter it is attempted to provide an overview over the diverse set of benchmarks that are publicly available for comparison of RGB-D based algorithms The findings are summarized in an overview table, Table 2.2 and compared for main distinguishable criteria. The table is sorted alphabetically for each research field, i.e. *SLAM*, Sect. 2.9 and *Object Recognition*, Sect. 2.10. I evaluated if the accelerometer of the Kinect was used (third column), if the data were annotated and which type of ground truth has been made available (fourth column). Finally I provided the link to the datasets (fifth columns). I tested the accessability in the middle of August. Some datasets may require login data, which however can be acquired by contacting the corresponding authors (instructions were published on the corresponding website in that case). In Sect. 2.11 I provide a critical view onto the diversity of the publicly available datasets and phrase suggestions for extending the state of the art in benchmarks. Statistics about the volume and impact of each dataset is provided in Fig. 2.4.

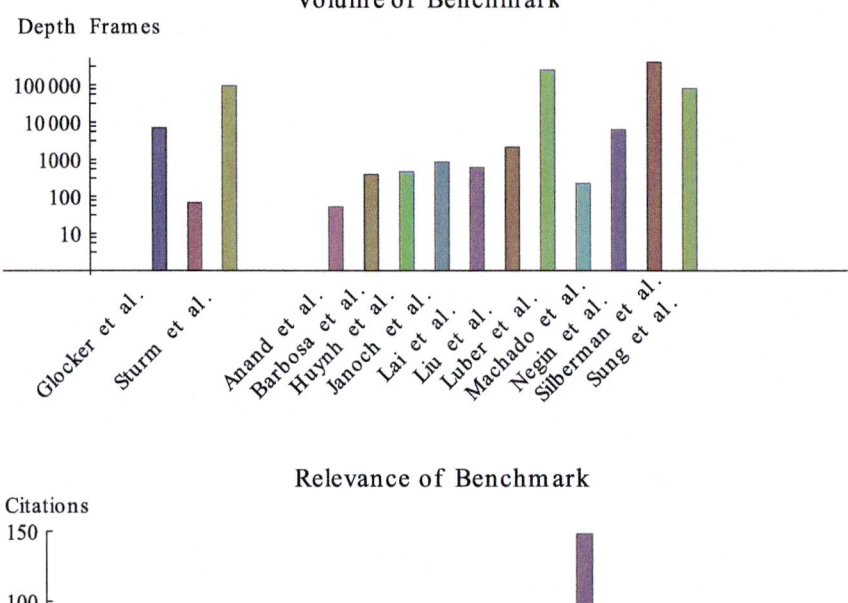

Fig. 2.4 *Left* This semi-logarithmic bar chart depicts the size of each published dataset in terms of absolute depth-images. The dataset presented by Silberman et al. [34] bears the most input images. *Right* This chart depicts the impact of each published dataset in the community. It is sorted alphabetically for each research field. The work by Lai et al. [21] has been considered most in the community

2.8 Annotation for Ground Truth Retrieval

Most datasets exceed a feasible size to be handled by a single user for annotation. Hence, with the increasing popoluratiy of internet freelance websites, most publications presented in this report have relied on Mechanical Turk, e.g. [18], for robust annotation of the datasets. Some rely on additional sensors to provide the ground truth, e.g. for the camera pose at a given frame [45, 46]. A sophisticated approach transforms the labeling in another space: instead of letting the user annotate in image space, the static scene captured with a moving Kinect is reconstructed in 3D and annotated in a 3D graphics tool once, e.g. [21]. The annotated point clouds are then simply reprojected into the input stream using the camera pose for the Kinect sensor at each frame.

2.9 SLAM

Highly accurate depth data are necessary for 3D reconstruction and simultaneous reconstruction and SLAM applications, although the requirements for mapping or localization can differ within the applicational context. It can be seen, that accuracy and the running time/framerates trade each other off. The Kinect is the first device that provides fast data acquisition at acceptable accuracy. In their work Sturm et al. [45, 46] release a 50 GB dataset conisisting of 39 RGB-D sequences captured with the Microsoft Kinect including the recorded accelerometer data with the intention to test SLAM algorithms on the input data. The authors provide ground truth via external per frame pose estimation of the Kinect within a global reference framework, which has been computed from the capturing of markers that have been attached to the Kinect beforehand. They used a MotionAnalysis capturing system at 100 Hz. Lieberknecht et al. [22] create also a benchmark for localisation and provide video data, from which the RGB and depth data can be extracted. However, they do not provide a dataset that contains annotations or additional data, e.g. accelerometric data. Glocker et al. [13] prvoide a dataset captured with a moving camera and use KinectFusion to generate the 3D scene and the camera path as ground truth for the benchmark. They provide seven different scenes including RGB, depth and pose data in a txt-file.

2.10 Object Recognition

Based on the Kinect's realtime output of accurate depth maps, it became possible to reconstruct 3D objects with the Kinect, e.g. by moving the sensor around the acquired object. For example, Tam and his colleagues [50] register point clouds captured with the Kinect to each other. Lai et al. [21] present an annotated dataset containing visual and depth images of 300 physically distinct objects ranging from fruits to tools. Their dataset was captured with the Primesense prototype and a Firewire RGB-camera from Pointgrey. Their approach to labeling the objects in the input sequences is somewhat innovative: they reconstruct the 3D scene from the moving RGB-D sensor setup while keeping track of its position over time. The objects of interest are then labeled once in the 3D scene by hand and then backprojected into the input streams. Liu and Shao [23] present a dataset for gesture recognition where 2,160 hand gesture sequences of 6 persons are captured with the Microsoft Kinect. The annotated dataset differentiates 10 hand gestures: circle (clockwise), triangle (anti-clockwise), up-down, right-left, wave, Z, cross, comehere, turnaround. As the Microsoft Kinect remains fixed during acquisition there is no additional accelerometric data in the dataset. Negin et al. [35] provide a dataset of human body movements represented by 3D positions of skeletal joints. As the Kinect sensor remained fixed, no accelerometric data is available, but the authors provide the complete tracking results gained from applying the Microsoft Kinect SDK to the RGB-D data as the ground truth for their benchmark. In the dataset 15 people conduct 10 different exercises. Barbosa et al. [5] capture 79 persons first for a distinctive signature, e.g. in a defined pose, and then in regular motion, e.g. walking across a floor. They provide both skeleton fits and .ply meshes alongside the RGB-D data. The goal of their dataset is to reindentify different humans captured with the Kinect. The humans may change their movement patterns or their clothes in between recordings. Machado and Ferreira [27] record several objects and models with the Kinect camera and let them annotate by human observers. The meshes are presented in various formats with the task to identify the object from the recorded shape. Luber et al. [25] present a pedestrian dataset captured with three Kinects which are placed such that their viewing cones do not interfere. The dataset is annotated in that the position of each pedestrian is bounded by a rectangle in the input views. Their dataset contains of walking and standing pedestrians seen from different orientations and with different levels of occlusions. Silberman et al. [34] present a dataset consisting of 1,449 labeled pairs of aligned RGB and depth images captured in indoor environments, such as bathrooms, basements, bedrooms, kitchens and playrooms. It includes the accelerometric data for each frame and also features a toolbox implemented in matlab that includes useful functions for manipulating the data and labels. Anand et al. [3] captured several indoor environments and labeled the depth data. They also present in bag files the output of RGBDSLAM for each scene, e.g. for each timestamp a transform-matrix for that frame that transforms the camera from the first frame accordingly. Janoch et al. [18] show a large dataset annotated with the help of Amazon's Mechanical Turk consisting of indoor environment items like chairs, monitors, cups, bottles, bowls, keyboards, mouses or phones. They do not provide additional accelerometer data. Dataset consisting of faces of 52 people (14 females, 38 males) captured with the Microsoft Kinect has been presented by Huynh et al. [16]. The faces are captured in nine different conditions (neutral face, smile, mouth open, face in left profile, face in right profile, partial occlusion of face parts, changing lighting conditions). They do not include the accelerometric data. Defined landmark points were manually identified in the input images. In their work about motion recognition Sung et al. [48] provide depthmaps and skeletons for four subjects (two male, two female, one left-handed) who were asked to perform different high-level activities, like making cereal, arranging objects or having a meal. The activities are label and subclassified for movements like reaching, opening, placing, or scrubbing.

2.11 Shortcomings

The authors believe that, although there is already quite a remarkable amount of publicly available datasets based on capturings conducted with the Kinect, certain aspects in use of the sensor seem to be underrepresented. While already one paper is published [30] that aims to extend the depth reconstruction capabilities from IR input stream data, a coherent dataset containing the IR data and additional ground truth depth information, e.g. from scene calibration or stereo, is missing. Also, arbitrary mesh reconstruction is in the datasets currently considered as byproduct of SLAM algorithms, Sect. 2.9, such that estimates with the accuracy of a few millimeters to a centimeter seem sufficient. However, recently publications have emerged to employ one or many Kinects for the accurate reconstruction of objects, e.g. based on depth, a combination of depth and texture cues in the RGB stream [31] or from IR input stream [37]. The reconstructed objects in these setups need explicitly not necessary be purely opaque [7, 26]. A ground truth dataset with a high-resolution laser scan alongside input frames from Kinect (depth, RGB and IR) with a pose reconstruction of the sensor position would be highly desirable.

2.12 Conclusion

In this chapter I have shown that, counter-intuitively, it is possible to use several Kinects in one capturing setup. Although each device projects the same pattern at the same wavelength into the scene and consequently contributes to confusion in processing the raw IR-data, several approaches, ranging from hardware fixes over intelligent software algorithms for mitigation to placing the Kinects such that the scene content acts as an occluding surface between each projection cone, have been discussed. The applicational context varied between motion capturing, the original purpose of the Kinect sensor, over scene reconstruction to tracking and recognition. Furthermore, I have provided an overview over the publicly available datasets generated for benchmark with the Microsoft Kinect. Several approaches, ranging from a steady single Kinect capturing setup over a moving Kinect in the scene to capturing setups that include multiple Kinects, have been discussed. The applicational context varied between SLAM, motion capturing and recognition. I have also phrased a critical view onto the diversity of current datasets with suggestions for extending the state of the art in benchmarks. With the deployment of the new *Kinect One* in the near future the authors assume that in the next years the amount of publicly available benchmark datasets will increase significantly. It has to be evaluated, though, if setups with multiple sensors in one capturing scenario are possible, but the authors predict that in the next years there will still be challenges for multiple RGB-D sensors relying on the emission of light to be addressed by the community

References

1. Ahmed N (2012) A system for 360 acquisition and 3D animation reconstruction using multiple RGB-D cameras
2. Alexiadis DS, Kordelas G, Apostolakis KC, Agapito JD, Vegas J, Izquierdo E, Daras P (2012) Reconstruction for 3D immersive virtual environments. In: 13th international workshop on image analysis for multimedia interactive services (WIAMIS). IEEE, pp 1–4

3. Anand A, Koppula HS, Joachims T, Saxena A (2013) Contextually guided semantic labeling and search for three-dimensional point clouds. Int J Robot Res 32(1):19–34
4. Asteriadis S, Chatzitofis A, Zarpalas D, Alexiadis DS, Daras P (2013) Estimating human motion from multiple kinect sensors. In: Proceedings of the 6th international conference on computer vision/computer graphics collaboration techniques and applications. ACM, p 3
5. Barbosa IB, Cristani M, Del Bue A, Bazzani L, Murino V (2012) Re-identification with RGB-D sensors. In: Computer vision-ECCV 2012. Workshops and demonstrations. Springer, pp 433–442
6. Berger K, Kastner M, Schroeder Y, Guthe S (2013) Using sparse optical flow for two-phase gas flow capturing with multiple kinects. Robotics: science and systems 2013 workshop on RGB-D: advanced reasoning with depth cameras, pp 1–8
7. Berger K, Ruhl K, Albers M, Schroder Y, Scholz A, Kokemuller J, Guthe S, Magnor M (2011) The capturing of turbulent gas flows using multiple kinects. In: IEEE international conference on computer vision workshops (ICCV workshops). IEEE, pp 1108–1113
8. Berger K, Ruhl K, Brümmer C, Schröder Y, Scholz A, Magnor M (2011) Markerless motion capture using multiple color-depth sensors. In Proceedings of vision, modeling and visualization (VMV), vol 2011, p 3
9. Butler DA, Izadi S, Hilliges O, Molyneaux D, Hodges S, Kim D (2012) Shake'n'sense: reducing interference for overlapping structured light depth cameras. In: Proceedings of the 2012 ACM annual conference on human factors in computing systems. ACM, pp 1933–1936
10. Caon M, Yue Y, Tscherrig J, Mugellini E, Abou Khaled O (2011) Context-aware 3D gesture interaction based on multiple kinects. In: AMBIENT 2011, the first international conference on ambient computing, applications, services and technologies, pp 7–12
11. Faion F, Friedberger S, Zea A, Hanebeck UD (2012) Intelligent sensor-scheduling for multi-kinect-tracking. In: IEEE/RSJ international conference on intelligent robots and systems (IROS). IEEE, pp 3993–3999
12. Fuhrmann AL, Kretz J, Burwik P (2013) Multi sensor tracking for live sound transformation
13. Glocker B, Izadi S, Shotton J, Criminisi A (2013) Real-time RGB-D camera relocalization. In: International symposium on mixed and augmented reality. Springer
14. Han J, Shao L, Xu D, Shotton J (2013) Enhanced computer vision with microsoft kinect sensor: a review
15. Hossny M, Filippidis D, Abdelrahman W, Zhou H, Fielding M, Mullins J, Wei L, Creighton D, Puri V, Nahavandi S (2012) Low cost multimodal facial recognition via kinect sensors. In: Proceedings of the land warfare conference (LWC): potent land force for a joint maritime strategy. Commonwealth of Australia, pp 77–86
16. Huynh T, Min R, Dugelay J-L (2013) An efficient LBP-based descriptor for facial depth images applied to gender recognition using RGB-D face data. In: Computer vision-ACCV 2012 workshops. Springer, pp 133–145
17. Izadi S, Newcombe R, Kim D, Hilliges O, Molyneaux D, Hodges S, Kohli P, Shotton J, Davison A, Fitzgibbon A (2011) Kinectfusion: real-time dynamic 3D surface reconstruction and interaction. In: ACM SIGGRAPH 2011 talks. ACM, p 23
18. Janoch A, Karayev S, Jia Y, Barron JT, Fritz M, Saenko K, Darrell T (2013) A category-level 3D object dataset: putting the kinect to work. In: Consumer depth cameras for computer vision. Springer, pp 141–165
19. Kainz B, Hauswiesner S, Reitmayr G, Steinberger M, Grasset R, Gruber L, Veas E, Kalkofen D, Seichter H, Schmalstieg D (2012) Omnikinect: real-time dense volumetric data acquisition and applications. In: Proceedings of the 18th ACM symposium on virtual reality software and technology. ACM, pp 25–32
20. Khoshelham K (2011) Accuracy analysis of kinect depth data. In: ISPRS workshop laser scanning, vol 38, p 1
21. Lai K, Bo L, Ren X, Fox D (2011) A large-scale hierarchical multi-view RGBD-D object dataset. In: IEEE international conference on robotics and automation (ICRA). IEEE, pp 1817–1824

22. Lieberknecht S, Huber A, Ilic S, Benhimane S (2011) RGB-D camera-based parallel tracking and meshing. In: ISMAR
23. Liu L, Shao L (2013) Learning discriminative representations from RGB-D video data. In: Proceedings of the international joint conference on artificial intelligence (IJCAI)
24. Lo R, Rampersad V, Huang J, Mann S (2013) Three dimensional high dynamic range veillance for 3D range-sensing cameras
25. Luber M, Spinello L, Arras KO (2011) People tracking in RGBD-D data with on-line boosted target models. In: IEEE/RSJ international conference on intelligent robots and systems (IROS). IEEE, pp 3844–3849
26. Lysenkov I, Eruhimov V, Bradski GR (2012) Recognition and pose estimation of rigid transparent objects with a kinect sensor. In: Robotics: science and systems
27. Machado J, Ferreira A (2013) Retrieval of objects captured with low-cost depth-sensing cameras. In: SHREC2013. Springer
28. Macknojia R, Chávez-Aragón A, Payeur P, Laganière R (2013) Calibration of a network of kinect sensors for robotic inspection over a large workspace. In: Proceedings of the IEEE workshop on robot vision (WoRV 2013)
29. Maimone A, Fuchs H (2012) Reducing interference between multiple structured light depth sensors using motion. In: Virtual reality workshops (VR). IEEE, pp 51–54
30. Martinez M, Stiefelhagen R (2013) Kinect unleashed: getting control over high resolution depth maps
31. Miao D, Fu J, Lu Y, Li S, Chen CW (2012) Texture-assisted kinect depth inpainting. In: IEEE international symposium on circuits and systems (ISCAS). IEEE, pp 604–607
32. Nakamura DALR Multiple 3D data acquisition system setup based on structured ligth technique for immersive videoconferencing applications
33. Nakazawa M, Mitsugami I, Makihara Y, Nakajima H, Habe H, Yamazoe H, Yagi Y (2012) Dynamic scene reconstruction using asynchronous multiple kinects. In: 21st international conference on pattern recognition (ICPR). IEEE, pp 469–472
34. Nathan Silberman PK, Hoiem D, Fergus R (2012) Indoor segmentation and support inference from RGBD images. In: ECCV
35. Negin F, Özdemir F, Akgül CB, Yüksel KA, Erçil A (2013) A decision forest based feature selection framework for action recognition from RGB-depth cameras. In: Image analysis and recognition. Springer, pp 648–657
36. Olesen SM, Lyder S, Kraft D, Krüger N, Jessen JB (2012) Real-time extraction of surface patches with associated uncertainties by means of kinect cameras. J Real-Time Image Process 1–14
37. Ou-Yang T-H, Tsai M-L, Yen C-T, Lin T-T (2011) An infrared range camera-based approach for three-dimensional locomotion tracking and pose reconstruction in a rodent. J Neurosci Methods 201(1):116–123
38. Pancham A, Tlale N, Bright G (2012) Mapping and tracking of moving objects in dynamic environments
39. Rafibakhsh N, Gong J, Siddiqui MK, Gordon C, Lee HF (2012) Analysis of xbox kinect sensor data for use on construction sites: depth accuracy and sensor interference assessment. In: Constitution research congress, pp 848–857
40. Santhanam A, Low D, Kupelian P (2011) Th-c-brc-11: 3D tracking of interfraction and intrafraction head and neck anatomy during radiotherapy using multiple kinect sensors. Med Phys 38:3858
41. Saputra MRU, Putra GD, Santosa PI et al (2012) Indoor human tracking application using multiple depth-cameras. In: International conference on advanced computer science and information systems (ICACSIS). IEEE, pp 307–312
42. Satta R, Pala F, Fumera G, Roli F (2013) Real-time appearance-based person re-identification over multiple kinect TM cameras
43. Satyavolu S, Bruder G, Willemsen P, Steinicke F (2012) Analysis of IR-based virtual reality tracking using multiple kinects. In: Virtual reality workshops (VR). IEEE, pp 149–150

44. Schröder Y, Scholz A, Berger K, Ruhl K, Guthe S, Magnor M (2011) Multiple kinect studies. Comput Graph
45. Sturm J, Engelhard N, Endres F, Burgard W, Cremers D (2012) A benchmark for the evaluation of RGB-D slam systems. In: Proceedings of the IEEE international conference on intelligent robot systems (IROS), pp 573–580
46. Sturm J, Magnenat S, Engelhard N, Pomerleau F, Colas F, Burgard W, Cremers D, Siegwart R (2011) Towards a benchmark for RGB-D slam evaluation. In: Proceedings of the RGB-D workshop on advanced reasoning with depth cameras at robotics: science and systems conference (RSS), vol 2. Los Angeles, USA, p 3
47. Sumar L, Bainbridge-Smith A (2014) Feasability of fast image processing using multiple kinect cameras on a portable platform. Department of electrical and computer engineering, University. Canterbury, New Zealand
48. Sung J, Ponce C, Selman B, Saxena A (2011) Human activity detection from RGBD images. In: plan, activity, and intent recognition
49. Susanto W, Rohrbach M, Schiele B (2012) 3D object detection with multiple kinects. In: Computer vision-ECCV 2012. Workshops and demonstrations. Springer, pp 93–102
50. Tam G, Cheng Z-Q, Lai Y-K, Langbein F, Liu Y, Marshall A, Martin R, Sun X-F, Rosin P (2012) Registration of 3D point clouds and meshes: a survey from rigid to non-rigid
51. Tong J, Zhou J, Liu L, Pan Z, Yan H (2012) Scanning 3D full human bodies using kinects. EEE Trans Visual Comput Graph 18(4):643–650
52. Wang J, Zhang C, Zhu W, Zhang Z, Xiong Z, Chou PA (2012) 3D scene reconstruction by multiple structured-light based commodity depth cameras. In: IEEE international conference on acoustics, speech and signal processing (ICASSP). IEEE, pp 5429–5432
53. Wilson AD, Benko H (2010) Combining multiple depth cameras and projectors for interactions on, above and between surfaces. In: Proceedings of the 23nd annual ACM symposium on user interface software and technology. ACM, pp 273–282
54. Ye G, Liu Y, Deng Y, Hasler N, Ji X, Dai Q, Theobalt C (2013) Free-viewpoint video of human actors using multiple handheld kinects. In: IEEE transactions on cybernetics
55. Zhang L, Sturm J, Cremers D, Lee D (2012) Real-time human motion tracking using multiple depth cameras. In: IEEE/RSJ international conference on intelligent robots and systems (IROS). IEEE, pp 2389–2395
56. Zhang Z (2012) Microsoft kinect sensor and its effect. IEEE Multimedia 19(2):4–10

Part II
Reconstruction, Mapping and Synthesis

Chapter 3
Calibration Between Depth and Color Sensors for Commodity Depth Cameras

Cha Zhang and Zhengyou Zhang

Abstract Commodity depth cameras have created many interesting new applications in the research community recently. These applications often require the calibration information between the color and the depth cameras. Traditional checkerboard-based calibration schemes fail to work well for the depth camera, since its corner features cannot be reliably detected in the depth image. In this chapter, we present a maximum likelihood solution for the joint depth and color calibration based on two principles. First, in the depth image, points on the checkerboard shall be coplanar, and the plane is known from color camera calibration. Second, additional point correspondences between the depth and color images may be manually specified or automatically established to help improve calibration accuracy. Uncertainty in depth values has been taken into account systematically. The proposed algorithm is reliable and accurate, as demonstrated by extensive experimental results on simulated and real-world examples.

3.1 Introduction

Recently, there has been an increasing number of depth cameras available at commodity prices, such as those from 3DV systems[1] and Microsoft Kinect.[2] These cameras can usually capture both color and depth images in real time. They have created a lot of interesting new research applications, such as 3D shape scanning [1], foreground/background segmentation [2], facial expression tracking [3], etc.

---

[1] 3DV Systems, http://www.3dvsystems.com/.
[2] Microsoft, http://www.xbox.com/en-US/kinect/.

C. Zhang (✉) · Z. Zhang
Microsoft Research, One Microsoft Way, Redmond, WA 98052, USA
e-mail: chazhang@microsoft.com

Z. Zhang
e-mail: zhang@microsoft.com

For many applications that use the color and the depth images jointly, it is critical to know the calibration parameters of the sensor pair. Such parameters include the intrinsic parameters of the color camera, its radial distortion parameters, the rotation and translation between the depth camera and the color camera, and parameters that help determine the depth values (e.g., in meters) of pixels in the depth image. Although color camera calibration has been thoroughly studied in the literature [4, 5], the joint calibration of depth and color images presents a few new challenges:

- Feature points such as the corners of checkerboard patterns are often indistinguishable from other surface points in the depth image, as shown in Fig. 3.1.
- Although depth discontinuity can be easily observed in the depth image, the boundary points are usually unreliable due to unknown depth reconstruction mechanisms used inside the depth camera.
- One may use the infrared image cocentered with the depth image to perform calibration. However, this may require external infrared illumination (e.g., the Kinect camera). In addition, the depth mapping function Eq. (3.28) of the depth image may not be calibrated with such a method.
- Most commodity depth cameras produce noisy depth images. Such noises need to be accurately modeled in order to obtain satisfactory results.

In this chapter, we present a maximum likelihood solution for joint depth and color calibration using commodity depth cameras. We use the popular checkerboard pattern adopted in color camera calibration (Fig. 3.1); thus, no extra hardware is needed. We utilize the fact that points on the checkerboard shall lie on a common plane; thus, their distance to the plane shall be minimized. Point correspondences between the depth and color images may be further added to help improve calibration accuracy. A maximum likelihood framework is presented with careful modeling of the sensor noise, particularly in the depth image. Extensive experimental results are presented to validate the proposed calibration method.

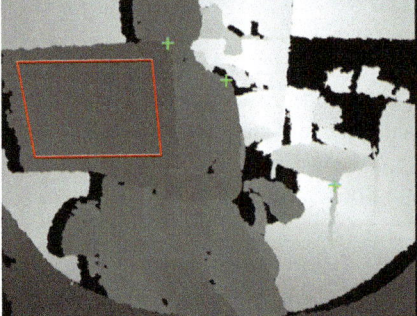

Fig. 3.1 The calibration pattern used in this chapter. The color image is shown on the *left*, and the depth image is shown on the *right*. The depth pixels inside the *red* rectangle shall lie on the model plane surface, though point correspondence is difficult to obtain. A few manually specified corresponding point pairs are also shown in the figure

The rest of the chapter is organized as follows. Related works are presented in Sect. 3.2. Notations used in this chapter are introduced in Sect. 3.3. The maximum likelihood solution is described in Sect. 3.4. Experimental results and conclusions are given in Sects. 3.5 and 3.6, respectively.

3.2 Related Works

Some of the earliest works on depth camera calibration are on time-of-flight (ToF) cameras. For instance, in Kuhnert and Stommel [6] and [7], simple linear or basic polynomial functions are used to determine the deviation between the measured depth information and ground truth. Fuchs and Hirzinger [8] focused on ToF cameras mounted on an external positioning system, and they modeled three types of errors for ToF sensors, including distance-related error, amplitude-related error, and a latency-related error and estimated them simultaneously. Lindner et al. [9] adopted a combined calibration approach that incorporates several separate models into one and realizes a reduction of complexity. Shim et al. [10] presented another ToF camera calibration scheme under a multiview acquisition setup, which is composed of ToF sensors and color cameras. Their approach employed optical features in estimating the pose of ToF sensors and color cameras and does not suffer from erroneous estimation in intrinsic parameters for the ToF sensors.

It is not until the availability of the Microsoft Kinect sensor in November 2010 that depth cameras become a commodity. Herrera et al. [11] and Zhang [12] independently proposed to use a planar checkerboard pattern to help calibrating the relative rotation and translation between the color and depth sensors in Kinect, in which this chapter is mostly based on. Herrera et al. [13] later extended their work to include a disparity distortion correction model that depends on the observed disparity, which could further improve accuracy. Raposo et al. [14] later proposed a few modifications to Herrera [13], improved stability, and decreased the number of input images and run-time for calibration.

Other interesting works on Kinect calibration include Liu et al. [15] and [16]. In Liu et al. [15] presented a method for Kinect calibration based on a one-dimensional object, which can be extracted easily even in the depth image. In Mikhelson et al. [16] still used a checkerboard, but relied more on the checkerboard boundary rather than interior points for the calibration, which again is observable or computable from the depth image.

3.3 Notations

Figure 3.2 illustrates the notations used during our calibration procedure. We assume the color camera's 3D coordinate system coincides with the world coordinate system. In the homogeneous representation, a 3D point in the world coordinate system is

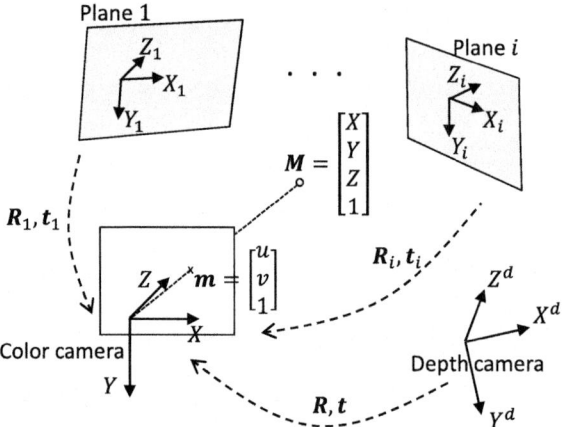

Fig. 3.2 Illustration of the notations used in the paper

denoted by $\mathbf{M} = [X, Y, Z, 1]^T$, and its corresponding 2D projection in the color image is $\mathbf{m} = [u, v, 1]^T$. We model the color camera by the usual pinhole model, i.e.,

$$s\mathbf{m} = \mathbf{A}[\mathbf{I}\ \mathbf{0}]\mathbf{M}, \tag{3.1}$$

where $\mathbf{I}$ is the identity matrix and $\mathbf{0}$ is the zero vector. s is a scale factor. In this particular case, $s = Z$. $\mathbf{A}$ is the camera's intrinsic matrix, given by Zhang [5]:

$$\mathbf{A} = \begin{bmatrix} \alpha & \gamma & u_0 \\ 0 & \beta & v_0 \\ 0 & 0 & 1 \end{bmatrix}, \tag{3.2}$$

where α and β are the scale factors in the image coordinate system, (u_0, v_0) are the coordinates of the principal point, and γ is the skewness of the two image axes.

The depth camera typically outputs an image with depth values, denoted by $\mathbf{x} = [u, v, z]^T$, where (u, v) are the pixel coordinates and z is the depth value. The mapping from $\mathbf{x}$ to the point in the depth camera's 3D coordinate system $\mathbf{M}^d = [X^d, Y^d, Z^d, 1]^T$ is usually known, denoted as $\mathbf{M}^d = \mathbf{f}(\mathbf{x})$. The rotation and translation between the color and the depth cameras are denoted by $\mathbf{R}$ and $\mathbf{t}$, i.e.,

$$\mathbf{M} = \begin{bmatrix} \mathbf{R} & \mathbf{t} \\ \mathbf{0}^T & 1 \end{bmatrix} \mathbf{M}^d. \tag{3.3}$$

3.4 Joint Depth/Color Camera Calibration

3.4.1 Problem Statement

During calibration, we assume the user moves a planar calibration board in front of the depth camera, similar to that in Zhang [5]. In total, there are n image pairs (color and depth) captured by the depth camera. The positions of the calibration board in the n images are different, as shown in Fig. 3.2. We set up local 3D coordinate system (X_i, Y_i, Z_i) for each position of the calibration model plane, such that the $Z_i = 0$ plane coincides with the model plane. In addition, we assume the model plane has a set of m feature points. Usually, they are the corners of a checkerboard pattern. We denote these feature points as $\mathbf{P}_j$, $j = 1, \ldots, m$. Note the 3D coordinates of these feature points in each model plane's local coordinate system are identical. Each feature point's local 3D coordinate is associated with the world coordinate as

$$\mathbf{M}_{ij} = \begin{bmatrix} \mathbf{R}_i & \mathbf{t}_i \\ \mathbf{0}^T & 1 \end{bmatrix} \mathbf{P}_j. \tag{3.4}$$

where $\mathbf{M}_{ij}$ is the jth feature point of the ith image in the world coordinate system and $\mathbf{R}_i$ and $\mathbf{t}_i$ are the rotation and translation from the ith model plane's local coordinate system to the world coordinate system. The feature points are observed in the color image as $\mathbf{m}_{ij}$, which are associated with $\mathbf{M}_{ij}$ through Eq. (3.1).

Given the set of feature points $\mathbf{P}_j$ and their projections $\mathbf{m}_{ij}$, our goal is to recover the intrinsic matrix $\mathbf{A}$, the model plane rotations and translations $\mathbf{R}_i, \mathbf{t}_i$, and the transform between the color and the depth cameras $\mathbf{R}$ and $\mathbf{t}$. It is well-known that given the set of color images, the intrinsic matrix $\mathbf{A}$ and the model plane positions $\mathbf{R}_i, \mathbf{t}_i$ can be computed [5]. It is unclear, however, whether the depth images can be used to reliably determine $\mathbf{R}$ and $\mathbf{t}$ automatically.

3.4.2 A Maximum Likelihood Solution

The calibration solution to the color image-only problem is well known [5]. Due to the pinhole camera model, we have

$$s_{ij}\mathbf{m}_{ij} = \mathbf{A}[\mathbf{R}_i \ \mathbf{t}_i]\mathbf{P}_j \tag{3.5}$$

In practice, the feature points on the color images are usually extracted with automatic algorithms and may have errors. Assume that $\mathbf{m}_{ij}$ follows a Gaussian distribution with the ground truth position as its mean, i.e.,

$$\mathbf{m}_{ij} \sim \mathcal{N}(\bar{\mathbf{m}}_{ij}, \Phi_{ij}). \tag{3.6}$$

The log likelihood function can be written as

$$L_1 = -\frac{1}{2nm} \sum_{i=1}^{n} \sum_{j=1}^{m} \epsilon_{ij}^{\mathrm{T}} \Phi_{ij}^{-1} \epsilon_{ij}, \qquad (3.7)$$

where

$$\epsilon_{ij} = \mathbf{m}_{ij} - \frac{1}{s_{ij}} \mathbf{A}[\mathbf{R}_i \ \mathbf{t}_i] \mathbf{P}_j. \qquad (3.8)$$

We next study terms related to the depth images. There are a set of points in the depth image that correspond to the model plane, as those inside the red quadrilateral in Fig. 3.1. We randomly sample K_i points within the quadrilateral, denoted by $\mathbf{M}_{ik_i}^d, i = 1, \ldots, n; k_i = 1, \ldots, K_i$. If the depth image is noise free, we shall have

$$[0\ 0\ 1\ 0] \begin{bmatrix} \mathbf{R}_i & \mathbf{t}_i \\ \mathbf{0}^{\mathrm{T}} & 1 \end{bmatrix}^{-1} \begin{bmatrix} \mathbf{R} & \mathbf{t} \\ \mathbf{0}^{\mathrm{T}} & 1 \end{bmatrix} \mathbf{M}_{ik_i}^d = 0, \qquad (3.9)$$

which states that if we transform these points to the local coordinate system of each model plane, the Z_i coordinate shall be zero.

Since the depth images are usually noisy, we assume $\mathbf{M}_{ik_i}^d$ follows a Gaussian distribution as

$$\mathbf{M}_{ik_i}^d \sim \mathcal{N}(\bar{\mathbf{M}}_{ik_i}^d, \Phi_{ik_i}^d). \qquad (3.10)$$

The log likelihood function can thus be written as

$$L_2 = -\frac{1}{2 \sum_{i=1}^{n} K_i} \sum_{i=1}^{n} \sum_{k_i=1}^{K_i} \frac{\varepsilon_{ik_i}^2}{\sigma_{ik_i}^2}, \qquad (3.11)$$

where

$$\varepsilon_{ik_i} = \mathbf{a}_i^{\mathrm{T}} \mathbf{M}_{ik_i}^d \qquad (3.12)$$

where

$$\mathbf{a}_i = \begin{bmatrix} \mathbf{R}^{\mathrm{T}} & \mathbf{0} \\ \mathbf{t}^{\mathrm{T}} & 1 \end{bmatrix} \begin{bmatrix} \mathbf{R}_i & \mathbf{0} \\ -\mathbf{t}_i^{\mathrm{T}} \mathbf{R}_i & 1 \end{bmatrix} \begin{bmatrix} 0 \\ 0 \\ 1 \\ 0 \end{bmatrix}, \qquad (3.13)$$

and

$$\sigma_{ik_i}^2 = \mathbf{a}_i^{\mathrm{T}} \Phi_{ik_i}^d \mathbf{a}_i. \qquad (3.14)$$

It is sometimes helpful to have a few corresponding point pairs in the color images and the depth images, as shown in Fig. 3.1. We denote such point pairs as $(\mathbf{m}_{ip_i}, \mathbf{M}_{ip_i}^d), i = 1, \ldots, n; p_i = 1, \ldots, P_i$. These point pairs shall satisfy

$$s_{ip_i} \mathbf{m}_{ip_i} = \mathbf{A}[\mathbf{R}\ \mathbf{t}]\mathbf{M}^d_{ip_i}. \tag{3.15}$$

Whether the point correspondences are manually labeled or automatically established, they may not be accurate. Assume

$$\mathbf{m}_{ip_i} \sim \mathcal{N}(\bar{\mathbf{m}}_{ip_i}, \Phi_{ip_i});\ \mathbf{M}^d_{ip_i} \sim \mathcal{N}(\bar{\mathbf{M}}^d_{ip_i}, \Phi^d_{ip_i}), \tag{3.16}$$

where Φ_{ip_i} models the inaccuracy of the point in the color image and $\Phi^d_{ip_i}$ models the uncertainty of the 3D point from the depth sensor. The log likelihood function can be written as

$$L_3 = -\frac{1}{2\sum_{i=1}^n P_i} \sum_{i=1}^n \sum_{p_i=1}^{P_i} \xi_{ip_i}^T \tilde{\Phi}_{ip_i}^{-1} \xi_{ip_i}, \tag{3.17}$$

where

$$\xi_{ip_i} = \mathbf{m}_{ip_i} - \mathbf{B}_{ip_i} \mathbf{M}^d_{ip_i}, \tag{3.18}$$

where

$$\mathbf{B}_{ip_i} = \frac{1}{s_{ip_i}} \mathbf{A}[\mathbf{R}\ \mathbf{t}], \tag{3.19}$$

and

$$\tilde{\Phi}_{ip_i} = \Phi_{ip_i} + \mathbf{B}_{ip_i} \Phi^d_{ip_i} \mathbf{B}^T_{ip_i}. \tag{3.20}$$

Combining all the information together, we maximize the overall log likelihood as

$$\max_{\mathbf{A}, \mathbf{R}_i, \mathbf{t}_i, \mathbf{R}, \mathbf{t}} \rho_1 L_1 + \rho_2 L_2 + \rho_3 L_3, \tag{3.21}$$

where $\rho_i, i = 1, 2, 3$ are weighting parameters. The above objective function is a non-linear least squares problem, which can be solved using the Levenberg–Marquardt method [17].

3.4.3 The Depth Mapping Function

There may be a few other parameters that need to be estimated during calibration. For instance, the color camera may exhibit significant lens distortions; thus, it is necessary to estimate them based on the observed model planes. Another set of unknown parameters may be in the depth mapping function $\mathbf{f}(\cdot)$. In the following, we present a model of the depth mapping function for the Kinect sensor.

The Kinect sensor uses structured light to perform depth reconstruction. The principle is described in Fig. 3.3. Let the baseline between the IR projector and the IR camera be b_0, and the IR camera's focal length be f_0. Based on triangulation,

Fig. 3.3 Depth computation of Kinect camera

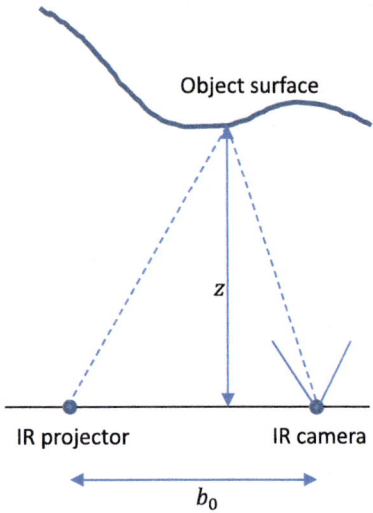

the object depth Z and the disparity between the IR projector and the IR camera δ have the simple relationship:

$$\frac{b_0}{Z} = \frac{\delta}{f_0}, \text{ or } Z = \frac{b_0 f_0}{\delta}. \tag{3.22}$$

All Kinect sensors go through in-factory calibration before they are shipped to customers. The calibration procedure is simple: The Kinect sensor is mounted in front of a flat white surface, which is at a distance $Z_0 = 1,000$ mm from the sensor. The captured image from the IR camera is stored in the firmware as a reference image I_0. During operation, the IR camera captures a new image I and computes the disparity between I and I_0. Let the disparity be $\delta(u, v)$, where (u, v) is the image coordinate in I; the Kinect will then output depth as

$$Z(u, v) = \frac{b_0 f_0}{\zeta_0 + \delta(u, v)}, \tag{3.23}$$

where $\zeta_0 = \frac{b_0 f_0}{Z_0}$. Note parameters b_0, f_0, and Z_0 are all preset values during depth reconstruction.

However, the in-factory calibration may not be very accurate. In addition, the Kinect sensor may become uncalibrated during transportation for various reasons, such as vibration, heat, etc. These factors cause the reported depth values from Kinect inaccurate. We would like to use a calibration procedure to correct such factors, in other words, to find a correct depth mapping function $\mathbf{f}(\cdot)$. For this purpose, we make the following two assumptions in this paper:

- The preset values, b_0, f_0, and Z_0, can be inaccurate.
- Between the IR projector and the IR camera, there could be small translation and rotation that happen during the transportation. Note if translation happens, it is equivalent to having an inaccurate b_0; thus, the translation case can be absorbed to the first case.

We approach the above modeling problem as follows. Assume, in the ideal case, the in-factory calibration is accurate, and the calibration remains accurate throughout transportation. In such a case, Eq. (3.23) would be the perfect solution to compute $Z(u, v)$. Let there be a flat wall in front of the Kinect at distance $Z(u, v) = Z_0$; we would have $\delta(u, v) = 0$. However, if the Kinect sensor lost its perfect calibration, even when we place a flat wall perfectly in front of the Kinect at distance Z_0, it will not report a constant $Z(u, v)$. In other words, $\delta(u, v)$ is no longer zero everywhere. Denote the current disparity values $\delta(u, v) = \delta_0(u, v)$. If $\delta_0(u, v)$ is known, then the corrected depth value of the scene shall be

$$\tilde{Z}(u, v) = \frac{b_0 f_0}{d_0 + \delta_0(u, v) + \delta(u, v)} = \frac{b_0 f_0}{\delta_0(u, v) + \frac{b_0 f_0}{Z(u,v)}}. \quad (3.24)$$

Note in the above equation, $Z(u, v)$ is the depth value reported by the Kinect sensor.

Let us further examine how to establish a model for $\delta_0(u, v)$. Assume that the preset values should indeed be b_1, f_1 and Z_1, and there is a small rotation $\Delta\theta$ between the IR projector and the IR camera during transportation. Note since the depth reconstruction is done by triangulation horizontally, only the yaw angle $\Delta\theta_y$ (rotation along the vertical axis) will cause systematic bias to $\delta_0(u, v)$. It could be computed that

$$\delta_0(u, v) \approx \frac{b_1 f_1}{Z_1} - \frac{b_0 f_0}{Z_0} + \frac{\partial u}{\partial \theta_y} \Delta\theta_y, \quad (3.25)$$

where

$$\frac{\partial u}{\partial \theta_y} = \frac{f_1 \partial \tan\theta_y}{\partial \theta_y} = \frac{(u - u_0)^2 + f_1^2}{f_1}, \quad (3.26)$$

where u_0 is the camera principle point's horizontal coordinate. Let $\omega = \frac{u-u_0}{f_1}$, which is the normalized horizontal coordinate. Plug Eqs. (3.25)–(3.24), we have a mathematical model for Kinect calibration as

$$\tilde{Z}(u, v) \approx \frac{1}{\eta_1 + \frac{1+\eta_2}{Z(u,v)} + \eta_3 \omega^2} \quad (3.27)$$

Thus, during calibration, parameters η_1, η_2, η_3 shall be estimated. Note if there is no distortion, we shall have $\eta_1 = \eta_2 = \eta_3 = 0$.

And the depth mapping function for Kinect shall be

$$\mathbf{f}(\mathbf{x}) = \begin{bmatrix} \left(\dfrac{1}{\eta_1 + \frac{1+\eta_2}{z} + \eta_3 \omega^2}\right) (\mathbf{A}^d)^{-1}[u, v, 1]^{\mathrm{T}} \\ 1 \end{bmatrix}, \qquad (3.28)$$

where $\mathbf{A}^d$ is the intrinsic matrix of the depth sensor. Usually, $\mathbf{A}^d$ is predetermined. The other parameters η_1, η_2, and η_3 can be estimated within the same maximum likelihood framework.

3.4.4 Solutions for Initialization

Since the overall likelihood function in Eq. (3.21) is nonlinear, it is very important to have good initialization for the unknown parameters. For the parameters related to the color camera, i.e., $\mathbf{A}$, $\mathbf{R}_i$ and $\mathbf{t}_i$, we may adopt the same initialization scheme as in [5]. In the following, we discuss methods to provide the initial estimation of the rotation $\mathbf{R}$ and translation $\mathbf{t}$ between the depth and color sensors. During the process, we assume $\mathbf{A}$, $\mathbf{R}_i$, and $\mathbf{t}_i$ of the color camera are known.

3.4.4.1 Initialization with Model Plane Matching

For most commodity depth cameras, the color camera and the depth camera are positioned very closely. It is therefore simple to automatically identify a set of points in each depth image that lies on the model plane. Let these points be $\mathbf{M}^d_{ik_i}$, $i = 1, \ldots, n$; $k_i = 1, \ldots, K_i$. For a given depth image i, if $K_i \geq 3$, it is possible to fit a plane to the points in that image. That is, given

$$\mathbf{H}_i \begin{bmatrix} \mathbf{n}^d_i \\ b^d_i \end{bmatrix} = \begin{bmatrix} (\mathbf{M}^d_{i1})^{\mathrm{T}} \\ (\mathbf{M}^d_{i2})^{\mathrm{T}} \\ \vdots \\ (\mathbf{M}^d_{iK_i})^{\mathrm{T}} \end{bmatrix} \begin{bmatrix} \mathbf{n}^d_i \\ b^d_i \end{bmatrix} = 0, \qquad (3.29)$$

where $\mathbf{n}^d_i$ is the normal of the model plane in the depth sensor's 3D coordinate system, $\|\mathbf{n}^d_i\|^2 = 1$, and b^d_i is the bias from the origin. $\|\mathbf{n}^d_i\|$ and b^d_i can be easily found through least squares fitting.

In the color sensor's coordinate system, the model plane can also be described by plane equation

$$[0\ 0\ 1\ 0] \begin{bmatrix} \mathbf{R}_i & \mathbf{t}_i \\ \mathbf{0}^{\mathrm{T}} & 1 \end{bmatrix}^{-1} \mathbf{M} = 0. \qquad (3.30)$$

Since $\mathbf{R}_i$ and $\mathbf{t}_i$ are known, we represent the plane's normal as $\mathbf{n}_i$, $\|\mathbf{n}_i\|^2 = 1$, and bias from the origin b_i.

We first solve the rotation matrix $\mathbf{R}$. Denote

$$\mathbf{R} = \begin{bmatrix} \mathbf{r}_1^T \\ \mathbf{r}_2^T \\ \mathbf{r}_3^T \end{bmatrix}. \tag{3.31}$$

We minimize the following objective function with constraint:

$$J(\mathbf{R}) = \sum_{i=1}^{n} \|\mathbf{n}_i - \mathbf{R}\mathbf{n}_i^d\| + \sum_{j=1}^{3} \lambda_j (\mathbf{r}_j^T \mathbf{r}_j - 1) \\ + 2\lambda_4 \mathbf{r}_1^T \mathbf{r}_2 + 2\lambda_5 \mathbf{r}_1^T \mathbf{r}_3 + 2\lambda_6 \mathbf{r}_2^T \mathbf{r}_3. \tag{3.32}$$

This objective function can be solved in close form [18]. Let

$$\mathbf{C} = \sum_{i=1}^{n} \mathbf{n}_i^d \mathbf{n}_i^T. \tag{3.33}$$

The singular value decomposition of $\mathbf{C}$ can be written as

$$\mathbf{C} = \mathbf{U}\mathbf{D}\mathbf{V}^T, \tag{3.34}$$

where $\mathbf{U}$ and $\mathbf{V}$ are orthonormal matrices and $\mathbf{D}$ is a diagonal matrix. The rotation matrix is simply

$$\mathbf{R} = \mathbf{V}\mathbf{U}^T. \tag{3.35}$$

The minimum number of images to determine the rotation matrix $\mathbf{R}$ is $n = 2$, provided that the two model planes are not parallel to each other.

For translation, we have the following relationship:

$$(\mathbf{n}_i^d)^T \mathbf{t} + b_i^d = b_i. \tag{3.36}$$

Thus, three non-parallel model planes will determine a unique $\mathbf{t}$. If $n > 3$, we may solve $\mathbf{t}$ through least squares fitting.

3.4.4.2 Initialization with Point Pair Matching

Another scheme to estimate the initial rotation $\mathbf{R}$ and translation $\mathbf{t}$ is through the knowledge of a set of point correspondences between the color images and the depth images. Denote such point pairs as $(\mathbf{m}_{ip_i}, \mathbf{M}_{ip_i}^d)$, $i = 1, \ldots, n$; $p_i = 1, \ldots, P_i$. We have the relationship

$$s_{ip_i}\mathbf{m}_{ip_i} = \mathbf{A}[\mathbf{R}\ \mathbf{t}]\mathbf{M}^d_{ip_i}. \tag{3.37}$$

Note the intrinsic matrix **A** is known. Such a problem has been studied extensively in the literature [19, 20]. It has been shown that given three point pairs, there are in general four solutions to the rotation and translation. When one has four or more non-coplanar point pairs, the so-called POSIT algorithm [21] can be used to find the initial value of **R** and **t**.

3.5 Experimental Results

The maximum likelihood solution in Eq. (3.21) can be used to calibrate all unknown parameters for the depth and color sensors. Due to space limitations, in this paper, we focus our attention on the parameters related to the depth sensor only, i.e., **R**, **t**, and $\mathbf{f}(\cdot)$ and assume $\mathbf{A}, \mathbf{R}_i, \mathbf{t}_i$ are known (or obtained separately from, say, maximizing Eq. (3.7) only [5]).

3.5.1 Simulated Results

The simulated depth/color camera has the following parameters. For the color camera, $\alpha = 750, \beta = 745, \gamma = 0, u_0 = 315, v_0 = 245$. The image resolution is 640×480. The rotation and translation from the depth camera to the color camera is represented by vector $[\theta_x, \theta_y, \theta_z, t_x, t_y, t_z]^T = [0.05, -0.01, 0.02, 25, 2, -2]^T$, where $[\theta_x, \theta_y, \theta_z]^T$ in radians represents rotation, which can be converted to **R** through the well-known Rodrigues' rotation formula, and the last three elements represent translation $\mathbf{t} = [t_x, t_y, t_z]^T$ in millimeters.

3.5.1.1 Performance w.r.t. the Noise Level

In this experiment, we examine the impact of the depth camera's noise level on the calibration accuracy. Three model planes are used in the experiment. The checkerboard pattern has 10×7 corners on a regular grid. The distance between neighboring corners is 37. The three model planes are located at $\left[\frac{\pi}{8}, 0, 0, -300, 25, 750\right]^T$, $\left[0, \frac{\pi}{8}, -\frac{\pi}{18}, -110, -100, 1150\right]^T$, and $\left[-\frac{\pi}{36}, 0, \frac{\pi}{6}, 120, -200, 800\right]^T$, respectively. Only the plane fitting likelihood term Eq. (3.11) is maximized to determine **R** and **t**, where $K_i = 1{,}000$. The covariance of the depth noise is assumed to be independent of the depth values (which is an acceptable assumption for ToF-based depth cameras). At each noise level, 500 trials were run and the standard deviations (STDs) of the errors are reported, as shown in Fig. 3.4. It can be seen that the STDs of the angular errors and translation errors increase linearly with the noise level. The mean of the

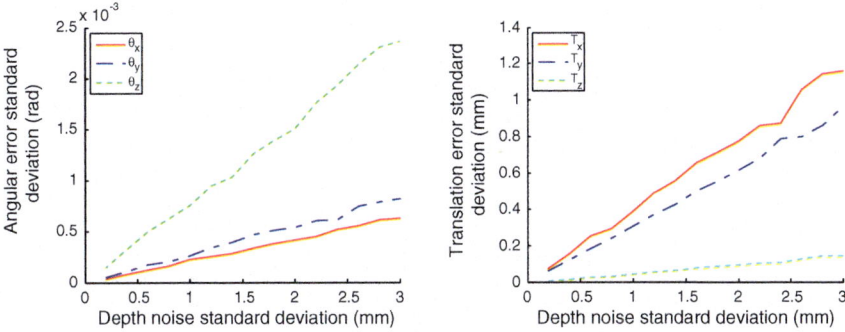

Fig. 3.4 Calibration accuracy versus depth camera noise level

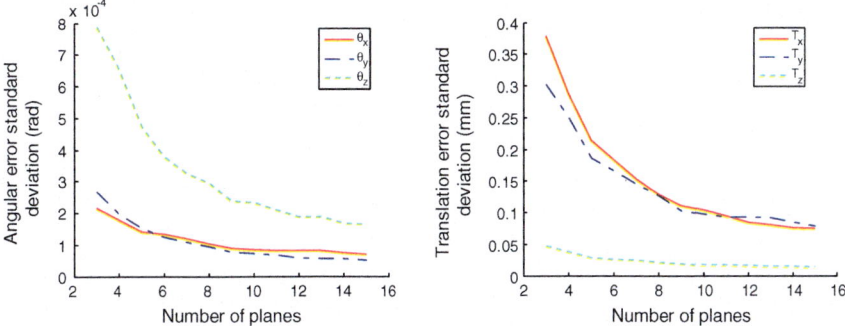

Fig. 3.5 Calibration accuracy versus number of model planes

errors are generally very close to zero (not shown in Fig. 3.4), and the STDs are very small, indicating satisfactory calibration accuracy and algorithm stability.

3.5.1.2 Performance w.r.t. the Number of Planes

In the second experiment, we examine whether increasing the number of model planes could improve calibration accuracy. We tested between 3 and 15 planes, as shown in Fig. 3.5. The first 3 planes are the same as those in Sect. 3.5.1.1. From the fourth image on, we randomly generate a vector on the unit sphere and apply a rotation with respect to the vector for an angle of $\frac{\pi}{6}$. Again only the plane fitting likelihood term Eq. (3.11) is maximized to determine **R** and **t**. The covariance of the depth noise is set to 1 throughout the experiment. For a given number of planes, we run 500 trials and report the STDs of the errors. From Fig. 3.5, it is obvious that increasing the number of planes leads to smaller STDs of the errors and thus better calibration accuracy. We recommend at least 8–10 planes to achieve sufficient accuracy during calibration.

3.5.1.3 Performance w.r.t. the Plane Orientations

Next, we study the impact of the model plane orientations. We again use three planes for calibration. The planes are generated as follows. We first randomly choose three vectors on the unit circle in the color camera's imaging plane, and we make sure the smallest angle between the three vectors is greater than $\frac{\pi}{9}$. We then apply a rotation with respect to the three vectors for a varying angle between 10° and 80° to generate three model planes for calibration. A total of 500 trials were run for each configuration in Fig. 3.6. It contains three groups of curves.

In the first group, only the plane fitting likelihood term Eq. (3.11) is maximized to determine **R** and **t**. It can be seen that when the plane orientations are small, the calibration errors are big. This is intuitive, since according to Sect. 3.4.4.1, parallel planes would not be effective in determining the rotation/translation between the depth and color sensors.

In the second group, we use the point pair likelihood term Eq. (3.17) to determine **R** and **t**. For this purpose, we assume the four corners of each model plane are known in both the color and the depth images; thus, we have a total of 12 point pairs. Noise of covariance 0.25^2 is added to the position of the point pairs to mimic the real-world scenario. It can be seen from Fig. 3.6 that with so few point pairs, the calibration error STDs are generally bigger than those generated by planning fitting. An exception is the cases of very small plane orientations, where the plane fitting only solution performs very poorly.

In the third group, we determine **R** and **t** based on the combination of plane fitting and point pair likelihood terms. We use $\rho_2 = 1$ and $\rho_3 = 0.2$. It can be seen that for small plane orientations, combining the two likelihood terms results in better performance than using only either. When the plane orientations are large, however, the plane fitting likelihood term alone seems to perform better. In practice, we also need to consider the calibration accuracy of the color camera parameters. It has been shown in [5] that color camera calibration will perform poorly if the model planes are

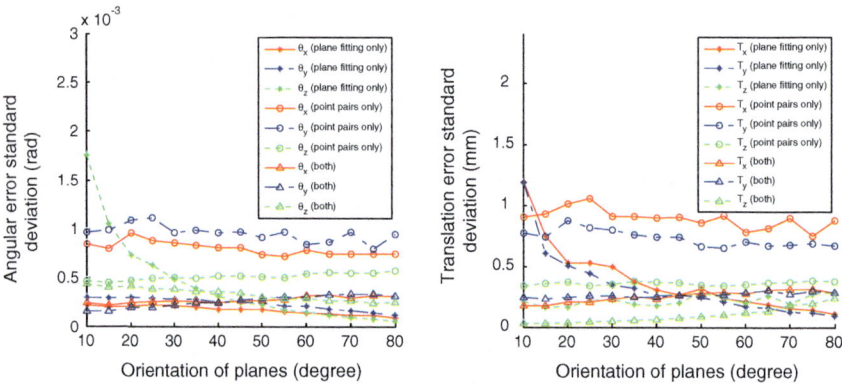

Fig. 3.6 Calibration accuracy versus plane orientations

near perpendicular to the color image's imaging plane. Therefore, we recommend to use model planes oriented about 30°–50° with respect to the color camera's imaging plane for better overall calibration quality.

3.5.1.4 Performance w.r.t. the Correct Noise Model

So far, we have assumed depth-independent noises in the depth image. This is acceptable for ToF depth cameras such as the ZCam from 3DV systems. However, for triangularization-based depth cameras such as the Kinect camera, the noise level is a quadratic function of the depth [3]. Both types of noises can be accommodated with our maximum likelihood solution in Sect. 3.4. On the other hand, applying the correct noise model would generally improve calibration performance. Here, we use the same setup as Sect. 3.5.1.1, except that the depth noise follows the formula in [3]:

$$\sigma \propto Z^2, \qquad (3.38)$$

and we assume the noise level at $Z = 1{,}000$ is known (adapting as the horizontal axis of Fig. 3.7). We ran two sets of experiments. In the first set, we assume the user is unaware of the sensor noise type and blindly assume that the noise is depth independent. In the second set, the correct noise model is applied. It can be seen from Fig. 3.7 that using the correct noise model results in better calibration performance.

3.5.2 Real-World Results

Finally, we test the proposed method on a real Kinect sensor. A set of 12 model planes at different positions and orientations is captured. One of the image pairs has been shown in Fig. 3.1. The color sensor's intrinsic parameters are first estimated

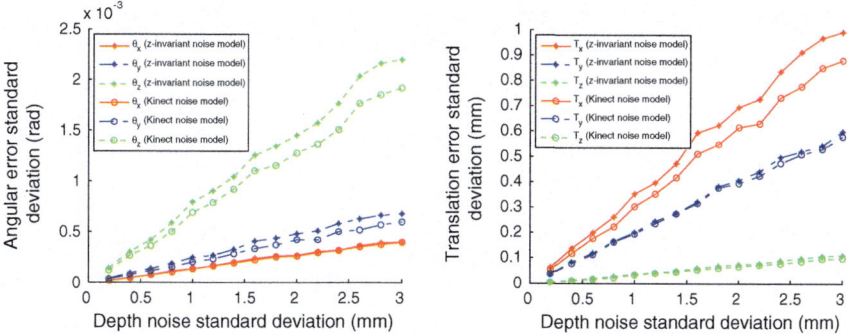

Fig. 3.7 Calibration accuracy versus correct noise model

with [5] as $\alpha = 528.32, \beta = 527.03, \gamma = 0, u_0 = 320.10, v_0 = 257.57$. We then apply the proposed technique to calibrate $\mathbf{R}$, $\mathbf{t}$, and $\mathbf{f}(\cdot)$, where $\mathbf{f}(\cdot)$ contains unknown parameters such as η_1, η_2, and η_3. The depth camera's intrinsic matrix $\mathbf{A}^d$ is preset to $\alpha^d = 575, \beta^d = 575, \gamma = 0, u_0^d = 320, v_0^d = 240$.

The calibration results with plane fitting alone are $[0.0063, 0.0029, 0.0066, -15.2278, 20.089, 5.6089]^T$ for rotation and translation, $\eta_1 = 0.000098$, $\eta_2 = -0.030588$, and $\eta_3 = 0.000040$ for the depth mapping model. To demonstrate the calibration accuracy, we warp the color images based on the calibrated parameters and overlay them onto the depth images to examine how well they align with each other, as shown in Fig. 3.8a. It can be seen that the alignment is very accurate.

As shown in Sect. 3.5.1.3, adding additional point correspondences between the color and the depth images may help improve calibration performance when the model planes do not have sufficient variations in orientation. Another benefit of adopting point correspondences is to expand the calibration effective zone. It is well known that for calibration to work well, the checkerboard shall be placed across the whole workspace. In Fig. 3.8a, we notice the chair region is not aligned well,

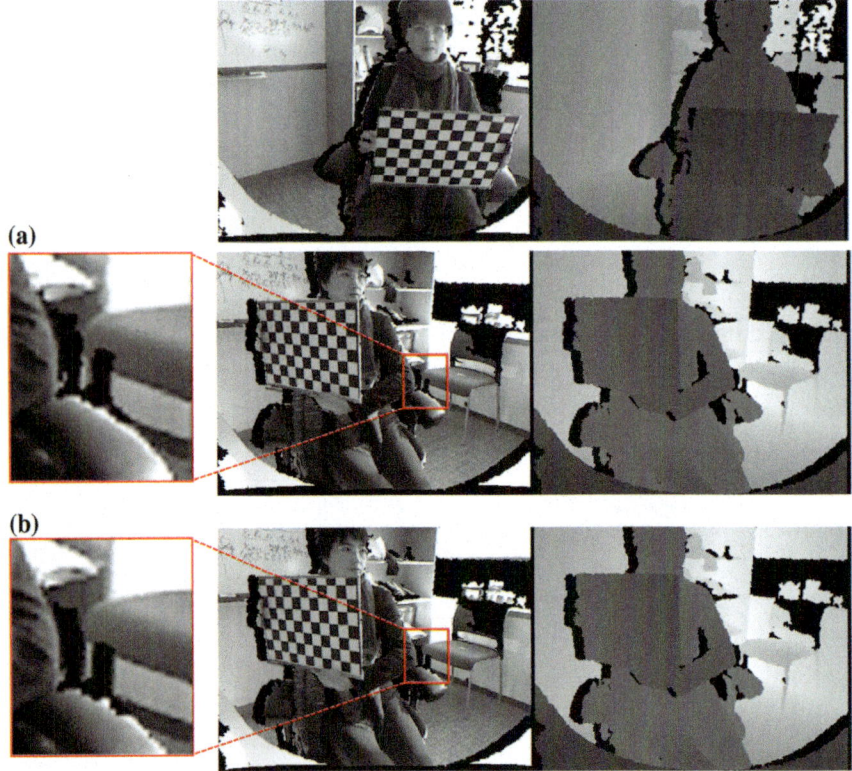

Fig. 3.8 Calibration results for a real scene. **a** Use plane fitting only. **b** Use both plane fitting and point pairs

since no checkerboard was placed there in the 12 images. We manually add 3–5 point correspondences for each image pair, some of them lying on the background of the scene (see Fig. 3.1). After using both plane fitting and point correspondences to calibrate, the results are $[-0.0080, 0.0019, 0.0083, -15.7976, 10.3564, 12.2657]^T$ for rotation and translation, $\eta_1 = 0.000095$, $\eta_2 = -0.031034$, and $\eta_3 = 0.000038$ for depth correction model. A warped result is shown in Fig. 3.8b. The improvement in the chair area is very obvious.

3.6 Conclusions and Future Work

In this chapter, we presented a novel algorithm to calibrate color and depth sensors jointly. The method is reliable and accurate, and it does not require additional hardware other than the easily available checkerboard pattern. Future work includes better modeling of the depth mapping function $\mathbf{f}(\cdot)$ and better understanding of the depth cameras' noise models.

References

1. Cui Y, Schuon S, Chan D, Thrun S, Theobalt C (2010) 3D shape scanning with a time-of-flight camera. In: CVPR
2. Crabb R, Tracey C, Puranik A, Davis J (2008) Real-time foreground segmentation via range and color imaging. In: CVPR workshop on ToF-camera based computer vision
3. Cai Q, Gallup D, Zhang C, Zhang Z (2010) 3D deformable face tracking with a commodity depth camera. In: ECCV
4. Tsai R (1987) A versatile camera calibration technique for high-accuracy 3D machine vision metrology using off-the-shelf tv cameras and lens. IEEE J Robot Autom RA–3(4):323–344
5. Zhang Z (2000) A flexible new technique for camera calibration. IEEE Trans Pattern Anal Mach Intell 22(11):1330–1334
6. Kuhnert KD, Stommel M (2006) Fusion of stereo-camera and pmd-camera data for real-time suited precise 3D environment reconstruction. In: Intelligent robots and systems, 2006 IEEE/RSJ international conference on, IEEE, pp 4780–4785
7. Beder C, Koch R (2008) Calibration of focal length and 3d pose based on the reflectance and depth image of a planar object. Int J Intell Syst Technol Appl 5(3):285–294
8. Fuchs S, Hirzinger G (2008) Extrinsic and depth calibration of tof-cameras. In: CVPR, IEEE, pp 1–6
9. Lindner M, Schiller I, Kolb A, Koch R (2010) Time-of-flight sensor calibration for accurate range sensing. Comput Vis Image Underst 114(12):1318–1328
10. Shim H, Adelsberger R, Kim JD, Rhee SM, Rhee T, Sim JY, Gross M, Kim C (2012) Time-of-flight sensor and color camera calibration for multi-view acquisition. Vis Comput 28(12):1139–1151
11. Herrera D, Kannala J, Heikkilä J (2011) Accurate and practical calibration of a depth and color camera pair. In: Computer analysis of images and patterns, Springer, pp 437–445
12. Zhang C, Zhang Z (2011) Calibration between depth and color sensors for commodity depth cameras. In: International workshop on hot topics in 3D, IEEE, pp 1–6
13. Herrera C, Kannala J, Heikkilä J et al (2012) Joint depth and color camera calibration with distortion correction. Pattern Anal Mach Intell, IEEE Trans 34(10):2058–2064

14. Raposo C, Barreto JP, Nunes U (2013) Fast and accurate calibration of a kinect sensor. In: 3DTV-conference, 2013 international conference on, IEEE, pp 342–349
15. Liu W, Fan Y, Zhong Z, Lei T (2012) A new method for calibrating depth and color camera pair based on kinect. In: Audio, language and image processing (ICALIP), 2012 international conference on, IEEE, pp 212–217
16. Mikhelson IV, Lee PG, Sahakian AV, Wu Y, Katsaggelos AK (2014) Automatic, fast, online calibration between depth and color cameras. J Vis Commun Image Represent 25(1):218–226
17. More J (1978) The Levenberg-Marquardt algorithm: implementation and theory. Numerl Anal, Lect Notes Math 630(1978):105–116
18. Arun K, Huang T, Blostein S (1987) Least-squares fitting of two 3-d point sets. IEEE Trans PAMI 9(5):698–700
19. Fischler MA, Bolles RC (1981) Random sample consensus: a paradigm for model fitting with applications to image analysis and automated cartography. Commun ACM 24(6):381–395
20. Yuan JS-C (1989) A general photogrammetric method for determining object position and orientation. IEEE Trans Robot Autom 5(2):129–142
21. Dementhon D, Davis L (1995) Model-based object pose in 25 lines of code. Int J Comput Vis 15(1):123–141

Chapter 4
Depth Map Denoising via CDT-Based Joint Bilateral Filter

Andreas Koschan and Mongi Abidi

Abstract Bi-modal image processing can be defined as a series of steps taken to enhance a target image with a guidance image. This is done by using exploitable information derived from acquiring two images of the same scene with different image modalities. However, while the potential benefit of bi-modal image processing may be significant, there is an inherent risk; if noise or defects in the guidance image are allowed to transfer to the target image, the target image could become corrupted rather than improved. In this chapter, we present a new method to enhance a noisy depth map from its color information via the joint bilateral filter (JBF) based on common distance transform (CDT). This method is composed of two main steps: CDT map generation and CDT-based JBF. In the first step, a CDT map is generated that represents the degree of pixel-modal similarity between a depth pixel and its corresponding color pixel. Then, based on the CDT map, JBF is carried out in order to enhance depth information with the aid of color information. Experimental results show that CDT-based JBF outperforms other conventional methods objectively and subjectively in terms of noise reduction, as well as inherent visual artifacts suppression.

4.1 Introduction

Following the significant advances in depth acquisition technologies over the last few years, high-performance active range sensors [5, 7, 17] have been developed. They capture per-pixel distance information of a real scene which is represented in the form of a depth map. In many applications, the depth map is used with its corresponding color image as a pair called video-plus-depth [10, 41]. The merit

---

A. Koschan (✉) · M. Abidi
Imaging, Robotics, and Intelligent Systems Laboratory, Department of Electrical Engineering and Computer Science, The University of Tennessee, Knoxville, TN, USA
e-mail: akoschan@utk.edu

of video-plus-depth is backward compatibility with current video transmission and display devices [11]. The three-dimensional (3D) image representation is expected to be applied to a variety of interactive applications related to 3DTV [19], entertainment [31], and human-computer interaction [25] in the near future.

For practical applications of video-plus-depth, accurate depth data is often required. However, the depth maps acquired by active range sensors are typically degraded by severe noise during the acquisition process. The noise usually occurs as a result of a non-linear response of physical sensors, mixed pixels in the region of an object boundary, or a different reflectivity caused by object color variations [8]. Due to low-quality depth map generation, the practical use of active range sensors is limited in applications involving foreground extraction [16] and motion tracking [31]. Depth map denoising is essential to enabling a large variety of applications.

A bilateral filter (BF) [9, 35, 39] has been introduced for denoising a depth map using a kernel regression function derived from differences in pixel positions and depth values between a pixel of interest and its neighboring pixels. A joint bilateral filter (JBF) [14, 24, 26] is used to improve the quality of a depth map by the additional usage of the color information. The kernel of the JBF is derived from differences of intensities in the color image. A deblurring method applying regularized locally-adaptive kernel regression was introduced in [33], a dictionary-learning method using wavelets for denoising was proposed in [38], and an overview of image denoising algorithms can be found in [30]. In order to examine the effects of the data-adaptive kernel regression filters for depth map enhancement, experiments were carried out using a ground truth depth map and its corresponding color image *monopoly* provided by the Middlebury stereo dataset [29].

Figure 4.1a shows the noisy depth map for the test image *monopoly*, where Gaussian noise with a standard deviation of 20 is artificially added to the ground truth depth image (Fig. 4.1c). Figure 4.1b shows its corresponding color image. Figure 4.1d–f show the results of BF, JBF, and the proposed CDT-based JBF, respectively. When we look at the close-ups of the rectangular regions in the third and fifth row, it is observed that JBF preserves important depth discontinuity along the edge between objects. However, homogenous and continuous depth information (in the region around the letters 'MONOPOLY' on the playing panel) is changed to discontinuous depth information during JBF. These distortions are called *visual artifacts* [14, 22, 27]. In case of BF, depth information is blurred at the object boundaries. The aim of this work is to provide a practical solution for reducing the noise present in a depth map. For this, we present here a method to denoise a depth map via common distance transform (CDT) based JBF. As shown in Fig. 4.1f, CDT-based JBF preserves important depth discontinuity in a depth map while suppressing visual artifacts.

The proposed method for depth data enhancement is composed of two main steps: *CDT map generation* and *CDT-based JBF*. The first step is to obtain a CDT map that represents the degree of pixel-modal similarity between a depth pixel and its corresponding color pixel. Then, a per-pixel weighting function is calculated based on a CDT map and is used to determine which depth map regions are processed by color data. Finally, based on the weighting function, JBF is carried out for filtering

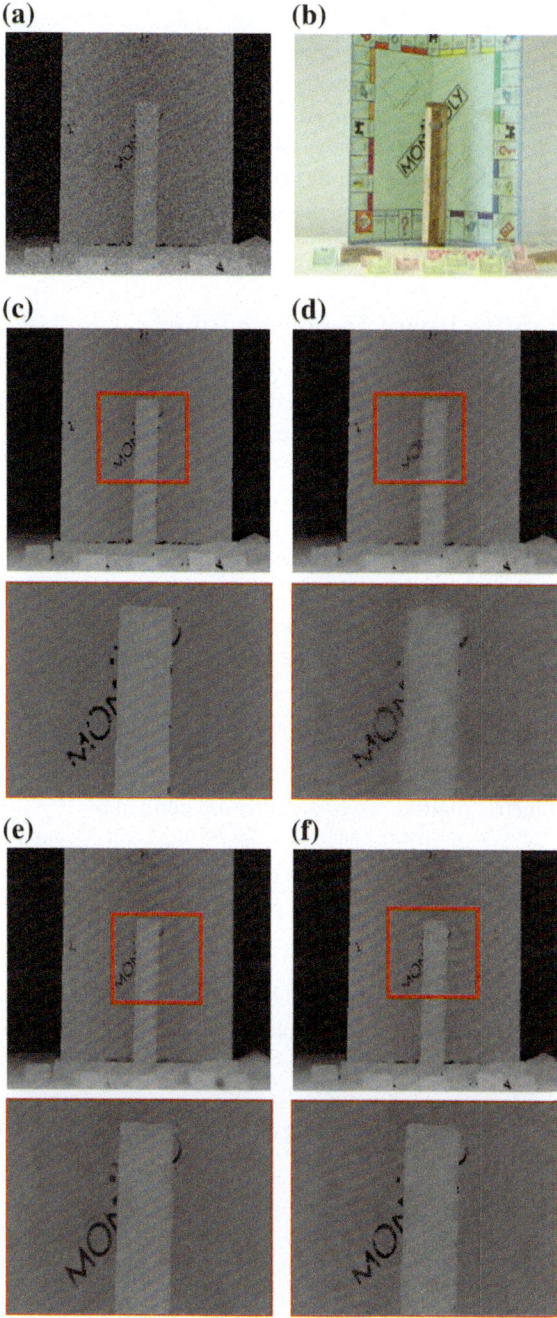

Fig. 4.1 Results of data-adaptive kernel regression filters for the test image *monopoly*; **a** input noisy depth map, **b** input color image, **c** ground truth depth map of (**a**), **d** result of BF, **e** result of JBF, and **f** result of the proposed CDT-based JBF

depth information with the aid of color data. The main contributions presented in this chapter are two-fold: (a) *developing an efficient method for depth map denoising via JBF while minimizing visual artifacts* and (b) *presenting a CDT map that represents the pixel-wise similarity of two different image modalities*.

This chapter is organized as follows. Section 4.2 introduces the related work of JBF. Then, Sect. 4.3 presents the proposed method in detail. Section 4.4 discusses the experimental results followed by conclusions in Sect. 4.5.

4.2 Data-Adaptive Image Denoising Filter

Suppose that (i_n, j_n) indicates the spatial coordinates of a pixel x_n and $z(x_n)$ is a regression function [36], a depth value d_n at x_n contaminated by a noise ε_n is expressed by

$$d_n = z(x_n) + \varepsilon_n \quad n = 1, \ldots, W \times W, \quad x_n = [i_n, j_n]^T \quad (4.1)$$

where $W \times W$ is the size of the local analysis window. Assuming that a regression function $z(x_n)$ is locally smooth to the 2nd order and a pixel x is close to x_n, we can represent $z(x_n)$ using the following Taylor series.

$$z(x_n) = \alpha_0 + \alpha_1^T (x_n - x) + \alpha_2^T \text{vech}\{(x_n - x)(x_n - x)\}^T, \quad (4.2)$$

where $(\cdot)$ is the distance between x_n and x. $\text{vech}\{\cdot\}$ is defined as the lower triangular portion of a symmetric matrix. α_0, α_1, and α_2 are defined by

$$\alpha_0 = z(x), \quad \alpha_1 = \nabla z(x) = \left[\frac{\partial z(x)}{\partial i} \frac{\partial z(x)}{\partial j}\right]^T, \quad \alpha_2 = \frac{1}{2}\left[\frac{\partial^2 z(x)}{\partial i^2} \frac{\partial^2 z(x)}{\partial i j} \frac{\partial^2 z(x)}{\partial j^2}\right]. \quad (4.3)$$

Note that the parameter α_0 is identical to $z(x)$ which is the estimated depth value at x. From Eq. (4.2), the optimization problem [2] to find the best depth value d_x^{new} is expressed by

$$\min \sum_{n \in W \times W} [\varepsilon_n]^2 = \min \sum_{n \in W \times W} [d_n - z(x_n)]^2$$
$$\approx \min \sum_{n \in W \times W} [d_n - \alpha_0$$
$$- \alpha_1^T (x_n - x) - \alpha_2^T \text{vech}\{(x_n - x)(x_n - x)^T\}]^2 K_H(x_n - x) \quad (4.4)$$

4 Depth Map Denoising via CDT-Based Joint Bilateral Filter

where K is the weighting function and H is the smoothing parameter. For example, if K is defined by a Gaussian function, H becomes its standard deviation. The minimum of the above term can be calculated by setting its derivative to zero.

Then, d_x^{new} can be written as

$$\alpha_0 \approx \hat{z}(x) = d_x^{\text{new}} = \frac{\sum_{n \in W \times W} K_H(x_n - x) d_n}{\sum_{n \in W \times W} K_H(x_n - x)}. \tag{4.5}$$

When a Gaussian function is used for K, the above equation is similar to a Gaussian low-pass filter [15]. It provides d_x^{new} by a weighted linear combination of the nearby samples. A higher order estimator such as the steering kernel filter (SKF) [13, 33] can be generally expressed in the weight-linear fashion as

$$d_x^{\text{new}} = \sum_{n \in W \times W} W_n(K, H, N, x_n - x) d_n \quad \text{where} \quad \sum_{n \in W \times W} W_n(\cdot) = 1 \tag{4.6}$$

and W_n is referred to as the equivalent kernel function.

A bilateral filter (BF) [9, 35, 39] uses photometric properties as well as spatial properties of a depth map. By considering the photometric difference between the depth value d_x at a pixel position x of interest and its neighbors $\{d_n\}$ at x_n, the BF is represented by

$$d_x^{\text{new}} = \frac{\sum_{n \in W \times W} K_S(x_n - x) K_P(d_n - d_x) d_n}{\sum_{n \in W \times W} K_S(x_n - x) K_P(d_n - d_x)}, \tag{4.7}$$

where S and P are the spatial and the photometric smoothing parameters, respectively.

Contrarily to the BF, the depth map is a *target image* and the color image becomes a *guidance image* in the *JBF* [14, 24, 26]. The fidelity of the color image is generally much better than the fidelity of the depth map because of the accuracy of the acquisition sensor. Hence, *JBF* is a process to enhance a noisy depth map from a color image. For the sake of simplicity we assume that the color image contains no noise even though to some degree every color image pixel is affected by noise.

If the photometric term of Eq. (4.7) is replaced by the color data, the JBF can be expressed by

$$d_x^{\text{new}} = \frac{\sum_{n \in W \times W} K_S(x_n - x) K_C(c_n - c_x) d_n}{\sum_{n \in W \times W} K_S(x_n - x) K_C(c_n - c_x)}, \tag{4.8}$$

where C is the photometric smoothing parameter of the color image. In addition, when photometric properties of a depth map and a color image are considered at the same time, an *adaptive JBF* [6, 21] is formulated as follows:

$$d_x^{\text{new}} = \frac{\sum_{n \in W \times W} K_S(x_n - x) K_C(c_n - c_x) K_P(d_n - d_x) d_n}{\sum_{n \in W \times W} K_S(x_n - x) K_C(c_n - c_x) K_P(d_n - d_x)}. \tag{4.9}$$

JBF has been widely used in various applications according to the structure of a guidance image. Petschnigg et al. [26] developed JBF to compute the edge-stopping function using the flash image and non-flash image. Kopf et al. [24] and Xiao et al. [37] employed JBF to upsample a low-resolution to high-resolution image. Tan et al. [34] and Yu et al. [42] also used JBF as a spatial filter to reduce noise on an image. Due to its satisfactory performance, JBF has even been used in other fields, such as compression [3] and matting [16].

In terms of depth map denoising using JBF, Riemens et al. [27] and Gangwal and Djapic [14] presented a JBF to upsample a depth map with its color information. Cho et al. [6] developed a method to remove optical noise on depth maps using adaptive JBF. Jachalsky et al. [18] regarded a confidence map representing reliable and occluded areas as a guidance image to refine a depth map. Kim et al. [20] used adaptive sampling and Gaussian smoothing for depth map enhancement in a range sensor system. Yang et al. [40] developed an iterative JBF method to increase spatial resolution of a depth map captured by a range sensor.

4.3 CDT-Based Joint Bilateral Filter

In the following sections, we will first introduce the CDT. Then we will explain the CDT map generation and define a JBF based on the CDT.

4.3.1 Common Distance Transforms

In order to prevent visual artifacts occurring from JBF, the depth map region affected by color information needs to be located. For this, distance transform (DT) [1, 12, 28] is employed in order to generate a DT map that contains the values of DT of an image. Since the DT map represents the distance between edges extracted from the image and all pixel positions in it, it is possible to determine whether a pixel belongs to a homogenous region or not.

Unlike the bilateral filter, the JBF utilizes depth data as well as color data. Therefore, we need to extend the distance transform to a new distance transform that can cover both data. For this, we present CDT to search out the similar DT value region between two different images. The CDT map is generated by an interaction of the DT maps of a depth map and a color image. As a consequence, a CDT map describes the degree of pixel-modal similarity between a depth pixel and its corresponding color pixel.

Figure 4.2 shows the overall framework of the proposed method which is implemented as follows: (1) Two edge maps, a depth edge map and a color edge map, are extracted from a depth map and a color image, (2) DT is performed on both edge maps, (3) A CDT map is derived by comparing the DT values of two depth maps, (4) A weighting function is derived by combining K_S, K_C, and K_P based on the

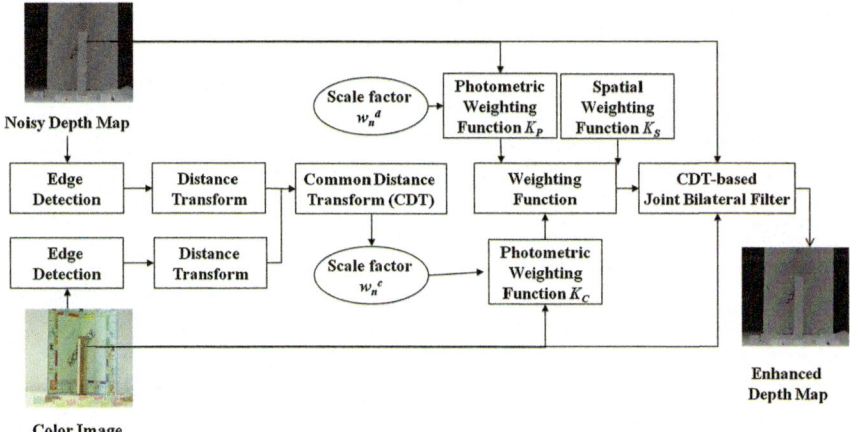

Fig. 4.2 Overall framework of depth map denoising

CDT map, and (5) JBF based on the weighting function is carried out adaptively to denoise a depth map.

4.3.2 CDT Map Generation

Prior to the distance transform, the *Canny* edge operator [4] is used to extract a color edge map E_C and a depth edge map E_D. Note that we ignore isolated edges during edge detection. For CDT map generation, we perform DT on E_C and E_D in order to obtain two DT maps. Initially, edge pixels in E_C and E_D are set to zero, while non-edge pixels are assigned infinity values, as shown in Fig. 4.3a. Then, based on a–b distance transform (a–b DT), the DT value $q^k(i, j)$ at iteration k is computed by

$$q^k(i, j) = \min\ [q^{k-1}(i-1, j-1) + b, q^{k-1}(i-1, j) + a, q^{k-1}(i-1, j+1) + b,$$
$$q^{k-1}(i, j-1) + a, q^{k-1}(i, j), q^{k-1}(i, j+1) + a,$$
$$q^{k-1}(i+1, j-1) + b, q^{k-1}(i+1, j) + a, q^{k-1}(i+1, j+1) + b]$$
(4.10)

where a and b control the strength of distance transform. b is empirically set to be $a + 1$. Figure 4.3 illustrates a DT map generation procedure using *1–2* DT.

In Fig. 4.3c, the DT value of the top-left corner pixel is 4. In contrast, the bottom-left pixel has a DT value of 1. This number indicates that the former may belong to a homogenous area whereas the latter may belong to a textured area. Suppose that there are the depth DT-value DT_x^D at x in a depth DT map DT^D and its corresponding color DT-value DT_x^C in a color DT map DT^C. If DT_x^D is equal to or similar with DT_x^C, both pixels may simultaneously belong to homogenous or textured areas.

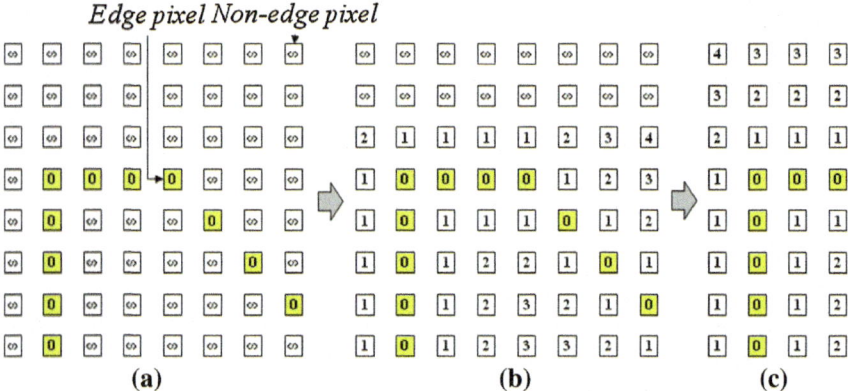

Fig. 4.3 DT map generation. **a** Initialization. **b** 1st iteration ($k = 1$). **c** 2nd iteration ($k = 2$)

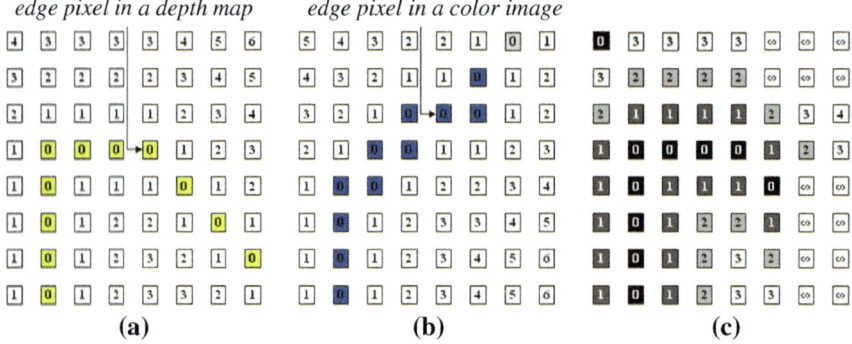

Fig. 4.4 CDT map generation procedure. **a** Depth DT map DT^D. **b** Color DT map DT^C. **c** CDT map DT^J

In order to measure pixel-wise similarity between a depth pixel and a color pixel based on a–b DT, a CDT value DT^J_x at x in the CDT map DT^J is calculated by

$$DT^J_x = \begin{cases} 0 & \text{if} & DT^D_x > T \, \& \, DT^C_x > T \\ DT^D_x & \text{if} & \left|DT^D_x - DT^C_x\right| \leq 2a \\ 255 & \text{otherwise} \end{cases}, \quad (4.11)$$

where T is the homogenous region detection threshold and $T > 2a$. Figure 4.4 depicts a CDT map generation procedure with $a = 1$ and $T = 4$. If both DT^D_x and DT^C_x are greater than 4, DT^J_x becomes zero.

If the absolute difference between DT^D_x and DT^C_x is smaller than 2, then DT^D_x is assigned to DT^J_x. Otherwise, DT^J_x is set to infinity (e.g., 255). As shown in Fig. 4.4c, a CDT map represents the degree of pixel-wise similarity between a depth pixel and a color pixel. If the CDT map value is zero or DT^D_x, the degree of pixel-wise similarity

4 Depth Map Denoising via CDT-Based Joint Bilateral Filter

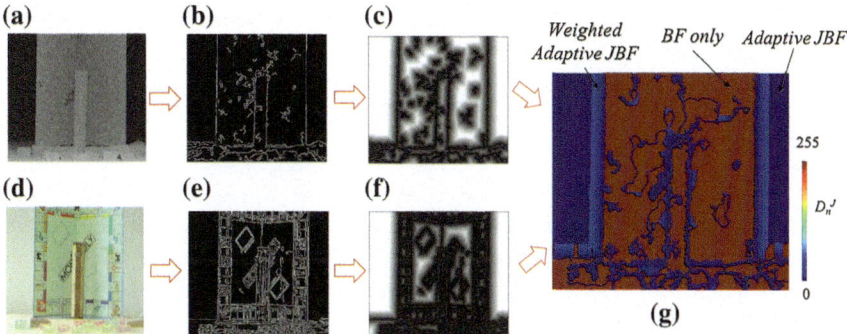

Fig. 4.5 Example of CDT map generation. **a** Noisy depth map. **b** Edge map E_D. **c** DT map DT^D. **d** Color image. **e** Edge map E_C. **f** DT map DT^C. **g** CDT map D^J

of both pixels is very high, i.e., the depth pixel is on a homogenous region in a depth map and its corresponding color pixel may be also a homogenous region in a color image, and vice versa. If the CDT value is infinity, the pixel modalities of both pixels are not identical. Figure 4.5 shows an example of CDT map generation for the image *monopoly* using *1–2* DT. DT values are multiplied by 10 for better visualization.

4.3.3 CDT-Based JBF

The CDT-based JBF enhances a noisy depth map with the aid of a color image based on a CDT map. The filter uses color information adaptively according to depth map regions. For example, in the CDT map of *monopoly* in Fig. 4.5g, the degree of pixel-wise similarity of a depth pixel and its color pixel is very high if DT_x^J is close to zero (dark blue color area). Therefore, the proposed filter directly uses the color information to enhance the depth information. In contrast, when DT_x^J is 255 (red color area), both pixels do not have a close bond with each other. In this case, the proposed filter only uses depth information. In a third case (graduated blue color area), the degree of pixel-wise similarity is moderate. Then, the amount of color information to be used is determined by DT_x^J. Basically, the greater DT_x^J is, the less the proposed filter uses color information. Formally, the CDT-based JBF is represented by

$$d_x^{\text{new}} = \begin{cases} \dfrac{\sum_{n \in W \times W} K_S(x_n - x) K_C(w_n^c \cdot (c_n - c_x)) K_P(w_n^d \cdot (d_n - d_x)) d_n}{\sum_{n \in W \times W} K_S(x_n - x) K_C(w_n^c \cdot (c_n - c_x)) K_P(w_n^d \cdot (d_n - d_x))} & \text{if } DT_n^J < T \\ \\ \dfrac{\sum_{n \in W \times W} K_S(x_n - x) K_P(d_n - d_x) d_n}{\sum_{n \in W \times W} K_S(x_n - x) K_P(d_n - d_x)} & \text{otherwise} \end{cases}$$

(4.12)

where w_n^c and w_n^d are scale factors for the photometric weighting functions K_C and K_P. $w_n^c \geq 1$ and $0.5 \leq w_n^d \leq 1$. Exponential functions are used for the definitions of K_S, K_C and K_P:

$$K_S(x) = e^{-\frac{x^2}{S^2}}, \quad K_C(x) = e^{-\frac{x^2}{C^2}}, \quad K_P(x) = e^{-\frac{x^2}{P^2}}, \quad (4.13)$$

where S, C, and P are smoothing parameters of K_S, K_C, and K_P, respectively. C is empirically set equal to P. In depth map denoising, the shapes of the functions for K_C and K_P should be much more precipitous than the one for K_S to strongly reflect the effect of photometric data [35]. In our experiments, we set the smoothing parameters as $S = 3.0$, $C = 0.1$, and $P = 0.1$. w_n^c is derived directly from DT_n^J in the CDT map.

$$w_n^c = \begin{cases} 1 & \text{if } \mathrm{DT}_n^J \leq a \\ e^{\frac{\log \beta}{T-a}(\mathrm{DT}_n^J - a)} & \text{if } \mathrm{DT}_n^J < T \end{cases}, \quad (4.14)$$

where a controls the strength of DT, β indicates the maximum scale factor with $\beta > 1$, and T is the threshold in Eq. (4.11).

If $a < \mathrm{DT}_n^J < T$, then $w_n^c > 1$. In this case, the degree of pixel-wise similarity of a depth pixel and its color pixel is not very high ($\mathrm{DT}_n^J \leq a$ and $w_n^c = 1$). In Eq. (4.12), w_n^c is multiplied by $(c_n - c_x)$ for moving K_C toward zero. Hence, the effect of color data reduces during depth map filtering in comparison with the case of $w_n^c = 1$. In contrast, if $0.5 \leq w_n^d < 1$, then K_P moves toward one. Consequently, the effect of depth data increases.

Figure 4.6 illustrates the comparison of GF, BF, JBF, and the proposed CDT-based JBF. In a 5×5 depth map (Fig. 4.6b), the pixel of interest, whose depth value is 8, is located at (3, 3). We assume that the gray pixels belong to an object and that three noisy pixels are present in this depth map. Two noisy pixels at (2, 1) and (4, 1) have a value of 8. Although their pixel values (8) are similar to other depth values, the pixels are isolated and out of the object represented by depth values 8 or 9. In addition, the other pixel located at (4, 4) is a noisy pixel because its depth value 6 is different from the object depth values 8 or 9. In GF, K_S (Fig. 4.6e) according to a weighting scale (Fig. 4.6a) is only used as shown in Fig. 4.6i.

The depth pixel at (4, 4) will be ignored in BF since the shape of K_P is so precipitous. Therefore, BF uses K_P (Fig. 4.6f) for depth map denoising like in Fig. 4.6j. In JBF, we use K_C instead of K_P as shown in Fig. 4.6k. In the proposed CDT-based JBF, K_C is changed to K_C' by multiplying it by w_n^c that is computed based on a CDT map in Fig. 4.6d. The result of the CDT-based JBF is shown in Fig. 4.6l. In this comparison, it is noticeable that the CDT-based JBF only uses noiseless depth pixels to estimate a new depth value at (3, 3), whereas the other filters use the noisy pixels at (2, 2), (4, 1), and (4, 4). As a result, the new depth value at (3, 3) computed by CDT-based JBF will be almost 9.

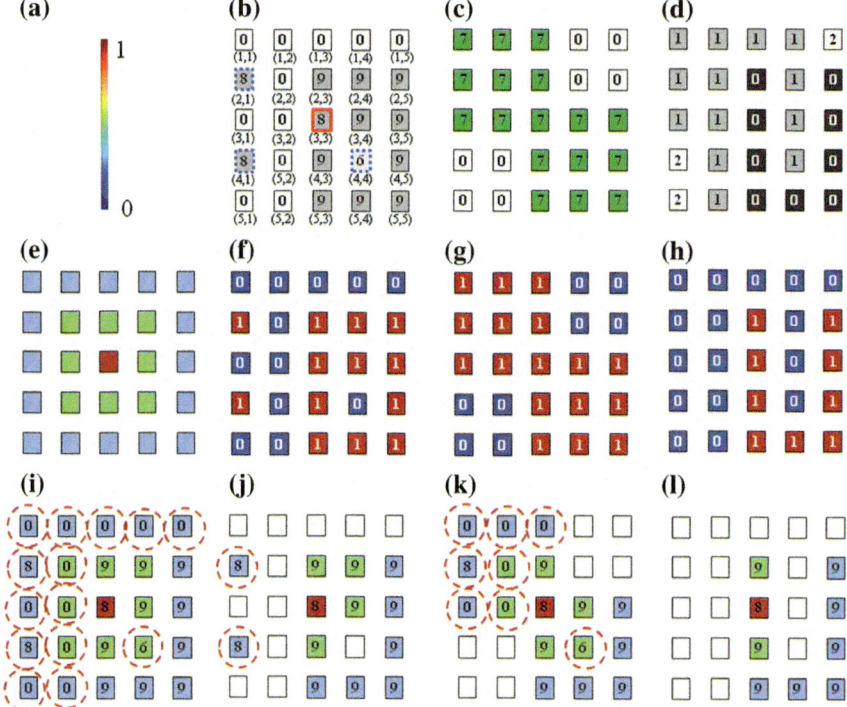

Fig. 4.6 Analysis of weighting functions. **a** Weighting scale. **b** Depth map. **c** Color image. **d** CDT map. **e** K_S. **f** K_P. **g** K_C. **h** K'_C scaled by w_n^c. **i** GF. **j** BF ($K_S \times K_P$). **k** JBF ($K_S \times K_C$). **l** Proposed ($K_S \times K'_C \times K_P$)

4.4 Experimental Results

In the following subsections, we first evaluate the performance of CDT-based JBF using 9 ground truth data sets. The results obtained are compared to those obtained with 5 competing methods with different noise levels. Comparisons of computational times needed to obtain filter results are presented. Second, we present results obtained when applying CDT-based JBF to a real data set acquired from a Kinect-type range sensor. Finally, we analyze the effect of the parameters on the results obtained with CDT-based JBF.

4.4.1 Performance Evaluation with Ground Truth Data Sets

For assessing the improvement of the depth accuracy via CDT-based JBF, we tested the method on ground truth data from the Middlebury stereo dataset [29]. The 9 datasets shown in Fig. 4.7 are *baby1, bowling, cloth, flowerpots, lampshade, midd1,*

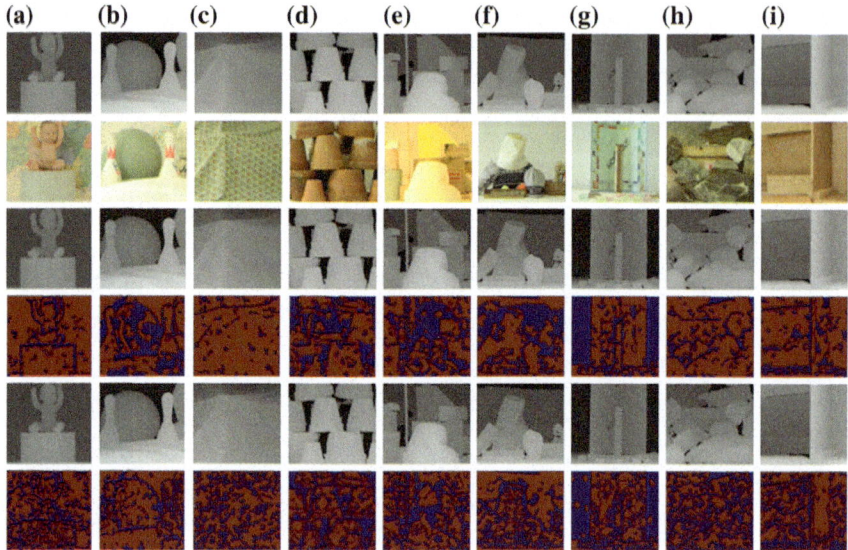

Fig. 4.7 Nine Synthetic test image sets and their CDT maps; *the first row* shows ground truth depth maps, *the second row* shows input color images, *the third row* shows noisy input depth maps with $\sigma = 20$, *the fourth row* shows the CDT maps of noisy input depth maps with $\sigma = 20$, *the fifth row* shows noisy input depth maps with $\sigma = 25$, *the last row* shows the CDT maps of noisy input depth maps with $\sigma = 25$: **a** baby1, **b** bowling, **c** cloth, **d** flowerpots, **e** lampshade, **f** midd1, **g** monopoly, **h** rocks, **i** wood1

monopoly, rocks1, and *wood1*. Each test image was downsampled from its original resolution of 437 × 370 pixels to 400 × 360 pixels for simplified implementation.

We added Gaussian noise (standard deviation $\sigma = 20$ or $\sigma = 25$) to the ground truth data to create noisy depth maps. In this experiment, the values of some parameters needed for depth map filtering are set as follows based on empirical evaluation: $\beta = 1.5$, $W = 7$ or 11, $S = 3$, $P = 0.1$, $C = 0.1$, $T = 10$, and $w_n^d = 0.8$. We used *1–2* DT to obtain a CDT map. Figure 4.7 shows the ground truth depth map, the input color image, the input noisy depth map, and their CDT maps for 9 test image sets.

Peak signal to noise ratio (PSNR) measurement was used for an objective evaluation of depth quality improvements. The proposed method was compared with the geometry-based Gaussian filter (GF) [20], BF [9], SKF [32], JBF [24, 26], and adaptive JBF (A-JBF) [6, 21]. For GF, the parameter of the spatial weighting function S is 3. For BF, we set the parameters $S = 3$ and $P = 0.1$. For JBF and A-JBF, $S = 3$, $P = 0.1$, and $C = 0.1$, which are the same as in the proposed method. The comparative methods expect SKF to be iterated twice in order to obtain refined depth maps. These methods usually have the best PSNR in the 2nd iteration whereas SKF requires more than 7 iterations. We carried out SKF up to twelve iterations to get the best PSNR. We used the 2nd order SKF [32] with global smoothing parameter 2.4, elongation parameter 1, and the structure sensitive parameter 0.5.

4 Depth Map Denoising via CDT-Based Joint Bilateral Filter

Table 4.1 PSNR comparison ($\sigma = 20$, $W = 7$, *unit* dB)

Test data	GF	BF	SKF	JBF	A-JBF	CDT-based JBF
Baby1	32.76	35.86	35.73	34.51	35.91	36.34
Bowling	32.02	35.43	35.16	32.58	35.95	36.21
Cloth	34.04	37.73	37.63	36.03	36.31	37.69
Flowerpots	29.01	33.80	32.71	28.78	34.29	34.29
Lampshade	31.85	34.82	34.91	32.69	35.63	35.70
Midd1	31.50	34.56	33.59	31.66	34.63	35.01
Monopoly	32.19	35.53	34.83	33.43	35.58	36.28
Rocks1	31.03	34.70	33.62	31.23	34.81	35.06
Wood1	32.03	36.18	36.06	33.59	36.42	36.52
Average	**31.83**	**35.41**	**34.92**	**32.72**	**33.51**	**35.90**

Table 4.2 PSNR comparison ($\sigma = 20$, $W = 11$, *unit* dB)

Test data	GF	BF	SKF	JBF	A-JBF	CDT-based JBF
baby1	31.70	31.83	36.92	31.83	36.84	37.05
bowling	33.69	36.11	36.17	34.33	36.67	36.89
cloth	37.61	39.40	40.67	38.37	38.04	39.21
flowerpots	27.38	33.88	32.91	27.98	34.73	34.59
lampshade	31.50	34.91	35.63	31.95	35.16	36.14
midd1	31.41	34.88	34.18	31.08	35.23	35.32
monopoly	31.95	35.97	35.32	33.17	36.60	37.02
rocks1	30.22	34.88	34.16	30.57	35.36	35.57
wood1	32.24	36.91	37.20	33.14	36.27	37.35
Average	**31.97**	**35.42**	**35.91**	**32.50**	**36.10**	**36.57**

Tables 4.1, 4.2, 4.3, 4.4 show the PSNR comparison for nine test images. In Tables 4.1 and 4.2, the average PSNRs of enhanced depth maps from noise addition with $\sigma = 20$ are 31.90 dB, 35.41, 35.41, 32.61, 34.80 and 36.23 for GF, BF, SKF, JBF, A-JBF and the proposed method, respectively. This result indicates that the proposed method outperforms other comparative methods by 4.78, 0.82, 0.82, 3.61, and 1.43 dB on average.

In the case of a noise addition of $\sigma = 25$, the averages of PSNRs are 30.98, 32.75, 31.77, 34.03, 32.67 and 33.46 dB for GF, BF, SKF, JBF, A-JBF and the proposed method, respectively. The PSNR of the proposed method is higher than the ones for GF, BF, JBF and A-JBF by 2.48, 0.71, 1.69, and 0.79 dB but lower than the ones of SKF by 0.57 dB. The CDT-based JBF could not use color information efficiently due to the failure of depth edge detection in a severe noise situation. The difference of CDT maps in the fourth and sixth rows of Fig. 4.7 illustrates this situation. In contrast, SKF was more robust to severe noise due to its higher order estimation.

Table 4.3 PSNR comparison ($\sigma = 25$, $W = 7$, *unit* dB)

Test data	GF	BF	SKF	JBF	A-JBF	CDT-based JBF
baby1	31.42	32.77	34.33	33.99	32.39	33.38
bowling	30.81	32.61	33.60	32.02	32.75	33.34
cloth	32.44	33.84	35.72	32.59	32.04	33.55
flowerpots	28.17	31.15	31.24	28.39	31.45	31.79
lampshade	30.64	31.96	33.41	32.23	32.34	32.91
midd1	30.39	31.97	32.46	31.18	31.65	32.39
monopoly	30.98	32.81	33.29	32.70	32.36	33.55
rocks1	29.97	31.84	32.45	30.83	31.55	32.35
wood1	30.78	32.78	34.48	33.08	32.90	33.41
Average	**30.63**	**32.42**	**33.44**	**31.90**	**32.16**	**32.96**

Table 4.4 PSNR comparison ($\sigma = 25$, $W = 11$, *unit* dB)

Test data	GF	BF	SKF	JBF	A-JB F	CDT-based JBF
baby1	33.13	33.54	35.90	34.16	33.45	34.49
bowling	31.14	33.40	34.79	31.45	33.91	34.34
cloth	36.03	35.10	38.76	33.13	33.41	35.16
flowerpots	27.02	31.70	31.57	27.68	32.16	32.39
lampshade	31.00	32.43	34.36	31.65	33.15	33.62
midd1	30.90	32.65	33.05	30.80	32.56	33.13
monopoly	31.27	32.62	33.91	32.62	33.38	34.65
rocks1	29.84	32.51	33.10	30.37	32.57	33.23
wood1	31.70	33.77	36.12	32.85	34.02	34.60
Average	**31.34**	**33.08**	**34.62**	**31.64**	**33.18**	**33.96**

In this experiment, altogether the PSNR gain of our method is approximately 3.63, 0.76, 2.65 and 1.11 dB more than GF, BF, JBF, and A-JBF and is similar with SKF.

Figures 4.8, 4.9 and 4.10 show the results of the comparative methods for the test images *bowling*, *midd1*, and *monopoly*, respectively. Each enhanced depth map was obtained from their noisy depth maps (Figs. 4.8b, 4.9b, 4.10b) artificially generated from the ground truth depth maps (Figs. 4.8a, 4.9a, 4.10a) using GF (Figs. 4.8c, 4.9, 4.10c), BF (Figs. 4.8d, 4.9d, 4.10d), SKF (Figs. 4.8e, 4.9e, 4.10e), JBF (Figs. 4.8f, 4.9f, 4.10f), A-JBF (Figs. 4.8g, 4.9g, 4.10g), and CDT-based JBF (Figs. 4.8h, 4.9h, 4.10h).

When we compare the magnified rectangular regions on the left bowling pin in Fig. 4.8, we can observe that the CDT-based JBF made the border; i.e. depth discontinuous area, between the bowling pin and the bowling ball sharper than GF, BF, and SKF. At the same time, CDT-based JBF led the depth homogenous area on the bowling pin smoother than JBF and A-JBF while reducing visual artifacts. From

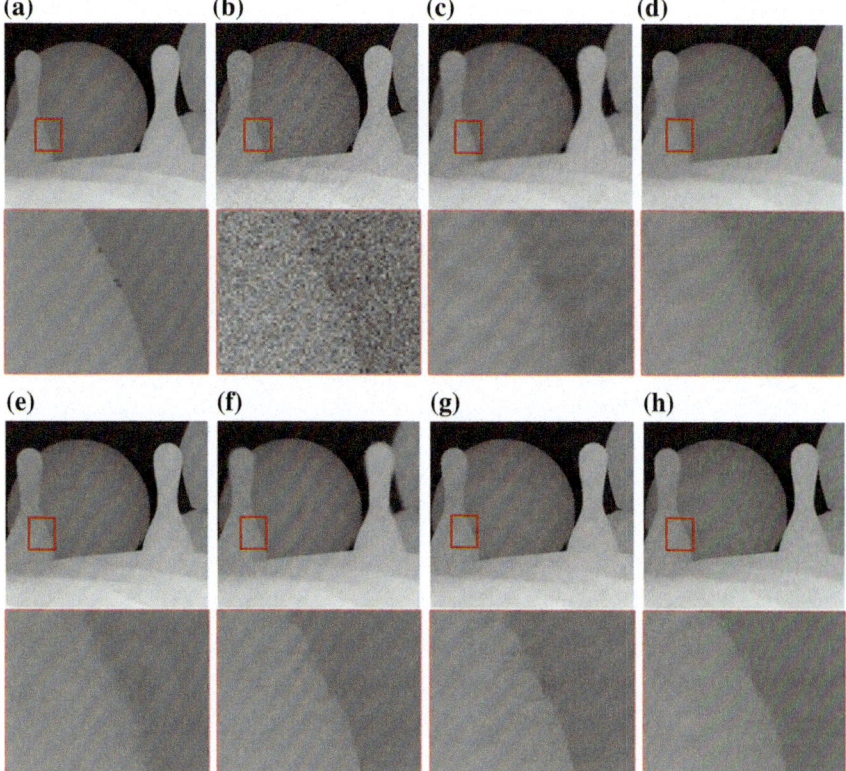

Fig. 4.8 Results for *bowling* ($\sigma = 20$, $W = 11$). **a** Ground truth. **b** Noisy depths image. **c** GF. **d** BF. **e** SKF. **f** JBF. **g** A-JBF. **h** CDT-based JBF

the results of *midd1* and *monopoly* in Figs. 4.9 and 4.10, we can observe the same effect for the CDT-based JBF.

To compare the computational time for comparative methods, we calculated the average processing time for the test data at $W = 7, 9, 11$ with 2 iterations. The processing time of SKF was estimated when it had the best PSNR during 12-time iterations. The test was done with an Intel(R) Core^{TM} 2 Duo CPU 3.00 GHz with 2.0 GB RAM. Table 4.5 shows computational times of the comparative methods.

The average computational time of GF, BF, JBF, A-JBF, SKF, and CDT-based JBF was 0.1, 1.1, 5.3, 6.0, 123.3, and 7.6 s, respectively. The CDT-based JBF was slower than GF, BF, JBF, and A-JBF by 7.5, 6.5, 2.3, and 1.6 s. The main reason for this was the additional processing time, about 2 s, needed for DT and CDT map generation. Meanwhile, CDT-based JBF was much faster than SKF as much as about 16 times.

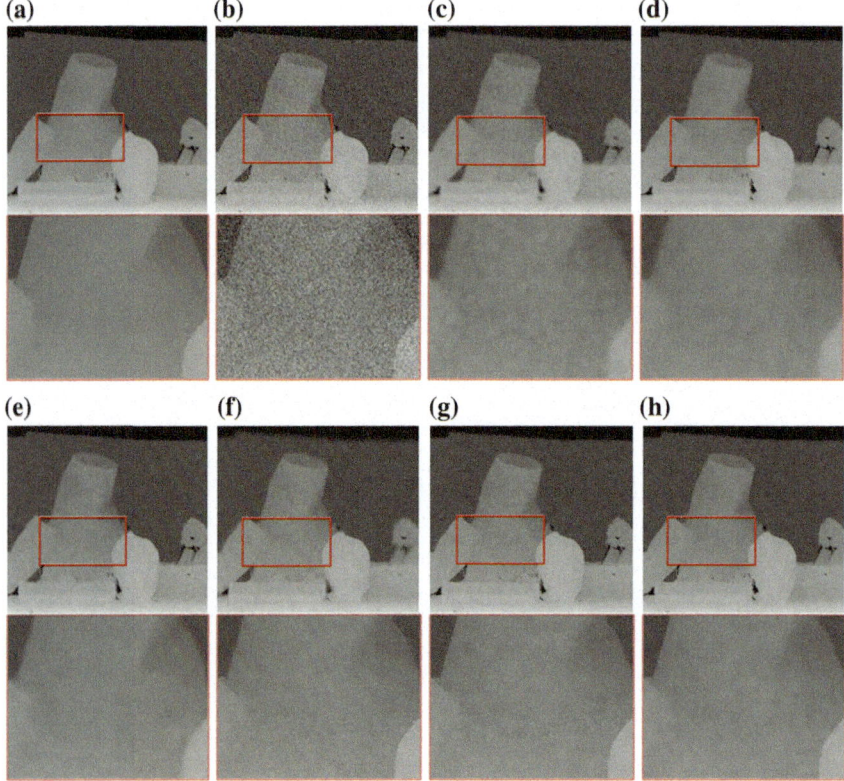

Fig. 4.9 Results for *midd1* ($\sigma = 20$, $W = 11$). **a** Ground truth. **b** Noisy depths image. **c** GF. **d** BF. **e** SKF. **f** JBF. **g** A-JBF. **h** CDT-based JBF

4.4.2 Performance Evaluation for Real Data

As mentioned in the introduction of this chapter, the practical use of many active range sensors is limited in computer vision applications involving foreground extraction [16] and motion tracking [31] due to the low-quality depth map generation. In order to evaluate the possibility of extending possible computer vision applications to 3D object and scene modeling, we applied CDT-based JBF to a real data set, *Actor*, acquired from a Kinect-type range sensor [25]. The *Actor* sequence is composed of 50 frames with 720×480 resolution. Figure 4.11 shows a color image, an original depth map, and the enhanced depth maps of the 1st frame obtained by BF, A-JBF, and the proposed method. The results of 3D scene reconstruction with its original and enhanced depth maps are shown in Fig. 4.12. For this, a hierarchical decomposition method for depth maps [23] was employed.

As shown in Fig. 4.12a, the quality of a 3D scene reconstructed by the original depth map is not satisfactory due to the presence of noise. The low-quality 3D scene

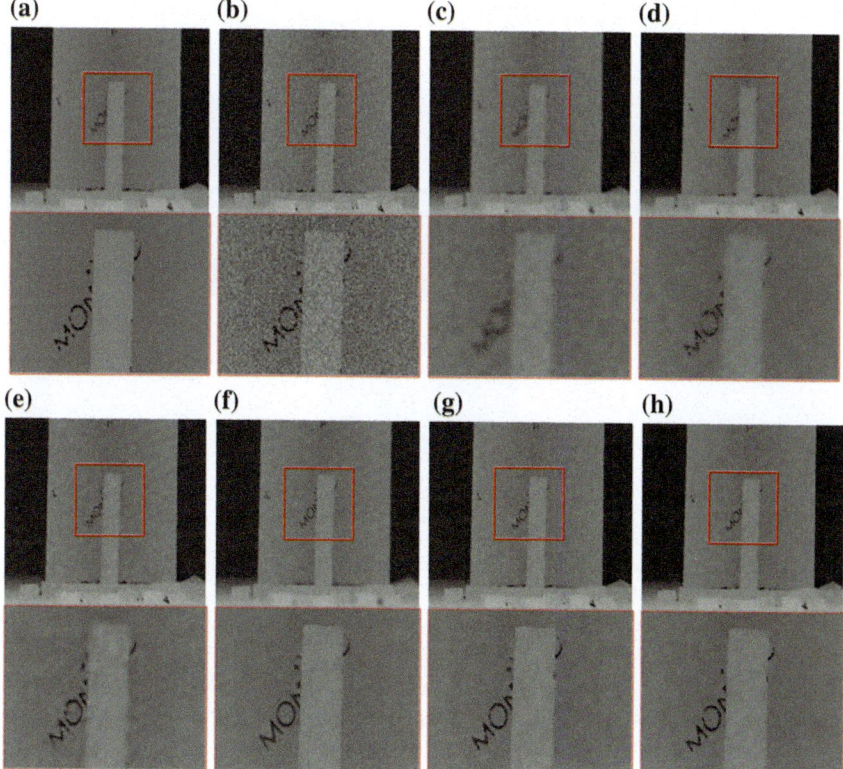

Fig. 4.10 Result of *monopoly* ($\sigma = 20$, $W = 11$). **a** Ground truth. **b** Noisy depths image. **c** GF. **d** BF. **e** SKF. **f** JBF. **g** A-JBF. **h** CDT-based JBF

Table 4.5 Comparison of computational times (*1–2* DT, 9 test data)

Test data	GF (s)	BF (s)	JBF (s)	A-JBF (s)	SKF (s)	CDT-based JBF (s)
$W = 7$	0.1	0.6	3.3	3.7	109.7	5.2
$W = 9$	0.1	1.1	5.5	6.2	117.0	8.5
$W = 11$	0.1	1.6	7.2	8.2	143.3	9.3
Average	**0.1**	**1.1**	**5.3**	**6.0**	**123.3**	**7.6**

could be enhanced by depth map denoising. In this experiment, we set the parameters as $\beta = 2.0$, $W = 11$, $S = 3$, $P = 0.1$, $C = 0.1$ and *1–2* DT. At the region of a table, a woman, and a chair marked by circles in Figs. 4.11 and 4.12, we could notice that the proposed method presented here preserved important depth discontinuity better than BF. Furthermore, it suppressed the visual artifact occurring from A-JBF efficiently. Figure 4.13 depicts the result of dynamic 3D scenes of the *Actor* sequence.

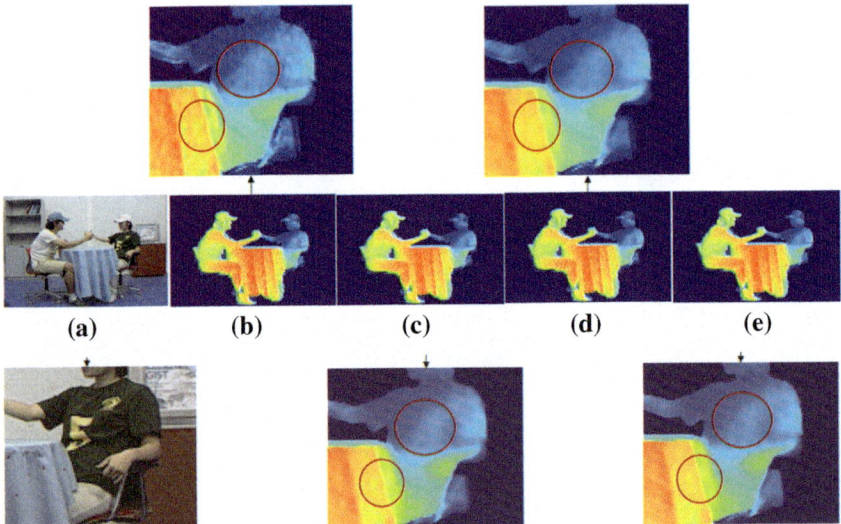

Fig. 4.11 Result for a selected frame of the *Actor* sequence. **a** Input color image. **b** Input depth image. **c** BF. **d** A-JBF. **e** CDT-based JBF

As shown in Fig. 4.12a, the quality of a 3D scene reconstructed by the original depth map is not satisfactory due to noise presence. The low-quality 3D scene could be enhanced by depth map denoising. In this experiment, we set the parameters as $\beta = 2.0$, $W = 11$, $S = 3$, $P = 0.1$, $C = 0.1$ and *1–2* DT. At the region of a table, a woman, and a chair marked by circles in Figs. 4.11 and 4.12, we can notice that CDT-based JBF preserved important depth discontinuity better than BF. Furthermore, it suppressed the visual artifact occurring from A-JBF efficiently. Figure 4.13 depicts the result of dynamic 3D scenes of *Actor* sequence. In this experiment, we could notice that the proposed CDT-based JBF outperformed other conventional methods objectively and subjectively in terms of the noise reduction as well as visual artifacts suppression.

4.4.3 Parameter Analysis for CDT-Based JBF

In the following experiments, the parameters of CDT-based JBF were analyzed. β in Eq. (4.14) was evaluated on various w_n^d in Eq. (4.12). β is the parameter of w_n^c in Eq. (4.12) and plays an important role to scale the photometric weighting function of color data, while w_n^d defines the strength of photometric weighting function of depth data. Table 4.6 shows the results.

When $\beta = 1.0$, we can study the effect of w_n^d by varying w_n^d from 0.5 to 1.0. In the test with *cloth*, its PSNR is the largest at $w_n^d = 0.7$ and 0.8. In the case of *monopoly*,

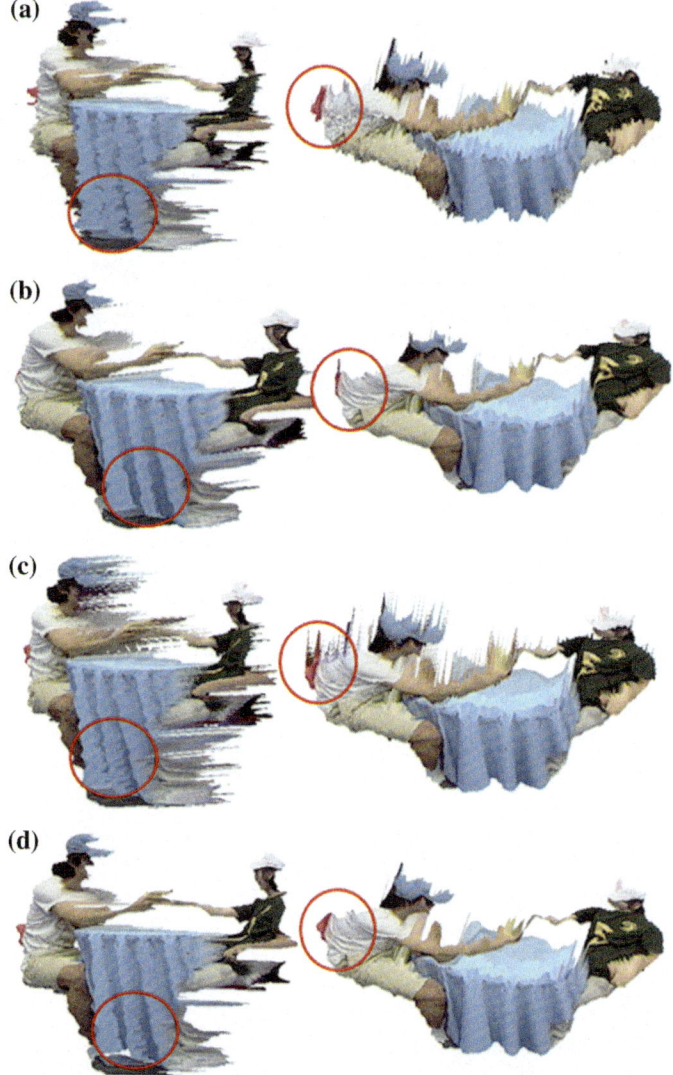

Fig. 4.12 Comparison with reconstructed 3D scenes. **a** Original data. **b** JF. **c** A-JBF. **d** CDT-based JBF

its PSNR is the largest at $w_n^d = 1.0$. If the CDT map of *cloth* (shown in the fourth row in Fig. 4.7c) is carefully observed, ignoring the red color area, it has more of the dark blue colored area than the graduated one. It means that the homogeneity of both color and depth data on the area is identical. On the other hand, the rate of the dark blue color area in the CDT map of *monopoly* in Fig. 4.11e is similar to the one of graduated blue color area. It means that the homogeneity of both color and depth data

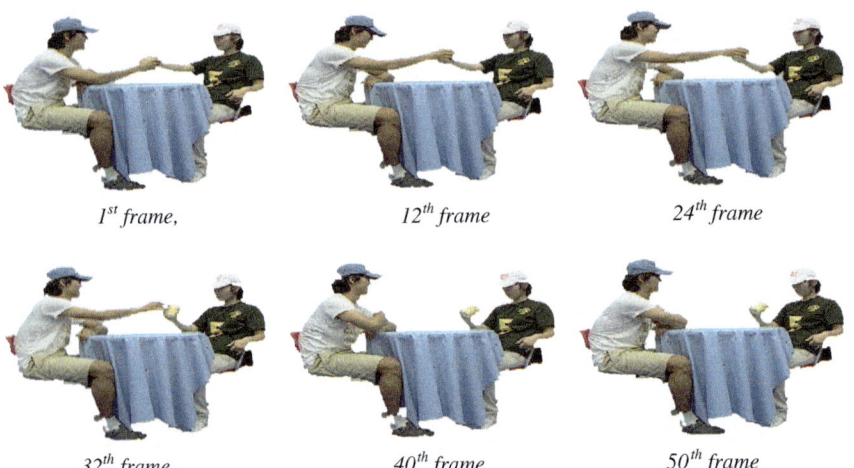

Fig. 4.13 Dynamic 3D scene reconstruction

Table 4.6 Evaluation of β and w_n^d (PSNR, *unit* dB)

w_n^d	bowling			midd1		
	$\beta = 1.0$	$\beta = 1.5$	$\beta = 2.0$	$\beta = 1.0$	$\beta = 1.5$	$\beta = 2.0$
1.0	36.68	36.68	36.68	35.19	35.19	35.19
0.9	36.73	36.73	36.73	35.21	35.22	35.22
0.8	36.76	36.76	36.76	35.22	**35.23**	**35.23**
0.7	36.76	**36.77**	**36.77**	35.22	35.22	35.22
0.6	36.75	36.76	36.76	35.18	35.18	35.18
0.5	36.71	36.71	36.72	35.10	35.11	35.11
w_n^d	monopoly			cloth		
	$\beta = 1.0$	$\beta = 1.5$	$\beta = 2.0$	$\beta = 1.0$	$\beta = 1.5$	$\beta = 2.0$
1.0	36.78	36.79	36.78	39.17	39.17	39.17
0.9	36.79	**36.80**	**36.80**	39.18	39.18	39.18
0.8	36.76	36.76	36.76	**39.19**	39.18	39.18
0.7	36.68	36.69	36.69	**39.19**	39.18	39.18
0.6	36.57	36.58	36.58	39.18	39.18	39.18
0.5	36.41	36.42	36.42	39.17	39.17	39.17

on the area is not identical but moderate. Therefore, the proposed filter enhanced the depth map by increasing the effect of depth data while reducing the effect of color data. The situation for the data sets *bowling* and *midd1* is in between the *cloth* and *monopoly* cases. As a consequence, their PSNRs converged at $w_n^d = 0.7$ or 0.8 with $\beta = 1.5$ or 2.0.

4 Depth Map Denoising via CDT-Based Joint Bilateral Filter

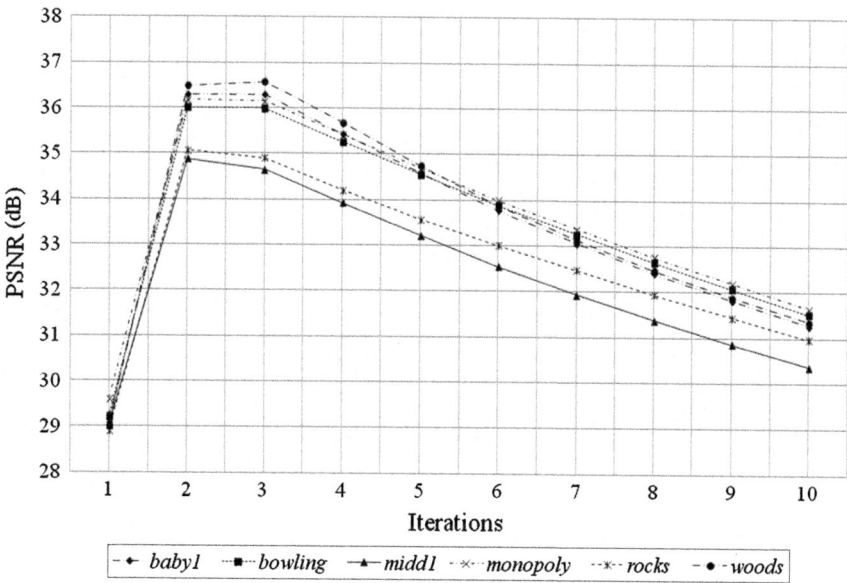

Fig. 4.14 Results of iteration variation

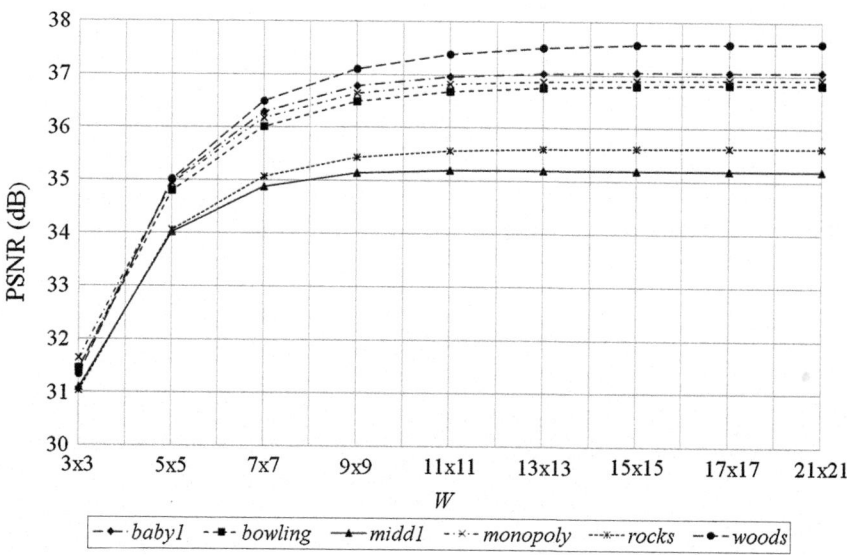

Fig. 4.15 Results of window size variation

In a second experiment, we studied the effect of the number of iterations and the window size W. Figure 4.14 shows the filter results obtained at different iterations for 6 images. In respect of best PSNR, the CDT-based JBF converged at the 2nd iteration. Figure 4.15 depicts the results with different window sizes. This graph indicates that

Table 4.7 Results of DT strength a and threshold T variation

T, a–b DT	bowling (PSNR, unit dB)					
	$a = 1,$ $b = 2$	$a = 3,$ $b = 4$	$a = 5,$ $b = 6$	$a = 7,$ $b = 8$	$a = 9,$ $b = 10$	$a = 11,$ $b = 12$
$T = 4 \times a$	36.79	36.76	36.72	36.72	36.73	36.73
$T = 6 \times a$	**36.80**	36.75	36.73	36.72	36.73	36.72
$T = 8 \times a$	**36.80**	36.75	36.73	36.72	36.72	36.72
$T = 10 \times a$	36.79	36.74	36.72	36.71	36.72	36.72
$T = 12 \times a$	36.78	36.73	36.72	36.71	36.72	36.72
$T, a - b$ DT	monopoly (PSNR, unit dB)					
	$a = 1,$ $b = 2$	$a = 3,$ $b = 4$	$a = 5,$ $b = 6$	$a = 7,$ $b = 8$	$a = 9,$ $b = 10$	$a = 11,$ $b = 12$
$T = 4 \times a$	36.78	36.76	36.78	36.77	36.77	36.76
$T = 6 \times a$	**36.79**	36.77	36.77	36.76	36.76	36.75
$T = 8 \times a$	**36.79**	36.76	36.76	36.75	36.75	36.75
$T = 10 \times a$	36.78	36.75	36.75	36.74	36.74	36.74
$T = 12 \times a$	36.77	36.75	36.75	36.74	36.74	36.74

11×11 pixels is a proper selection of the window size. From evaluations of β, w_n^d and W, empirically-recommended parameters of CDT-based JBF are $\beta = 0.8$, $w_n^d = 1.5$, and $W = 11$ for depth map denoising.

In a third experiment, the quality of the filtered depth maps was examined via varying T in Eq. (4.14). T is set in proportion to DT strength a. We tested the images *bowling* and *monopoly* with $\sigma = 20$, $W = 11$, $\beta = 0.8$, and $w_n^d = 1.5$. Table 4.7 shows the results of this experiment. CDT-based JBF had the best performance at $a = 1$ and $T = 6 \times a$. In addition, if T is fixed, then the quality of the filtered depth maps is degraded slightly as a increases. If a is fixed, then the quality of depth maps declines slightly as T increases. Here, the maximum difference of PSNRs in Table 4.7 is only 0.09 dB (maximum PSNR: 36.80 dB, minimum PSNR: 36.71 dB). This means that if T increases proportionally by a, then there is not much difference in the depth value quality.

Finally, based on the results of Table 4.7, the computational time of the CDT-based JBF was evaluated via varying a–b DT. Table 4.8 shows the results of computation time variation according to a–b DT. From this result, the processing time is reduced by 2.8 s on average when *11–12* DT is used instead of *1–2* DT. In this case, the depth quality degradation was 0.07 dB on average.

Table 4.8 Computational time by a–b DT variation ($T = 6 \times a$, $W = 11$)

	$a = 1$, $b = 2$ (s)	$a = 3$, $b = 4$ (s)	$a = 5$, $b = 6$ (s)	$a = 7$, $b = 8$ (s)	$a = 9$, $b = 10$ (s)	$a = 11$, $b = 12$ (s)
baby1	8.1	7.9	6.8	6.3	6.0	5.9
bowling	11.0	9.3	8.4	7.7	7.4	7.1
cloth	5.3	5.1	5.0	4.9	4.9	4.9
flowerpots	10.8	10.7	9.7	8.6	8.0	7.7
lampshade	10.6	9.2	8.4	7.7	7.4	7.2
midd1	10.2	8.4	7.6	7.1	6.9	6.8
monopoly	9.8	9.3	7.8	7.0	6.5	6.4
rocks1	7.4	7.3	7.0	6.7	6.5	6.5
wood1	10.1	9.2	7.8	6.6	6.2	6.0
Average	**9.3**	**8.5**	**7.6**	**7.0**	**6.6**	**6.5**

4.5 Conclusion

We introduced a method to enhance depth information using color information via CDT-based JBF. In this work, we selected depth map regions filtered by color information based on a CDT map for visual artifacts suppression. Based on the nine test depth maps, the PSNR gain of our method is approximately 3.63, 0.76, 2.65, and 1.11 dB more than GF, BF, JBF, and A-JBF and is similar to SKF. In comparison of computational time for depth map filtering, the proposed method was faster than SKF by as much as 16 times. In analysis of CDT-based JBF, we empirically recommended its parameters in terms of depth quality and real-time filter design. We hope that the proposed idea can present new directions for further research related to bi-modal image processing and will be used in its applications.

Acknowledgments This work was supported in part by the U.S. Air Force under Grant FA8650-10-1-5902. The views and conclusions contained herein are those of the authors and should not be interpreted as necessarily representing the official policies or endorsements, either expressed or implied, of Air Force Research Laboratory or the U.S. Government. We are thankful to Dr. Sung-Yeol Kim for the implementation and evaluation of various filters.

References

1. Borgefors G (1988) Hierarchical chamfer matching: a parametric edge matching algorithm. IEEE Trans Pattern Anal Mach Intell 10(6):849–865
2. Bose K, Ahuja N (2006) Superresolution and noise filtering using moving least squares. IEEE Trans Image Process 15(8):2239–2248
3. Brooks S, Saunders I, Dodgson NA (2007) Image compression using sparse colour sampling combined with non-linear image processing. In: Proceedings of electronic imaging: human vision and electronic imaging, vol XII

4. Canny J (1986) A computational approach to edge detection. IEEE Trans Pattern Anal Mach Intell 8(6):679–698
5. Chiabrando F, Chiabrando R, Piatti D, Rinaudo F (2009) Sensors for 3D imaging: metric evaluation and calibration of a CCD/CMOS time-of-flight camera. Sensors 9(12):10080–10096
6. Cho J, Kim S-Y, Ho YS, Lee KH (2008) Dynamic 3D human actor generation method using a time-of-flight depth camera. IEEE Trans Consum Electron 54(4):1514–1521
7. Diebel J, Thrun S (2005) An application of Markov random fields to range sensing. In: Proceedings of advances in neural information processing systems, pp 291–298
8. Dorrington AA, Payne AD, Cree MJ (2010) An evaluation of time-of-flight cameras for close range methodology applications. International archives of photogrammetry, remote sensing and spatial information sciences, vol. XXXVIII, Part 5 Commission V Symposium
9. Elad M (2002) On the origin of the bilateral filter and ways to improve it. IEEE Trans Image Process 11(10):1141–1150
10. Fehn C (2003) A 3D-TV system based on video plus depth information. In: Proceedings of asilomar conference on signals, systems and computers, vol 2, pp 1529–1533
11. Fehn C, Barré R, Pastoor S (2006) Interactive 3-D TV- concepts and key technologies. Proc. IEEE 94(3):524–538
12. Felzenszwalb PF, Huttenlocher DP (2004) Distance transforms of sampled functions. Cornell computing and information science, TR2004-1963
13. Feng X, Milanfar P (2002) Multiscale principal components analysis for image local orientation estimation. In: Proceedings of asilomar conference on signals, systems and computers, pp 478–482
14. Gangwal OP, Djapic B (2010) Real-time implementation of depth map post-processing for 3D-TV in dedicated hardware. In: Proceedings of international conference on consumer electronics
15. Gonzalez RC, Woods RE (2002) Digital image processing. Prentice Hall, Englewood Cliffs
16. Grabb R, Tracey C, Puranik A, Davis J (2008) Real-time foreground segmentation via range and color imaging. In: Proceedings of IEEE computer vision and pattern recognition workshops, pp 1–5
17. Iddan GJ, Yahav G (2001) 3D imaging in the studio and elsewhere. In: Proceedings of SPIE videometrics and optical methods for 3D shape measurements, pp 48–55
18. Jachalsky J, Schlosser M, Gandolph D (2010) Reliability aware cross multilateral filtering for robust disparity map refinement. In: Proceedings of 3DTV conference
19. Kauff P, Atzpadin N, Fehn C, Müller M, Schreer O, Smolic A, Tanger R (2007) Depth map creation and image-based rendering for advanced 3D-TV services providing interoperability and scalability. Signal Process. Image Commun. 22(2):217–234
20. Kim SM, Cha J, Ryu J, Lee KH (2006) Depth video enhancement for haptic interaction using a smooth surface reconstruction. IEICE Trans Inf Syst E89-D(1):37–44
21. Kim S-Y, Cho J, Koschan A, Abidi M (2010) Spatial and temporal enhancement of depth images captured by a time-of-flight depth sensor. In: Proceedings of IEEE international conference on pattern recognition, pp 2358–2361
22. Kim S-Y, Cho W, Koschan A, Abidi M (2011) Depth map enhancement using adaptive steering kernel regression based on distance transform. In: Proceedings of international symposium and visual computing, vol 6938. Lecture notes in computer science, pp 291–300
23. Kim S-Y, Lee SB, Ho YS (2006) Three-dimensional natural video system based on layered representation of depth maps. IEEE Trans Consum Electron 52(3):1035–1042
24. Kopf J, Cohen MF, Lischinski D, Uyttendaele M (2007) Joint bilateral upsampling. ACM Trans Comput Graph 26(3):1–6
25. Lee EK, Ho YS (2011) Generation of high-quality depth maps using hybrid camera system for 3-D video. J Vis Commun Image Represent 22:73–84
26. Petschnigg G, Agrawala M, Hoppe H, Szeliski R, Cohen M, Toyama K (2004) Digital photography with flash and no-flash image pairs. ACM Trans Comput Graph 23(3):664–672
27. Riemens AK, Gangwal OP, Barenbrug B, Berretty RM (2009) Multi-step joint bilateral depth upsampling. In Proceedings of electronic imaging: visual communications and image processing

28. Rosenfeld A, Pfaltz J (1968) Distance functions in digital pictures. Pattern Recognit 1:33–61
29. Scharstein D, Szeliski R (2002) A taxonomy and evaluation of dense two-frame stereo correspondence algorithms. Int J Comput Vision 47(1–3):7–42
30. Shao L, Yan R, Li X, Liu Y (2014) From heuristic optimization to dictionary learning: a review and comprehensive comparison of image denoising algorithms. IEEE Trans Cybern. doi:10.1109/TCYB.2013.2278548
31. Shotton J, Fitzgibbon A, Cook M, Blake A (2011) Real-time human pose recognition in parts from single depth images. In: Proceedings of IEEE computer vision and pattern recognition, pp 1297–1304
32. Takeda H, Farsiu S, Milanfar P (2007) Kernel regression for image processing and reconstruction. IEEE Trans Image Process 16(2):349–366
33. Takeda H, Farsiu S, Milanfar P (2008) Deblurring using regularized locally-adaptive kernel regression. IEEE Trans Image Process 17(4):550–563
34. Tan H, Tian F, Qiu Y, Wang S, Zhang J (2010) Multihypothesis recursive video denoising based on separation of motion state. IET Image Process 4(4):261–268
35. Tomasi C, Manduchi R (1998) Bilateral filtering for gray and color images. In: Proceedings of IEEE international conference on computer vision, pp 839–846
36. Wand MP, Jones MC (1995) Kernel smoothing, ser. Monographs on statistics and applied probability. Chapman and Hall, London
37. Xiao C, Nie Y, Hua W, Zheng W (2010) Fast multi-scale joint bilateral texture upsampling. Visual Comput 26(3):263–275
38. Yan R, Shao L, Liu Y (2013) Nonlocal hierarchical dictionary learning using wavelets for image denoising. IEEE Trans Image Process 22(12):4689–4698
39. Yang Q, Tan KH, Ahuja N (2009) Real-time O(1) bilateral filtering. In: Proceedings of IEEE computer vision and pattern recognition, pp 557–564
40. Yang Q, Yang R, Davis J, Nistér D (2007) Spatial-depth super resolution for range images. In: Proceedings of IEEE computer vision and pattern recognition, pp 1–8
41. Yoon SU, Ho YS (2007) Multiple color and depth video coding using a hierarchical representation. IEEE Trans. Circ. Syst. Video Technol. 17(11):1450–1460
42. Yu H, Zhao L, Wang H (2009) Image denoising using trivariate shrinkage filter in the wavelet domain and joint bilateral filter in the spatial domain. IEEE Trans Image Process 18(10):2364–2369

Chapter 5
Human Performance Capture Using Multiple Handheld Kinects

Yebin Liu, Genzhi Ye, Yangang Wang, Qionghai Dai and Christian Theobalt

Abstract Capturing real performances of human actors has been an important topic in the fields of computer graphics and computer vision in the last few decades. The reconstructed 3D performance can be used for character animation and free-viewpoint video. While most of the available performance capture approaches rely on a 3D video studio with tens of RGB cameras, this chapter presents a method for marker-less performance capture of single or multiple human characters using only three handheld Kinects. Compared with the RGB camera approaches, the proposed method is more convenient with respect to data acquisition, allowing for much fewer cameras and carry-on camera capture. The method introduced in this chapter reconstructs human skeletal poses, deforming surface geometry and camera poses for every time step of the depth video. It succeeds on general uncontrolled indoor scenes with potentially dynamic background, and it succeeds even for reconstruction of multiple closely interacting characters.

5.1 Introduction

In recent years, the field of marker-less motion estimation has seen great progress. Two important lines of research have recently emerged in this domain. On the one side, there are multi-view motion capture approaches that reconstruct skeleton motion and possibly simple body shape of people in skintight clothing from a set of video recordings that were taken from around the scene, e.g., [1–6]. Human performance capture approaches take one step further and not only reconstruct a motion model (like a skeleton) but also detailed dynamic surface geometry as well as detailed texture, e.g., [7–12]. However, these approaches are still limited to mostly controlled studio settings and static frame-synchronized multi-video systems which often feature 10 or more cameras.

Y. Liu (✉) · G. Ye · Y. Wang · Q. Dai · C. Theobalt
Tsinghua University, Beijing, China
e-mail: liuyebin@tsinghua.edu.cn

© Springer International Publishing Switzerland 2014
L. Shao et al. (eds.), *Computer Vision and Machine Learning with RGB-D Sensors*,
Advances in Computer Vision and Pattern Recognition,
DOI: 10.1007/978-3-319-08651-4_5

On the other end of the spectrum are methods for marker-less motion capture from a single camera view at interactive or near real-time frame rates. Estimation of complex poses from a single video stream is still a very challenging task. The recent advent of depth cameras, such as time-of-flight sensors [13] and the Microsoft Kinect, has opened up new possibilities. These cameras measure 2.5D depth information at real-time frame rates and, as for the Kinect, video as well. This makes them ideal sensors for pose estimation, but they suffer from significant noise and have, at best, moderate resolution. Therefore, (using a single depth camera) it has been difficult to capture 3D models of a complexity and detail comparable to multi-view performance capture results.

This chapter introduces a method to do full performance capture of moving humans using just three handheld, thus potentially moving, Kinect cameras. It reconstructs detailed time-varying surface geometry of humans in general apparel, as well as the motion of the underlying skeleton without any markers in the scene. It can handle fast and complex motion with many self-occlusions. By resorting to depth sensors, it can be applied to more general uncontrolled indoor scenes and is not limited to studios with controlled lighting and many stationary cameras. Also, it requires only three handheld sensors to produce results that rival reconstructions obtained with recent state-of-the-art multi-view performance capture methods [14, 15].

The key technology in this method is a tracking algorithm that tracks the motion of the handheld cameras and aligns the RGB-D data and that simultaneously aligns the surface and skeleton of each tracked performer to the captured RGB-D data. The algorithm also needs to be robust against the sensor noise, as well as missing data due to multi-Kinect interference and occlusions in the scene. It therefore introduces an efficient geometric 3D point-to-vertex assignment strategy to match the Kinect RGB-D data points to the geometric model of each performer. The assignment criterion is stable under missing data due to interference and occlusions between persons. Based on this criterion, a segmentation of the scene into performers, ground plane, and background is implicitly achieved. As a second correspondence criterion, it detects and tracks SIFT features in the background part of each video frame. Based on these model-to-data assignment criteria, the pose parameters of the performers and the poses and orientations of the Kinects are jointly estimated in a combined optimization framework. Finally, the nonlinear objective function can be linearized and effectively minimized through a quasi-Newton method.

The experimental section shows results on several challenging single- and multi-person motions including dance and martial arts. Also, quantitative proof of the accuracy of the reconstruction method is given by comparing it to an available video-based performance capture approach [12].

The technique presented in this chapter is a revision of former published papers [16, 17].[1]

---

[1] [2014] IEEE. Reprinted, with permission, from [Genzhi Ye, Yebin Liu, Yue Deng, Nils Hasler, Xiangyang Ji, Qionghai Dai, Christian Theobalt, Free-viewpoint Video of Human Actors using Multiple Handheld Kinects, IEEE Trans. Cybernetics, 43(5), pp 1370–1382, 2013].

5.2 Related Works

Most human performance capture approaches reconstruct human skeletal motion in controlled studios with a large number of cameras [3, 18, 19]. They usually employ a template skeleton with simple shape primitives [2, 5, 20] to fit the image data by optimizing an energy function parameterized by the template skeleton. This energy function usually exploits motion cues, such as silhouette, edge, and salient features. Typically, they are solved by local [2] or global optimization [20, 21], or the combine of the two [12].

Some advanced methods further reconstruct a detailed 3D deforming surface [7, 12, 22] of people in more general clothing. All these methods take advantage of a more elaborate shape and skeleton template, to improve the tracking accuracy while enforcing some surface refinement [12] or shading refinement [23] for better geometry reconstruction, or possibly reflectance reconstruction [24]. Recently, Wu et al. [22] proposed the integration of shading cues and develop the local linear optimization for more reliable skeletal pose tracking from indoor multi-view video.

The recent trend of marker-less motion capture aims to simplify the capture setup, e.g., by reducing the number of cameras, capturing in outdoor scenes, or using handheld devices. Outdoor marker-less motion capture with handheld cameras is studied in the pioneering work by Hasler et al. [25], but the accuracy of their method is restricted by the limited silhouette cues. Under the assumption of fixed distant global illumination, Wu et al. [26] employed a handheld stereo rig for performance capture in front of a general background, which significantly broadens the operation range of marker-less motion capture. But their local optimization and fixed global illumination model is only demonstrated for relatively restricted camera motion. However, only a frontal view of depth information from a binocular camera cannot guarantee a robust tracking under fast motion and serious occlusions. Wei et al. [27] further studied motion tracking from a monocular video. This challenging problem requires intensive manual interventions.

The prevalence of consumer depth cameras, such as the Microsoft Kinect camera, opens up new opportunities to solve fundamental problems in computer vision [28] and especially in human pose estimation [29, 30] and motion tracking [31]. Shotton et al. [32] and Ganapathi et al. [33] developed real-time motion estimation systems for indoor scenes captured recorded by a depth camera, which enables enormous applications in human–computer interaction and gaming. Typically, to achieve real-time performance, discriminative methods [34, 35] are applied to predict skeleton pose directly from the depth map by a trained regression model. Some recent works [31, 36, 37] further improved these discriminative methods with local optimization-based motion tracking. However, pose tracking with a single depth camera is far from robust and accurate and is challenged by motions with serious self-occlusions.

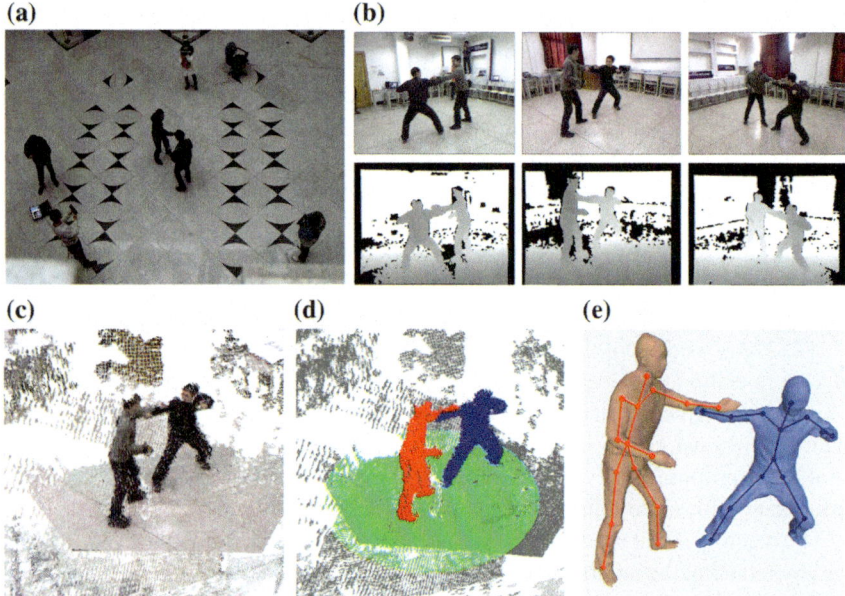

Fig. 5.1 Overview of the processing pipeline. **a** Overhead view of typical recording setup: three camera operators (*circled in red*) film the moving people in the center (*blue*); **b** input to the algorithm – RGB images and the depth images from three views; **c** Registered RGB-D point cloud from all cameras; **d** segmented RGB-D point cloud–color labels correspond to background, ground plane (*green*), and interacting humans (*red, blue*); **e** reconstructed surface models and skeletons

5.3 Data Capture and Scene Representation

For the data capture, one or more moving humans are recorded by $C = 3$ individuals (camera operators) that stand around the scene. Each of the operators holds a Kinect camera and points it toward the center of the recording volume. They are free to move the cameras during recording. The performance capture method can handle a certain amount of moving scene elements in the background. To improve the practicability of the whole system, we rely on simple and convenient software synchronization since hardware synchronization of multiple Kinects so far is not possible. Each Kinect is connected to a notebook computer, and all recording notebooks are connected through WiFi. One computer serves as a master that sends a *start recording* signal to all other computers. The cameras are set to a frame rate of 30fps, and with the software solution, the captured data of all cameras are frame-synchronized with at most 10 ms temporal difference.

Each Kinect captures a 640×480 video frame and an aligned depth frame at every time step t, Fig. 5.1b, which yields a combined RGB-D point cloud. The intrinsics of both the depth and the video cameras are calibrated off-line using a checkerboard [38]. Depth and color data are aligned with each other using the OpenNI API [39].

For each RGB-D point p, we store a triplet of values $p = \{x_p, n_p, l_p\}$. Here, x_p is the 3D position of the point, n_p is the local 3D normal, and l_p is a RGB color triplet. The normal orientations are found by PCA-based plane fitting to local 3D point neighborhoods. Note that the 3D point locations are given with respect to each camera's local coordinate system. For performance capture, the points from all cameras are required to be aligned into a global system. Since the Kinects are allowed to move in our setting, the extrinsic camera parameters Λ_c^t (position and orientation) of each Kinect c at every time step of video t, i.e., the combined extrinsic set $\Lambda^t = \{\Lambda_c^t\}_{c=1}^C$, need to be solved for. Fig. 5.1c shows the merged point set at time t after solving for the extrinsics using the method later described in this chapter. Also, due to occlusions in the scene and interference between several Kinects, 3D points corresponding to some Kinect camera pixels cannot reliably be reconstructed. The joint camera tracking and performance capture method thus need to be robust against such missing measurements.

For each of the $k = 1, \ldots, K$ performers in the scene, a template model is defined. Similar to [12, 14], a template model comprises a surface mesh M_k with an embedded kinematic bone skeleton (see Fig. 5.1e). A laser scanner is used to get a static surface mesh of the person. Alternatively, image-based reconstruction methods could be used or the mesh could be reconstructed from the aligned Kinect data [40–42]. The surface models are remeshed to have around $N_k = 5,000$ vertices. Each vertex is also assigned a color that can change over time, as described in Sect. 5.4.3. Henceforth, the 3D positions of vertices of mesh k with attached colors at time t are denoted by the set $V_k^t = \{v_{k,i}^t\}_{i=1}^{N_k}$. To stabilize simultaneous 3D human shape and Kinect position tracking, the ground plane is also explicitly modeled as a planar mesh V_0^t with circular boundary. The ground plane model has a fixed radius of 3m, and during initialization, it is centered below the combined center of gravity of the human models (see Fig. 5.1d). In total, this yields a combined set of vertex positions $V^t = \{\{V_k^t\}_{k=0}^K\}$ that need to be reconstructed at each time step. This excludes the ground plane vertices as their position is fixed in world space. Its apparent motion is modeled by moving the cameras.

A kinematic skeleton with $n = 31°$ of freedom (DoFs) is manually placed into each human mesh, and surface skinning weighs are computed using a similar process as [12, 14]. Skeleton poses $\chi^t = (\xi^t, \Theta^t) = (\theta_0 \hat{\xi}, \theta_1, \ldots, \theta_n)$ are parameterized using the twist and exponential maps parameterizations [2, 12]. $\theta_0 \hat{\xi}$ is the twist for the global rigid body transform of the skeleton, and Θ^t is the vector of the remaining angles. Using linear blend skinning, the configuration of a vertex of human mesh M_k in skeleton pose χ_k^t is then determined by

$$v_i\left(\chi_k^t\right) = \sum_{m=1}^{n} \left(w_i^m \prod_{j \in Parent(m)} \exp\left(\theta_j \hat{\xi}_j\right) \right) v_i. \quad (5.1)$$

Here, w_i^m is the skinning weight of vertex i with respect to the m-th DoF. Further on, $Parent(m)$ is the set of all the DoFs in the kinematic chain that influences the m-th DoF, i.e., all the parents of m-th DoF. In addition to $\Lambda^t = \{\Lambda_c^t\}_{c=1}^C$, the performance capture approach thus needs to solve for the joint parameters of all persons at each time step, $X^t = \{\chi_k^t\}_{k=1}^K$.

5.4 Human Performance Capture

Performance capture from 3D point data is only feasible if the RGB-D data from all Kinects are correctly registered. In the beginning, for each time step, the correct extrinsics Λ_t are unknown. A traditional approach to track camera extrinsics is structure from motion (SfM) performed on the background of the sequence [25]. However, in our multiple Kinect recording setting, the moving subjects fill most of the visible area in each video frame and thus, a different approach has to be used. In such a setting, human pose capture and camera pose estimation are performed simultaneously, leading to more robust results. In other words, the optimization tries to mutually align all point clouds and fit the poses of the actors to the RGB-D data. At the same time, feature correspondences in the background are exploited similarly to SfM, since they provide additional evidence for correct reconstruction. Camera and body poses are therefore simultaneously computed, and the solution is regularized to additional feature correspondences found in the video frame.

In the first frame of multi-view RGB-D video, camera extrinsics are initialized interactively and the template models are fitted to each person's depth map. The initialization pose in the data sequence is guaranteed to be close to the scanned pose. Thereafter, the algorithm runs in a frame-by-frame manner applying the processing pipeline from Fig. 5.1c–e to each time step. For a time step t, the steps are as follows: The Kinect RGB-D point clouds are first aligned according to the extrinsics Λ^{t-1} from the previous frame. Starting with the pose parameters X^{t-1} and resulting mesh configurations and vertex colors from the previous frame, a matching algorithm is introduced to match the Kinect point data to the model vertices. During this matching, the RGB-D data are also implicitly segmented into classes for *ground plane*, *background*, and one class for each *person*, Sect. 5.4.1 (Fig. 5.1d). Thereafter, a second set of 3D correspondences is found by matching points from the *ground plane* and the *background* via SIFT features, Sect. 5.4.1.

Based on these correspondences, Sect. 5.4.2 simultaneously solves for Kinect and skeleton poses for the current frame. Correspondence finding and reconstruction are iterated several times, and the model poses and point cloud alignments are continuously updated (Fig. 5.1c). Non-rigid deformations of the human surface, e.g., due to cloth deformation, are not explained by skeleton-driven deformation alone. In a final step, the meshes M_k are thus non-rigidly deformed into the aligned point clouds via Laplacian deformation and the vertex colors of the mesh model(s) are updated (Fig. 5.1e). The following section explains each step in the algorithm for a specific time t, and it omits the index t for legibility.

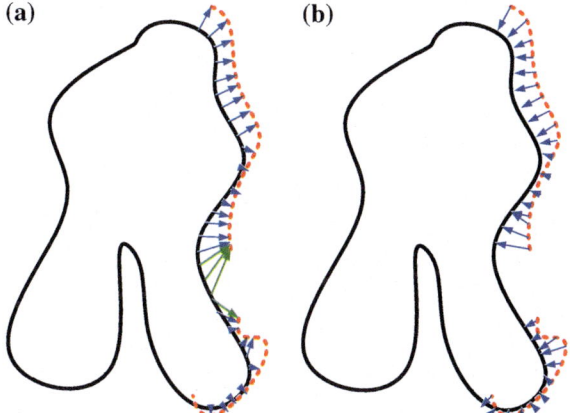

Fig. 5.2 Comparison of forward matching and inverse matching when Kinect data occlusion happens. The *red* points are Kinect data, and the *black lines* are model surface. The *blue arrows* and *green arrows* are matching. **a** forward matching. *Green* matching are error correspondences. **b** inverse matching

5.4.1 Point Data Correspondence and Labeling

The reconstructed 3D human models should matched to the RGB-D point clouds. Therefore, an error function that measures the alignment of the RGB-D point clouds with the 3D human models is minimized for finding the correct camera and body configurations, Sect. 5.4.2. To evaluate this error, for all scene model vertices V, plausible correspondences to the RGB-D points P need to be defined. With these correspondences, the alignment error can be evaluated, as it was also used in video-based performance capture to measure alignment in the image domain [12].

Due to mutual occlusions, the Kinect point cloud P will not always sample every part of the body surfaces. Additionally, interference between several Kinects renders some 3D points unreliable. That is, in this scenario, matching model vertices V to Kinect point clouds P tends to be unstable. Also, the matching term should ensure that each 3D human template is explained by the point data. Therefore, as shown in Fig. 5.2, reverse matching is much more robust since all the foreground points physically exist and, in theory, can all be explained by the model surface, although there is noise and outliers in the captured data. Thus, the closest mesh vertices for all RGB-D points are proposed as matches.

Here, we define the metric F for the searching of a model vertex v to a given 3D point p. Such metric simultaneously measures the color distance and a geometric distance as follows:

$$F(v, p) = \Delta\left(\|l_v - l_p\|, \theta_l\right) \Delta\left(\|x_v - x_p\|, \theta_x\right) \max\left(n_v n_p, 0\right) \quad (5.2)$$

where

$$\Delta(x, \theta) = \max\left(1 - \frac{x}{\theta}, 0\right) \quad (5.3)$$

Here, x_p, l_p, n_p and x_v, l_v, n_v denote the position, color, and normal of a Kinect point and a mesh vertex, respectively. The first part in F is a color term enforces color similarity between the mesh vertex and the corresponding Kinect point, with the maximum color difference θ_l is experimentally set to 100. The second part in F is a geometry term, and it only matches RGB-D points and vertices that are spatially close and have similar normal orientation. The maximum distance a mesh vertex is allowed to move θ_x is also experimentally set to 100 mm.

Based on F, we first select the points corresponding to the persons and the ground plane as:

$$Z_V^k = \left\{(v, p) \,|\, v = \underset{v}{\operatorname{argmax}}\, F(v, p), F(v, p) > 0, v \in M_k\right\} \quad (5.4)$$

and

$$Z_G = \left\{(v, p) \,|\, v = \underset{v}{\operatorname{argmax}}\, F(v, p), F(v, p) > 0, v \in V_0\right\}. \quad (5.5)$$

For each point p, the vertex v is first selected from V to maximize F. If the maximum $F > 0$, according to the label of v, the correspondence (p, v) is classified into a person correspondence set Z_V^k of person k, or into the ground plane correspondence set Z_G. After the correspondences $Z_V = \{Z_V^k\}_{k=1}^K$ and Z_G are established, the RGB-D point cloud is thus implicitly segmented into one class for each *person*, *ground plane*, and *background* for all RGB-D points that were not assigned a corresponding point in V.

As stated in the beginning, the reconstruction error is also based on feature correspondences in the scene background, similar to classical structure-from-motion approaches. The method from Sect. 5.4.1 provides a classification of background RGB-D points and thus corresponding RGB pixels in each Kinect video image. SIFT features are detected on the background regions of the RGB images from $t-1$ and t and then converted into 3D correspondences $Z_S = \{(p', p)\} \,|\, p' \in P^{t-1}, p \in P^t, (p', p)$ matched via SIFT$\}$ through the available depth. As stated earlier, background correspondences are not always fully reliable. Measurement accuracy decreases with increasing distance from the camera, and moving objects in the background lead to erroneous correspondences. Thus, the error function additionally measures point-to-model correspondences in the foreground. Fig. 5.3b shows that alignment based on SIFT features in the background alone will not suffice.

Fig. 5.3 Comparison of RGB-D point data fusion at frame t before and after joint skeleton and Kinect optimization. **a** Fusion using extrinsics from the former time. **b** Fusion based on SIFT features alone fails. **c** Fusion using extrinsics solved by the combined human and camera pose optimization produces much better results

5.4.2 Joint Skeleton and Kinect Tracking

After the computing of correspondence sets Z_V, Z_G, and Z_S, a geometric error function can be defined and minimized in the space of skeleton pose X and camera extrinsics Λ:

$$E(X, \Lambda) = \arg\min_{X, \Lambda} \left\{ \sum_{(p,v) \in Z_S} \frac{\|p(\Lambda) - v(X)\|^2}{\|Z_V\|} + \sum_{(p,v) \in Z_G} \frac{\|p(\Lambda) - v\|^2}{\|Z_G\|} + \sum_{(p,p') \in Z_S} \frac{\|p(\Lambda) - p'\|^2}{\|Z_S\|} \right\} \quad (5.6)$$

Here, $\|Z\|$ is the number of elements in set Z. This function is solved through linearization within an iterative quasi-Newton minimization. Using Taylor expansion of the exponential map, the transformation of Λ on point p leads to a linear formulation

$$p(\Lambda) = Rp + T = e^{\theta \hat{\xi}} p \approx \left(I + \theta \hat{\xi}\right) p \quad (5.7)$$

For the body pose, we can perform the similar expansion. Specifically, Eq. (5.1) can be linearized as

$$v(X) = \left(I + \theta_0 \hat{\xi}_0 + \sum_{m=1}^{n} \left(\sum_{j \in Children(m)} w_j \right) \theta_m \hat{\xi}_m \right) v, \quad (5.8)$$

where, $Children(m)$ is the set of DoFs corresponding to the children DoFs of the m-th DoF.

Robust correspondence finding and pose optimization are iterated for 20 times. After each iteration, the normals of the fused point cloud points n_p are updated. Fig. 5.3 shows the comparison of the fused data before pose optimization (a) and after pose optimization (c). Please note that even using state-of-the-art techniques, direct fusion of the point data without the aid of a 3D model is extremely difficult and error prone because of the small overlap region between the different Kinects [43].

5.4.3 Surface Geometry Optimization

After tracking and skinned deformation of the skeleton-driven model of each character, mesh deformation is performed to refine the surface geometry of the performers and capture non-rigid deformation effects, such as cloth motion. Similar to [8], for each person k, surface deformation is formulated as:

$$\arg\min_{v}\{\|Lv - \delta\|_2^2 + \|Cv - p\|_2^2\} \quad (5.9)$$

Here, v denotes the vector of vertices on human body mesh M_k. L is the discrete Laplace operator, and δ is the differential coordinates of the current mesh vertices. The Laplace operator is defined as [44]

$$L = \begin{cases} d_i & i = j \\ -1 & (i, j) \in E \\ 0 & \text{otherwise} \end{cases} \quad (5.10)$$

and δ is usually defined as

$$\delta_i = \frac{1}{d_i} \sum_{j \in N(i)} (v_i - v_j). \quad (5.11)$$

Here, $(i, j) \in E$ means vertex v_i and v_j are on the same edge and d_i is the number of neighbor vertices of v_i. The definition of δ is upgraded to cotangent weights in this work, please refer to [44] for detail. In (5.9), C is a diagonal matrix with nonzero entries $c_{jj} = \alpha$ (α=0.1) for vertices in correspondence set Z_{pv}^k. p is the vector with nonzero position entries for those p in Z_V^k.

After non-rigid mesh deformation, the color of each vertex is updated according to a linear interpolation between the previous color and the current color using

$$l_v = \frac{t}{t+1} l_v + \frac{1}{t+1} l_{nn} \quad (5.12)$$

where l_{nn} is the color of the nearest RGB-D neighbor point of v.

5.5 Experimental Results

This section verifies the performance capture system from both the perspectives of qualitative analysis and quantitative evaluations. The data were recorded with three moving Kinects at a resolution of 640 × 480 pixels and at a frame rate of 30fps. The sequence is consisted of a wide range of different motions, including

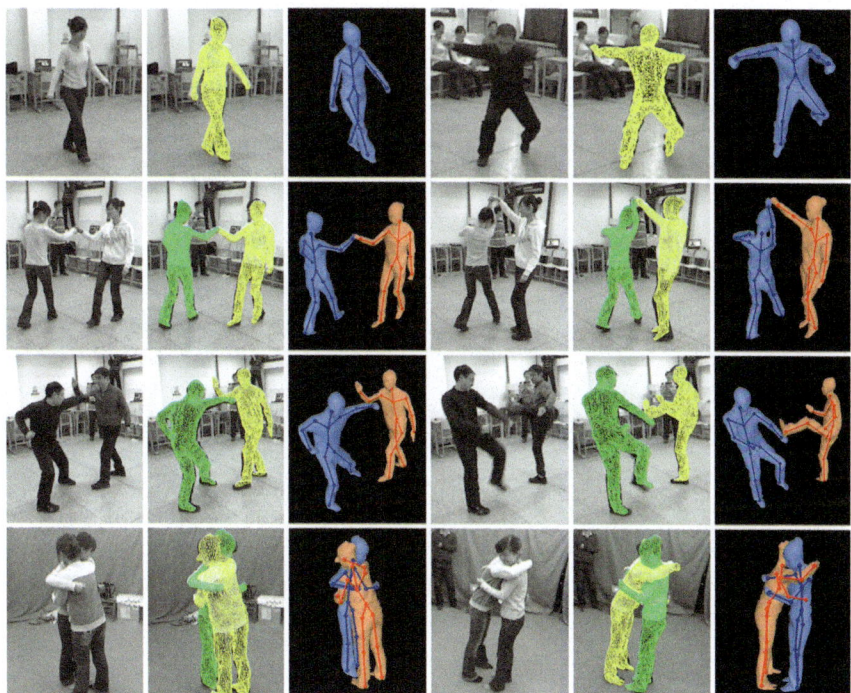

Fig. 5.4 Performance capture results on a variety of sequences: one of the input image, layered geometry, reconstructed geometry, and skeleton. Each row shows two results

dancing, fighting, and jumping, see Fig. 5.4, and accompanying video.[2] The motions were performed by five different persons wearing casual clothing. There are also two evaluation sequences where the performer was simultaneously tracked by a multi-view video system and also three evaluation sequences where one of the two human actors is wearing a marker suit for simultaneous optical motion capture. The configurations of the acquisition setups for all these sequences are shown in Table 5.1.

5.5.1 Qualitative Evaluation

Figure 5.4 shows several results produced by the system. The approach enables fully automatic reconstruction of skeletal pose and shape of two persons, even if they are as closely interacting as in martial arts fight, hug, or while dancing, see Fig. 5.4 and the accompanying video. Despite notable noise in the captured depth maps, the method successfully captures pose and deforming surface geometry of persons in

---

[2] The accompanying video is available at: www.media.au.tsinghua.edu.cn/kinectfvv.mp4.

Table 5.1 Description of the capture sequences

Sequence	Frame rate	Number of performers (K)	Number of Kinects (C)	Number of frames	Kinect status	Comparison
Dancing walk	30	1	3	300	Moving	No
Kungfu	30	1	3	300	Moving	No
Couple dance	30	2	3	300	Moving	No
Fight	30	2	3	300	Moving	No
Hug	30	2	3	250	Moving	No
Arm crossing	30	1	3	400	Static	No
Rolling	15	1	3	200	Static	Multi-view Video
Jump	15	1	3	200	Static	Multi-view Video
Exercise1	30	1	3	450	Static	Marker based
Exercise2	30	1	3	450	Moving	Marker based
Exercise3	30	2	3	450	Moving	Marker based

loose apparel. With a capturing frame rate of only 30fps, the introduced approach can also handle very fast motions, see the jump and kicking motions in Fig. 5.4.

5.5.2 Comparison to Vision-Based Motion Capture

To compare against a vision-based motion capture system, two sequences are captured in a multi-view video studio with 10 calibrated cameras (15fps, 1024 × 768) and a green screen in the background. The Kinect data were temporally aligned to the multi-view video data at frame-level accuracy using event synchronization. Although the synchronization of the video camera system and the Kinect system is not guaranteed at subframe accuracy, the evaluation of the difference between the two results still presents a conservative performance evaluation of the proposed algorithm.

Since the multi-view video system runs at 15fps, a sequence "rolling" is captured with slow motion and a sequence "jump" with fast motion. The Kinect system runs at 30fps, so the frames from the multiple Kinect system are subsampled by factor two and compared to the performance captured with multi-view video-based tracking (MVT) [12]. Figure 5.5 visually demonstrates the results of the two systems on the basis of four frames selected at regular equidistant intervals from the "rolling" sequence. Since the MVT requires a green screen for clean background subtraction and it, thus, does not work with extra camera operators in the scene background, the three Kinects are fixed in the MVT studio during data capture. With these fixed Kinects, the introduced algorithm can be validated by comparing the optimized Kinect extrinsics in the later frames with those of the first frame. The average distance from the Kinect center in the first frame to the Kinect center of other frames (both "rolling" and "jump") for each of the Kinects are 10.66 mm, 7.28 mm and

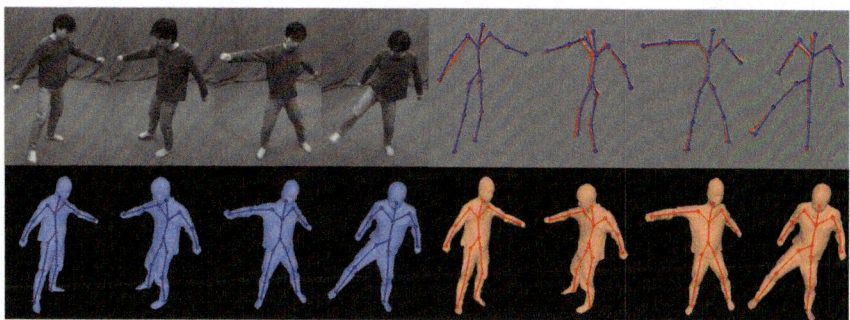

Fig. 5.5 Comparison with multi-view video-based tracking (MVT) approach on the "rolling" sequence. The *top left* are four input images of the multi-view video sequence. The *top right* shows the close overlap of the two skeletons tracked with MVT (*blue*) and the multiple Kinect-based approach (*red*). The *bottom left* is the reconstructed surface with the skeleton using MVT, and the *bottom right* is the results from the multiple Kinect-based approach. Quantitative and visual comparisons show that MVT-based and Kinect-based reconstructions are very similar

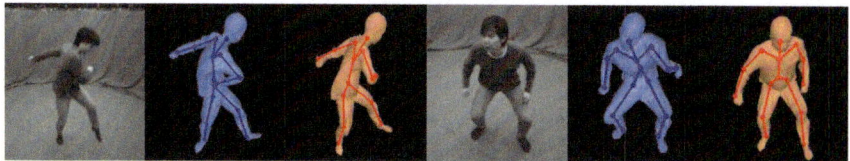

Fig. 5.6 Comparison with multi-view video-based tracking (MVT) approach on the *"jump"* sequence. The *left* three and the *right* three are input image, result of MVT, and result of the Kinect-based approach. On this fast motion, Kinect-based tracking succeeds, while MVT fails to capture the arm motion

6.67 mm, respectively. For the slow motion sequence "rolling", the result from the multiple Kinect system closely matches the input images and the result of the MVT system, see Fig. 5.5. In addition, the differences on the joint centers of these results from the two systems are computed. The average distance between the corresponding joint positions across all 200 frames of the sequence is 21.42 mm with a standard deviation of 27.49 mm. This distance also includes the synchronization differences between the two systems. For the fast motion sequences, the MVT even fails despite a much higher number of cameras, while the Kinect-based tracking is able to track the whole sequence, see Fig. 5.6.

5.5.3 Comparison to Marker-Based Motion Capture

Most of the commercial motion capture systems apply marker-based techniques since they provide comparably robust and accurate performance. In this chapter, a quantitative evaluation on the accuracy of simultaneous skeleton motion capture and

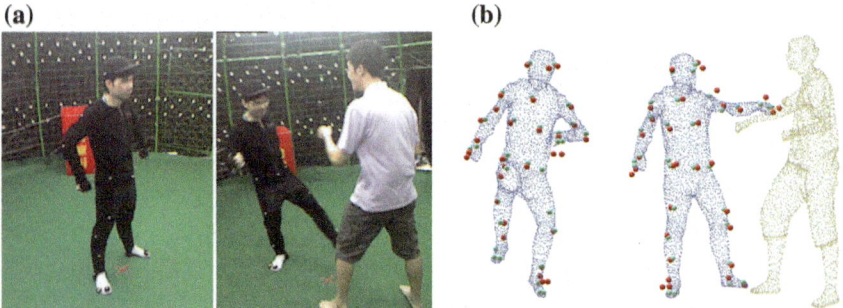

Fig. 5.7 The capturing environment with the OptiTrack motion capture system **a** and comparison between this marker-based Mocap system and our algorithm **b**. *Red* dots represent the ground truth marker position and the *green* dots are their corresponding vertice on the body model. The distance between them is evaluated

geometry reconstruction with the proposed system against a marker-based system is conducted. One sample image showing the capturing environment of the marker system is provided in Fig. 5.7a. In our setting, OptiTrack marker-based motion capture system [45] is adopted for comparison. Besides three handheld Kinects in the capture environment, 34 optical markers were attached to one of the persons, whose motions were captured with the marker-based system. Since it is impossible to synchronize the two systems, both of the two systems run at 30fps and the start frames are manually aligned. The synchronization error is then within 1/30 s.

The error metric is defined as the average distance between the markers and their corresponding vertices on the template model across all the frames of the sequence. The corresponding vertices are found in the first frame when the markers and the 3D model template is well aligned. The error metric not only accounts for the performance of skeleton tracking, but also the accuracy of the geometry reconstruction. Figure 5.7b and the accompany video show the ground truth marker positions and their corresponding vertices on the recovered models. Our experiments show that the multiple Kinect-based system produces reasonable and similar tracking performances as the marker system. In cases of occlusions between two persons, the tracking result is also robust and accurate. Quantitative evaluations are also performed, as shown in Fig. 5.8. The average distance and the standard derivations of the distance between each marker and their corresponding vertices on the 3D model are calculated. The results are shown in Fig. 5.8. The average error between the two systems is about 38 mm. Considering that the two systems are not strictly synchronized, this geometry accuracy is plausible. Compared with available single depth camera-based motion capture systems such as Ganapathi et al. [33], which report an average tracking error about 200 mm, the multiple Kinect-based system provides much lower tracking errors. This improvement is achieved through the combination of multiple depth cameras and the delicate algorithm design. From the quantitative evaluation on "Exercise 1"(static cameras) and "Exercise 2"(handheld cameras), it

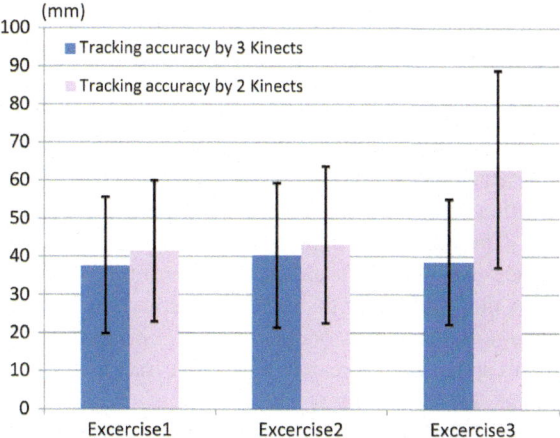

Fig. 5.8 The quantitative comparison of the Kinect-based tracking accuracy with the marker-based result (*ground truth*). The *blue* bars and *pink* bars show the accuracy and standard derivations (*std*) with three Kinects and two Kinects, respectively

is also interesting to note that, compared with static capture, handheld capture does not obviously damage system performance.

All the experiments discussed above are implemented with three Kinect cameras. To verify the robustness of the multiple Kinect-based system, the number of cameras is decreased to show how the final results are affected by the number of Kinects. The accuracy achieved with two Kinects is shown with the pink bars in Fig. 5.8. This shows that the accuracy obtained with two Kinects and three Kinects is very similar for one body tracking (for "Exercise 1" and "Exercise 2"). However, the accuracy decreases significantly by using two cameras for the "Exercise 3." This is because in "Exercise 3," occlusion between the two persons is more serious. Using only two cameras could not sufficiently capture the whole scenario and therefore results in a relatively low tracking quality.

5.6 Discussion

Interference: Currently, multiple Kinects aiming at the same scene may introduce interferences between each other and degrade the depth quality. In our case, the Kinects are very sparse with any of the two Kinects covering a viewing angle of about 120°. Such a baseline with such a large angle causes only about 10% of the whole pixels surfers interference for a camera in the experiments, compared with the case of single Kinect. Moreover, the Kinect will not return depth values for pixels with interference, so interference will not produce erroneous 3D point data to degrade the tracking accuracy. To adapt for more Kinects working together, multiple depth sensors may share the same lighting source to infer depth information while reducing interference.

Complexity: Computational complexity does not starkly depend on the number of subjects in the scene. It takes about 10 s for single person tracking of a frame and 12 s for the two persons tracking on a standard PC using unoptimized code. The system uses local optimization, and the run time of the system mainly depends on the number of captured points. The number of captured points decides the time complexity of both correspondence establishment and the pose estimation. The correspondence establishment takes more than half of the total time and could be optimized using more efficient data structures, like octrees, to decrease the searching number of matching vertices to speed up the search. Real-time tracking is possible with code optimization and parallel computing.

Alternative Optimization Approach: Since the method introduced is based on local optimization, the tracking may fail when serious occlusions happen or when the motion is too fast. Alternatively, a global optimization approach [12] can be employed based on the local optimization results, similar to the method proposed for multi-view video-based tracking. Such global optimization is, for instance, based on analysis by synthesis, that is, sampling on the skeleton and camera pose space and retrieving the one that best matched to the input data in a particle swarm optimization (PSO) [46] or interacting simulated annealing (ISA) [21] optimization. Theoretically, the tracking results will be comparably more robust than local optimization approach; however, the computation complexity is greatly increased and the temporal smoothness of the tracking results will be degraded.

5.7 Conclusions

This chapter introduces a method for human performance capture using several handheld Kinects. The method adopts a local optimization approach to simultaneously solve for the skeleton parameters and camera pose by driving them to fit to the input point data from the Kinects. The tracking approach is based on iterating robust matching of the tracked 3D models and the input Kinect data and a quasi-Newton optimization on Kinect poses and skeleton poses. This joint optimization enables us to reliably and accurately capture shape and pose of multiple performers. In summary, the proposed technique removes the common constraint in traditional multi-view motion capture systems that cameras have to be static and scenes need to be filmed in controlled studio settings. Instead, the introduced system allows users to hold the Kinects for motion capture and 3D reconstruction of performers. This enriches the practical application, especially when considering the anticipated introduction of depth cameras in consumer devices like tablets.

References

1. Deutscher J, Blake A, Reid I (2000) Articulated body motion capture by annealed particle filtering. In: IEEE conference on computer vision pattern recognition, pp 1144–1149
2. Bregler C, Malik J, Pullen K (2004) Twist based acquisition and tracking of animal and human kinematics. IJCV 56:179–194
3. Sigal L, Black M (2006) Humaneva: synchronized video and motion capture dataset for evaluation of articulated human motion. Technical Report CS-06-08, Brown University
4. Balan A, Sigal L, Black M, Davis J, Haussecker H (2007) Detailed human shape and pose from images. In: IEEE conference on computer vision pattern recognition, pp 1–8
5. Stoll C, Hasler N, Gall J, Seidel HP, Theobalt C (2011) Fast articulated motion tracking using a sums of gaussians body model. In: IEEE international conference on computer vision, pp 951–958
6. Poppe R (2007) Vision-based human motion analysis: an overview. CVIU 108:4–18
7. Vlasic D, Baran I, Matusik W, Popović J (2008) Articulated mesh animation from multi-view silhouettes. ACM Trans Graph 27:1–9
8. De Aguiar E, Stoll C, Theobalt C, Ahmed N, Seidel H, Thrun S (2008) Performance capture from sparse multi-view video. In: ACM Transactions on Graphics (TOG). vol 27, p 98
9. Ballan L, Cortelazzo G (2008) Marker-less motion capture of skinned models in a four camera set-up using optical flow and silhouettes. In: 3DPVT, vol 37
10. Cagniart C, Boyer E, Ilic S (2010) Free-form mesh tracking: a patch-based approach. In: IEEE conference on computer vision pattern recognition, pp 1339–1346
11. Starck J, Hilton A (2007) Surface capture for performance based animation. IEEE Comput Graph Appl 27(3):21–31
12. Gall J, Stoll C, De Aguiar E, Theobalt C, Rosenhahn B, Seidel H (2009) Motion capture using joint skeleton tracking and surface estimation. In: IEEE conference on computer vision pattern recognition, pp 1746–1753
13. Kolb A, Barth E, Koch R, Larsen R (2010) Time-of-flight cameras in computer graphics. Comput Graph Forum 29:141–159
14. Liu Y, Stoll C, Gall J, Seidel HP, Theobalt C (2011) Markerless motion capture of interacting characters using multi-view image segmentation. In: IEEE conference on computer vision pattern recognition, pp 1249–1256
15. Liu Y, Gall J, Stoll C, Dai Q, Seidel HP, Theobalt C (2013) Markerless motion capture of multiple characters using multiview image segmentation. IEEE Trans Pattern Anal Mach Intell 35:2720–2735
16. Ye G, Liu Y, Hasler N, Ji X, Dai Q, Theobalt C (2012) Performance capture of interacting characters with handheld kinects. In: IEEE conference on computer vision ECCV. Springer, Berlin, pp 828–841
17. Ye G, Liu Y, Deng Y, Hasler N, Ji X, Dai Q, Theobalt C (2013) Free-viewpoint video of human actors using multiple handheld kinects. IEEE T Cybern 43:1370–1382
18. Moeslund TB, Hilton A, Krüger V (2006) A survey of advances in vision-based human motion capture and analysis. Comput vis image underst 104:90–126
19. Poppe R (2007) Vision-based human motion analysis: an overview. Comput vis image underst 108:4–18
20. Deutscher J, Blake A, Reid I (200) Articulated body motion capture by annealed particle filtering. In: Proceedings of the IEEE Conference on computer vision and pattern recognition, Vol 2, pp 126–133
21. Gall J, Rosenhahn B, Brox T, Seidel HP (2010) Optimization and filtering for human motion capture. Int j comput vis 87:75–92
22. Wu C, Varanasi K, Theobalt C (2012) Full body performance capture under uncontrolled and varying illumination: a shading-based approach. Springer, New York, pp 757–770
23. Wu C, Varanasi K, Liu Y, Seidel HP, Theobalt C (2011) Shading-based dynamic shape refinement from multi-view video under general illumination. In: IEEE international conference on computer vision (ICCV), pp 1108–1115

24. Li G, Wu C, Stoll C, Liu Y, Varanasi K, Dai Q, Theobalt C (2013) Capturing relightable human performances under general uncontrolled illumination. Comput Graph Forum 32:275–284
25. Hasler N, Rosenhahn B, Thormählen T, Wand M, Gall J, Seidel HP (2009) Markerless motion capture with unsynchronized moving cameras. In: IEEE international conference on computer vision pattern recognition, pp 224–231
26. Wu C, Stoll C, Valgaerts L, Theobalt C (2013) On-set performance capture of multiple actors with a stereo camera. ACM Trans Graph (TOG) 32:161
27. Wei X, Chai J (2010) Videomocap: modeling physically realistic human motion from monocular video sequences. ACM Trans Graph (TOG) 29:42
28. Han J, Shao L, Xu D, Shotton J (2013) Enhanced computer vision with microsoft kinect sensor: a review. IEEE T Cybernet 43:1318–1334
29. Shum HPH, Ho ESL, Jiang Y, Takagi S (2013) Real-time posture reconstruction for microsoft kinect. IEEE T Cybernet 43:1357–1369
30. Ni B, Pei Y, Moulin P, Yan S (2013) Multilevel depth and image fusion for human activity detection. IEEE T Cybernet 43:1383–1394
31. Baak A, Müller M, Bharaj G, Seidel HP, Theobalt C (2013) A data-driven approach for real-time full body pose reconstruction from a depth camera. In: Consumer depth cameras for computer vision. Springer, New York, pp 71–98
32. Shotton J, Fitzgibbon AW, Cook M, Sharp T, Finocchio M, Moore R, Kipman A, Blake A (2011) Real-time human pose recognition in parts from single depth images. In: IEEE international conference on computer vision pattern recognition, pp 1297–1304
33. Ganapathi V, Plagemann C, Koller D, Thrun S (2010) Real time motion capture using a single time-of-flight camera. In: IEEE international conference on computer vision pattern recognition, pp 755–762
34. Agarwal A, Triggs B (2004) 3d human pose from silhouettes by relevance vector regression. In: Proceedings of the IEEE computer society conference on computer vision and Pattern Recognition, vol 2, p 882
35. Ye M, Wang X, Yang R, Ren L, Pollefeys M (2011) Accurate 3d pose estimation from a single depth image. In: IEEE international conference on computer vision, pp 731–738
36. Taylor J, Shotton J, Sharp T, Fitzgibbon A (2012) The vitruvian manifold: inferring dense correspondences for one-shot human pose estimation. In: IEEE conference on computer vision and pattern recognition (CVPR), pp 103–110
37. Wei X, Zhang P, Chai J (2012) Accurate realtime full-body motion capture using a single depth camera. ACM Trans Graph (TOG) 31:188
38. Bouguet JY (2004) Camera calibration toolbox for matlab
39. OpenNI: (http://www.openni.org/)
40. Barmpoutis A (2013) Tensor body: real-time reconstruction of the human body and avatar synthesis from rgb-d. IEEE T Cybernet 43:1347–1356
41. Tong J, Zhou J, Liu L, Pan Z, Yan H (2012) Scanning 3d full human bodies using kinects. IEEE Trans Vis Comput Graph 18:643–650
42. Li H, Vouga E, Gudym A, Luo L, Barron JT, Gusev G (2013) 3d self-portraits. ACM Trans Graph 32:187
43. Aiger D, Mitra NJ, Cohen-Or D (2008) 4-points congruent sets for robust surface registration. ACM Trans Graph 27(85):1–10
44. Sorkine O (2006) Differential representations for mesh processing. Comput Graph Forum 25:789–807
45. OptiTrack: (http://www.naturalpoint.com/optitrack/)
46. Oikonomidis I, Kyriazis N, Argyros AA (2011) Efficient model-based 3d tracking of hand articulations using kinect. In: IEEE international conference on BMVC, pp 1–11

Chapter 6
Human-Centered 3D Home Applications via Low-Cost RGBD Cameras

Zhenbao Liu, Shuhui Bu and Junwei Han

Abstract In this chapter, we will introduce three human-centered home 3D applications realized by virtue of low-cost RGBD cameras. The first application is personalized avatar for user via multiple Kinects, which can reconstruct a real human and provide personalized avatars for everyday users and enhance interactive experience in game and virtual reality environments. The second application automatically evaluates energy consumption of users in gaming scenarios by a model with tracked skeleton, which may help users to know their exercise effects and even diet or reduce their weights. The final application presents a real-time system that automatically classifies the human action acquired by consumer-priced RGBD sensor.

6.1 Personalized Avatar for User via Multiple Kinects

In traditional human-centered games and virtual reality applications, skeleton of human is commonly captured via consumer-priced cameras or professional motion capture devices to animate an avatar to follow his movements. In this section, we

---

Z. Liu and S. Bu were supported by NSFC (61003137, 61202185), Fundamental Research Funds for the Central Universities(310201401JCQ01012, 310201401JCQ01009), Shaanxi NSF(2012JQ8037), and Open Fund from State Key Lab of CAD&CG of Zhejiang University. J. Han was supported by the NSFC under Grant 61005018 and 91120005, NPU-FFR-JC20120237 and Program for New Century Excellent Talents in University under grant NCET-10-0079.

Z. Liu · S. Bu (✉) · J. Han
Northwestern Polytechnical University, Xi'an, China
e-mail: bushuhui@nwpu.edu.cn

Z. Liu
e-mail: liuzhenbao@nwpu.edu.cn

J. Han
e-mail: jhan@nwpu.edu.cn

propose a novel application that automatically reconstructs a real 3D moving human captured from multiple Kinect RGBD cameras in the form of polygonal mesh, which may help users to really enter a virtual environment or even collaborative immersive environments. Compared to 3D point cloud, 3D polygonal mesh is commonly adopted to represent objects or characters in games and virtual reality applications. The vivid 3D human mesh can enormously promote the immersion when he interacts with a computer. The proposed method includes three key steps to dynamically realize 3D human reconstruction from noisy RGB image and depth data captured in a distant distance. We first recover 3D scene represented in point cloud from scanned RGBD data. We then filter noisy and unorganized point cloud and obtain a relatively clean 3D human point cloud. A complete 3D human mesh is reconstructed from the filtered point cloud using Delaunay triangulation and Poisson surface reconstruction. A group of experiments demonstrates the reconstructed 3D human meshes, and these dynamic meshes with different poses are placed in a virtual environment. It could be used to provide personalized avatars for everyday users and enhance interactive experience in game and virtual reality environments.

6.1.1 Introduction

Real 3D scene and human reconstruction from a professional 3D scanner have been well studied in multimedia, virtual reality, and computer graphics [1]. It has generated satisfactory results adaptable to industrial inverse engineering and production design based on virtual reality. However, the technique cannot be directly applied in home-centered amusements because of high price, large volume, difficult operation, and computational burden. In recent years, portable RGBD cameras with low cost and easy operation, for example, Kinect [2], is highly appealing and becoming more widespread. Han et al. [3] investigate recent Kinect-based computer vision algorithms and applications and classify these algorithms according to the type of vision problems. These topics include preprocessing, object tracking and recognition, human activity analysis, hand gesture analysis, and indoor 3D mapping. However, the type of cameras generates low-quality color and depth images, which becomes a main constraint on providing fully immersive and virtual applications. Many researchers have payed close attention to recent developments on high-quality scene and human generation.

There have been several pioneering works focusing on interesting 3D virtual applications of RGBD sensors. Alexiadis et al. [4] build a real-time automatic system of dance performance evaluation via Kinect RGBD sensor and provide visual feedback to beginners in a 3D virtual scene. Bleiweiss et al. [5] propose a solution to animating in-game avatars using real-time motion capture data and blend actual movements of players with pre-defined animation sequences. Pedersoli et al. [6] provide a framework for Kinect enabling more natural and intuitive hand gesture communication between human and computer devices. Tong et al. [7] present a novel scanning system for capturing different parts of a human body at a close distance, and then reconstructing 3D full human body.

Ye et al. [8] propose an algorithm for creating free-viewpoint video of interacting humans using three handheld Kinect cameras. They reconstruct deforming surface geometry and temporal varying texture of humans through estimation of human poses and camera poses for every time step of the RGBD video. Barmpoutis [9] reconstruct 3D model of the human body from a sequence of RGB-D frames by means of parameterization of cylindrical-type objects using Cartesian tensor and b-spline bases along the radial and longitudinal dimension. The reconstruction is performed in real time, while the human subject moves arbitrarily in front of the camera. The tensor body is fitted to the input data using segmentation of different body regions, robust filtering, and energy-based optimization.

Differently from the above applications, we attempt to solve the problem of dynamic 3D human reconstruction from data acquired by means of multiple RGBD sensors located in a distant distance. This is a similar scene setting as home game. Nevertheless, several major difficulties must be faced, which include (1) RGB image and depth data simultaneously sampled from the same RGBD sensor in a low resolution is difficult to be calibrated and coupled to 3D textured point cloud without distortion and (2) the coupled point cloud is too sparse and noisy to reconstruct a detailed and smooth mesh. In order to overcome these problems, we first propose several 3D human filters to extract relatively pure point cloud of human from a whole 3D scene. An initial triangulation with holes and burrs is then reconstructed based on the point cloud. We finally fill all the holes and smooth the surface via poisson surface reconstruction. The reconstructed 3D human is dynamically placed into a virtual environment and able to follow the movements of users. See Fig. 6.1 for an illustration.

The section is organized as follows. The colored point cloud of scene is first generated in Sect. 6.1.2. Section 6.1.3 illustrates how we filter the noisy and unorganized 3D scene point cloud to get a relatively clean human point cloud. We introduce two steps to convert the point cloud to 3D mesh in Sect. 6.1.4. Section 6.1.5 demonstrates personalized avatar of user in a virtual scene.

6.1.2 Point Cloud Generation

We adopt the dataset captured by five Microsoft Kinects and their registration parameters, which are provided by 3DLife/Huawei Grand Challenge of ACM Multimedia 2013 [10]. The dataset contains five groups of Kinect data recording the same scene. The five Kinect sensors are, respectively, placed in different positions and different directions. Each Kinect outputs a sequence of depth and color images, which are encoded with video format. Each one of the five captured videos only records a part view of the whole 3D scene due to the limited visual angle of Kinect camera. The raw depth map and its corresponding color map of each view are separately extracted by means of OpenNI develop toolkit. Both depth and color images have the same

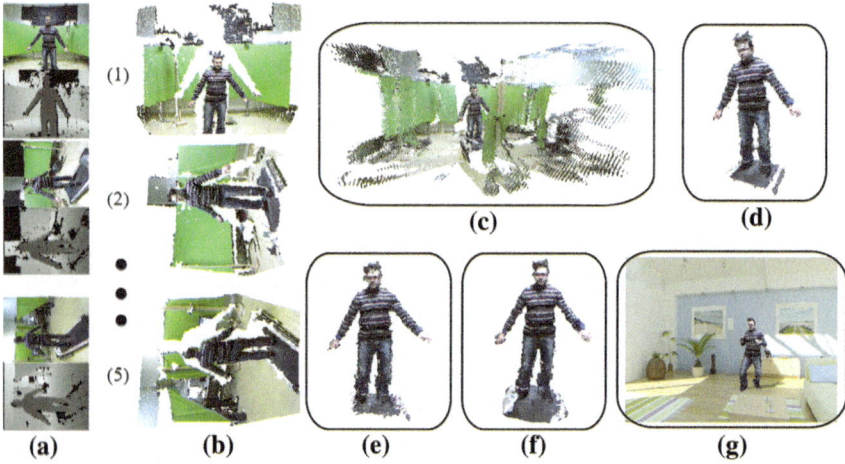

Fig. 6.1 Overview of the steps in our personalized avatar implementation. **a** RGB and depth images from (*1*) to (*5*) captured from five Kinects. **b** Five respective RGB-D calibrated images. **c** Registered point cloud of scene. **d** Filtered 3D human point cloud. **e** Delaunay triangulation. **f** Poisson mesh reconstruction. **g** Movement of personalized avatar in a virtual scene

Fig. 6.2 Registered whole scene in the form of 3D point cloud. We first calibrate the depth and color map using a recent algorithm [11] for each Kinect data and map the color map to the depth map using camera parameters to get five colored point clouds. The five point clouds are then registered into one whole 3D scene

resolution with 480 × 640 pixels. Because depth and color images come from different cameras on the same Kinect and are not completely overlapped, we adopt a recent algorithm [11] to calibrate them in advance. The calibration model does not use depth discontinuities in the depth image and accordingly is flexible and robust to noise. We use the calibrated camera parameters to recover the five 3D partial views, and then register the five 3D partial views into one whole 3D point cloud scene. The reconstructed whole 3D scene in the form of point cloud is shown in Fig. 6.2.

6.1.3 3D Human Filters

Although the color and depth images have been calibrated and registered into 3D point cloud without distortion, it can be seen that the point cloud is still very noisy and mixed with a lot of isolated points and wrongly colored points. This leads to the difficulty in reconstructing the point cloud to a clean polygonal mesh. Moreover, many details representing realistic effects of a user, for example, face and clothes, should be recovered in a high-quality way.

In order to attain the above objective, we first have to extract a whole human from the 3D scene point cloud. Because many noisy points and background points have been mixed into the point cloud of human in the step of scene generation, we consider how to remove these redundant points and extract a relatively clean point cloud of human from the whole 3D scene. We propose three simple and efficient filters to finish the task, which are band-pass filter $F(b)$, background color filter $F(c)$, and distance filter $F(d)$.

We first use a band-pass filter $F(b)$ to get a coarse human point cloud. It is expressed as the following form.

$$F(b) * p_i = \begin{cases} p_i, & x \in [x_0, x_1], y \in [y_0, y_1], z \in [z_0, z_1] \\ 0, & \text{otherwise} \end{cases} \quad (6.1)$$

where $\{[x_0, x_1], [y_0, y_1], [z_0, z_1]\}$ denotes a bounding box of the human point cloud. p_i is a point in the point cloud. $F(b) * p_i$ means applying the filter to the point p_i.

Here, the bounding box is built by virtue of a recent high-level skeleton tracking algorithm [15]. The algorithm designs an intermediate body parts representation that maps the difficult pose estimation problem into a simpler per-pixel classification problem. Its classifier is trained by efficient randomized decision forests, considering a large number of characters from short to tall and thin to fat, many poses, models with different hair styles and clothing. Once we get the positions of the skeleton joints tracked, the bounding box of the whole skeleton is simply computed by utilizing the maximum and minimum values of all the joint coordinates. We empirically enlarge the bounding box of skeleton by 10 filter $F(b)$. The filter passes a coarse human point cloud as shown in Fig. 6.3a and reject outside points. We see the point cloud is still disturbed by background noises. In order to keep a better point cloud for next mesh reconstruction, we refine the boundary of coarse human point cloud. A background color filter $F(c)$ is considered to get rid of the noisy background color points on the boundary. Finally, we use another distance filter $F(d)$ to delete the isolated points which may cause wrong faces in mesh reconstruction.

$$F(d) * p_i = \begin{cases} p_i, & d(p_i) < d_0 \\ 0, & \text{otherwise} \end{cases} \quad (6.2)$$

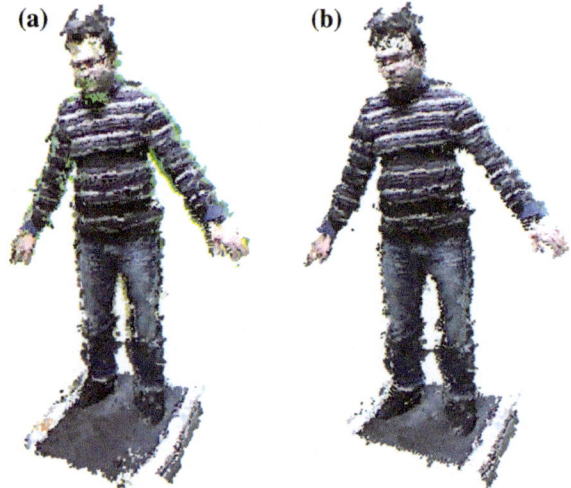

Fig. 6.3 **a** Coarse human point cloud. **b** Final human point cloud. We first use a band-pass filter to get the coarse human point cloud (**a**). By applying other two filters, background color filter and distance filter, the final point cloud (**b**) is obtained

$d(p_i)$ is the distance between p_i and its nearest point, and we practically set the constant threshold value d_0 to 10. After passing these three filters, a relatively fine scattered point cloud is generated for next mesh reconstruction, as shown in Fig. 6.3b.

6.1.4 Human Mesh Reconstruction

The human point cloud with color generated above has three defective problems, which may cause incorrect mesh reconstruction. We first solve the organization problem of these unordered 3D points and adopt polygonal form to topologically connect these points. The second problem to be addressed is that there are many holes in the point cloud because of low image resolution of Kinect, placement of Kinect in a distant distance, and missed points while scanning human in different directions. Another problem we find is that the point cloud is not smooth and contains a lot of burrs on the boundary.

Therefore, we attempt to introduce a two-stage solution to these low-quality problems. In the first stage of mesh reconstruction, we preliminarily triangulate the unorganized point cloud and make these massive points connect with spatial neighbors. We solve the problem of holes and burrs in the second stage, and it can be cast as an issue of Poisson surface reconstruction. Because global Poisson equation considers all the points simultaneously, it is considered highly robust to small data noises.

During the first stage, we topologically connect and triangulate the unorganized point cloud by means of Delaunay triangulation [12] to get a coarse human mesh from

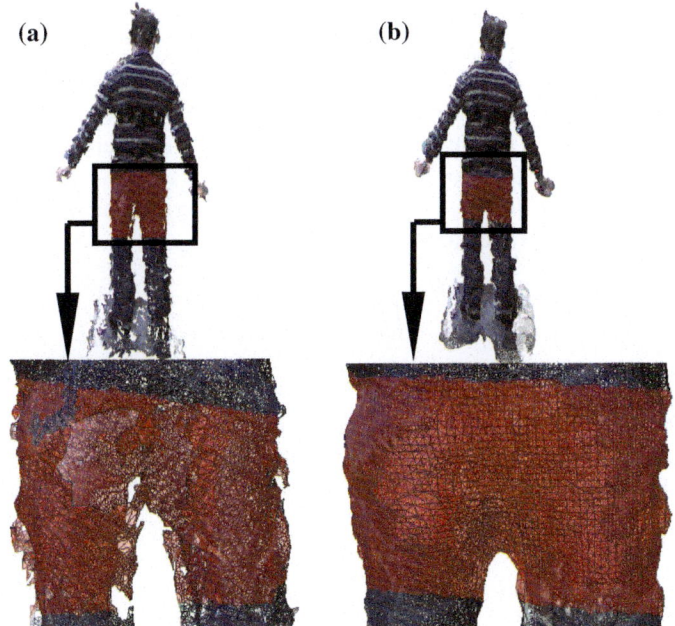

Fig. 6.4 a Local amplification in Delaunay triangulation. **b** Local amplification in Poisson surface reconstruction. It can be seen the surface is smoothed after introducing Poisson reconstruction

the scattered point cloud. In order to obtain an adaptive human mesh, it is feasible to adjust the density of triangles according to the amount of points in different parts of human. However, we find that Delaunay triangulation is susceptible to undersampling and outliers. For example, there are some holes and burrs in the triangulated human mesh shown in Fig. 6.4a.

In order to overcome the problem, in the second step, we adopt the Poisson mesh reconstruction [13] to refine the initial mesh, fill the holes on the surface, and remesh it. The surface reconstruction is seen as the solution to a Poisson equation of isosurface as follows.

$$\Delta \phi = \nabla \cdot \mathbf{V}, \tag{6.3}$$

where ϕ is an indicator function and Δ denotes its Laplace operator. The divergence ∇ of a vector field $\mathbf{V}$ equals Laplacian of the scalar function. The above Poisson equation is actually equivalent to expected approximation and reconstruction:

$$\phi = \mathrm{argmin} \, \| \nabla \phi - \mathbf{V} \|, \tag{6.4}$$

which means the gradient of the implicit function ϕ of an input point cloud $\{p_i\}$ fits the vector field based on these points and their normal vectors $\{\mathbf{v}_i\}$. The form of the vector field is discretized in a subdivision octree as follows.

$$\mathbf{V} = \sum_{p_i} \sum_{j \in n(p_i)} \alpha_{ij} b_j(p_i) \mathbf{v}_i, \qquad (6.5)$$

where $n(p_i)$ denotes the set of the eight closest octree nodes of each point p_i and j is the node index. α_{ij} is the interpolation weight. $b_j(p_i)$ is a transformed function on each octree node n_j. It is worth noting that it is similar as wavelet built on the 3D regular grid. More specifically, each transformed function is obtained by translating and scaling a fixed basis function

$$b_j(p_i) = b\left(\frac{p_i - c(n_j)}{w(n_j)}\right) \frac{1}{w(n_j)^3}, \qquad (6.6)$$

where $b(p_i)$ denotes the fixed basis. $c(n_j)$ is the center of the node n_j and $w(n_j)$ is its width. The basis function has a uniform form, that is, the convolution with a box filter $f(x)$ (or $f(y)$, $f(z)$) t times separately on each dimensional coordinate $\{x, y, z\}$. The convolution can be expressed as

$$b(x, y, z) = (f(x) * f(x))^t (f(y) * f(y))^t (f(z) * f(z))^t, \qquad (6.7)$$

where each box filter, for example, $f(x)$, has the following form

$$f(x) = \begin{cases} 1, & |x| < 0.5 \\ 0, & \text{otherwise} \end{cases} \qquad (6.8)$$

The approximation problem in Eq. 6.4 can be converted by projecting it onto the space spanned by bases b_j, $j \in [1, |T|]$. $|T|$ is the number of octree nodes. The solution to ϕ is equivalent to minimizing

$$\begin{aligned} &\sum_j \|\langle \Delta \phi - \nabla \cdot \mathbf{V}, b_j \rangle\|^2 \\ &= \sum_j \|\langle \Delta \phi, b_j \rangle - \langle \nabla \cdot \mathbf{V}, b_j \rangle\|^2, \end{aligned} \qquad (6.9)$$

which can be written in a matrix form, and the Laplace matrix L with $|T| \times |T|$ elements is defined so that $L\phi$ returns the dot product of the Laplacian with each base b_j. Each element of the sparse and symmetric matrix has the following expression

$$L_{jk} = \left\langle \frac{\partial^2 b_j}{\partial x^2}, b_k \right\rangle + \left\langle \frac{\partial^2 b_j}{\partial y^2}, b_k \right\rangle + \left\langle \frac{\partial^2 b_j}{\partial z^2}, b_k \right\rangle. \qquad (6.10)$$

Then, the Poisson equation reduces to a well-conditioned sparse linear system

$$L\phi = \mathbf{v}, \qquad (6.11)$$

where $\mathbf{v}$ is a $|T|$-dimensional vector whose element is

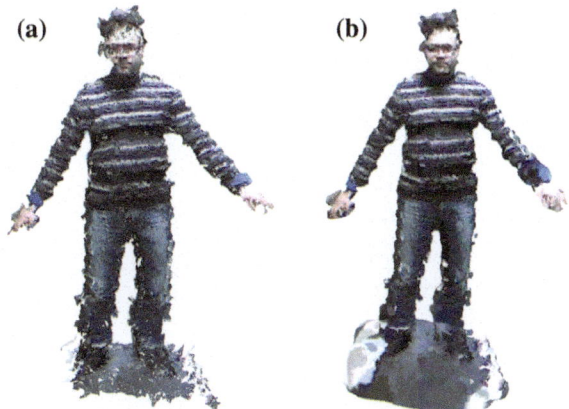

Fig. 6.5 a Delaunay triangulation. **b** Poisson surface reconstruction. Delaunay mesh is an initial result only by triangulating the human point cloud. It can be seen that the mesh contains a lot of holes and burrs. Poisson surface is then approximated from the Delaunay triangles as a way to refine the initial mesh. These holes and burrs are filled and smoothed, respectively, in the remeshing result

$$v_j = \langle \nabla \cdot \mathbf{V}, b_j \rangle. \tag{6.12}$$

The above linear system is solved using a conjugate gradient solver. After obtaining the indicator function ϕ, Marching Cubes [14] based on octree representations are adopted to extract the iso-surface and build a 3D human mesh. The solution can create a smooth surface that robustly approximate noisy points, as illustrated in Fig. 6.4b. The reconstruction comparison between the initial Delaunay triangulation and Poisson surface reconstruction is shown in Fig. 6.5. In the parameter settings, the maximum depth of octree is empirically set to be eight for achieving balance between reconstruction quality and run time.

Since Poisson surface reconstruction does not allow the color information attached to the point cloud, which is very important for recovering a realistic human, we regain the texture of the reconstructed mesh by searching the correspondence between points before reconstruction and vertices on the reconstructed surface. An efficient kd-tree algorithm is designed to realize this task. Finally, we obtain a relatively smooth textured mesh without holes, as illustrated in Fig. 6.5b. See Fig. 6.6 for more reconstruction results.

6.1.5 Experimental Results

We implemented the proposed dynamic personalized avatar algorithm from noisy RGBD data based on C++, OpenNI [17], and OpenCV [16]. OpenNI packages are first employed to obtain the raw depth and color maps from the provided dataset. By slightly modifying the code provided by OpenNI develop toolkit, we compute the

Fig. 6.6 The reconstruction examples of three users with different poses

RGB value of each pixel in the color map and the distance of each pixel in depth map to Kinect. Because there exist offsets between color values and depth values, we align the depth and color maps with the aid of a recent calibration method [11]. And then, five camera images are registered to be a large 3D scene in the form of point cloud in OpenCV. 3D human filters are introduced to obtain a relatively clean 3D human point cloud, and we reconstruct its 3D mesh via Delaunay triangulation and Poisson surface reconstruction. The averaged time for reconstruction of human is 0.47 seconds on a modern computer with i7 CPU with 16G memory, and the implementation can be seen as a near real-time solution to personalized avatar for user via multiple Kinects. It should be noted that in practical applications, the reconstruction of realistic 3D human mesh can be performed only once, for example, in the stage of system initialization.

Fig. 6.7 a Reconstructed boxing action. **b** Reconstructed waving action. The reconstructed realistic 3D human is placed in a virtual scene and follows user movements

The movement of skeleton can be mapped onto the preliminary 3D human in real time.

In order to further demonstrate the realistic effect of personalized avatar, we dynamically reconstruct a 3D human mesh for each frame in these videos and visualize the sequential results in a gaming development software, Unity [18]. We reconstructed a sequence of moving 3D human meshes with different postures to test our method, as shown in Fig. 6.7. These 3D human meshes are dynamically imported into a virtual scene built in Unity and compose a realistic and meaningful action which approximates the actual human movements in the scene of game or virtual reality. It will enhance the interactive experience of users in practical applications.

6.1.6 Conclusion

In this section, we discussed the novel proposal about personalized avatar for user via multiple Kinects. The core of the implementation process lies in how to reconstruct a realistic human from noisy RGB data. The process is composed of three key steps, that is, point cloud generation, 3D human filters, and human mesh reconstruction. This novel application could help a user to see himself in a virtual scene using low-cost RGB-D cameras. This will increase the interactive experience with the computer in a virtual world. In the future, we will concentrate on continuing to improve the quality of reconstructed human mesh from sparse RGB-D data in a noisy environment. Neighbor frames will be considered as complementary information and several reconstructed human in a non-rigid form will be registered to a more complete 3D mesh. We also try to realize its practical applications such as virtual fitting room for validating its performance further.

6.2 Evaluating User's Energy Consumption Using Kinect-Based Skeleton Tracking

In this section, we propose a refreshing application that automatically evaluates player's energy consumption in gaming scenarios by a model with tracked skeleton, which may help users to know their exercise effects and even diet or reduce their weights. We develop a program to compute the energy consumption in real time by analyzing data captured from Microsoft Kinect and also give a cue in the dynamic interaction. We model 3D human skeleton by joining different body parts with 15 nodes and decompose player action into rigid body motions of these parts. Amount of energy consumed in the action is calculated as the sum of powers required to overcome gravity of each part. Experimental results show that instantaneous and total energy consumption of different dancers can be stably calculated. The hardware system is based on low-price Kinect and easily accepted by users. The proposed application also provides a quantitative approach which help users to control their dining and exercise intensity.

6.2.1 Introduction

Home-oriented virtual reality technologies become increasingly important in real-time realistic interaction games. They bring players rich experience by placing players in virtual environments. As a new kind of devices based on infrared structured light, depth sensors with low price such as Microsoft Kinect [2] have attracted much attention among not only game users but also researchers and developers. It is possible to use depth sensors like Microsoft Kinect to capture human motion in an easy and robust way. This will help many interactive games to animate an avatar and promote user experience in games.

Some researchers have begun to use depth sensor data to construct 3D virtual applications. Tong et al. [7] present a novel scanning system for accurately capturing 3D full human body model by using multiple Kinects, which could be used to provide personalized avatars for everyday users. Bleiweiss et al. [5] blend player's actual movements tracked using a depth sensor with pre-defined animation sequences. They aim at visually enhancing the player's motion to display exaggerated and supernatural motions. Suma et al. [20] provide us a middleware to facilitate integration of full-body control with virtual reality applications and video games using OpenNI-compliant depth sensors. Alexiadis et al. [4] propose an interesting application and evaluate dance performances of students against a gold-standard performance and provide visual feedback to the student dancer in a 3D virtual environment.

Different from above applications, we propose a novel system that automatically evaluates player's energy consumption in gaming scenarios, which may help users to know their exercise effects and even diet or reduce their weights. We attempt to solve the problem of real-time computation of energy consumption while dancing and also give a numerical feedback in the interaction environment. We model 3D human skeleton by connecting different body parts using 15 joints and decompose player's action into rigid body motions of these parts. Amount of energy consumed in the action is calculated as the sum of powers required to overcome gravitational potential energy. The dancing action is seen as the process of burning calories or fat. We stably obtain quantitative energy consumption of each dancer and convert it to the value of burned fat. Players could interactively know the exercise effects during dance.

The section is organized as follows. Section 6.2.2 describes how to track the skeleton of Kinect captured data. We provide a energy consumption model by introducing power of rigid motion in Sect. 6.2.3. We demonstrate the capability of stably computing energy consumption of users by a group of experiments in Sect. 6.2.4 and allow players to interactively know their exercise effects.

6.2.2 Kinect Skeleton Tracking

We use the provided dancer dataset captured using a Microsoft Kinect in 3DLife/ Huawei Challenge of ACM Multimedia. We take 10 dancers' videos from the set of dance videos. Each video is composed of a sequence of depth images, which are encoded with video format. By means of the high-level skeleton tracking method [15], we remove the background and extract the skeleton from the captured images. This tracking method generates the positions of 17 joints, which include head, neck, torso, left and right collars, light and right shoulders, left and right elbows, left and right wrists, left and right hips, left and right knees, and left and right foot. Different from using extra user calibration [4], we infer information about the user's height and body characteristics. It helps us to accurately obtain the changed skeletons in each frame, as shown in Fig. 6.8. We also omit the joints of left and right foot because we consider their weights can be incorporated into shank.

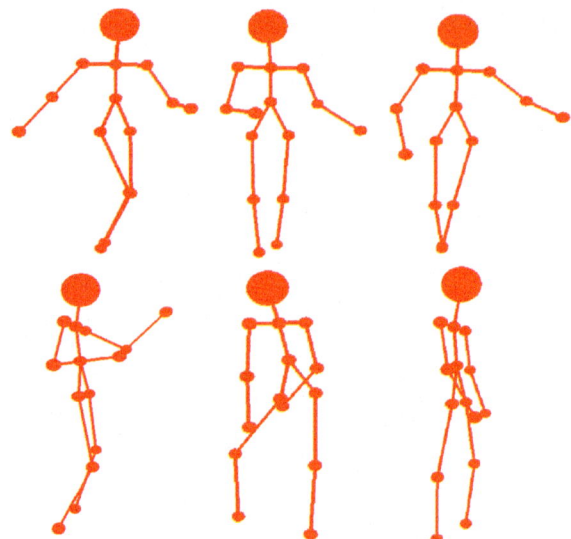

Fig. 6.8 We obtain a depth image of the environment from infrared light sensors, segment, and extract the articulated skeleton from the background. The human body is connected via 15 joints, and the mass is placed on 10 parts (head, torso, left and right forearms, left and right upper arms, left and right thighs, left and right shanks). Compared with original skeleton generated by [15], we omit two joints of feet because we consider their weights can be incorporated into shank. The dance actions captured include walk, hand gesture, jump, rock, and rotation. These actions are represented by a series of equivalent rigid body motions in our method. Therefore, each dance's action can be converted to the movements of body parts, resulting in energy requirements

Table 6.1 We record every part's percentage of the body weight according to the knowledge of human factors engineering. For example, the torso has 58 % body weight

Body part	Weight proportion (%)
Head	23.1
Forearm	1.8
Upper arm	3.5
Thigh	9.4
Shank	4.2
Torso	58

We define a typical human model with 175 cm height and 65 kg weight by a normal relation $W = H - 110$ between height H and weight W. According to human factors engineering, every body part has a percentage of the body weight as listed in the Table 6.1. For example, the torso is 58 weight. In our work, human body contains 10 main mass parts, head, torso, left and right forearms, left and right upper arms, left and right thighs, left and right shanks. They are connected as shown in Fig. 6.8. The weight of neck is incorporated into head, and the weight of left and right foot is incorporated into shank. In the next step, we will use this proportion to compute the power required to move each part.

6.2.3 Energy Consumption Model

Here, we focus on describing the energy consumption model adopted in the application. We use this model to provide dancers with their energy consumption values in each frame and added up each frame's energy consumption to obtain the total consumption. According to the human model previously generated, each dancing action is composed of the motions of all the body parts. Every body part is considered as a rigid part, and these rigid parts are connected by 15 nodes. Energy consumption of each motion is approximately equivalent to the required power to overcome gravitational potential energy of moving parts. The power is obtained by tracking the position change of each body part, and the powers of all the parts are summed up. Certainly, we view each body part as a rigid body with uniform mass distribution.

In order to acquire the kinetic energy of each moving part, its motion is firstly decomposed into two directional movements in vertical plane and horizontal plane. In the model, the vertical coordinate axis is defined as y axis, horizontal coordinate axis is defined as x axis, and z axis points outside the display. We have known that the body is composed of k mass parts $\{m_1, ..., m_i, ..., m_k\}$. Here, k is set to 10 because the human body contains 10 main mass parts mentioned in the previous section. Assume each part has two end joints l, r. The height change of this part between the frame $t+1$ and the frame t is defined as $\Delta h(t)$. The power E_v of moving part m_i in the vertical plane is given by

$$E_v(i) = m_i g \Delta h(t) = m_i g \frac{\Delta y_l(t) - \Delta y_r(t)}{2}. \tag{6.13}$$

where $\Delta y_l(t)$ and $\Delta y_r(t)$ are y coordinate variations of the end node l, r between time $t+1$ and t. Because gravity does not work during fall from the viewpoint of energy consumption, we only take into account the gravitational potential energy while rising. That is, the following condition should be satisfied

$$\Delta h(t) > 0. \tag{6.14}$$

We deduce the required power E_h during movement in the horizontal plane and represent it via the kinetic energy in the horizontal plane

$$E_h(i) = E_x(i) + E_z(i) = \frac{1}{2} m_i (v_x(i)^2 + v_z(i)^2). \tag{6.15}$$

where i means the ith mass part. $E_x(i)$ is the kinetic energy along x-axis, and $E_z(i)$ is the kinetic energy along z-axis. $v_x(i)$ is the moving speed of the mass part in the x direction, and $v_z(i)$ is the speed in the z direction. Here, the speed in x direction is obtained by differentiating its position as follows

$$v_x(i) = \frac{\Delta x_l(t) - \Delta x_r(t)}{\Delta t}. \tag{6.16}$$

where $\Delta x_l(t)$ and $\Delta x_r(t)$ are x coordinate variations of the end nodes l and r between time $t+1$ and t. Similar as the speed calculation in the x direction, the speed in z direction can be obtained by

$$v_z(i) = \frac{\Delta z_l(t) - \Delta z_r(t)}{\Delta t}. \qquad (6.17)$$

where $\Delta z_l(t)$ and $\Delta z_r(t)$ are z coordinate variations of the end nodes l and r between time $t+1$ and t.

Finally, the total power $E(i)$ of the ith part between two frames is computed as the summation of powers $E_v(i)$ and $E_h(i)$ in the two planes. We consider that intervals between two frames are uniform, and hence, we see movement of rigid part as uniform linear motion. The total energy consumption E of the body at time t is the energy summation of all the parts.

6.2.4 Experimental Results

We implemented the application based on C++, and the skeleton movements are visualized and confirmed in OpenGL. We programmed the computation process of energy consumption using C++ and visualize the interaction in a gaming development software, Unity [18].

We totally experimented ten dancers' depth images and extracted their skeletons. Every skeleton is used to drive a 3D human, and the joints connect corresponding body parts. The instantaneous and total energy consumption are calculated in real time. We obtained energy consumption in each frame and illustrate the relationship between energy consumption and time. The cumulative energy consumption curves of the first five dancers are drawn in the Fig. 6.9a. Another five dancers' curves are shown in the Fig. 6.9b. Curves with larger slope show that these dancers consume more energy at this frame because their dances need more motions of body parts. In order to interactively visualize the result, we also map the dancer' motions onto a photo-realistic avatar and place the avatar into Unity development environment [18]. And then, the system provides a vivid description of energy consumption, that is, we suggest a conversion of dancers' energy consumption to fat consumption per minute (FCPM). It is known that 1 g fat contains the energy of 37.67 kilojoule. Player's motion interactively gives the dynamic value of fat consumption per minute, for example, 0.427 g, as illustrated in Fig. 6.10.

6.2.5 Conclusion

In this section, we discussed our proposal about a real-time evaluation system of energy consumption while playing an interactive game or dancing. This novel

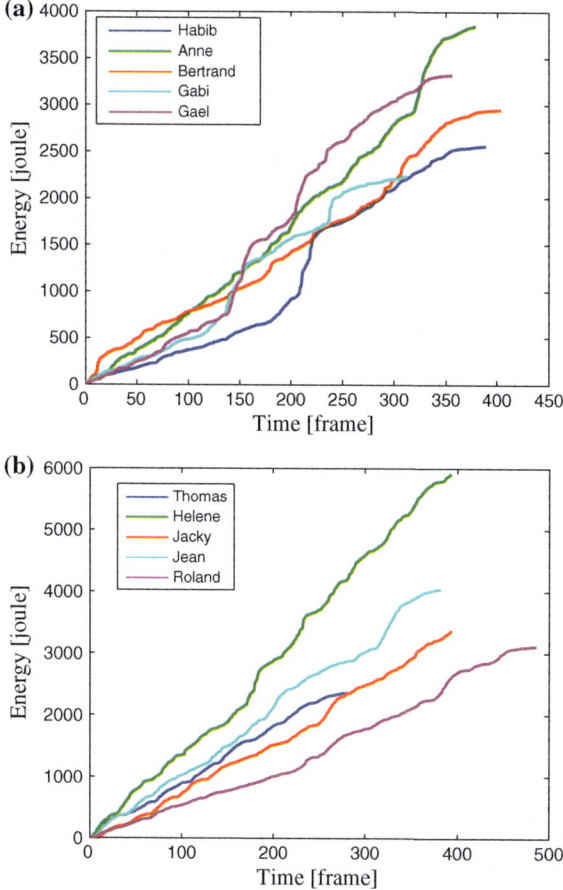

Fig. 6.9 We calculate the cumulative energy consumption curves for all 10 dancers. **a** The cumulative energy consumption curves of first five dancers during the whole dancing process. **b** The cumulative energy consumption curves of another five dancers. The unit of the *horizontal axis* is frame (30 frames per second), and the unit of *vertical axis* is joule. Because the ten dancers' dancing time is different, the horizontal axis of each curve has different length from others. Curves with larger slope show that these dancers consume more energy because their dances need more movements of human body

application could help players to understand their energy status in real time and reduce their weights and plan healthy diet. We tested ten dancers' motions and generated their energy consumption curves stably. The energy consumption is converted into the value of burned fat so that players could interactively know the exercise effects during dance. In the future, we consider introducing a 3D human model construction method by extending the process of 3D freeform model design proposed by Igarashi et al. [22]. The extracted skeleton from depth sensors is dilated into a 3D human model with accurate body proportion, which will be directly placed in the

Fig. 6.10 Visualization result in one frame. In each captured image, the power of movements per minute is converted to fat consumption per minute. And fat consumption per minute (FCPM) is displayed in the *left top corner*. The unit of FCPM is gram. Players could interactively know the exercise effect in burning fat in real time

interactive environment to promote user experience. High-quality 3D human model construction with multiple Kinects will be also considered in our future research because the error between real players and a mean human model used in our system is possible to be avoided.

6.3 Efficient Recognition of 3D Human Actions Captured from Kinect

With the development of computer, people want to use computer in a lively and intuitive manner. In order to improve user experience with computers, we require some methods to make computer recognize action automatically. In order to interact with computer by action command, we propose a new real-time system that automatically classifies the human action acquired by consumer-priced RGBD sensor. The main contributions include two effective features extracted from RGBD low-quality videos, average geometric feature and moving body part feature, which represent action in certain degree. Classification experiments show that using these two features, the accuracy of action recognition is acceptable. Users are capable of interacting with computers through human action under Kinect environment.

6.3.1 Introduction

With the development of 3D capturer such as the Microsoft Kinect, users hope to intuitively interact with computers, instead of traditional mouse and keyboard. Compared with the depth of the traditional camera and motion capture system, more game players and researchers use the Kinect because of its low price. It is possible to use depth sensors like the Kinect to capture human motion in an easy and robust way. This will help many interactive games to animate an avatar and promote user experiences in games.

Existing approaches to human action and gesture recognition can be coarsely grouped into two classes. The first uses 2D image sequences, e.g., Schudlt et al. [27] use bag-of-words representations of the videos that discard much of the spatial structure of the data, which have proved effective in the classification of simple human actions, e.g., walking, running, and boxing. The second approach uses 3D information provides many benefits over the pure image based methods. Using the data of industrial motion capture, Mller et al. [25] transform motions into time-varying geometric feature relationships to achieve low dimensionality and robustness in the matching process. Their approach is scalable and efficient for noise-free motion capture data. Because of high cost of industrial motion capture system, it seems impossible to be widely used. An alternative way is Kinect, which also provides relatively robust motion capture at a low cost. Using the motion capture of Kinect, Raptis et al. [26] propose a complete system which uses a novel angular skeleton representation, a cascaded correlation-based max-likelihood multivariate classifier, and a space–time contract–expand distance metric to process robust action recognition.

A lot of somatic games such as XBOX 360 Kinect sports change the way of game, but these somatic games always focus on motion track rather than motion recognition. Our aim is to expand substantially the interaction with computer, by using simple actions to control the computer. To achieve this objective, we propose a novel system that automatically identifies actions captured by Kinect, which may help users to interact with computer more intuitively and easily. We model 3D human skeleton [15] by connecting different body parts using 15 joints and extract the feature from it. Then, we train a k-nearest neighbors (k-NN) classifier which is used to recognize the action automatically.

Feature is a key to recognize action. **Geometric feature** [24] is used first to convert the spatial information to boolean values. By analyzing geometric feature, we discover two new features: average **geometric feature** and **moving body parts feature**, which have a good representative of action.

The remainder of this section is organized as follows. We describe the proposed features of RGBD data in Sect. 6.3.2. In Sect. 6.3.3, we describe how to use the feature to build a classifier. In Section 6.3.4, we use 83 motion clips in 10 classes to test our method.

6.3.2 Action Feature

The first step of our method is to extract the skeleton from the captured images. We first extract the skeleton from the captured images. Then, its geometric feature will be computed. Based on the geometric feature, we introduce average geometric feature and moving body part feature.

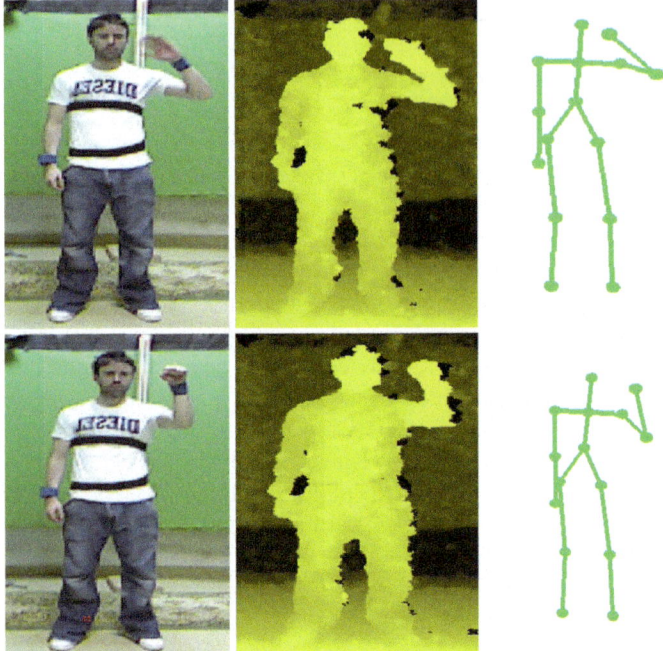

Fig. 6.11 We compute a depth image of the environment from infrared light sensors, segment, and extract the articulated skeleton from the background. The human body is connected via 15 joints. Each image from *left* to *right* represents RGB image, depth image, and skeleton. The *upper row* is a single frame of waving hand, and the *bottom row* is a frame of knocking the door

Kinect Skeleton Tracking. We follow Shotton's [15] method to extract the skeleton from the captured images. Through the depth sensor, we get depth image which is used to process skeleton tracking. We obtain the skeleton with 15 nodes, which include head, neck, torso, light and right shoulders, left and right elbows, left and right wrists, left and right hips, left and right knees, and left and right foot, as shown in Fig. 6.11.

Average Geometric Feature. In order to analyze the motion with fixed standard, we follow the idea of Mller et al. [24] to describe geometric relations between some nodes of a pose. For example, consider a fixed pose, which we test whether the right foot lies in front of (feature value is zero) or behind (feature value is one) the plane spanned by the center of the torso, the left hip joint, and the right hip joint. Another way to calculate geometric feature is measuring the distance of nodes. For example, the distance of both hands is below (feature value is one) or above a certain distance threshold. Threshold is set by hand or position of skeleton nodes. A motion clip with K frames yields a feature matrix G with the size of $K \times D$. $G_i = 0$ or 1, D is the dimension of feature. In our work, D is set to 13. See details in Table 6.2.

The geometric feature used above only contains the information of single frame. For example, the single-frame skeleton in Fig. 6.12, it may be punching, clapping, or

Table 6.2 The geometric feature used in our work

Body part	Threshold	Geometric feature
Arm part	[0° 150°]	Left arms bent
Arm part	[0° 150°]	Right arms bent
Arm part	0.150 m	Left hand approaching left hip
Arm part	0.150 m	Right hand approaching right hip
Arm part	0.200 m	Left hand approaching head
Arm part	0.200 m	Right hand approaching head
Arm part	head height	Left hand raised
Arm part	head height	Right hand raised
Arm part	0.150 m	Hand approaching
Mid part	[15° 180°]	Back bent
Leg part	Right knee height	Left foot raised
Leg part	Left knee height	Right foot raised
Leg part	0.525 m	Foot approaching each other in horizontal plane

We calculate 13-dimensional geometric feature of arm, middle, and leg body parts. The middle column is threshold value. The right column shows the meaning of geometric feature

Fig. 6.12 The *upper row* shows single frame of punching action; however, it may be a clapping action or one of other actions. The *lower row* represents single frame of punching and kicking action, and its left leg rises compared to punching action

other actions. It shows that the single frame may be classified incorrectly. Because continuous action can provide much more information, we want to find feature which can distinguish between actions better. The average value of geometric feature can summarize the change rule; therefore, it is a representative feature for action recognition. For example, the waving hand action's arm is always bending, so the average value of geometric feature correspondence to this arm is close to 1; in contrast, the same average feature of the knocking action is about 0.7 because the arm sometimes unbend in this action. We can infer that the average value of geometric feature is a simple but robust feature. After extracting the geometric feature of a motion clip, we calculate the average value AG of every dimension, the element value of AG ranges from zero to one. So a motion clip has an average geometric feature vector which size is D.

Moving Body Part Feature. Each class of action has specific moving parts of body that means each class of action has typical numbers which accounts the number of nonzero geometric features. Actions with different moving body part should not belong to the same class. For example, if legs in one motion clip keep static, while legs in another motion clip have obvious changes, these two motion clips should not belong to the same class, as shown in Fig. 6.12. Our geometric feature is calculated due to the moving degree of body parts, each class may have a special number of moving body parts. Based on this observation, we calculate the number of moving arm parts, central body part, leg parts of every motion clip according to geometric feature, respectively. Each motion clip has the moving body part feature M with the size of 3, as shown in Fig. 6.13. We can conclude that the number of moving body parts in most action classes is constant. A few action classes may have some fluctuation, e.g., in the jumping jacks, and the number of moving arm parts varies. This is caused by the all-body movement. And we can also discover that only in specific action classes, certain body parts have movements. Such as middle body parts, only punch and kick, and weight lift, have changes.

6.3.3 Action Recognition

In this section, we will first train a k-NN classifier by using the features proposed in the above section. Then, we use the trained classifier to realize action recognition. We adopt a k-NN classifier, and the classifier is trained from a set of hand-labeled motion clips. These motion clips contain complete action and incomplete action. The difference between complete action and incomplete action is the length of action. For example, the average number of punching frames is about 50. Hence, a motion clip of punching lasts for 40 frames and can be defined as complete action. However, if a clip has only 20 frames, we classify the clip into incomplete action. Both complete and incomplete action clips will be used for training. Then, the average geometric feature combines with moving body part feature, and accordingly we get a feature vector S with the size of 16. Each feature S of motion clip is regarded as the input

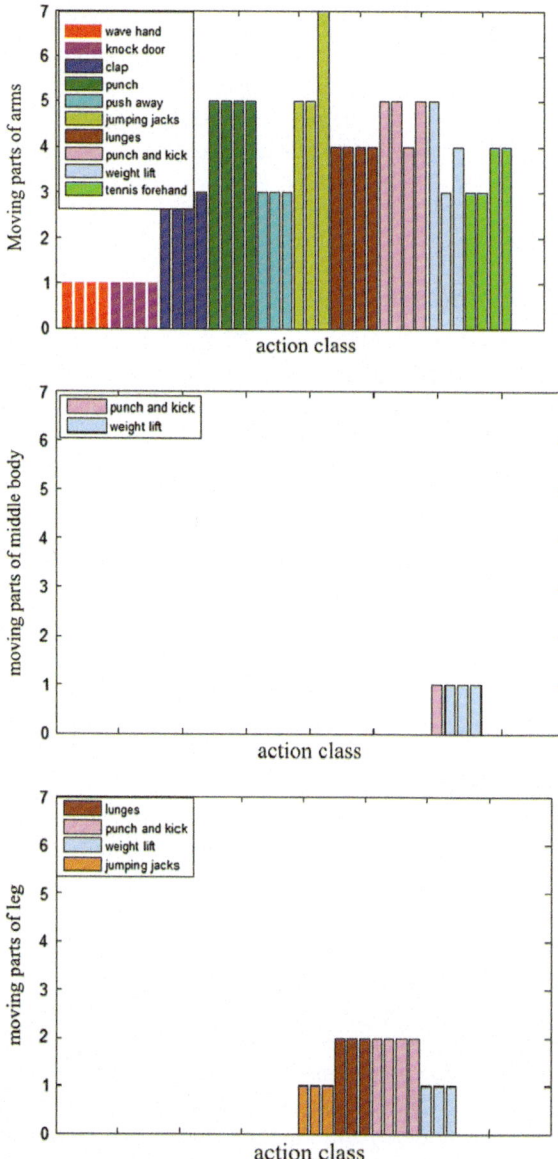

Fig. 6.13 The *upper table* shows the number of moving parts of arms. The *middle table* shows the number of moving parts of middle body. The *bottom* of table illustrates the number of moving parts of legs

of classifier. The classifier parameters are fixed via training and will be employed to recognize novel actions on line.

Once the classifier is trained, labeling motion clip is an automatic process. In order to get a label of motion clip, we extract the features as the same as the training process. Then through examining the labels on each of the closest samples, the label of testing motion clip can be determined. In order to examine our feature further, a SVM classifier is also trained to perform classification. k-NN classifier can be compared with SVM.

6.3.4 Experimental Results

We programmed the algorithm of action recognition using C++. We used the provided dataset captured using a Kinect by 3DLife/Huawei Grand Challenge [10]. Our classifier was trained on 85 motion clips which contain 10 classes. And the testing data are composed of 83 motion clips. Both training data and testing data contain different frames which represent the completeness of the action. The number of nearest neighbors is set to 4 in our work. The average time of extracting feature and recognition by using the motion clip with average 30 frames is shown in Table 6.3. The classification performance is computed in four cases: (1) motion clips with high completeness; (2) motion clips with low completeness; (3) using only the average geometric feature AG; (4) using both the average geometric feature AG and moving body part feature M. The results are summarized in Tables 6.4 and 6.5. We also used SVM classifier to test our two features. The test data contains both incomplete action and complete action. The result is shown in Table 6.6, and the classification accuracy of SVM is clearly lower than that of k-NN.

We can find that (1) by using moving body part feature, the classification accuracy increases by about 10 %. Moving body part feature is validated useful to discriminate the motion which average geometric feature is similar to another. In Fig. 6.12, without moving body part feature, the action of punching and kicking is always recognized as punching, because of the short length of kick action. The average value of leg geometric feature is also small. However, with feature of the body parts, we solved this problem when counting the number of moving parts of the body can discriminate two actions. (2) We compared classification accuracy between motion clips with low completeness and high completeness, the motion clip with high completeness achieved higher accuracy. The incomplete motion clip is similar to single-frame action, which contains ambiguous information resulting in incorrect classification. The result also accords with the rule that the longer action is more possible to be identified, which is similar as the viewpoint of human. (3) Recognition of jumping

Table 6.3 Average time of feature extraction and action recognition

Process	Average time
Feature extraction	0.076 s
Recognition	0.850 s

Table 6.4 The classification accuracy of incomplete motion clip

Action	AG + M (%)	AG (%)
Hand waving	60	40
Knocking door	75	75
Clapping	75	75
Punching	75	75
Push away	25	25
Jumping jacks	100	100
Lunges	100	100
Punching and kicking	66.7	0
Weight lifting	100	100
Tennis forehead	50	75
Average	72.57	64.86

The middle column is the classification accuracy using both average geometric feature AG and moving body part feature M, and the right is the accuracy using only average geometric feature

Table 6.5 The classification accuracy of complete motion clip

Action	AG + M (%)	AG (%)
Hand waving	80	80
Knocking door	25	25
Clapping	75	75
Punching	75	60
Push away	80	40
Jumping jacks	100	100
Lunges	100	100
Punching and kicking	100	50
weight lifting	100	80
Tennis forehead	75	50
Average	80.43	67.35

Table 6.6 The classification accuracy of action

	AG + M (%)	AG (%)
Average accuracy	59.01	38.89

jacks, lunges, and weight lifting obtains very high accuracy. The reason is that both average geometric feature and moving body part feature in these three actions are very different, which leads to higher discrimination. (4) Our method did not perform well in the action of knocking the door illustrated in Fig. 6.11. This action is commonly misclassified as waving hand because their geometric features are close. (5) The time of recognition is fast, and it is possible to implement the real-time applications.

6.3.5 Conclusion

In this section, we proposed a real-time human action recognition system used for Kinect applications. Two new features, average geometric feature and body part feature, were introduced to represent different actions. These features were classified with k-NN classifier to achieve high classification accuracy. However, our method does not perform well in ambiguous action classes. In the future, we plan to extract more robust and discriminative features to improve the accuracy, and structural classifier such as latent structural SVM will also be investigated to enhance classification performance.

References

1. Berger M, Levine JA, Nonato LG, Taubin G, Silva CT (2013) A benchmark for surface reconstruction. ACM Trans Graph 32(2):20
2. Microsoft Kinect (2010) http://www.xbox.com/kinect
3. Han J, Shao L, Xu D, Shotton J (2013) Enhanced computer vision with Microsoft Kinect sensor: a review. IEEE Trans Cybern 43(5)
4. Alexiadis D, Daras P, Kelly P, O'Connor NE, Boubekeur T, Moussa MB (2011) Evaluating a dancer's performance using Kinect-based skeleton tracking. In: Proceedings of ACM multimedia
5. Bleiweiss A, Eshar D, Kutliroff G, Lerner A, Oshrat Y, Yanai Y (2010) Enhanced interactive gaming by blending full-body tracking and gesture animation. In: Proceedings of ACM SIGGRAPH Asia sketches
6. Pedersoli F, Adami N, Benini S, Leonardi R (2012) XKin-: eXtendable hand pose and gesture recognition library for Kinect. In: Proceedings of ACM multimedia
7. Tong J, Zhou J, Liu L, Pan Z, Yan H (2012) Scanning 3D full human bodies using Kinects. IEEE Trans Vis Comput Graph 18(4):643–650
8. Ye G, Liu Y, Deng Y, Hasler N, Ji X, Dai Q, Theobalt C (2013) Free-viewpoint video of human actors using multiple handheld Kinects. IEEE Trans Cybern 43(5)
9. Barmpoutis A (2013) Tensor body: real-time reconstruction of the human body and avatar synthesis from RGB-D. IEEE Trans Cybern 43(5):1347–1356
10. ACM Multimedia 2013 Huawei/3DLife Grand Challenge. http://mmv.eecs.qmul.ac.uk/mmgc2013/
11. Daniel HC, Juho K, Janne H (2012) Joint depth and color camera calibration with distortion correction. IEEE Trans Pattern Anal Mach Intell 34(10):2058–2064
12. Cignoni P, Montani C, Scopigno R (1998) DeWall: a fast divide and conquer Delaunay triangulation algorithm in Ed. Comput Aided Des 30(5):333–341
13. Kazhdan M, Bolitho M, Hoppe H (2006) Poisson surface reconstruction. In: Proceedings of eurographics symposium on geometry processing
14. Lorensen W, Cline H (1987) Marching cubes: a high resolution 3D surface reconstruction algorithm. In: Proceedings of ACM SIGGRAPH
15. Shotton J, Fitzgibbon A, Cook M, Sharp T, Finocchio M, Moore R, Kipman A, Blake A (2011) Real-Time human pose recognition in parts from single depth images. In: Proceedings of IEEE conference on computer vision and pattern recognition
16. OpenCV. http://www.opencv.org
17. http://www.openni.org
18. Unity. http://www.unity3d.com

19. 3DLife/Huawei ACM MM grand challenge. http://perso.telecom-paristech.fr/essid/3dlife-gc-12/
20. Suma EA, Lange B, Rizzo A, Krum DM, Bolas M (2011) FAAST: the flexible action and articulated skeleton toolkit. In: Proceedings of IEEE virtual reality conference
21. OpenGL. http://www.opengl.org
22. Igarashi T, Matsuoka S, Tanaka H (2007) Teddy: a sketching interface for 3D freeform design. In: Proceedings of ACM SIGGRAPH courses
23. 3DLife/Huawei ACM MM Grand Challenge. http://mmv.eecs.qmul.ac.uk/mmgc2013/
24. Mller M, Rder T, Clausen M (2005) Efficient content-based retrieval of motion capture data. ACM Trans Graph 24(3):677–685
25. Mller M, Rder T (2006) Motion templates for automatic classification and retrieval of motion capture data. In: Proceedings of ACM SIGGRAPH/Eurographics symposium on computer animation, pp 137–146
26. Raptis M, Kirovski D, Hoppe H (2011) Real-time classification of dance gestures from skeleton animation. In: Proceedings of ACM SIGGRAPH/Eurographics symposium on computer animation, pp 147–156
27. Schuldt C, Laptev I, Caputo B (2004) Recognizing human actions: a local SVM approach. In: Proceedings of international conference on pattern recognition, pp 32–36

Chapter 7
Matching of 3D Objects Based on 3D Curves

Christian Feinen, Joanna Czajkowska, Marcin Grzegorzek and Longin Jan Latecki

Abstract In this chapter, we introduce a novel approach to 3D object retrieval capable to match query objects generated by a user with those captured by a depth device (RGB-D). Our processing pipeline consists of several steps. In the preprocessing step, we first detect edges in the depth image and merge them to 2D object curves which allows a back-projection to 3D space. Then, we estimate a local coordinate system for these 3D curves. In the next step, distinctive feature points are localised and shortest paths between these points are determined. Subsequently, the shortest paths are represented by robust descriptors invariant to rotation, scaling, and translation. Finally, all the information collected to describe the object is used for matching. The matching process is transformed to the problem of Maximum Weight Subgraph search. Excellent retrieval results achieved in a comprehensive setup of challenging experiments show the benefits of our method comparing to the state-of-the-art.

7.1 Introduction

3D objects captured by 2D imaging systems are usually classified by texture, 2D shape, or colour features. Often, the object has to be segmented from the background first, which is a highly challenging task in complex scenes. The features extracted in the next step have to posses discriminative power with regard to certain properties. Although many state-of-the-art methods for 3D object recognition using 2D visual

---

C. Feinen · J. Czajkowska · M. Grzegorzek (✉)
Pattern Recognition Group, University of Siegen, 57076 Siegen, Germany
e-mail: marcin.grzegorzek@uni-siegen.de
http://www.pr.informatik.uni-siegen.de

L.J. Latecki
Department of Computer and Information Sciences, Temple University,
Philadelphia, PA 19122, USA
e-mail: latecki@temple.edu

© Springer International Publishing Switzerland 2014
L. Shao et al. (eds.), *Computer Vision and Machine Learning with RGB-D Sensors*,
Advances in Computer Vision and Pattern Recognition,
DOI: 10.1007/978-3-319-08651-4_7

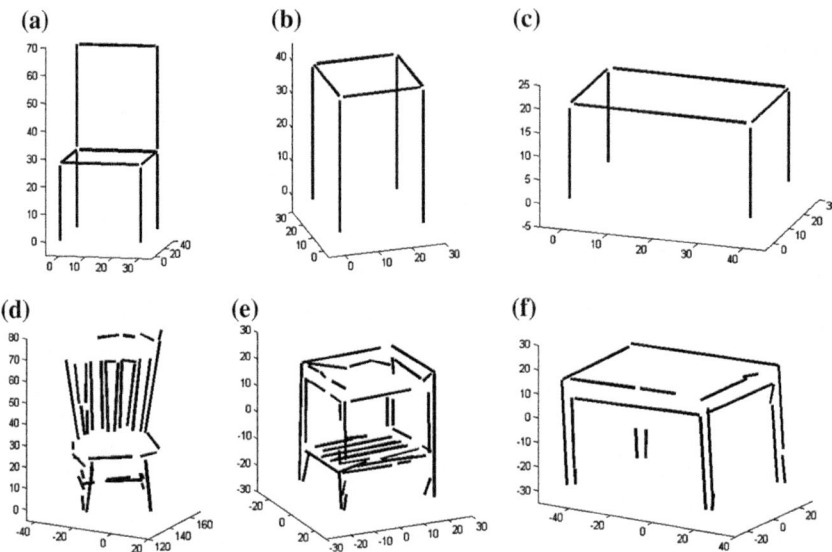

Fig. 7.1 Objects used during our evaluation. The columns are showing from *left* to *right*: the chair, the stand and the table. The *upper* row shows the query object, generated by a user, while the *lower* one illustrates the corresponding target. **a–c** Query. **d–f** Target

sensors report on excellent classification rates [12, 19, 27], they often suffer from changing light conditions, cluttered backgrounds, occlusions, etc. Moreover, due to new and more complex requirements most of the methods are not applicable to 3D. For instance, while the ordering of points is trivial in 2D, it is tough in 3D.

In our work, a single 2.5D image is taken by a depth device (Kinect) and used for representing an arbitrary scene including all of its 3D objects. We focus on using 3D curves derived by 2D contours as a feature distinguishing objects. While native contour description techniques have been comprehensively investigated in the 2D space, their extensions to 3D still need to be conceptualised. The advantages of the contour descriptors are, e.g., the low computational requirements as well as their invariance to colour and texture changes. Their disadvantage lies in their sensitivity with regard to changing viewpoints. To overcome this problem, 3D curves are used instead of the 2D contours themselves.

In this chapter we introduce a novel technique for 3D object retrieval based on 3D curve configurations. The method matches a highly abstracted 3D query object generated by a user (Fig. 7.1a–c) with those captured by a depth device (Fig. 7.1d–f). This results in great advantages. First, it works stable and leads to a good accuracy even under significant view point changes as proved in Sect. 7.9. Second, the user-generated query model can be easily replaced by any other model without generating a new and large training set in order to adapt the method to a new object class. However, since our approach highly relies on the feature points which are distinctive for each object class, the used fixed and single view approach limits us in the range of objects. Nevertheless, the method can be easily extended to multiple views in combination with techniques from the field of 3D reconstruction. This enables us to merge the 3D curves of all views and would result in one fully reconstructed 3D curve model. Moreover, it can be assumed that the data provides a high accuracy as well as more reliable lines compared to the current ones. Besides this, articulated objects can not be handled in its natural way, but, theoretically, one could provide a specified query object for a certain articulation as input for a successful matching.

The chapter is structured as follows. We start with a comprehensive state-of-the-art summary in Sect. 7.2. Then, in Sect. 7.3, a brief method overview shortly explaining all steps of the processing pipeline and their dependencies between each other is given. Sections 7.4–7.8 describe the proposed matching method in detail. A thorough quantitative evaluation of our methodology is documented in Sect. 7.9. Finally, our work is concluded in Sect. 7.10.

7.2 Related Work

Researchers early realised that accuracy and robustness of the object segmentation, detection, and recognition can be remarkably increased, if 2D data is enriched with 2.5D or 3D information. Supported by the recent development of range-measurement devices, many approaches that, similar to us, exploit depth for 3D object recognition purposes have been published.

> [Topics affected by that new technology include, e.g.,] preprocessing, object tracking and recognition, human activity analysis, hand gesture analysis, and 3D indoor mapping [13].

The work of Han et al. [13] provides a very detailed and complete overview about most recent projects initiated or enhanced by employing a Kinect device.

Contour-Based Methods: The most related work was published by Ma et al. [22]. In our approach, we employ the same 3D line segment data structure to represent 3D objects. However, instead of using a correspondence graph of all pairs of 3D line segments, we first detect feature points and subsequently use them for computing the Maximum Weight Subgraph. The work by Nguyen et al. [24] introduced an algorithm that combines 2D images and 3D point clouds. In our approach, 2D lines are first extracted from a 2D image and then back-projected to get a set of 3D points for each line. Based on these point sets, 3D lines are estimated. Another relevant method has been proposed by Stiene et al. [29]. The authors use range data for reliable silhouette extraction that represents an object for recognition. Payet and Todorovic [25] address view-invariant object detection and pose estimation from a single image by using contours as basis features. In this approach, a few view-dependent shape templates are jointly used for detecting object occurrences and estimating their 3D poses. However, their work requires training examples of arbitrary views of an object to learn a sparse object model.

Approaches Operating on Point Clouds: Drost et al. [8] propose a novel method that creates a global model description based on oriented point pair features to detect rigid 3D objects in 3D point clouds. By employing a fast voting scheme this model can be matched locally. In [26] the authors describe an algorithm to recognise object categories in point clouds. Here, 3D SURF local descriptors are computed on partial 3D shapes extracted from point clouds. Subsequently, these descriptors are used to generate a vocabulary of 3D visual words.

Kernel-Based Algorithms: Bo et al. [4] introduce a kernel-based object recognition approach. Here, a set of kernel features, e.g., size, shape and depth edges (extracted from the point cloud and the depth image) are proposed. In [3] the same authors developed hierarchical kernel descriptors that recursively apply kernel descriptors in order to form image-level features. Another kernel-based object recognition approach operating on range images was introduced by Li and Guskov [20]. They employ local shape descriptors computed on surface patches defined by detected salient features. The similarities between input 3D images are estimated by matching their descriptors with a pyramid kernel function.

Surface-Based Approaches: A plethora of approaches exploit surface properties for object recognition. Spin images, introduced by Johnson and Hebert [15], are one of the most popular features in this area. Further relevant examples are the work on surface patch representation proposed by Chen and Bhanu [7] or the scale-invariant local 3D shape descriptors [2, 23], where the local surface patches of the model are represented by tensors. Global and local surface features have been comprehensively investigated in the past (overview in [6]). In [30] histograms of oriented normal vectors (HONV) are presented as features for local geometric properties based on 2.5D data. Here the *azimuthal* and *zenith* angle is computed for each normal vector and voted into a 2D histogram. Through concatenation of this histogram, the HOVN feature is generated. This representation is strongly related to our work, refer Sect. 7.7.

RGB-D-Based Approaches: In Lai et al. [16] present a large RGB-D dataset where the instances of each object class are captured from multiple views (51 classes and 300 objects). Moreover, they propose a comprehensive evaluation based on state-of-the-art methods where they use the RGB as well as the 2.5D image for the purpose of feature extraction. Later, the same authors also provided a sparse distance learning approach and proposed a distance function allowing data adaption by assigning weights to each feature and each view [17]. In [28] an adaptive fusion scheme for RBG-D data is introduced, realised by a two-tier mixture of local experts architecture. Here two different gating functions weight the confidence of each detector and adjust the relative importance of each sensory cue with respect to the other one, respectively.

Unsupervised Dictionary-Based Approach: According to the authors in [5] all so-called "hand-designed representations" are insufficient for robust object recognition purposes. Thus, they propose an unsupervised feature learning approach using a hierarchical matching pursuit (HMP) . In more detail, dictionaries are first learnt for different data channels based on pixel patches (first layer). Afterwards, the second layer of the proposed HMP employs the first layer to represent observations as sparse, linear combination of these codewords.

Path Similarity Skeleton Graph Matching: A highly related 2D skeleton matching approach was proposed by Bai and Latecki [1]. They match skeletons based on dissimilarities between the shortest paths connecting their endpoints. For this, each shortest path is sampled by a fixed number of points. Each such point is represented by a radius of a maximum disc that was determined for it during the skeletonization process. In this way, every shortest path is represented by a vector of radii. Subsequently, matching costs for all pairs of skeleton endpoints are calculated. This is done by an approach called Optimal Subsequence Bijection (OSB). Afterwards, all output values of the OSB are rearranged and given as input to the Hungarian algorithm, where the matching problem is reduced to a classical assignment problem of a bipartite graph.

7.3 Method Overview

The whole processing pipeline of our approach consists of multiple steps as depicted in Fig. 7.2. The input to our approach is a depth image preprocessed by the methods proposed in [31] and [22]. In more detail, the ground plane is detected and the camera is moved to the scene's top pointing to the ground. In this view, the scene is clustered into objects based on the distance information stored in the 2.5D image. Afterwards, the Canny edge detector is run on the depth image itself, the edge fragments are combined to object contours and these, in turn, are back-projected into 3D by incorporating both, the depth and the cluster data. After this preprocessing step, we start to approximate a local coordinate system (LCS) for each scene object (Sect. 7.4). This is critical for all subsequent tasks and has to be as accurate as possible. For this, a PCA is performed on the pixel coordinates of each cluster. The principal components lead to a first initial alignment of the x and the y axis, where the z axis is assumed to be perpendicular to them. To stabilise the whole procedure, the orientations of x and y are refined by involving the z coordinate of all 3D curves. In the third step (Sect. 7.5), representative feature points are computed. This is done iteratively by combining already localised features with unknown object points. By taking this set as well as the LCS, the point combinations are analysed in terms of triangular and rectangular constraints. After retrieving all feature points, shortest paths between them are computed. Caused by the symmetry of our objects and by measurement inaccuracies, some of these paths are ambiguous. Hence, in Sect. 7.6,

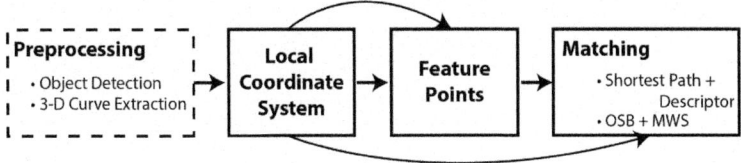

Fig. 7.2 Processing pipeline of the proposed approach

we propose a modification of the well-known Dijkstra algorithm to tackle this problem. In the fourth step a shortest path descriptor is generated based on relative angles (Sect. 7.7). Induced by that structure, our method becomes invariant to rotation, scaling and translation. Finally, in Sect. 7.8, we use all information collected before and perform the matching. For this, the process is transformed into a more generic and more challenging problem, namely the search of Maximum Weight Subgraphs (MWS)—known to be NP-hard. By incorporating mutual exclusions the dimensionality of the search space can be reduced. In addition to that, the algorithm is more flexible and more accurate. At the end, the actual matching process is performed with an abstracted and user generated query model (Fig. 7.6) matched to the ones captured by the depth device.

7.4 Object Local Coordinate System

The estimation of the object's LCS is necessary, because a LCS increases the information content of a 3D curve set drastically. However, this task is not trivial and, thus, two assumptions must be incorporated. First, the object is symmetric in terms that its geometry can be approximated with cuboids. Second, the object is assumed to be in its dedicated pose—one axis is fixed. Although the latter assumption reduces our problem to 2D space, we also incorporate the 3D part later. The LCS estimation directly follows the output of the approach described in [31]. This method results in clustered regions derived from the scene's top view (as shown in Fig. 7.3). Each cluster represents one object inside the scene. By taking all pixel coordinates covered by the cluster region, we determine the two principal components (k_1, k_2). These eigenvectors provide us with a rough approximation of the coordinate system. In order to achieve a more robust and accurate result, we additionally introduce a LCS refinement step. In contrast to the previous step, it operates on the set of 3D curves. In more detail, operating from the centre of gravity (COG), we sample the neighbourhood of k_1 by rotating it with following angles $\gamma \in \{\pi/4, \ldots, 0, \ldots, -\pi/4\}$. For each rotated version $k_1^{(\gamma)}$, the start and the endpoints of all 3D curves, indicated by Λ, are separated along this axis in two disjoint point sets $A^{(\gamma)}$ and $B^{(\gamma)}$:

Fig. 7.3 *Left* currently observed scene. *Centre* detected ground plane. *Right top view* on the scene achieved by camera translation pointing to the ground

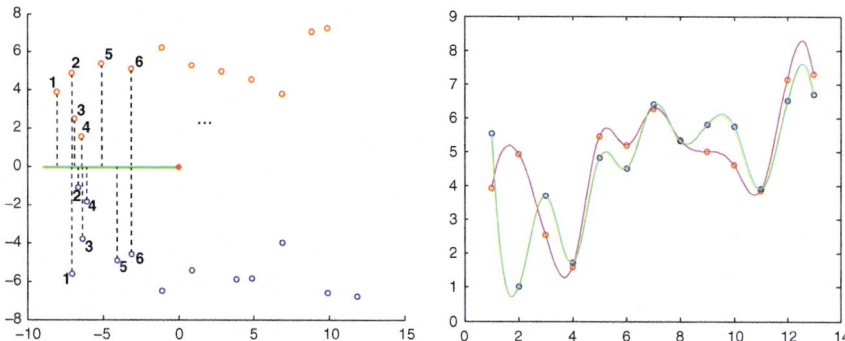

Fig. 7.4 LCS refinement. *Left* one possible rotation γ of k_1 and COG shown in *green* and *red*. By projecting the points on $k_1^{(\gamma)}$, a natural point order is retrieved. *Right* plot of point-to-axis distances in relation to the order obtained previously

$$\forall \gamma \quad A^{(\gamma)} \cap B^{(\gamma)} = \emptyset \quad \text{and} \quad A^{(\gamma)} \cup B^{(\gamma)} = \Lambda. \tag{7.1}$$

Afterwards, the points of $A^{(\gamma)}$ and $B^{(\gamma)}$ are projected on $k_1^{(\gamma)}$, respectively. These values lead to a natural order of all points in each subset according to their projection value (see Fig. 7.4). Moreover, the point-to-axis distances can be easily retrieved. Finally, a distance measurement approach [e.g., Dynamic Time Warping (DTW) or Earth Mover's Distance (EMD)] is used to calculate how symmetric $A^{(\gamma)}$ and $B^{(\gamma)}$ are to each other. The advantage of using the EMD is the consideration of the z coordinate of each 3D curve. This means, in addition to the ground distance matrix, we also pass the z coordinate of each point, interpreted as weight, to the method. The final $k_1^{(\gamma)}$ is the one that separates $A^{(\gamma)}$ and $B^{(\gamma)}$ with the lowest distance and provides the best orientation of the x axis for our LCS. The whole procedure completes by changing the positive orientation of the x axis pointing to object area with the higher point density (e.g. in case of a chair, to its back).

7.5 Object Feature Points

Our proposed matching procedure utilises the concept of shortest paths introduced in [1]. Consequently, object features are necessary, because they act like the skeleton end nodes described in the original method. The computation of features, without using any a priori knowledge, is a challenging task. In order to simplify it, we assume that the objects are symmetric and are approximable by cube-similar geometries. Our algorithm starts by localising a set of initial feature points, valid for all object classes. To determine this set, we select the farthest neighbour for each point in Λ leading to $\Theta = \{\hat{x}_1, \ldots, \hat{x}_n, \ldots, \hat{x}_N\}$:

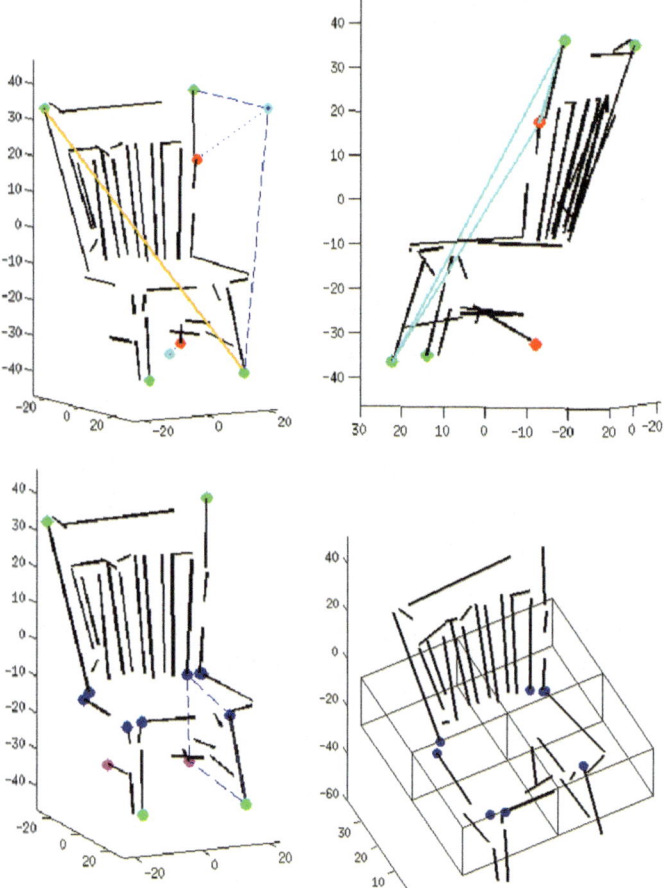

Fig. 7.5 Proposed feature detection pipeline. *Top left* initial feature points shown in *green*; virtual ones in cyan and their closest object correspondences in *red* + imaginary diagonal in orange. *Top right* False positive removal by enforcing (7.3) at each feature point location (*red*). *Bottom left* Valid feature points after false positive removal (*pink*) as well as corner point candidates (*blue*) after rectangular fitting. *Bottom right* 2D cluster scheme for mid-level features according to their position inside the LCS

$$\Theta = \{\hat{x} \,|\, \hat{x} \in \Lambda, \exists x \in \Lambda : \hat{x} \neq x \quad \wedge \quad \forall \check{x} \in \Lambda \setminus \{x, \hat{x}\} \to |x - \hat{x}| > |x - \check{x}|\}. \tag{7.2}$$

where $N \ll |\Lambda|$. This leads to the start and endpoint of the imaginary diagonals inside the object (Fig. 7.5, drawn in orange). To tackle the emergence of phantom features caused by outliers, we additionally enforce

7 Matching of 3D Objects Based on 3D Curves

$$\Theta' = \{\hat{x}_k \mid \exists\, \hat{x}_j, \hat{x}_h : f(\hat{x}_k, \hat{x}_j, \hat{x}_h) = 1 \wedge k \neq j \neq h\} \quad \text{where}$$

$$f(x_l, x_m, x_n) = \begin{cases} 1, & \text{if } \left|\frac{\pi}{2} - \arccos(\langle x_m - x_l, x_n - x_l\rangle)\right| < T \\ 0, & \text{else} \end{cases} \quad (7.3)$$

Afterwards, a non-maximum suppression (NMS) is conducted, which is explained later in this section. For now, it is assumed that $|\Theta'| \geq 2$ in order to start a dimension analysis. During this step, all feature point pairs, whose coordinates differ significantly in two dimensions while they remain very similar in one, are detected:

$$(p_1 - q_1)(p_2 - q_2)(p_3 - q_3) \approx 0 \wedge |(p_1 - q_1)(p_2 - q_2) + (p_1 - q_1)(p_3 - q_3) + (p_2 - q_2)(p_3 - q_3)| \gg 0. \quad (7.4)$$

where $\boldsymbol{p} = (p_1, p_2, p_3)^\mathrm{T}$ and $\boldsymbol{q} = (q_1, q_2, q_3)^\mathrm{T}$. It has to be noted that this procedure can only be realised thanks to the LCSE in Sect. 7.4. Then, new feature points get detected by swapping one of the coordinates analysed as dissimilar. This results in two virtual points $\boldsymbol{p}' = (q_1, p_2, p_3)^\mathrm{T}$ and $\boldsymbol{q}' = (p_1, q_2, q_3)^\mathrm{T}$ which are employed to find their closest object correspondences. To remove false positives appearing during that step (Fig. 7.5), all points have to fulfil again our constraint defined in (7.3). The valid ones ($\Theta'' = \{x_k \mid \exists\, x_j, x_h \in \Theta' : f(x_k, x_j, x_h) = 1 \wedge k \neq j \neq h\}$) are added to the feature set: $\Theta = \Theta' \cup \Theta''$. This procedure is repeated until no further candidates have been found and completes with a further NMS. The results as well as the virtual points are shown in Fig. 7.5.

By introducing a further extension to our method, namely a rectangular fitting technique, we now try to detect the seat corner points, being important, e.g., in case of a chair. The fitting procedure expects four input arguments which encompass two features $\hat{x}_m, \hat{x}_n \in \Theta$ as well as two object points $x_k, x_l \in \Lambda$ ($m \neq n \neq k \neq l$). The points x_k, x_l are stored in Θ, if this combination forms a rectangular structure. The outcome is shown in Fig. 7.5. This leads to an over-representation of each corner and is handled by the proposed two step NMS clustering approach. First, the features have to be clustered along the z axis. Second, each of the sets determined in the first step is clustered in 2D according to the quadrants of the LCS. The z clustering is realised by determining the maximum and minimum z axis value ($z^\mathrm{max}, z^\mathrm{min}$) of all feature points, which is sufficient for stands and tables. However, in case of chairs a third level is necessary: $z^\mathrm{mid} = (z^\mathrm{max} - z^\mathrm{min})/2$. Section 7.8 describes an automatic way to estimate the best number of z levels. Then, each feature $\hat{x}$ must be assigned to one z level:

$$g(\boldsymbol{q}) = \begin{cases} z^\mathrm{max}, & \text{if } |p_3 - z^\mathrm{max}| < |p_3 - z^\mathrm{mid}| \\ z^\mathrm{mid}, & \text{if } |p_3 - z^\mathrm{mid}| < |p_3 - z^\mathrm{max}| \wedge |p_3 - z^\mathrm{mid}| < |p_3 - z^\mathrm{min}| \\ z^\mathrm{min}, & \text{if } |p_3 - z^\mathrm{min}| < |p_3 - z^\mathrm{mid}| \end{cases} \quad (7.5)$$

where $\boldsymbol{q} = (q_1, q_2, q_3)^\mathrm{T}$. The resulting z clusters are processed subsequently in the 2D space, where each cluster point can easily be assigned to its corresponding quadrant of the LCS (Fig. 7.5):

$$h(q') = \begin{cases} 1, & \text{if } 0 \leq \Psi(q'_2, q'_1) < \frac{\pi}{2} \\ 2, & \text{if } \frac{\pi}{2} \leq \Psi(q'_2, q'_1) < \pi \\ 3, & \text{if } 0 > \Psi(q'_2, q'_1) > -\frac{\pi}{2} \\ 4, & \text{if } -\frac{\pi}{2} \geq \Psi(q'_2, q'_1) \geq -\pi \end{cases}. \quad (7.6)$$

where $\Psi(y, x) = 2\arctan(y/(\sqrt{x^2 + y^2} + x))$, $\boldsymbol{q} = (q_1, q_2, q_3)^\mathrm{T}$ and $\boldsymbol{q}' = (q'_1, q'_2)^\mathrm{T}$. Finally, we check whether one of the clusters already accommodate a feature point. If it is the case, all cluster points are skipped. If not, the point with the highest distance to the centre of gravity is selected.

In order to perform the shortest path analysis, feature connections need to be established. Therefore, we search for 3D curves, which can be interpreted as possible links between two points. Thus, all 3D curves have to be taken into account for each feature point pair, with the aim to find at least one segment satisfying the following constraints. Firstly, the length of the curve has to be greater than the average of all line lengths. Secondly, the ratio of lengths between the 3D curve and the virtual link has to be greater than $T^{(R)}$. Thirdly, the distance of the curve's orientation to the one of the virtual segment has to be below $T^{(W)}$. Fourthly, the closest distance from the currently observed feature point to either start or endpoint of the curve (used for verifying the virtual link), has to be below $T^{(C)}$. If all these constraints are fulfilled, the observed feature pair is marked as connected. Even if the result is suffering from a small amount of wrong connections, it does not decrease the robustness of our methodology due to our modified shortest path algorithm.

7.6 Modified Dijkstra Algorithm

As shown in Sect. 7.9, the proposed feature localisation method leads to good results. However, even if we assume that both objects belong to the same class, it can happen that paths are not similar or ambiguous, although all features are found and connections are established correctly. For example, in case of the user-generated chair model, there are at least two paths from the lower left front leg to the upper right back with identical lengths. If there is no appropriate criterion, the algorithm has to choose non-deterministically one of these paths. Other kinds of path irritations are caused by inaccuracies occurring during the depth acquisition, the line approximation or the curve back-projection. Consequently, there is a high risk to retrieve another result as the actual shortest path. Thus, the dissimilarity would increase drastically and the whole matching algorithm would fail. To tackle this problem, we propose two additional mechanisms to improve the result of the Dijkstra algorithm. Firstly, all shortest paths of the query object are monitored. This is done by a simple description in terms of left/right, up/down and front/back derived from object's LCS with the objective to depict the paths taken during the computation. These path descriptors are given then as input to the shortest path computation of the target object. However, if connections are missing, it is not possible to follow the instructions of the path descriptor anymore. For these situations, we formulated a second rule: The algorithm is allowed to establish one missing feature connection based on the information given by the query path descriptor. If this new connection does not support the further path computation, the algorithm terminates.

7.7 Shortest Path Representation

The shortest path representation is a crucial factor regarding the actual matching process (Sect. 7.8). It constitutes the only way to compute the cost values that are required to match feature pairs. For this, a feature vector is introduced consisting of K' tuples $r_m = ((\alpha, \beta)_{m,1}, \ldots, (\alpha, \beta)_{m,K'})^{\mathrm{T}}$, where α and β denote angles and m is the corresponding path. By employing these two angles, we are able to uniquely describe a 3D point. Therefore, we firstly compute the angle α between the point vector and z-axis of our LCS. Secondly, the point is projected onto the x, y-plane, where we calculate β as shown in Fig. 7.6. In order to describe the whole path m based on this angle constellation, it is sampled by K' equidistantly distributed points (see Fig. 7.6). Afterwards, each sample point is linked with the feature point from which the path is emanating with the result of K' sample vectors, which get finally described by α and β. Attributable to the use of relative angles based on the object's LCS, our path descriptor is invariant to rotation, translation and scaling (RTS). The actual dissimilarity between the paths is calculated based on their representation vectors. Therefore, the vector r_m is separated into two sub-vectors $r_m^{(\alpha)}$ and $r_m^{(\beta)}$. The sub-vectors, in turn, are given as input to a distance measurement approach, e.g., DTW or EMD.

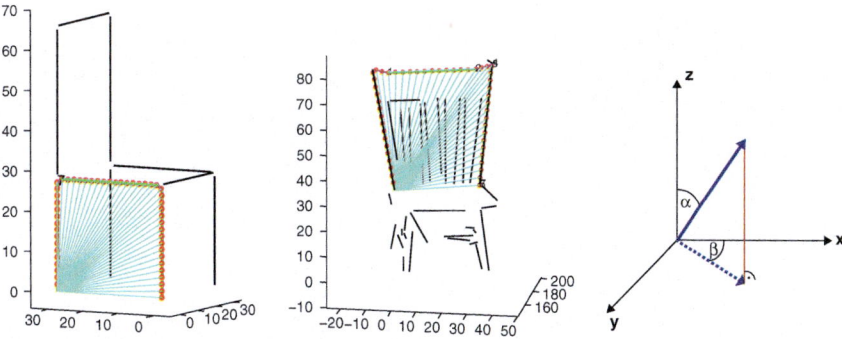

Fig. 7.6 Demonstration of our path representation. The *red circles* indicate the position of the sample points, the lines drawn in *cyan* are the sample vectors ($|g_i|$) between the currently observed feature and each sample point on the path used for the descriptor

7.8 Feature Point Matching

This section describes our 3D object matching procedure, which delivers the required similarity values for retrieval. These values, in turn, are based on cost values that have been needed for the matching of feature point pairs. The proposed matching principle works in analogy to the Path Similarity Skeleton Graph Matching algorithm proposed in [1], but we adapted it to depth sensory data and a completely different object representation.

Our matching strategy also involves the OSB procedure proposed by Latecki et al. [18]. OSB can be used for elastic matching of sequences of different lengths. It is similar to the DTW and the Longest Common Subsequence (LCSS) algorithms, but outperformed these methods during a comprehensive evaluation. Its key property is its capability to exclude outliers from the matching. Moreover, it is suitable for partial matching and it preserves the order of points during traversing the graph.

Ordering Feature Points: Attributed to the use of the OSB, our method requires a deterministic and reproducible scheme regarding the order of feature points; a problem that can easily be solved in 2D, but not in 3D. Simple solutions like distance-to-ground or distance-to-camera have no meaning in our context. At least the latter could be adapted by aligning the objects based on their LCS. However, in order to guarantee a deterministic order, the following scheme is proposed and also employed in Sect. 7.4 to determine the best number of z levels. First, the z coordinates p_z of all features are extracted $\boldsymbol{p}_{i=1,\ldots,|\Theta|} = (p_{i,x}, p_{i,y}, p_{i,z})^\mathrm{T}$ and arranged in descending order inside a vector $\boldsymbol{s}$. By subtracting neighbouring elements in $\boldsymbol{s}$, we retrieve a new vector $\boldsymbol{s}' = (s_1 - s_2, s_2 - s_3, \ldots, s_{|\Theta|-1} - s_{|\Theta|})^\mathrm{T}$, where the difference values are analysed in terms of peak occurrences as shown in Fig. 7.7 (Please note, that objects

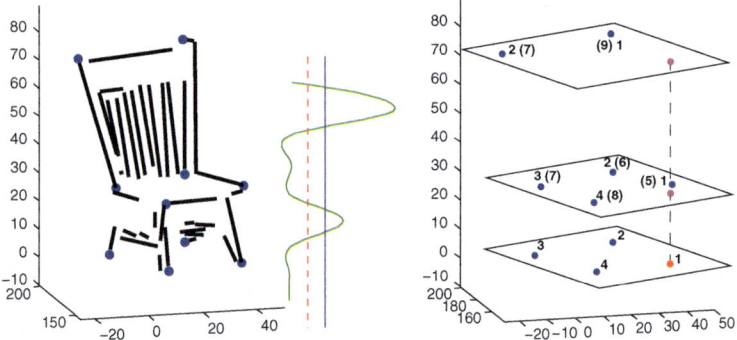

Fig. 7.7 *Left* chair object and its feature points (*blue*). The plot next to it visualises the values stored in $\boldsymbol{s}'$; peaks can be detected by using the average (*red dashed line*) or the standard derivation (blue line) of $\boldsymbol{s}'$. *Right* feature points (*blue*) clustered according to the peaks in $\boldsymbol{s}'$. The points in each cluster are ordered counter-clockwise in relation to the currently processed point (*red*), that is projected (*pink*) into the remaining clusters

are assumed to be in their dedicated pose). For each peak a z value is computed based on the two elements in s leading to this peak. Afterwards, these z values are used to cluster the features along the z-axis (Sect. 7.4). Finally, the points inside each cluster are ordered counter-clockwise in 2D. The technique completes with recombining all clusters. Therefore, the currently processed feature point, accommodated in one of the z clusters, is projected in the 2D space of the remaining ones, respectively (Fig. 7.7). The closest point to this projection identifies the start for the counting operation.

Maximum Weight Subgraphs (MWS): In order to compute the final feature matching and the overall similarity, we use the algorithm proposed in [21] that computes MWS considering mutual exclusion (mutex) constraints on weighted graphs. MWS can be expressed as an integer quadratic problem:

$$\max g(x) = x^T A x \quad \text{subject to} \quad x \in P, \quad x \in \{0,1\}^n. \quad (7.7)$$

where A is a symmetric $n \times n$ affinity matrix with $\forall i, j = 1\ldots, n : A_{i,j} \geq 0$, and P consists of constraints. Since the authors focus on quadratic equality constraints, a slightly more general form of (7.7) has to be introduced, where $M \in \{0,1\}^{n \times n}$ represents a symmetric mutex matrix:

$$\max g(x) = x^T A x \quad \text{subject to} \quad x^T M x = 0, \quad x \in \{0,1\}^n. \quad (7.8)$$

Using (7.8) a subset of vertices of graph G is selected, such that g is maximised and the mutex constraints are satisfied. Mutex constraints are an important utility regarding the degree of freedom of modelling. Moreover, they mark incompatible vertices and thus, they are reducing the search space. However, the integer quadratic program shown in (7.8) is NP-hard. To handle this problem, the authors relax the integer constraints to continuous ones and also relax the mutex constraints by moving them to the target function:

$$\max f(x) = x^T W x = x^T A x - x^T M x \quad \text{subject to} \quad x \in \{0,1\}^n. \quad (7.9)$$

where $W = A - M$. That guarantees us that all mutex constraints are satisfied for a discrete solution.

In the following, we describe how to determine the affinity matrix, where the size of A corresponds to the number of feature points that have been detected. For the population of the diagonal entries of A, we use the output values obtained by the OSB. Since A expects similarity data, the OSB cost values have to be converted. For this, a Gaussian function is used with $\mu = 0.2$ and $\sigma = 10$. The weights of the edges are encoded as off-diagonal elements in A. Therefore, the Euclidean distance $d(i, j)$ is used to generate a pairwise distance consistency:

$$A(u, v) = \exp\left(\frac{(d(i, j) - d(i', j'))^2}{2\sigma^2}\right). \tag{7.10}$$

where $u = (i, i')$ and $v = (j, j')$ are the two assignments.

Qualitative Spatial Mutual Exclusion: As stated above, the mutex matrix is employed to model relations which are preserved during the feature matching. In our case, we enforce a one-to-one matching for the proposed 3D object retrieval setup. Consequently, we obtain a logical defined matrix. In order to generate the mutex configuration, we collaborate with geometrical relations like up/down, front/back and left/right based on the object's LCS. Thus, we always retrieve the same relations for all the objects unconstrained by rotation, translation or scaling. If an assignment pair does not fulfil these constrains, it has to be skipped in the MWS. However, a threshold is introduced that removes all points whose distance is too close to each other. This requirement prevents the inclusion of incorrect information caused by measurement uncertainties.

7.9 Experiments

To be comparable to other methods, we evaluated our methodology on the same chair database as used in [22] consisting of 213 objects. Regarding the set of *stands* with 40 instances, we decided to extend it by further 67 objects. Additionally, we introduced a third dataset consisting of tables that encompasses 70 objects. All objects have been recorded with a RGB-D device (Kinect) from different viewpoints within complex real-world scenes. Hence, some parts of the objects are occluded, missing or distorted by outliers. Example images can be seen in Fig. 7.8. Our ground truth data was generated manually and each entry corresponds to one scene object that is described in terms of "chair", "stand", "table" and "undefined". The similarity values obtained with our method used for object retrieval and precision-recall graphs were generated for quantitative evaluation. Furthermore, we also assessed the average precision (AP) as introduced in [9]. All thresholds used in our experiments are based on the mean and on the standard deviation derived by incorporating all 3D curves.

Fig. 7.8 Example images used for evaluation

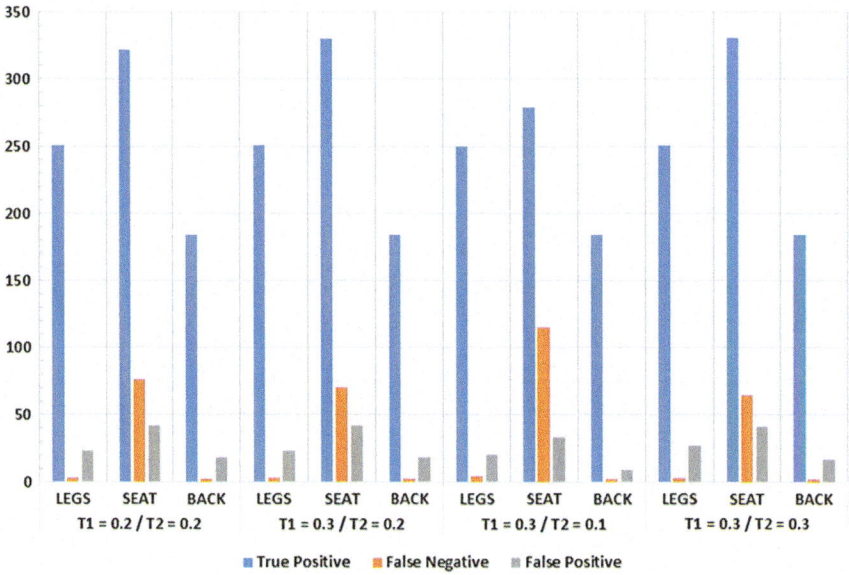

Fig. 7.9 Overview about four different threshold combinations (*horizontally plotted*) regarding their power in terms of detected features (*vertically plotted*). All of them perform as expected and lead to good results, expect the configuration T1 = 0.3 and T2 = 0.1

During our experiments we used the DTW as well as the Earth Mover's Distance to calculate the distances between the paths (Sect. 7.7) and to estimate the object LCS (Sect. 7.4).

Point Detection: To evaluate the robustness and accuracy of our feature detection method, a feature ground truth has been created for the most challenging object type in

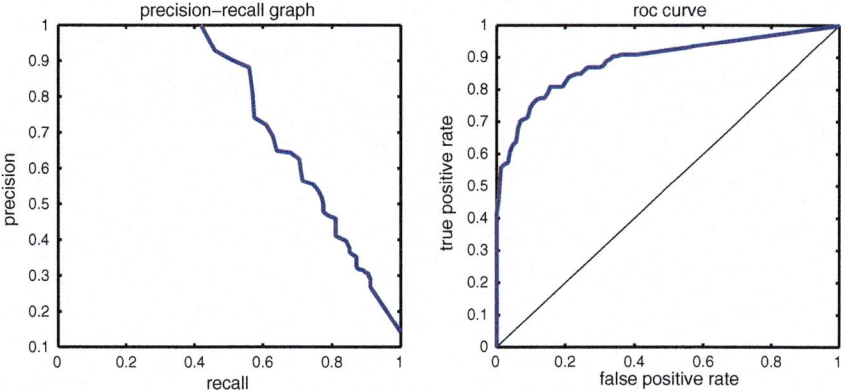

Fig. 7.10 Recall-precision graph (*left*) and ROC Curve (*right*) for the chair database used in [22]

Table 7.1 The table shows the average precision of our method compared to other state-of-the-art approaches

Method	Average precision
Our method	0.760
Ma et al. [22]	0.714
Janoch et al. [14]	0.438
Felzenszwalb et al. [10]	0.419
Ferrari et al. [11]	0.351

The most interesting information is its comparison to Ma et al. since their approach is the most related one to ours

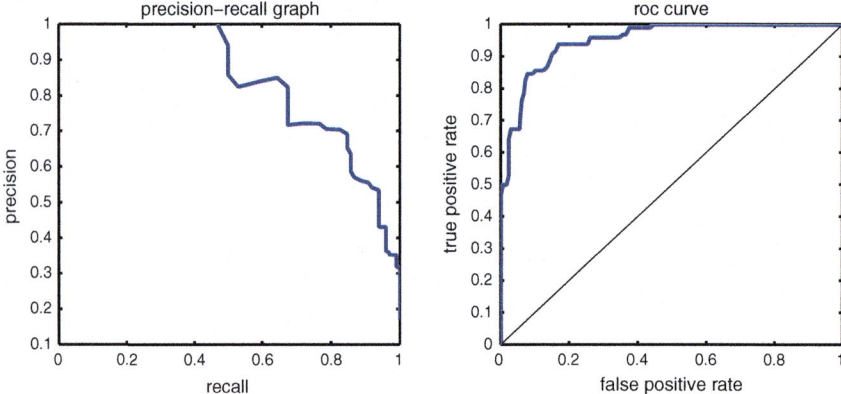

Fig. 7.11 Recall-precision graph (*left*) and ROC Curve (*right*) for the stand database, AP $= 0.8484$

our dataset, namely the chair. As presented in Fig. 7.9, we obtained excellent results, especially, if one considers the quality of our data. The threshold T1 is responsible for the triangular and T2 for the rectangular fitting. All configurations led to good results, except $T1 = 0.3$ and $T2 = 0.1$, where the rectangular fitting threshold is too restrictive.

Chair Database: First, we evaluated our approach on the chair database used in [22]. This database is a real challenge for our method, since many chairs are of poor quality and accommodate heavy outliers. Moreover, the dataset includes objects which principally cannot be recognised by our method, e.g., office chairs. However, even in presence of these negative factors, we have been able to obtain very good results as shown in Fig. 7.10. Moreover, the proposed method outperforms all of its competitors. Table 7.1 shows the AP of our approach compared to several state-of-the-art methods.

Stand Database: Fig. 7.11 shows the results of our stand database evaluation. Even in this case, we obtained excellent results, although we expected more irritations caused by our path descriptor. Nevertheless, despite the fact that we extended the database

7 Matching of 3D Objects Based on 3D Curves

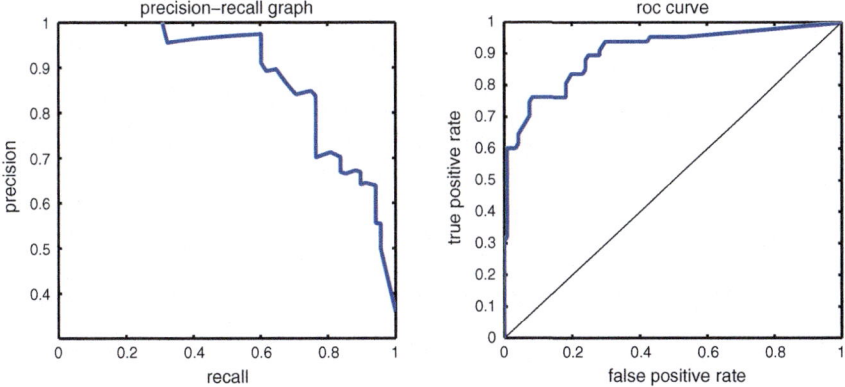

Fig. 7.12 Recall-Precision Graph (*left*) and ROC Curve (*right*) for the table database, AP = 0.8840

with new objects, it only includes half of the amount of true positives compared to the previous one.

Table Database: This evaluation was operating on our own database. It is the smallest database in our evaluation. However, it has been chosen deliberately, since this object class also provides a high risk of being ambiguous to the other ones. This makes it even more attractable that we retrieve very promising results as shown in Fig. 7.12. It seems, that the different object proportions can be represented adequately by our path descriptor.

7.10 Conclusion

The main scientific contribution of the approach presented in this chapter is the method for robust and generic 3D object recognition based on 3D curves. To underline the generic aspect, a user-generated and, hence, strongly abstracted model is introduced as a query object. Moreover, since this model is processed equally compared to the target one, the query can be easily replaced by other objects. This flexibility constitutes a great advantage in all areas where quick reaction is required. Furthermore, we propose an intelligent method to localise feature points by incorporating a local coordinate system. Finally, we demonstrate how these steps are combined to recognise 3D objects. The chapter concludes with a quantitative evaluation of our system based on a highly challenging database consisting of chairs, stands and tables captured in natural environments. Summarised, we achieved excellent results. Moreover, we even outperformed popular state-of-the-art methods. However, we are aware of the ambiguity potential of our RTS- invariant approach that could lead to irritations in cases where a stand or tables could also be interpreted as a top occluded chair.

To decrease this risk, we will investigate the possibility to encode also the proportions of objects. Therefore, e.g., the Earth Mover's Distance could be easily reused. Besides of this, it turned out that the followed fixed-view approach disables the selection of object classes. Thus, we will investigate new capabilities, i.e. 3D reconstruction, for a wider object handling. Without any major changes, our method is able to perform on 3D curve sets that have been generated by merging different views. Additionally, the surface curvature will be also considered in the future to increase substantially the power of discrimination.

Acknowledgments We would like to thank the German Research Foundation for financing the research work of Christian Feinen and Joanna Czajkowska within the Research Training Group 1564 "Imaging New Modalities": http://www.grk1564.uni-siegen.de/en.

References

1. Bai X, Latecki LJ (2008) Path similarity skeleton graph matching. IEEE PAMI 30(7):1282–1292
2. Bariya P, Nishino K (2010) Scale-hierarchical 3D object recognition in cluttered scenes. In: CVPR, p 1657–1664
3. Bo L, Lai K, Ren X, Fox D (2011) Object recognition with hierarchical Kernel descriptors. In: CVPR, p 1729–1736
4. Bo L, Ren X., Fox D (2011) Depth kernel descriptors for object recognition. In: 2011 IEEE international conference on robotics and automation (ICRA), IEEE, pp 821–826
5. Bo L, Ren X, Fox D (2012) Unsupervised feature learning for RGB-D based object recognition. In: International symposium on experimental robotics (ISER), Springer, pp 387–402
6. Campbell RJ, Flynn PJ (2001) A survey of free-form object representation and recognition techniques. Comput Vis Image Underst 81(2):166–210
7. Chen H, Bhanu B (2007) 3D free-form object recognition in range images using local surface patches. Pattern Recogn Lett 28(10):1252–1262
8. Drost B, Ulrich M, Navab N, Ilic S (2010) Model globally, match locally: efficient and robust 3D object recognition. In: CVPR, p 998–1005
9. Everingham M, Gool L, Williams CK, Winn J, Zisserman A (2010) The pascal visual object classes (VOC) challenge. Int J Comput Vis 88(2):303–338
10. Felzenszwalb P, Girshick R, McAllester D, Ramanan D (2010) Object detection with discriminatively trained part-based models. IEEE Trans Pattern Anal Machine Intell 32(9):1627–1645
11. Ferrari V, Jurie F, Schmid C (2010) From images to shape models for object detection. Int J Computer Vis 87(3):284–303
12. Grzegorzek M, Sav S, Izquierdo E, O'Connor NE (2010) Local wavelet features for statistical object classification and localisation. IEEE Multimedia 17(1):56–66
13. Han J, Shao L, Xu D, Shotton J (2013) Enhanced computer vision with microsoft kinect sensor: a review. Cybern IEEE Trans 43(5):1318–1334
14. Janoch A, Karayev S, Jia Y, Barron J, Fritz M, Saenko K, Darrell T (2011) A categorylevel 3-d object dataset: putting the kinect to work. In: Computer vision workshops (ICCVworkshops), 2011 IEEE International Conference on, pp 1168–1174
15. Johnson AE, Hebert MH (1999) Using spin images for efficient object recognition in cluttered 3D scenes. PAMI 21(5):433–449
16. Lai K, Bo L, Ren X, Fox D (2011) A large-scale hierarchical multi-view RGB-D object dataset. In: 2011 IEEE international conference on robotics and automation (ICRA), IEEE, pp 1817–1824

17. Lai K, Bo L, Ren X, Fox D (2011) Sparse distance learning for object recognition combining RGB and depth information. In: 2011 IEEE international conference on robotics and automation (ICRA), pp 4007–4013
18. Latecki LJ, Wang Q, Koknar-Tezel S, Megalooikonomou V (2007) Optimal subsequence bijection. In: International conference on data mining (ICDM), pp 565–570
19. Li C, Shirahama K, Grzegorzek M, Ma F, Zhou B (2013) Classification of environmental microorganisms in microscopic images using shape features and support vector machines. In: IEEE international conference on image processing. IEEE computer society, Melbourne, Australia, pp 2435–2439
20. Li X, Guskov I (2007) 3D object recognition from range images using pyramid matching. In: ICCV, pp 1–6
21. Ma T, Latecki LJ (2012) Maximum weight cliques with mutex constraints for video object segmentation. In: CVPR, pp 670–677
22. Ma T, Yi M, Latecki LJ (2013) View-invariant object detection by matching 3D contours. In: Park JI, Kim J (eds) ACCV workshops, lecture notes in computer science, vol 7729, Springer, Berlin, Heidelberg, pp 183–196
23. Mian A, Bennamoun M, Owens R (2006) Three-dimensional model-based object recognition and segmentation in cluttered scenes. PAMI 28(10):1584–1601
24. Nguyen TB, Sukhan L (2009) Accurate 3D lines detection using stereo camera. In: International symposium on assembly and manufacturing (ISAM), pp 304–309
25. Payet N, Todorovic S (2011) From contours to 3D object detection and pose estimation. In: ICCV, pp. 983–990
26. Redondo-Cabrera C, Lopez-Sastre R, Acevedo-Rodriguez J, Maldonado-Bascon S (2012) Surfing the point clouds: selective 3D spatial pyramids for category-level object recognition. In: CVPR, pp 3458–3465
27. Reinhold M, Grzegorzek M, Denzler J, Niemann H (2005) Appearance-based recognition of 3-D objects by cluttered background and occlusions. Pattern Recogn 38(5):739–753
28. Spinello L, Arras KO (2012) Leveraging RGB-D data: adaptive fusion and domain adaptation for object detection. In: 2012 IEEE International Conference on robotics and automation (ICRA), pp 4469–4474
29. Stiene S, Lingemann K, Nuchter A, Hertzberg J (2006) Contour-based object detection in range images. In: International symposium on 3D data processing, visualization, and transmission, pp 168–175
30. Tang S, Wang X, Lv X, Han TX, Keller J, He Z, Skubic M, Lao S (2013) Histogram of oriented normal vectors for object recognition with a depth sensor. In: Proceedings of the 11th Asian conference on computer vision ACCV'12, volume part II, Springer-Verlag, Berlin, Heidelberg, pp 525–538
31. Yi M, Yang Y, Qi W, Zhou Y, Li Y, Pizlo Z, Latecki LJ (2013) Navigation toward non-static target object using footprint detection based tracking. In: Proceedings of the 11th ACCV, Springer, pp 389–400

Chapter 8
Using Sparse Optical Flow for Two-Phase Gas Flow Capturing with Multiple Kinect

Kai Berger, Marc Kastner, Yannic Schroeder and Stefan Guthe

Abstract The use of multiple Microsoft Kinect has become prominent in the last 2 years and enjoyed widespread acceptance. While several work has been published to mitigate quality degradations in the precomputed depth image, this work focuses on employing an optical flow suitable for dot patterns as employed in the Kinect to retrieve subtle scene data alterations for reconstruction. The method is employed in a multiple Kinect vision architecture to detect the interface of propane flow around occluding objects in air.

8.1 Introduction

With the advent of the Microsoft Kinect not only the human–computer interaction in the consumer market has been shifted to a new level, the interaction based on motion capturing, but also computer-vision-based research has experienced a sparked since the release. Ranging from advances in motion capturing and real-time self-localization and mapping to robust face capturing, the bandwidth of the research volume related to the Kinect is surprisingly broad. A nice overview about these articles can be found, e.g., in the following state-of-the-art reports by Khoshelham et al. [13], Han et al. [11], or Zhang et al. [22].

K. Berger (✉)
OeRC, University of Oxford, Oxford, UK
e-mail: kai.berger@oerc.ox.ac.uk

M. Kastner · Y. Schroeder · S. Guthe
TU Braunschweig, Braunschweig, Germany
e-mail: marc.kastner@gmail.com

Y. Schroeder
e-mail: schroeder@cg.cs.tu-bs.de

S. Guthe
e-mail: guthe@cg.cs.tu-bs.de

© Springer International Publishing Switzerland 2014
L. Shao et al. (eds.), *Computer Vision and Machine Learning with RGB-D Sensors*,
Advances in Computer Vision and Pattern Recognition,
DOI: 10.1007/978-3-319-08651-4_8

While most approaches have focused on preprocessed data of the sensor, i.e., a considerably accurate depth estimate of the scene, only few have actually considered the raw IR stream for their data processing. This article exploits the use of the IR footage, containing gray-level information about the scene together with sparsely distributed spots emitted from the IR laser component of the Kinect. While the nondisclosed algorithm of the Kinect computes a dense depth image of the scene from considerably shifted positions of the laser spots, the proposed algorithm will detect subtle alterations introduced on the captured spots image, e.g., in the scenario of small light path deviations introduced by a refractive medium. The resulting information is equivalent to an optical flow image as it quantitatively denotes the alteration, i.e., pixel movement, introduced on each spot. It, however, differs from state-of-the-art optical flow images as it considers only a sparse discrete set of spots, projected into the scene from a IR laser component and captured with the Kinect's IR camera, which are represented by its barycentric position in the image and its distincitve shape. Furthermore, the information about the projected pattern allows a computation *independent* from the actual resolution of the underlying image stream, Sect. 8.4. We will test the algorithm in a capturing setup consisting of multiple Microsoft Kinect. The refractive index gradient in the scene is generated by letting propane flow through the intersecting volume of their viewing cones, Fig. 8.1.

The remainder of the article is structured as follows: After a revision of the state of the art in active-light-based computer vision research with a focus on optical flow capturing, Sect. 8.2, we examine the characteristics of the spot pattern projected by the Kinect and derive an abstract model in Sect. 8.3 that allows us to compute an accurate estimate of the spot position on the image plane *independent* from the actual resolution of the underlying image stream. Afterward, we introduce the sub-pixel accurate optical flow computation for detecting subtle changes in the captured IR stream, Sect. 8.4. Note that the proposed algorithms differ significantly from

Fig. 8.1 We examine small pixel deviations in the IR stream of the Microsoft Kinect as they are introduced by an index gradient present in the scene. In our capturing setup, we place a propane gas nozzle (*left*) in the center of three Kinect (*middle*) and place projection walls at a fixed distance opposite to each Kinect. The index gradient causes light path deviations both between the projector and the projection wall and between the projection wall and the camera (indicated by *colored cones*). Note that the stickers on the Kinect are placed to act as external diaphragm. To reconstruct the underlying gas flow using the proposed optical flow algorithm, we register each sensor to one common world space (*right*) and reconstruct the visual from silhouettes enclosing the deflected pixel regions in each sensor's IR image

state-of-the-art optical flow computation as it considers only sparse samples of the input images. A global optimization-based approach is therefore not feasible.

The presented method is then applied in the scenario of capturing the interface of two-phase gas flows, Fig. 8.1, Sects. 8.5, and 8.5.2. Finally, we discuss the results, Sect. 8.6, and conclude, Sect. 8.7.

8.2 Related Work

A variety of approaches have been proposed to capture and visualize the dynamics of gases and fluids, e.g., in wind tunnels. Mostly, two-phase flows are hard to discriminate by imaging tools, because their color appearance is quite similar. A straightforward approach is to enhance the contrast by inserting seeding particles into the flow. Their buoyancy and density have to match the measured fluids. The particles are usually illuminated in a way that only a 2D intersection plane is imaged. The technique is known as particle image velocimetry (PIV), an introduction can be found in the monograph by [21]. Particle tracking velocimetry (PTV) introduced by Cowen and Monismith [7] is similar to the PIV but incorporates tracking algorithms for particles over several images. Other approaches are noninvasive. Wetzstein et al. [20] recently proposed to use lenslets with attached color-field printouts to physically map light path deviation to color when holding them behind a gas and imaging them. Atcheson et al. [1] designed a high-frequency background pattern for background-oriented schlieren (BOS) detection of gas flows. This approach was refined by Berger et al. [3, 5] to enable the capturing of gas flows with occluding objects. They, however, showed that purely image-based methods are limited, and occluders could not be segmented out crisply. Therefore, Berger et al. [4] introduced the usage of Kinect for capturing gas flows around occluders. They imaged gas-introduced differences in the captured depth stream. When the scene was captured with multiple Kinect, a reconstruction of the visual hull of the gas was possible, but it was limited to superpixel resolution. Their work is the closest to ours, as we consider the same capturing scenario. We, however, advance it in the following way: We introduce a new sparse spot-based optical flow to work directly on the IR input stream of the sensor and thus are to work on subpixel accurate light path deviation data.

8.3 Spot Model Derivation

As the pattern projected by the Microsoft Kinect has a unique distinctive shape, it allows for analyzing the geometric properties of the underlying pattern elements, the *spots*. Each projected spot pattern is set up in the same way: In a 3 × 3 repeated regular matrix, certain circularly shaped holes in a mask are filled with opaque matter, while others are left unfilled, so that light beams may pass through. This matrix is applied to the optical element of the Kinect's IR emitter such that a coded light pattern emerges and projects into the scene. We analyze the IR pattern by letting the emitter projected orthogonally onto a wall at 3 m distance and capturing a statistically significant area of the wall with a digital single-lens reflex (dSLR) camera at a resolution of 4,368 × 2,912 px at a distance of 2 m. This way, one imaged projected spot would approximately comprise 128 × 128 px. After image rectification, we calculate the mean intensity distribution over all captured spots and the moments with the intention to fit a suitable continuous 2D distribution function that characterizes the properties of all spots best. The function would then represent the mean spot. This is reasoned by the fact that we want to perform the optical flow computation on the image plane independent from the actual image resolution. Note that this mean distribution would be used for fitting to each spot in each IR image in order to locate the center position of each spot. The computed discrete distribution resembles a 2D Gaussian profile. However, the distribution shows a skew behavior and 8 small local peaks in the neighborhood of the mean. The latter is due to the factory process of the matrix, and the holes filled with opaque matter may transmit a small but measurable intensity of light. We opt for representing the continuous distribution by a weighted combination of continuous 2D skew Gaussian distributions. Such multivariate distribution can be formalized as follows [10].

Consider a multivariate variable $\mathscr{Z}$ with each component being skew-normal with skewness vector λ, $\lambda_i \in (-\infty, \infty)$, written as:

$$\mathscr{Z} \sim \mathscr{SN}_k(\lambda, \Phi) \tag{8.1}$$

with multivariate density function f_k of dimensionality k

$$f_k(z) = 2\phi_k(z; \Omega) \Phi\left(\alpha^T z\right) \quad \left(z \in R^k\right), \tag{8.2}$$

where ϕ denotes the $\mathscr{N}(0, 1)$ density function and Φ denotes the $\mathscr{N}(0, 1)$ distribution $\cdot$ Ω is defined as

$$\Omega = \text{diag}\left(\left(1 - \delta_1^2\right)^{\frac{1}{2}}, \ldots, \left(1 - \delta_k^2\right)^{\frac{1}{2}}\right) \tag{8.3}$$

$$\cdot \left(\Psi + \lambda\lambda^T\right) \tag{8.4}$$

$$\cdot \text{diag}\left(\left(1 - \delta_1^2\right)^{\frac{1}{2}}, \ldots, \left(1 - \delta_k^2\right)^{\frac{1}{2}}\right) \tag{8.5}$$

with Ψ the $k \times k$ correlation matrix and

$$\delta = \frac{\lambda}{\left(1 + \lambda^2\right)^{\frac{1}{2}}} \tag{8.6}$$

α^T is defined as

$$\alpha^T = \frac{\lambda^T \Psi^{-1} \text{diag}\left(\left(1 - \delta_1^2\right)^{\frac{1}{2}}, \ldots, \left(1 - \delta_k^2\right)^{\frac{1}{2}}\right)^{-1}}{\left(1 + \lambda^T \Psi^{-1} \lambda\right)^{\frac{1}{2}}} \tag{8.7}$$

8 Using Sparse Optical Flow for Two-Phase Gas Flow...

We will focus on the bivariate case in order to model the intensity distribution on the image plane. The density function can be expressed as

$$f_2(z_1, z_2) = 2\psi_2(z_1, z_2; \omega) \Psi(\alpha_1 z_1 + \alpha_2 z_2), \tag{8.8}$$

with ω denoting the off-diagonal element of $\Omega \cdot \alpha_1$ and α_2 can be expressed as:

$$\alpha_1 = \frac{\delta_1 - \delta_2 \omega}{\left((1-\omega^2)\left(1 - \omega^2 - \delta_1^2 - \delta_2^2 + 2\delta_1\delta_2\omega\right)\right)^{\frac{1}{2}}} \tag{8.9}$$

and

$$\alpha_2 = \frac{\delta_2 - \delta_1 \omega}{\left((1-\omega^2)\left(1 - \omega^2 - \delta_1^2 - \delta_2^2 + 2\delta_1\delta_2\omega\right)\right)^{\frac{1}{2}}} \tag{8.10}$$

Note that ω satisfies

$$\delta_1\delta_2 - \left((1-\delta_1^2)(1-\delta_2^2)\right)^{\frac{1}{2}} < \omega < \delta_1\delta_2 + \left((1-\delta_1^2)(1-\delta_2^2)\right)^{\frac{1}{2}} \tag{8.11}$$

8.4 Proposed Flow Computation for Captured Spot Pattern-Based Active Light Video Data

Based on the distribution that we derived in Sect. 8.3, we compute frame-to-frame alterations to emitted spot pattern introduced by the scene content. Note that this sparse flow computation has a focus on subtle movements that may be smaller than one pixel of the captured image resolution and thus distinguishes from state-of the art approaches that focus on the local disparity estimate in order to compute scene depth. We approximate Eq. 8.8 with a 128 × 128 px kernel that we then use to characterize the mean spot, Fig. 8.2. The 128 × 128 px kernel of a generic spot is built from the dSLR closeup images from Sect. 8.3. This kernel is then used at each time a Kinect IR stream is read out later. We filter the input images to determine the center position for each spot by fitting the 128 × 128 px kernel to all intensity peaks present in the input image. The sparse optical flow is then computed between the computed spot center positions for two subsequent images in the IR stream in a least squares sense, assuming that the pixel deviations introduced on the spot pattern are smaller than the radial distance between two spots in the image. The local optimum is found by applying a gradient descent approach

$$x_{n+1} = x_n - \gamma_n \nabla F(x_n), n \geq 0, \tag{8.12}$$

where x_n spans the domain, in this case the position on the image plane, and F is a bivariate function with defined and differentiable neighborhood. The gray-level

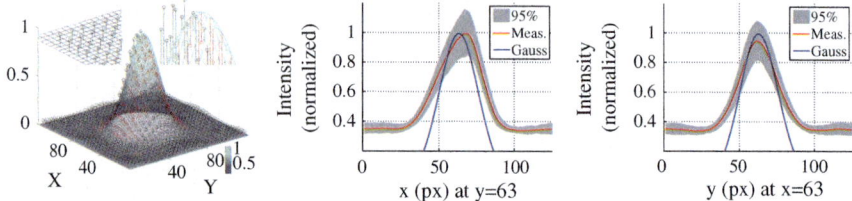

Fig. 8.2 The intensity profile of a measured spot in the projected IR pattern differs considerably from the profile of a standard Gaussian laser beam (*left, black* and *red error bars* and *slices, middle* and *right*). In this plot, a 50 mW laser spot is assumed that is shone onto a planar surface from 3 m distance and sampled with a 128 × 128 px grid. We thus discretize a skew Gaussian distribution to a 128 × 128 px kernel and fit it to the spots in the captured spot pattern to arrive at a discretized mean intensity distribution. The discretized kernel is later used for our spot-based optical computation

image is denoted F, and the gradient can be provided as a 2D vector. To account for the low sampling rate, the region of interest, usually a 5 × 5 px region, is upsampled. We use a bilinear kernel for upsampling. The stepsize γ is set to a small value, usually 0.5 px. The convergence criterion is an intensity difference of <0.01, and the maximum number of iterations is set to 100. We assume small spot deviations in the range of <1–3 pixel in x and y direction. Note, again, that the resulting optical flow is sparse as well.

8.5 Application: Capturing of Two-Phase Gas Flows

In our setup, we place three Kinect in an half-arc around the gas flow with projection walls placed opposite to each Kinect at ≈2 m distance. We may introduce occluders into the flow. The Kinect are calibrated to a common world space and aligned to frame accuracy. They are automatically focused on the scene center, i.e., the gas valve, Fig. 8.3. We let the gas valve vent for several seconds and capture the gas flow with the Kinect. The captured images of the IR stream, Fig. 8.4, are processed in the following. The 128 × 128 px kernel for the sparse optical flow computation in the IR pattern has been captured by a dSLR beforehand.

8.5.1 Projector Image Reprojection

We exploit both the sensor information of the infrared camera and the infrared emitter for the reconstruction. This way we can also use the shadowgraph regions in the IR image for optical flow calculation and consequently for a silhouette generation that helps refining the final visual hull enclosing the gas flow. Usually, the detected flow directions in the shadowgraph regions are inverted compared to the regions

8 Using Sparse Optical Flow for Two-Phase Gas Flow... 163

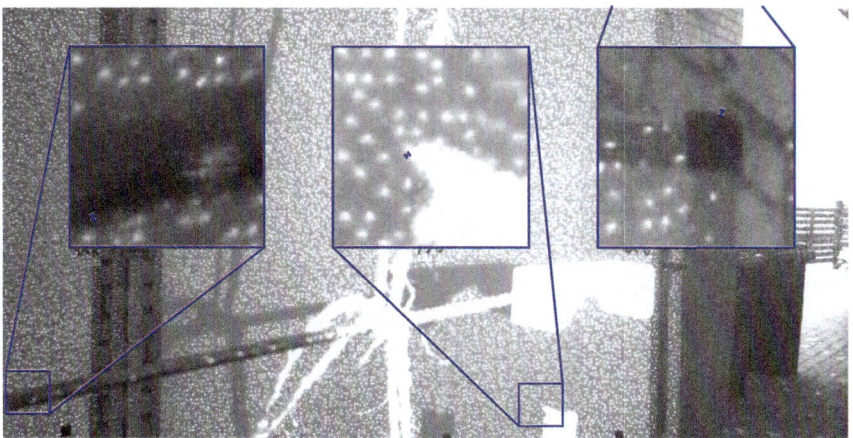

Fig. 8.3 In our setup, the camera is focused on the valve, i.e., its edge is smoothed over 5 pixels (*middle* closeup, 3x enlarged) compared to 12 pixels for the projection board (*right*closeup, 3x enlarged) and 9 pixels for the frontmost part of the metallic holder (*left* closeup, 3× enlarged)

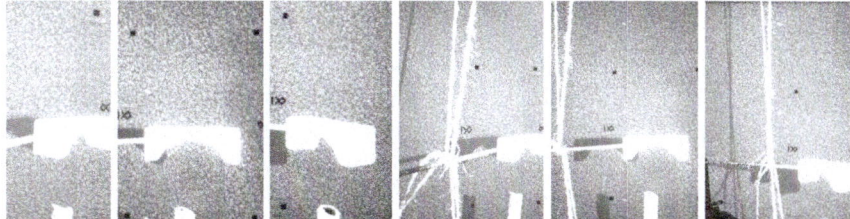

Fig. 8.4 The input images of the capturing setup for two-phase gas flows (*left three*) and their warped projector images (*right three*). The gas flows out of a valve (*bottom*) and is imaged from three Kinect placed in an half-arc around it. An occluder is placed above the valve to introduce turbulence to the gas flow. We examine both the deflections introduced on the way between projector and wall (*right three shadowgraphs*, i.e., enclosed regions between the shadows of the gas valve and the occluder) and on the way between wall and camera (*left three*)

that image light path deviations between the projection wall and the camera. The projector image is generated by reprojecting the infrared camera image into the projector image space. The calibration between projector and camera is done by identifying the spot subpatterns of the pattern projected onto the planar projection walls in the recorded image that form a rectangle in the projector space. Note that the deviations from a perfectly planar surface are negligible for the projection walls at the distance considered in our setup. Then, the corners are identified by using Fofi et al. approach [9] in order to calculate the image homography between the camera image and the projector image space. Effectively, thus, we can double the number of viewpoints in order to get a better fit of the visual hull.

8.5.2 GPU-Based Reconstruction

The reconstruction follows a GPU-based approach from Ladikos et al. [14], where silhouettes of the detected gas flow are downsampled so that every voxel projects into a single pixel. This way the projection of the voxel center point suffices for the lookup in the silhouette images. Note that the silhouettes need not necessarily be coherent regions of genus 0. In our case, we simply performed an opening on the spot regions with sufficiently large optical flow to arrive at a binary mask that we used as silhouette input for the hull generation. The downsampling is done by Gaussian smoothing followed by a downscaling. The kernel is then executed for every voxel by deriving the 3D position from its id and by projecting the voxel center point into the image. Early rejection based on image occupancy is performed to ease computational burden.

8.6 Discussion

8.6.1 Optical Flow Comparison

We compared the subpixel accurate sparse pattern-based distortion detection against Horn-Schunck [12], Lucas-Kanade [15], Drulea-Nedevschi [8], Deqing Sun [18], and Brox [6] with a synthetic spot image and the same image modulated by the Groove2 flowmap from the Middlebury database that have been altered with varying noise and increasing amount of blurriness. We evaluated the average angular error (AAE) compared to the ground truth and found that the proposed method shows a lower AAE with increasing image degradation compared to the other flow algorithms, Fig. 8.5. It can also be noticed that OF algorithms with an emphasis on global smoothness underperform on the sparse dataset. Thus, the proposed algorithm is more robust against the noise introduced by the capturing setup.

8.6.2 Comparison to Depth-Deviation-Based Approaches

Note that a direct ground truth comparison between our method and [4] on the same gas flow is not possible because the USB communication protocol forces a decision between accessing the depth stream or a high-resolution IR stream (a low-resolution IR stream bears aliasing artifacts and is not feasible for evaluation with our method). However, it is possible to use a block-matching based approach [17] for synthesizing the depth map closest to a depth map that the Kinect would have streamed for a given high-resolution IR image, Fig. 8.6. An exemplary comparison between the proposed approach and the depth-based approach on a synthesized depth map is visualized in Fig. 8.7: The middle and right plots show a visualization of the

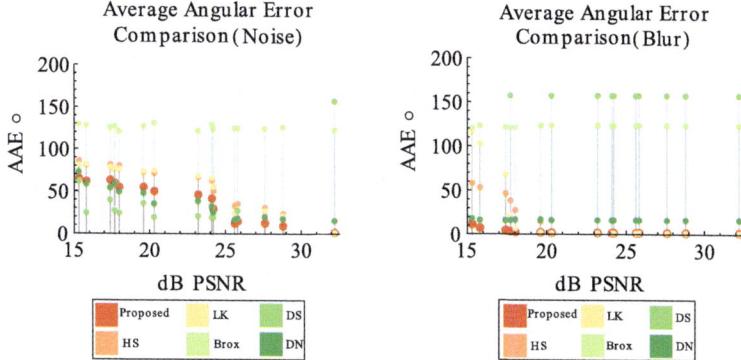

Fig. 8.5 Comparison of state-of-the-art optical flows to the proposed spot-based optical flow for varying levels of noise (*left*) and blur (*right*) applied to a synthetic spot pattern. The ground truth optical flow is generated with the *groove2* dataset from the Middlebury database. The proposed approach (*red, large dots*) outperforms the state-of-the-art approaches (Horn-Schunck (HS), Lucas-Kanade (LK), Drulea-Nedevshi (DN), Deqing Sun (DS), and Brox) in the range relevant for Kinect data stream processing (35–22 dB)

Fig. 8.6 We synthesized disparity values for the high-resolution IR image streams (*left*) using a block-matching approach [17]. A trade-off for the block sizes can be seen: A block size of 19×19 (*middle*) results in a less blurry but more sparse result than that with a block size of 31×31 (*right*) which is regarded as being closer to an expected disparity map from the Kinect

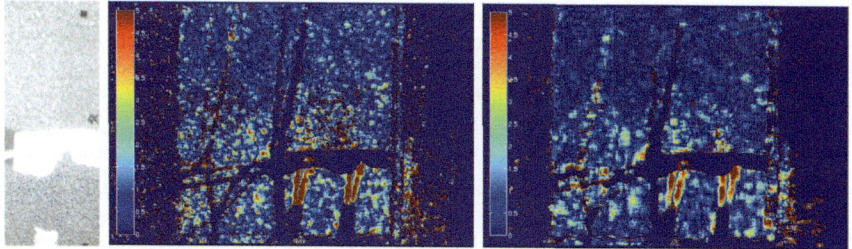

Fig. 8.7 In a direct comparison to the proposed method (quiver plot, *left*), it can be noticed that with the depth-based approach, a visualization of the main gas flow stream is robustly possible, but the signal discriminates only by five different values in both directions. Also, the signal-to-noise ratio is reduced. With a block size of 19×19 (*middle*), more noise either by scene depth variation or by sensor-/block-matching noise is visible than with a block size of 31×31 (*right*). Some small deviations introduced by the gas above the bridge occluder are not mapped by the depth-based approach

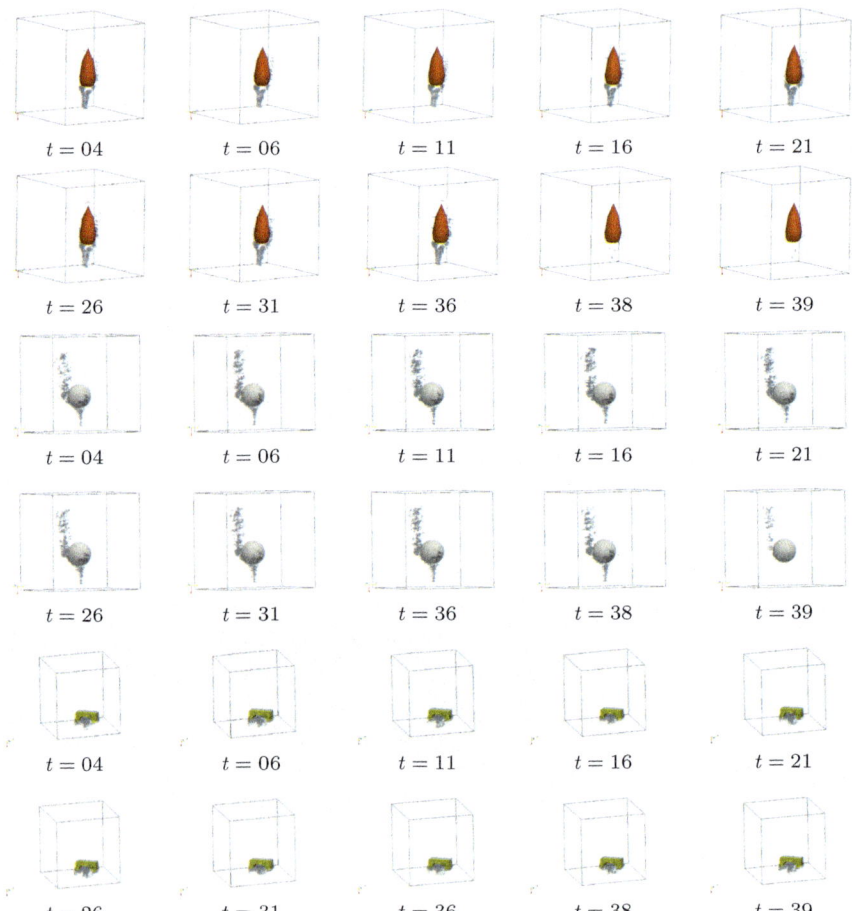

Fig. 8.8 A sequence of 39 frames captured with three Microsoft Kinect and processed with the proposed algorithm for propane gas flowing around obstructing objects with different aerodynamic properties. The voxel volumes have resolution 128^3, each input image roughly consists of 2,000 spots in the region of interest. While the droplet occluder (*first row*) is smoothly surrounded by the flow, the golf ball (*second row*) forces the gas to direct leftward. The bridge occluder completely obstructs the gas flow, and its flow direction is inverted downward

difference image between a frame with and without flowing, as computed by Berger et al. [4]. While the main gas stream is mapped as expected, parts above the occluder and to both lower sides of the occluder seem to not have been captured by the depth-based approach. Also, it is noticeable that the small range of five values in both directions results in a lower signal-to-noise ratio. Some patches in the image, introduced, e.g., by ambiguities in the block-matching approach result in high values in the difference image used for depth-based reconstruction. The proposed approach results on average in 20 different values in u- and v-direction in the range $[-0.9, 0.9]$ pixels and discriminates between 1/100 of a pixel.

8.6.3 Gas Flow and Occluder Segmentation

The occluders have been segmented out by removing the overexposed regions in the input image. The projected area of the gas flow could be determined accurately to subpixel level in the input images for both the original IR camera image and the warped projector image.

8.6.4 GPU-Based Reconstruction

The reconstruction is written in C for CUDA and performs in 52.76 ms at 64^3 voxel, in 417.79 ms at 128^3 voxel, and in 3,033.89 ms at 256^3 voxel on an Intel Corei7-3960X (Six Core Extreme, 15 MB Cache) Overclocked up to 4.0 Ghz with a 4 GB GDDR5 NVIDIA GeForce GTX 690 graphics card. Significant gain in performance can be achieved by using an octree-based approach. An exemplary visualization of the reconstructed volumes is depicted in Fig. 8.8 for different occluders: We captured a sequence of 39 frames with three Microsoft Kinect and processed it as proposed. It can be seen that the droplet occluder (first row) smoothly introduces into the flow, while the golf ball (second row) forces the gas to direct leftward. The bridge occluder obstructs the gas flow and forces the flow to be inverted downward.

8.7 Conclusion

We presented a new method for subpixel accurate flow detection for sparse image data such as the Microsoft Kinect spot pattern. We found that the discretized skew Gaussian approach outperforms traditional and current optical flow approaches in the context of the Kinect's IR image stream. We tested the algorithm in a multiple Kinect vision architecture to detect the interface of propane flow around occluding objects in air. In that use case scenario, we sought to reconstruct the geometric extend of gas flows under the presence of occluders captured with three Kinect placed in an half-arc around the flow with projection walls placed at a fixed distance opposite to each Kinect. We exploited the sparse spot detection algorithm to provide masks for a GPU-based visual hull reconstruction. By incorporating the projector extrinsics, we doubled the reprojection information in order to increase accuracy.

Acknowledgments Supplementary Videos are accessible under https://dl.dropbox.com/u/21912442/supplementary.zip. The authors would like to thank Manuel Martinez from KIT, Karlsruhe, who helped with generating synthetic depth images from the spot pattern images.

References

1. Atcheson B, Ihrke I, Heidrich W, Tevs A, Bradley D, Magnor M, Seidel H (2008) Time-resolved 3D capture of non-stationary gas flows. In: ACM transactions on graphics (TOG), vol 27. ACM, New York, p 132
2. Azzalini A, Dalla Valle A (1996) The multivariate skew-normal distribution. Biometrika 83:715–726
3. Berger K, Ihrke I, Atcheson B, Heidrich W, Magnor M et al (2009) Tomographic 4D reconstruction of gas flows in the presence of occluders. In: Vision, modeling, and visualization workshop (VMV), pp 29–36
4. Berger K, Ruhl K, Albers M, Schroder Y, Scholz A, Guthe S, Magnor M (2011) The capturing of turbulent gas flows using multiple kinects. In: Proceedings on CDC4CV, November 2011, IEEE, ISBN: 978-1- 4673-0061-2
5. Berger K, Ruhl K. Schroeder Y, Bruemmer C, Scholz AL, Magnor M Markerless motion capture using multiple color-depth sensors
6. Brox T, Bruhn A, Papenberg N. Weickert J In: High accuracy optical flow estimation based on a theory for warping European conference on computer vision ECCV
7. Cowen E, Monismith S, Cowen E, Monismith S (1997) A hybrid digital particle tracking velocimetry technique. Exp Fluids 22(3):199211
8. Drulea M, Nedevschi S (2011) Total variation regularization of local-global optical flow (accepted to ITSC 2011)
9. Falcao G, Hurtos N, Massich J, Fofi D (2009) Projector-camera calibration toolbox. http://code.google.com/p/procamcalib
10. Gupta A, Gonzlez-Faras G (2004) A multivariate skew normal distribution. J Multivar Anal 89(1):181–190
11. Han J, Shao L, Xu D, Shotton, J (2013) Enhanced computer vision with Microsoft Kinect sensor:a review. IEEE Trans Cybern
12. Horn BKP, Schunck BG (1981) Determining optical flow. Artif Intell 17:185–203
13. Khoshelham K (2011) Accuracy analysis of kinect depth data. In: ISPRS workshop laser scanning, vol 38(5). p W12
14. Ladikos A, Benhimane S, Navab N (2008) Efficient visual hull computation for real-time 3D reconstruction using CUDA. In: IEEE computer society conference on computer vision and pattern recognition, Anchorage, Alaska (USA), June 2008. Workshop on visual computer vision on GPUs (CVGPU)
15. Lucas BD, Kanade T (1981) An iterative image registration technique with an application to stereo vision. In: Proceedings of imaging understanding workshop, pp 121–130
16. Lulu Chen, Hong Wei, James Ferryman (2013) A survey of human motion analysis using depth imagery. Pattern Recogn Lett 34(15):1995–2006. ISSN 0167–8655, http://dx.doi.org/10.1016/j.patrec.2013.02.006
17. Martinez M, Stiefelhagen R (2013) Kinect unleashed: setting control over high resolution depth maps
18. Sun D, Roth S, Lewis JP, Black M In: Learning optical flow European conference on computer vision, ECCV

19. Svoboda T, Martinec D, Pajdla T (2005) A convenient multicamera self-calibration for virtual environments. Presence Teleoper Virtual Environ 14(4):407422
20. Wetzstein G, Raskar R, Heidrich W (2011) Hand-held schlieren photography with light field probes. In: IEEE international conference on computational photography (ICCP), 2011
21. Willert C, Gharib M (1991) Digital particle image velocimetry. Exp Fluids 10(4):181193
22. Zhang Z (2012) Microsoft kinect sensor and its effect. MultiMedia IEEE 19(2):4–10

Part III
Detection, Segmentation and Tracking

Chapter 9
RGB-D Sensor-Based Computer Vision Assistive Technology for Visually Impaired Persons

Yingli Tian

Abstract A computer vision-based wayfinding and navigation aid can improve the mobility of blind and visually impaired people to travel independently. In this chapter, we focus on RGB-D sensor-based computer vision technologies in application to assist blind and visually impaired persons. We first briefly review the existing computer vision based assistive technology for the visually impaired. Then we provide a detailed description of the recent RGB-D sensor based assistive technology to help blind or visually impaired people. Next, we present the prototype system to detect and recognize stairs and pedestrian crosswalks based on RGB-D images. Since both stairs and pedestrian crosswalks are featured by a group of parallel lines, Hough transform is applied to extract the concurrent parallel lines based on the RGB (Red, Green, and Blue) channels. Then, the Depth channel is employed to recognize pedestrian crosswalks and stairs. The detected stairs are further identified as stairs going up (upstairs) and stairs going down (downstairs). The distance between the camera and stairs is also estimated for blind users. The detection and recognition results on our collected datasets demonstrate the effectiveness and efficiency of our developed prototype. We conclude the chapter by the discussion of the future directions.

9.1 Introduction

Of the 314 million visually impaired people worldwide, 45 million are blind [1]. In the USA, the 2008 National Health Interview Survey (NHIS) reported that an estimated 25.2 million adult Americans (over 8 %) are blind or visually impaired [2]. This number is increasing rapidly as the baby boomer generation ages. Recent developments in computer vision, digital cameras, and portable computers make it

Y. Tian (✉)
Department of Electrical Engineering, The City College of New York,
New York, NY 10031, USA
e-mail: ytian@ccny.cuny.edu

© Springer International Publishing Switzerland 2014
L. Shao et al. (eds.), *Computer Vision and Machine Learning with RGB-D Sensors*,
Advances in Computer Vision and Pattern Recognition,
DOI: 10.1007/978-3-319-08651-4_9

feasible to assist these individuals by developing camera-based products that combine computer vision technology with other existing commercial products such optical character recognition (OCR), GPS systems.

Independent travel and active interactions with the dynamic surrounding environment are well known to present significant challenges for individuals with severe vision impairment, thereby reducing quality of life and compromising safety. In order to improve the ability of people who are blind or have significant visual impairments to access, understand, and explore surrounding environments, many assistant technologies and devices have been developed to accomplish specific navigation goals, obstacle detection, or wayfinding tasks.

We note that electronic technology developed over the last 50 years has been an enormous boon for visually impaired people, allowing access to text through video magnification [3], reading machines [4], text-to-speech (TTS) and screen readers [5], increasing quality of life for millions of individuals with vision loss by allowing independent and private access to text. However, few of them use these for navigation and travel. For navigation and travel, nearly all blind people use a cane at least some of the time due to the effectiveness, convenience, and low cost, even if they rely on another mobility aid. The user typically scans left and right along their forward directional path, gathering information about obstacles from tactile and sonic information. Additionally, it gives information about drop-offs, stairs, ground textures, and type of flooring. It also serves as an identifier so that sighted people may avoid collisions with the blind traveler. However, the long cane is not able to detect obstacles higher off the ground. We think that the cane is most likely to remain useful to blind users for the foreseeable future, together with other high-tech assistive devices.

Many efforts have been made in development of electronic assistive devices to help blind persons navigate, which can be found in recent surveys [6–9, 59, 61]. In addition to develop effective, reliable, and robust technology, friendly human interface design is even more important for successful assistive devices. There are two central and persistent issues in the human interface design: (1) how easy a system can be operated by the user, and (2) how the system can best present nonvisual information to the user.

A computer vision-based assistive system can improve the mobility of blind and visually impaired people to reduce risks and avoid dangers, enhance independent living, and improve quality of life. Our research efforts are focused on developing a computer vision-based navigation aid, because we believe this approach holds the greatest long-term promise, given the continually rapid growth in capabilities of computer and robotic technology fields of computer vision and robotics [10, 11]. The need for robots to navigate in the environment, in particular, is fueling the development of computer vision techniques for object recognition and scene analysis, along with localization and mapping. As imaging techniques advance, such as RGB-D cameras of Microsoft Kinect [12] and ASUS Xtion Pro Live [13], it has become practical to capture RGB sequences as well as depth maps in real time. Depth maps are able to provide additional information of object shape and distance compared to traditional RGB cameras. It has therefore motivated recent research work to investigate computer vision-based assistive technology using RGB-D cameras.

In this chapter, we focus on RGB-D sensor-based computer vision technologies in application to assist blind and visually impaired persons. We first briefly review the existing computer vision-based assistive technology for the visually impaired. Then, we provide a detailed description of the recent RGB-D sensor-based assistive technology to help blind or visually impaired people. Next, we present the prototype system we developed to detect and recognize stairs and pedestrian crosswalks based on RGB-D images. We conclude the chapter by the discussion of the future directions.

9.2 Related Work of Computer Vision-Based Assistive Technology for Visually Impaired

Many electronic mobility assistant systems are developed based on converting sonar information into an audible signal for the visually impaired persons to interpret [14–18]. However, they only provide limited information. Recently, researchers have focused on interpreting the visual information into a high-level representation before sending it to the visually impaired persons.

The "vOICe" system [19] is a commercially available vision-based travel aid that displays imagery through sound using videos captured by a head-mounted camera to help them build a mental image about the environment. However, the vOICe system translates images into corresponding sounds through stereo headphones, which will seriously block and distract the blind users' hearing sense. In addition, a training and education process is must conducted to understand the meanings of different tones and pitches of sounds about the environment. For example, if a short beep indicates a bright speck of light, three specks will produces three beeps. A vertical line is a stack of specks, sounding all at the same time but all with different pitches since they are at different heights. In real situation, an environment generally contains different objects, the vOICe system will generate a complex and "noisy" sound map that will be too complex for blind users to build the mental image.

Very recently, the US Food and Drug Administration approved for sale a new device—the Argus II retinal prosthesis [20], from Second Sight Medical Products—comprised of a small video camera mounted on the nose bridge of a pair of sunglasses, a transmitter mounted near one temple of the sunglasses, a worn or carried video-processing unit, and a 60-electrode array that is intended to replace the function of degenerated photoreceptor cells in the retinas of those with the disease retinitis pigmentosa. Although it does not fully restore vision, the Argus II can improve ability to perceive lights, images, and movement, using the video-processing unit to transform images from the video camera into image data that are wirelessly transmitted to the retinal electrode array. However, the temporal dynamics of electrical retinal stimulation are likely very different from those of a normal retina, the image is extremely low resolution relative to normal vision, and most important, the user must aim the head rather than the eye, to move an object into the field of view.

VizWiz [21] is a free iPhone app to provide answers to questions asked by blind users about their surroundings through anonymous web workers and social network members. Based on the statistic data about 50,000 questions, most questions were answered in a minute or less. With VizWiz, a user takes a picture and records a question on their mobile phone, then sends their question to anonymous workers, object recognition software—IQ [22], Twitter, or an email contact. Once an answer is received from any of those services, it is sent back to the users' phone. The advantage of VizWiz is the fusion of automatic image processing software with human replies from other members in user's social network. However, there are several main limitations for blind navigation and wayfinding: (1) For blind users, it is very hard to aim their iPhone to the targeted objects; (2) for the answers the user received, there is not a way to validate whether the answer is accurate; (3) some questions may not be answered; and (4) questions may take some time to answer.

A product in development called BrainPort (from Wicab Inc.) and recently approved for sale in Europe [23] uses a camera mounted on a pair of sunglasses as its input device. After image processing, images are displayed on the tongue via a "lollipop"-like display as shown in Fig. 9.1. The "image" has been described as "tasting" a bit like effervescent champagne bubble on the tongue. Studies have demonstrated that blind and blindfolded sighted subjects can localize and identify some objects [24, 25] and avoid obstacles while navigating [26] under favorable conditions of contrast and lighting. Drawbacks of this system are that it requires use of the mouth, which precludes concurrently engaging in other lingual activities such as speaking and eating, and its spatial resolution is still far worse (by orders of magnitude) than that of the visual system, posing limits to object recognition.

Coughlan and Shen [27] developed a method of finding crosswalks based on figure-ground segmentation, which they built in a graphical model framework for grouping geometric features into a coherent structure. As shown in Fig. 9.2,

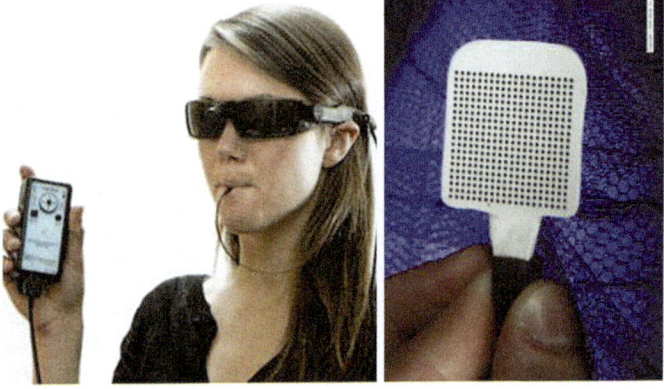

Fig. 9.1 BrainPort vision substitution device [23]

Fig. 9.2 Crosswatch system for providing guidance to visually impaired pedestrians at traffic intersections by panning a cell phone camera *left* and *right*; the system provides feedback to help user align him/herself to crosswalk before entering it [28]

Ivanchenko et al. [28] further extended the algorithm to detect the location and orientation of pedestrian crosswalks for a blind or visually impaired person using a cell phone camera. The prototype of the system can run in real time on an off-the-shelf Nokia N95 camera phone. The cell phone automatically took several images per second, analyzed each image in a fraction of a second, and sounded an audio tone when it detected a pedestrian crosswalk.

Advanyi et al. [29] employed the bionic eyeglasses to provide the blind or visually impaired individuals the navigation and orientation information based on an enhanced color preprocessing through mean shift segmentation. Then, detection of pedestrian crosswalks was carried out via a partially adaptive cellular nanoscale networks algorithm. Se [30] proposed a method to detect zebra crosswalks. They first detected the crossing lines by looking for groups of concurrent lines. Edges were then partitioned using intensity variation information. Se and Brady [31] also developed a Gabor filter-based texture detection method to detect distant stair cases. When the stairs are close enough, stair cases were then detected by looking for groups of concurrent lines, where convex and concave edges were portioned using intensity variation information. The pose of stairs was also estimated by a homograph search model. Uddin et al. [32] proposed a bipolarity-based segmentation and projective invariant-based method to detect zebra crosswalks. They first segmented the image on the basis of bipolarity and selected the candidates on the basis of area, then extracted feature points on the candidate area based on the Fisher criterion. The authors recognized zebra crosswalks based on the projective invariants.

Our own research group has developed a series of computer vision-based methods for blind people to recognize text and signage [33–36], recognize objects and clothes patterns [37–39], independently access and navigate unfamiliar environments [40–43], and under interface study [44]. Text and signage play important role in blind navigation and wayfinding. Tian et al. [40] developed a proof-of-concept computer vision-based wayfinding aid for blind people to independently access unfamiliar indoor environments. In order to find different rooms (e.g., an office, a lab, or a bathroom) and other building amenities (e.g., an exit or an elevator), the object detection is integrated with text recognition. A robust and efficient algorithm is developed to detect doors, elevators, and cabinets based on their general geometric shape which combines edges and corners. Then, the text information associated with the detected objects is extracted and recognized. For text recognition, they first extracted text regions from signs with multiple colors and possibly complex backgrounds and then applied character localization and topological analysis to filter out background interference. The extracted text is recognized using off-the-shelf (OCR) software products. The object type, orientation, location, and text information are presented to the blind traveler as speech. Some example results of door detection and text signage recognition are demonstrated in Fig. 9.3. The first row of Fig. 9.3 shows the detected door and signage regions. The second row displays the binarized signage. The last row displays that recognized text from OCR as readable codes on the extracted and binarized text regions.

Reading is obviously essential in today's society. Printed text is everywhere in the form of reports, receipts, bank statements, restaurant menus, classroom handouts, product packages, instructions on medicine bottles, etc. And while optical aids, video magnifiers and screen readers can help blind users and those with low vision to access documents, there are few devices that can provide good access to common hand-held objects such as product packages, and objects printed with text such as prescription medication bottles. The ability of people who are blind or have significant visual impairments to read printed labels and product packages will enhance independent living, and foster economic and social self-sufficiency.

Our group proposed a camera-based assistive framework to help blind persons to read text labels from hand-held objects in their daily life. As shown in Fig. 9.4, a blind user wearing a camera captures the hand-held object from the cluttered background or other neutral objects in the camera view by slightly shaking the object for 1 or 2 s. This process solves the aiming problem for blind users. The hand-held object is

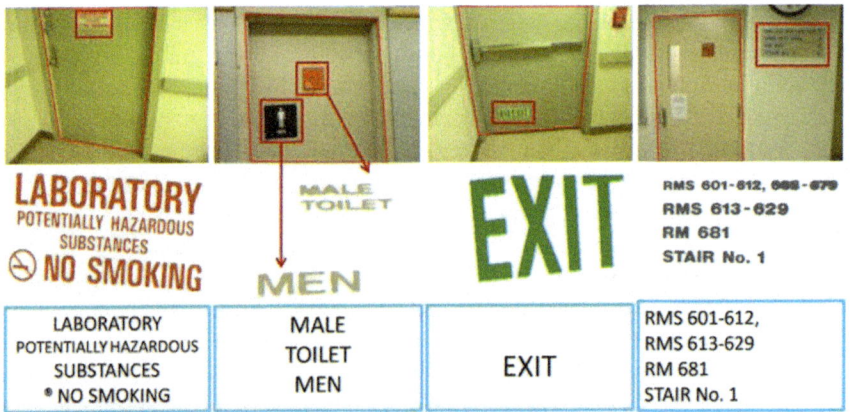

Fig. 9.3 *Top row* Detected doors and regions containing text information. *Middle row* Extracted and binarized text regions. *Bottom row* Text recognition results of OCR in text regions [40]

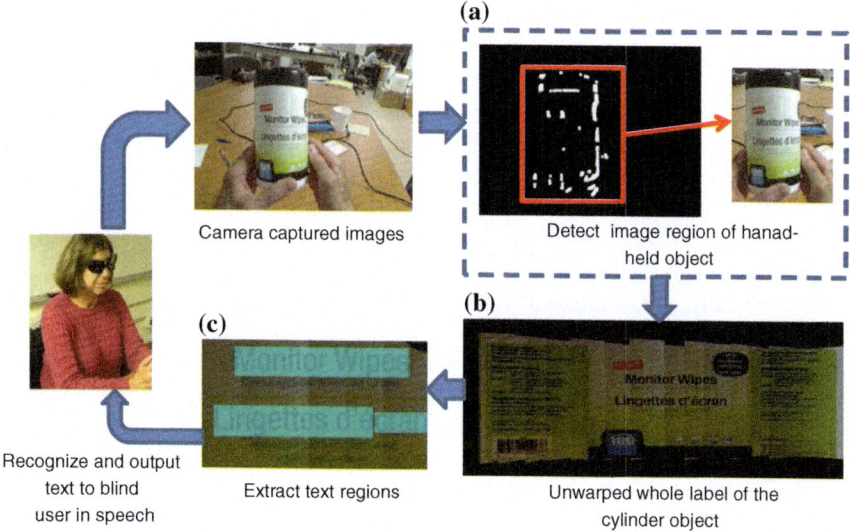

Fig. 9.4 Flowchart of the framework to read labels from hand-held objects for blind users [36]

detected from the background or other surrounding objects in the camera view by motion detection. Then, a mosaic model is applied to unwarp the text label on the object surface and reconstruct the whole label for recognizing text information. This model can handle cylinder objects in any orientations and scales. The text information is then extracted from the unwarped and flatted labels. In the text localization method, the basic processing cells are rectangle image patches with fixed ratio, where features of text can be obtained from both stroke orientations and edge distributions [45–47]. The extracted text regions are then recognized by OCR software and communicate with the blind user in speech.

9.3 RGB-D Sensor-Based Computer Vision Assistive Technology for Visually Impaired

As the release of RGB-D sensors and corresponding development toolkits, the applications of RGB-D sensor-based computer vision technology have been extended far beyond gaming and entertainment. More reviews of the applications for multimedia and object recognition can be found in [62, 63]. In this section, we only focus on the research related to RGB-D camera-based assistive technology to help visually impaired people. Compared to the traditional RGB cameras or the stereo cameras, RGB-D sensors have the following advantages: (a) RGB-D cameras contain both an RGB channel and a 3D depth channel, which can provide more information of the scene; (b) they work well in a low-light environment; (c) they are low cost; and (d) they are efficient for real-time processing. Currently, the RGB-D camera captures both RGB images and depth maps at a resolution of 640 × 480 pixels with 30 frames per second. The effective depth range of the Kinect RGB-D camera is from 0.8 to 4 m. Although the Kinect for Windows Hardware can be switched to near mode that provides a range of 0.5–3 m, currently the near mode is not supported for an Xbox Kinect for Windows SDK. The RGB-D camera field of view is about 60°. Since the RGB-D sensors use infrared, they cannot be used reliably for obstacle avoidance of transparent objects such as glass doors. Also they will not work in outdoor environments with direct sunlight.

Theoretically, the traditional RGB camera-based assistive technology for blind persons can be implemented using RGB-D sensors. However, since the limited resolution (640 × 480 pixels) of the current RGB-D sensors, some technologies may not work such as text detection and recognition especially for text with small size. In this section, we briefly summarize RGB-D sensor-based technology for applications to assist visually impaired people.

Khan et al. [48] developed a real-time human and obstacle detection system for a blind or visually impaired user using a Xtion Pro Live RGB-D sensor. As shown in Fig. 9.5, the prototype system includes a Xtion Pro live (Kinect) sensor, waist assembly to mount the Kinect, a laptop for processing and transducing the data, a backpack to hold the laptop, and a set of headphone for providing feedback to the user. The system runs in two modes: (1) track and/or detect multiple humans and moving objects and transduce the information to the user; and (2) avoid obstacles for safe navigation for a blind or visually impaired user in an indoor environment. They also presented a preliminary user study with some blindfolded users to measure the efficiency and robustness of their algorithms.

Tang et al. [50] presented an RGB-D sensor-based computer vision device to improve the performance of visual prostheses. First, a patch-based method is employed to generate a dense depth map with region-based representations. The patch-based method generates both a surface-based RGB and depth (RGB-D) segmentation instead of just 3D point clouds; therefore, it carries more meaningful information and it is easier to convey the information to the visually impaired. Then, they

 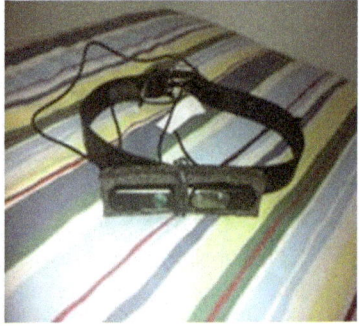

Fig. 9.5 The Xtion Pro Live-Waist assemblies for detecting humans and obstacles [48]

Fig. 9.6 The RGB-D camera-based navigation aid for the visually impaired, which includes an RGB-D camera and a tactile vest interface device [52]

applied a smart sampling method to transduce the important/highlighted information, and/or remove background information, before presenting to visually impaired people. They also reported some preliminary experiments with the BrainPort V100 [23] to investigate the effectiveness of both recognition and navigation that blind people can perform using such a low-resolution tactile device.

Lee and Medioni [52] developed a wearable RGB-D camera-based navigation aid for the visually impaired to navigate low-textured environment as shown in Fig. 9.6. To extract orientational information of the blind users, a visual odometer and feature-based metric topological simultaneous localization and mapping (SLAM) are incorporated. A vest-type interface device with 4 tactile feedback effectors is used to communicate with the user for the presence of obstacles and provide the blind user with guidance along the generated safe path from the SLAM.

Park and Howard [58] presented some preliminary results of development of a real-time haptic telepresence robotic system for the visually impaired to reach specific objects using an RGB-D sensor. As shown in Fig. 9.7, Tamjidi et al. [59] developed a smart cane prototype by adding a SwissRanger SR4000 3D camera [60] for camera's pose estimation and object/obstacle detection in an indoor environment. The SR4000 is an RGB-D sensor and provides intensity and range data of the scene. The SR4000 has a spatial resolution of 176×144 pixels and a field of view of $43.6 \times 34.6°$.

In assistive system development, the user interface design plays a very important role. Without a friendly user interface, it is impossible for blind users to use the device even though the technology is perfect. How the system can best present spatial information nonvisually to the user is one of the center issues together these comprise the human interface for blind users. Ribeiro et al. [49] developed a new approach for representing visual information with spatial audio to help a blind user building mental maps from the acoustic signals and associating them with spatial data. As shown in Fig. 9.8, the prototype device includes a Kinect RGB-D camera, an accelerometer,

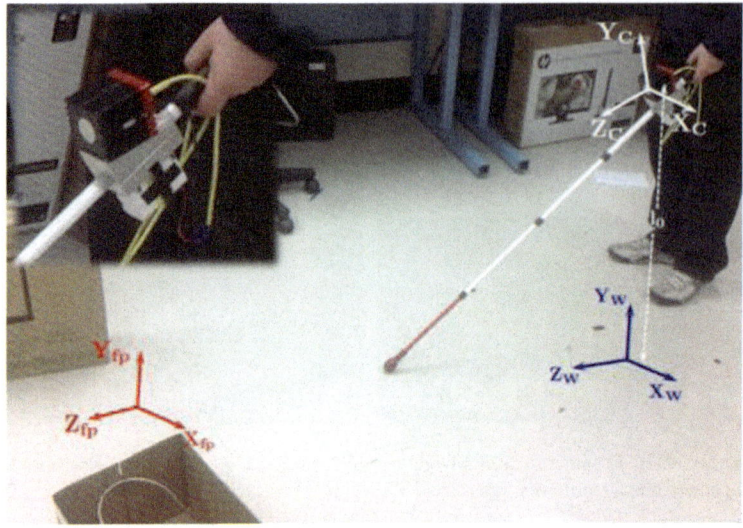

Fig. 9.7 The Smart Cane prototype with a SwissRanger SR4000 3D camera [59]

a gyroscope, and open-ear headphones. They applied computer vision methods for plane decomposition, navigable floor mapping and object detection. Unlike previous work to create acoustic scenes by transducing low-level (e.g., pixel-based) visual information, their method only identifies high-level features of interest in an RGB-

Fig. 9.8 The prototype device of the auditory augmented reality proposed in [49]

D stream. Then, they rendered the location of an object by synthesizing a virtual sound source at its corresponding real-world coordinates. By sonifying high-level spatial features with 3D audio, users can use their inherent capacity for sound source localization to identify the position of virtual objects.

9.4 RGB-D Image-Based Stair and Pedestrian Crosswalk Detection

9.4.1 System Overview

In this section, we describe an RGB-D-based framework to detect staircases and pedestrian crosswalks for blind persons by integrating an RGB-D camera, a microphone, a portable computer, and a speaker connected by Bluetooth for audio description of objects identified. In our prototype system, a mini laptop is employed to conduct image processing and data analysis. The RGB-D camera mounted on the user's belt is used to capture videos of the environment and connected to the mini laptop via a USB connection. The user can control the system by speech input via a microphone. Compared to existing work of staircase detection that only depends on RGB videos or stereo cameras [53–55], our proposed method is more robust and efficient to detect staircases and crosswalks.

As shown in Fig. 9.9, our whole framework consists of stair and crosswalk detection and recognition. First, a group of parallel lines are detected via Hough transform and line fitting with geometric constraints from RGB information. In order to distinguish stairs and pedestrian crosswalks, we extract the feature of one-dimensional depth information according to the direction of the longest detected line from the depth image. Then, the feature of one-dimensional depth information is employed as the input of a support vector machine (SVM)-based classifier [56] to recognize stairs and pedestrian crosswalks. For stairs, a further detection of the upstairs and downstairs is conducted. Furthermore, we estimate the distance between the camera and stairs for the blind user.

9.4.2 Detecting Candidates of Pedestrian Crosswalks and Stairs from RGB Images

There are various kinds of staircases and pedestrian crosswalks. In the application of blind navigation and wayfinding, we focus on detecting stairs or pedestrian crosswalks in a close distance for stair cases with uniform trend and steps, and pedestrian crosswalks of the most regular zebra crosswalks with alternating white bands.

Stairs consist of a sequence of steps that can be regarded as a group of consecutive curb edges, and pedestrian crosswalks can be characterized as an alternating pattern

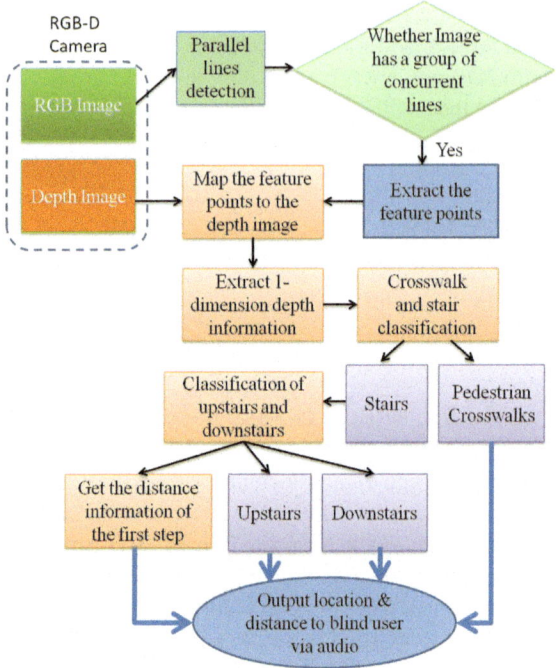

Fig. 9.9 Flowchart of our proposed algorithm for stair and pedestrian crosswalk detection and recognition

of black and white stripes. To extract these features, we first obtain the edge map from RGB image of the scene and then perform a Hough transform to extract the lines in the extracted edge map image. These lines are parallel for stairs and pedestrian crosswalks. Therefore, a group of concurrent parallel lines represent the structure of stairs and pedestrian crosswalks. In order to eliminate the noise from unrelated lines, we add constraints including the number of concurrent lines, line length, etc. We apply Hough transform to detect straight lines based on the edge points by the following steps:

Step1: Detect edge maps from the RGB image by edge detection.
Step2: Compute the Hough transform of the RGB image to obtain the direction of the line.
Step3: Calculate the peaks in the Hough transform matrix.
Step4: Extract lines in the RGB image.
Step5: Detect a group of parallel lines based on constraints such as the length and total number of detected lines of stairs and pedestrian crosswalks.

As shown in Fig. 9.10c, the detected parallel lines of stairs and pedestrian crosswalks are marked as green, while yellow dots and red dots represent the staring points and the ending points of the lines, respectively. However, these lines are often sepa-

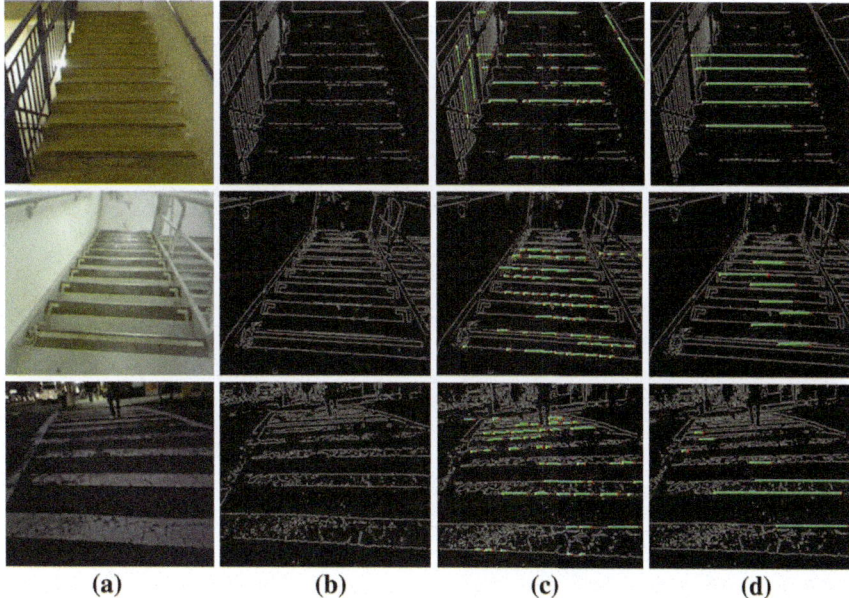

Fig. 9.10 Example of upstairs (*row* 1), downstairs (*row* 2), and pedestrian crosswalks (*row* 3). **a** Original image; **b** edge detection; **c** line detection; **d** concurrent parallel lines detection (*yellow dots* represent the starting points, *red dots* represent the ending points of the lines, and *green lines* represent the detected lines)

rated with small gaps caused by noises, so we group the line fragments as the same line if the gap is less than a threshold. In general, stairs and pedestrian crosswalks contain multiple parallel lines with a reasonable length. If the length of a line is less than a threshold (set as 60 pixels in our system), then the line does not belong to the line group. And if the number of parallel lines is less than 5 (more than two stair steps), the scene image does not contain stairs and pedestrian crosswalks.

9.4.3 Recognizing Pedestrian Crosswalks and Stairs from Depth Images

By detecting parallel lines under the constraints in a scene image captured by an RGB-D camera, we can detect the candidates of stairs and pedestrian crosswalks. From the depth images, we observe that upstairs have rising steps and downstairs have descending steps, and pedestrian crosswalks are flat with smooth depth change as shown in Fig. 9.11. Considering the safeness for the visually impaired people, it is necessary to classify the different stairs and pedestrian crosswalks into the correct categories.

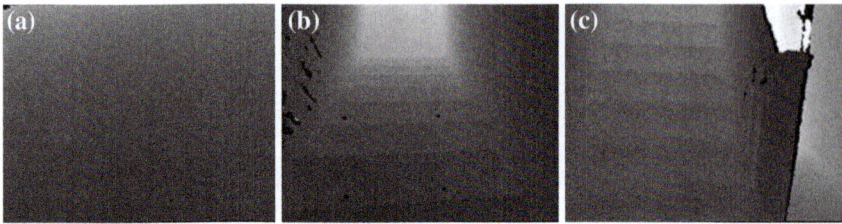

Fig. 9.11 Depth images of **a** crosswalks, **b** downstairs, and **c** upstairs

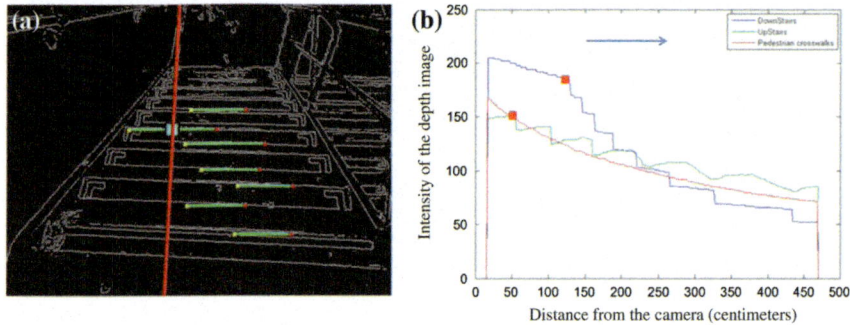

Fig. 9.12 a The orientation and position of the feature line to extract one-dimensional depth features from the edge image. The *blue square* indicates the middle point of the longest line and the *red line* shows the orientation, which is perpendicular to the detected parallel lines. **b** One-dimensional depth feature for upstairs (*green curve*), downstairs (*blue curve*), and pedestrian crosswalks (*red curve*). The *red squares* indicate the first turning points of the one-dimensional depth features of upstairs and downstairs

In order to distinguish stairs and pedestrian crosswalks, we first calculate the orientation and position of the feature line in the edge image to extract the one-dimensional feature from depth information. As shown in Fig. 9.12a, the orientation of the feature line is perpendicular to the parallel lines detected from RGB images. The position of the feature line is determined by the middle point of the longest line of the parallel lines. In Fig. 9.12a, the blue square indicates the middle point of the longest line and the red line is the feature line that indicates the orientation to calculate the one-dimensional depth feature. The typical one-dimensional depth feature for upstairs (green curve), downstairs (blue curve), and pedestrian crosswalks (red curve) is demonstrated in Fig. 9.12b.

The resolution of depth images captured by an RGB-D camera [12, 13] in Fig. 9.11 is 640×480 pixels. The effective depth range of the RGB-D camera is about 0.15–4.7 m. The intensity value range of the depth images is [0, 255]. Therefore, as shown in Fig. 9.12b, the intensities of the one-dimensional depth feature for upstairs, downstairs, and crosswalks are between 50 and 220 (the vertical axis) but are 0 if the distance is out of the depth range of an RGB-D camera. Therefore, the one-dimensional depth feature is a feature vector with 480 dimensions. We observe that the curve for crosswalks is very flat while the curves of upstairs and downstairs are with intensity changes of step shape, which can be used to distinguish stairs and crosswalks. In order to classify upstairs, downstairs, and pedestrian crosswalks, we employ a hierarchical SVM structure by using the extracted one-dimensional depth feature vector as the input. The classification processing includes two steps: (1) one classifier to identify pedestrian crosswalks from stairs. (2) For those detected stairs, one more classifier to further identify upstairs and downstairs.

9.4.4 Estimating Distance Between Stairs and the Camera

When walking on stairs, we should adjust our walking speed and foot height as the stairs have a steep rising or decreasing. For blind users, stairs, in particular downstairs, may cause injury if they fall. Therefore, it is essential to provide the distance information of the first step of the stairs to the blind or visually impaired individuals (i.e., the camera position) to remind them when they should adjust their walking speed and foot height. In our method, the distance information between the first step of the stairs and the camera position is calculated by detecting the first turning point from the one-dimensional depth feature as shown in Fig. 9.12b marked as the red squares.

From the near distance to far distance (e.g., from left side to the right side) as the blue line with arrow shown in Fig. 9.12b along the one-dimensional depth feature, a point x satisfies the following two conditions is considered as a turning point:

$$\|f(x) - f(x-1)\| > \lambda \quad \text{and} \quad \|f'(x) - f'(x-1)\| > \varepsilon$$

where $f(x)$ is the intensity value of the depth information, λ and are the thresholds that are determined by the RGB-D camera configuration. In our experiment, we observe that the best results can be obtained with $\lambda = 8$ and $\varepsilon = 50$.

After we obtain the position of the turning point that indicates the first step of the stairs, the distance information from the camera and the first step of the stairs can be read from the original RGB-D depth data and provided to the blind traveler by speech.

9.4.5 Experiment Results for Stair and Crosswalk Detection and Recognition

Stair and Crosswalk Database: To evaluate the effectiveness and efficiency of the proposed method, we have collected a database for stair and crosswalk detection and recognition using an RGB-D camera [13]. The database is randomly divided into two subsets: a testing dataset and a training dataset. The training dataset contains 30 images for each category (i.e., upstairs, downstairs, crosswalks, and negative images that contain neither stairs nor pedestrian crosswalks) to train the SVM classifiers. Then, the remaining images are used for testing which contains 106 stairs including

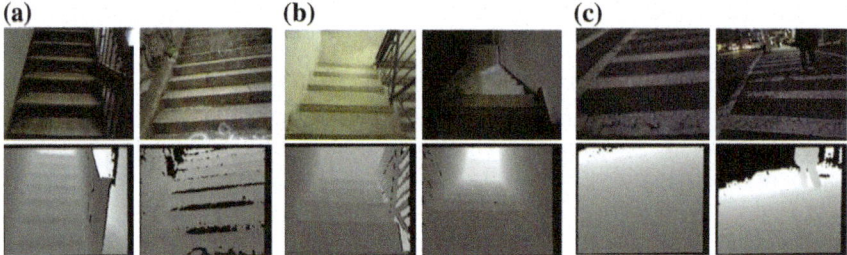

Fig. 9.13 Examples of RGB (*1st row*) and depth images (*2nd row*) for **a** upstairs, **b** downstairs, and **c** pedestrian crosswalks in our database

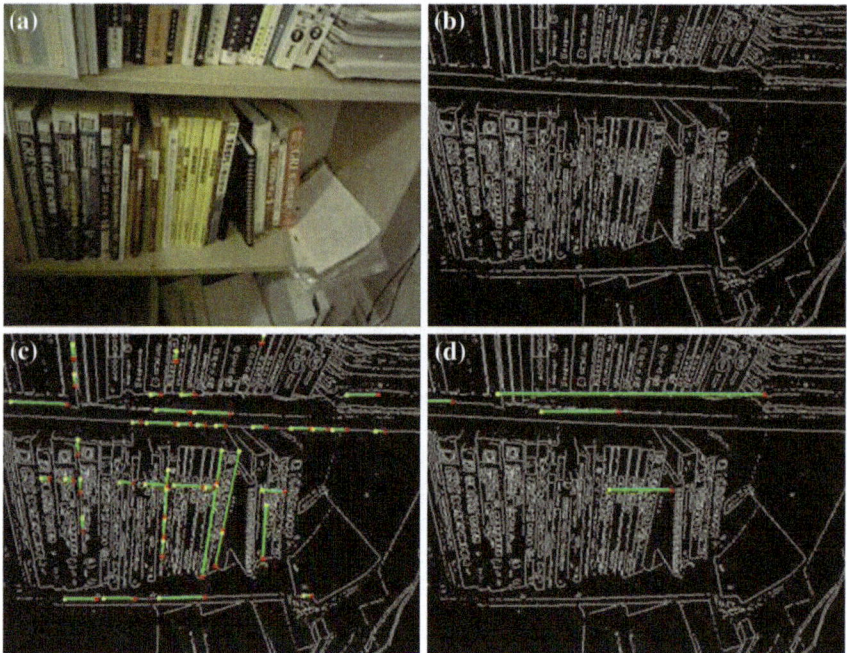

Fig. 9.14 Negative examples of a bookshelf that has similar parallel edge lines to stairs and crosswalks. **a** Original RGB image, **b** edge image, **c** line detection, **d** concurrent parallel lines detection (Yellow dots represent the starting points, red dots represent the ending points of the lines, and green lines represent the detected lines.)

56 upstairs and 50 downstairs, 52 pedestrian crosswalks, and 70 negative images. Here, positive image samples indicate images containing either stairs or pedestrian crosswalks, and negative image samples indicate images containing neither stairs nor pedestrian crosswalks. Some of the negative images contain objects structured with a group of parallel lines such as bookshelves as shown in Fig. 9.14. The images in the dataset include small changes of camera view angels $[-30°, 30°]$. Some of the experiment examples used in our algorithm are shown in Fig. 9.13. The first row

Table 9.1 Detection accuracy of candidates of stairs and pedestrian crosswalks

Classes	No. of samples	Correctly detected	Missed	Detection accuracy (%)
Stairs	106	103	3	97.2
Crosswalks	52	41	11	78.9
Negative samples	70	70	0	100
Total	**228**	**214**	**14**	**93.9**

displays some RGB images of upstairs (Fig. 9.13a), downstairs (Fig. 9.13b), and crosswalks (Fig. 9.13c) with different camera angles and the second row shows the corresponding depth images.

Experiment Results We have evaluated the accuracy of the detection and the classification of our proposed method. The proposed algorithm achieves an accuracy of detection rate at 91.14 % among the positive image samples and 0 % false positive rate as shown in Table 9.1. For the detection of candidates of stairs and crosswalks, we correctly detect 103 stairs from 106 images, and 41 pedestrian crosswalks from 52 images of pedestrian crosswalks. Some of the negative samples are constructed similar edges as stairs and pedestrian crosswalks as shown in Fig. 9.14. With the current RGB-D camera configuration, in general, only one to two shelves can be captured. The detected parallel lines do not meet the constraint conditions. Therefore, the bookshelves are not detected as candidates of stairs and pedestrian crosswalks.

In order to classify stairs and pedestrian crosswalks, the detected candidates of stairs and crosswalks are input into an SVM-based classifier. As shown in Table 9.2, our method achieves a classification rate for the stairs and pedestrian crosswalks at 95.8 % which correctly classified 138 images from 144 detected candidates. A total of 6 images of stairs are wrongly classified as pedestrian crosswalks. All the detected pedestrian crosswalks are correctly classified.

For stairs, we further classify them as upstairs or downstairs by inputting the one-dimensional depth feature into a different SVM classifier. We achieve an accuracy rate of 90.2 %. More details of the classification of upstairs and downstairs are listed in Table 9.3.

Our system is implemented by using MATLAB without optimization. The average processing time for stair and crosswalk detection and recognition of each image is about 0.2 s on a computer with 2.4 GHz processor. This can be easily sped up 10–100 times in C++ with optimization.

Limitations of the Proposed Method of Stair and Crosswalk Recognition In database capture, we observe that it is hard to capture good quality depth images of pedestrian crosswalks compared to capture images of stairs. The main reason is the current RGB-D cameras cannot obtain good depth information for outdoor scenes if the sunshine is too bright. Therefore, the field of view of the obtained depth maps is restricted compared to the RGB images. Some of the images our method cannot handle are shown in Fig. 9.15. For example, the depth information of some parts of the images is missing. Furthermore, as shown in Fig. 9.15c, the zebra patterns of

Table 9.2 Accuracy of classification between stairs and pedestrian crosswalks

Category	Total	Classified as stairs	Classified as crosswalks
Stairs	103	97	6
Crosswalks	41	0	41

In a total of 144 detected candidates of stairs (103) and crosswalks (41), all 41 crosswalks and 97 stairs are correctly classified. Six stairs are wrongly classified as crosswalks

Table 9.3 Accuracy of classification between upstairs and downstairs

Category	Total	Classified as upstairs	Classified as downstairs
Upstairs	53	48	5
Downstairs	50	5	45

In a total of 103 detected candidates of stairs (53 for upstairs and 50 for downstairs), 48 upstairs and 45 downstairs are correctly classified. Five upstairs and five downstairs are wrongly classified

Fig. 9.15 Examples of our proposed method of stair and crosswalk detection fails. **a** Downstairs with poor illumination. **b** Upstairs with less detected lines caused by noise. **c** Pedestrian crosswalks with missing zebra patterns; and **d** Stairs with less steps

pedestrian crosswalks are not always visible caused by the long-time use. In this case, it is hard to extract enough number of parallel lines to satisfy the candidate detection constraints for stair and crosswalk detection. In our method, stairs with less than 3 steps (only have 3 or 4 parallel lines) cannot be detected, as shown in Fig. 9.15d.

9.5 Conclusions and Future Work

In this chapter, we have reviewed several computer vision-based assistive systems and approaches for blind or visually impaired people, especially using RGB-D sensors. There are mainly three main limitations for current RGB-D sensor-based computer vision technology for the application of blind wayfinding and navigation: (1) It is difficult to achieve 100 % accuracy to apply only computer vision-based technology due to the complex environments and lighting changes. Based on the survey we conducted with blind users, we find that most of blind users prefer higher detection accuracy but are willing to accept more meaningful information especially for users who recently lost their vision. (2) For the current available RGB-D sensors, the size is still too large; the resolution is not high enough; the depth range is too short. In addition, they will not work in outdoor environments with direct sunlight. We believe that these limitations will be partially solved with design of next generation of RGB-D sensors. (3) It is hard to develop effective and efficient nonvisual display to blind users due to the huge amount of information images contain. Therefore, the user should be always included in the loop of the computer vision-based blind assistive device.

Theoretically, higher detection accuracy is always better. However, in reality, it is very hard to achieve 100 % detection accuracy in particular for computer vision-based methods due to the complex situations and the lighting changes. For the application to assist blind users, a high detection accuracy and a lower false-negative rate are more desirable. Therefore, it is very important to design a user-friendly interface to provide meaningful feedback to blind users with the detected important information.

We think that an assistive system is not intended to replace the white cane while most blind users using. Instead, a navigation aid can help blind users to gain improved perception and better understanding of the environment so that they can aware the dynamic situation changes. Blind users are the final decision makers who make travel decision and react to local events within the range of several meters. The future research should be focused on enhancing the robustness and accuracy of the computer vision technology as well as more user interface study for blind users.

Acknowledgments This work was supported in part by NSF Grant No. EFRI-1137172, IIP-1343402, FHWA DTFH61-12-H-00002, and Microsoft Research.

References

1. 10 facts about blindness and visual impairment, World Health Organization (2009) Blindness and visual impairment (2009) www.who.int/features/factfiles/blindness/blindness_facts/en/index.html
2. Advance Data Reports from the National Health Interview Survey (2008) http://www.cdc.gov/nchs/nhis/nhis_ad.htm
3. Genensky SM, Baran P, Moshin H, Steingold H (1968) A closed circuit TV system for the visually handicapped
4. Kurzweil R (1976) The Kurzweil reading machine: a technical overview. Sci, Technol Handicapped, pp 3–11
5. Arditi A, Gillman A (1986) Computing for the blind user. Byte 11(3):199–211
6. Dakopoulos D, Bourbakis NG (2010) Wearable obstacle avoidance electronic travel aids for blind: a survey. IEEE Trans Syst Man Cybern Part C Appl Rev 40:25–35
7. Giudice N, Legge GE (2008) Blind navigation and the role of technology. In: Helal A, Mokhtari M, Abdulrazak B (eds) The engineering handbook of smart technology for aging, disability, and independence. Wiley, Hoboken
8. Manduchi R, Coughlan J (2012) Computer vision without sight. Commun ACM 55(1):96–104
9. Roentgen UR, Gelderblom GJ, Soede M, de Witte LP (2008) Inventory of electronic mobility aids for persons with visual impairments: a literature review. J Vis Impairment Blindness 102:702–724
10. Bonin-Font F, Ortiz A, Oliver G (2008) Visual navigation for mobile robots: a survey. J Intell Robot Syst 53(3):263–296

11. DeSouza GN, Kak AC (2002) Vision for mobile robot navigation: a survey. IEEE Trans Pattern Anal Mach Intell 24(2):237–267
12. Microsoft (2010) http://www.xbox.com/en-US/kinect
13. PrimeSense http://www.primesense.com
14. Bousbia-Salah M, Redjati A, Fezari M, Bettayeb M (2007) An ultrasonic navigation system for blind people. IEEE international conference on signal processing and communications (ICSPC), pp 1003–1006
15. Kao G (1996) FM sonar modeling for navigation. Department of Engineering Science, University of Oxford, Technical Report
16. Kuc R (2002) A sonar aid to enhance spatial perception of the blind: engineering design and evaluation. IEEE Trans Biomed Eng 49(10):1173–1180
17. Laurent B, Christian T (2007) A sonar system modeled after spatial hearing and echolocating bats for blind mobility aid. Int J Phys Sci 2 (4):104–111
18. Morland C, Mountain D (2008) Design of a sonar system for visually impaired humans. The 14th international conference on auditory display, June 2008
19. Seeing with Sound—The vOICe:http://www.seeingwithdound.com
20. The Argus II retinal prosthesis system. Available: http://www2-sight.eu/en/product-en
21. VizWiz—Take a Picture, Speak a Question, and Get an Answer". Available: http://www.vizwiz.org/
22. Image Recognition APIs for photo albums and mobile commerce | IQ Engines. Available: https://www.iqengines.com
23. BrainPort lets you see with your tongue, might actually make it to market. Available: http://www.engadget.com/2009/08/14/brainport-lets-you-see-with-your-tongue-might-actually-make-it
24. Chebat DR, Rainville C, Kupers R, Ptito M (2007) Tactile—visual acuity of the tongue in early blind individuals. Neuro Report 18(18):1901–1904
25. Williams MD, Ray CT, Griffith J, De l 'Aune W (2011) The use of a tactile-vision sensory substitution system as an augmentative tool for individuals with visual impairments. J. Vis Impairment Blindness, 105(1):45–50
26. Chebat DR, Schneider FC, Kupers R, Ptito M (2011) Navigation with a sensory substitution device in congenitally blind individuals. Neuro Report 22(7):342–347
27. Coughlan J, Shen HA (2006) Fast algorithm for finding crosswalks using figure-ground segmentation. The 2nd workshop on applications of computer vision, in conjunction with ECCV, 2006
28. Ivanchenko V, Coughlan J, Shen H (2008) Detecting and locating crosswalks using a camera phone. Computers Helping People with Special Needs. (Lecture notes in computer science), 5105:1122–1128
29. Advanyi R, Varga B, Karacs K (2010) Advanced crosswalk detection for the bionic eyeglass. In: Proceedings of the 12th international workshop on cellular nanoscale networks and their applications (CNNA) 2010, pp 1–5
30. Se S (2000) Zebra-crossing Detection for the Partially Sighted. IEEE Conf Comput Vis Pattern Recogn 2:211–217
31. Se S, Brady M (2000) Vision-based detection of stair-cases. In: Proceedings of fourth asian conference on computer vision (ACCV) 2000, pp 535–540
32. Uddin M, Shioyama T (2005) Bipolarity and projective invariant-based Zebra-crossing detection for the visually impaired. 1st IEEE Workshop on computer vision applications for the visually impaired, 2005
33. C Yi, Tian Y, (2011) Assistive text reading from complex background for blind persons. The 4th international workshop on camera-based document analysis and recognition (CBDAR), 2011
34. Wang S, Yi CY, Tian Y (2012) Signage detection and recognition for blind per-sons to access unfamiliar environments. J Comput Vis Image Process 2(2)
35. Yi C, Tian Y, Arditi A, (2013) Portable camera-based assistive text and product label reading from hand-held objects for blind persons. IEEE/ASME Trans Mechatron Accepted, 2013 http://dx.doi.org/10.1109/TMECH.2013.2261083

36. Ye Z, Yi C, Tian Y (2013) Reading labels of cylinder objects for blind persons, IEEE international conference on multimedia & Expo (ICME), 2013
37. Yuan S, Tian Y, Arditi A (2011) Clothing matching for visually impaired persons. Technol Disabil 23:75–85
38. Hasanuzzaman F, Yang X, Tian Y (2012) Robust and effective component-based banknote recognition for the blind. IEEE Trans Syst Man Cybern Part C: Appl Rev, Jan 2012
39. Yang X, Yuan S, Tian Y, (2013) Assistive clothing pattern recognition for visually impaired people. IEEE Trans Hum Mach Syst. Accepted, 2013
40. Tian Y, Yang X, Yi C, Arditi A (2102) Toward a computer vision-based wayfinding aid for blind persons to access unfamiliar indoor environments. Mach Vis Appl, 2012
41. Pan H, Yi C, Tian Y (2103) A primary travelling assistant system of bus detection and recognition for visually impaired people. IEEE Workshop on multimodal and alternative perception for visually impaired people (MAP4VIP), in conjunction with ICME 2013
42. Joseph S, Zhang X, Dryanovski I, Xiao J, Yi C, Tian Y (2013) Semantic indoor navigation with a blind-user oriented augmented reality. IEEE International conference on systems, man, and cybernetics, 2013
43. Wang S, Pan H, Zhang C, Tian Y (2014) RGB-D image-based detection of stairs, pedestrian crosswalks and traffic signs. J Vis Commun Image Represent (JVCIR), 25:263–272, http://dx.doi.org/10.1016/j.jvcir.2013.11.005
44. Arditi A Tian Y (2013) User interface preferences in the design of a camera-based navigation and wayfinding aid. J Vis Impairment Blindness, 107(2):118–129
45. Yi C, Tian Y (2011) Text string detection from natural scenes by structure-based partition and grouping. IEEE Trans Image Process 20(9):2594
46. Yi C, Tian Y (2012) Localizing text in scene images by boundary clustering, stroke segmentation, and string fragment classification. IEEE Trans Image Process 21(9):4256–4268
47. Yi C, Tian Y (2013) Text extraction from scene images by character appearance and structure modeling. Comput Vision Image Underst 117(2):182–194
48. Khan A, Moideen F, Khoo W, Zhu Z, Lopez J, KinDetect: kinect detecting objects. In: Proceedings of the 13th international conference on computers helping people with special needs, 7383, Miesenberger K, Karshmer A, Penaz P, Zagler W (2012) Springer, Berlin Heidelberg, Linz, Austria, July 11–13, 2012, 588–595
49. Ribeiro F, Florêncio D, Chou PA, Zhang Z, (2012) Auditory augmented reality: object sonification for the visually impaired. IEEE 14th international workshop on multimedia signal processing (MMSP), 2012
50. Tang H, Vincent M, Ro T, Zhu Z (2013) From RGB-D to low resolution tactile: smark sampling and early testing. IEEE workshop on multimodal and alternative perception for visually impaired people (MAP4VIP), in conjunction with ICME 2013
51. Wang Z, Liu H, Wang X, Qian Y (2014) Segment and label indoor scene Based on RGB-D for the visually impaired. MultiMedia modeling, Lecture Notes in Computer Science 8325:449–460
52. Lee YH, Medioni G (2011) A RGB-D camera based navigation for the visually impaired. RGB-D: advanced reasoning with depth camera work-shop, June 2011
53. Lee YH, Leung T, Médioni G (2012) Real-time staircase detection from a wearable stereo system. ICPR, Japan
54. Lu X, Manduchi, R (2005) Detection and localization of curbs and stairways using stereo vision ICRA, 2005
55. Wang S, Wang H (2009) 2D staircase detection using real adaboost. Information, communications and signal processing (ICICS), 2009
56. Chang C, Lin C (2001) LIBSVM: a Library for support vector machine, 2001. http://www.csie.ntu.edu.tw/~cjlin/libsvm
57. Velazquez R (2010) Wearable assistive devices for the blind. Book chapter In Lay-Ekuakille A Mukhopadhyay SC (Eds), Wearable and autonomous biomedical devices and systems for smart environment: issues and characterization, LNEE 75, Springer, pp 331–349, 2010

58. Park CH, Howard AM (2013) Real-time haptic rendering and haptic telepresence robotic system for the visually impaired. World haptics conference (WHC), 2013
59. Tamjidi A, Ye C, Hong S (2013) 6-DOF pose estimation of a portable navigation aid for the visually impaired. IEEE international symposium on robotic and sensors environments, 2013
60. SR4000 User Manual (http://www.mesa-imaging)
61. Marion AH, Michael AJ (Eds) (2008) Assistive technology for visually impaired and blind people. Springer, London
62. Zhang Z (2012) Microsoft kinect sensor and its effect. IEEE MultiMedia 19(2):4–10
63. Han J, Shao L, Xu D, Shotton J (2013) Enhanced computer vision with microsoft kinect sensor: a review. IEEE Trans Cybern, Oct 2013

Chapter 10
RGB-D Human Identification and Tracking in a Smart Environment

Jungong Han and Junwei Han

Abstract Elderly and disabled people can particularly benefit from smart environments with integrated sensors, as they offer basic assistive functionalities enabling personal independence and increased safety. In a smart environment, the key issue is to quickly sense the location and identity of its users. In this paper, we aim at enhancing the robustness of human detection and identification algorithm in a home environment based on the Kinect, which is a new and multimodal sensor. The contribution of our work is that we employ different cameras for different algorithmic modules, based on investigating the suitability of each camera in Kinect for a specific processing task, resulting in an efficient and robust human detection, tracking and re-identification system. The total system consists of three processing modules: (1) object labeling and human detection based on depth data, (2) human reentry identification based on both RGB and depth information, and (3) human tracking based on RGB data. Experimental results show that each algorithmic module works well, and the complete system can accurately track up to three persons in a real situation.

10.1 Introduction

The concept of smart environments or ambient intelligence refers to physical spaces equipped with sensors feeding into adaptive algorithms that enable the environment to become sensitive and responsive to the presence of people. It is a vision on an imminent future to be brought about by the confluence of consumer electronics,

---

The major work was done while Jungong Han was working in CWI.

J. Han (✉)
Civolution Technology, Eindhoven, The Netherlands
e-mail: jungonghan77@gmail.com

J. Han
School of Automation, Northwestern Polytechnical University, Xi'an, China

distributed networking, and intelligent computing. In a smart environment, people carry out their everyday activities in easy and comfortable way using information and intelligence that is hidden in the network connecting devices and sensors. The concept of smart environment has been verified and provided to consumers recently. There are various example homes over the world with such embedded intelligent networks, where societies experiment with such technologies. Elderly and disabled people can particularly benefit from such environments, as they offer basic assistive functionalities, enabling personal independence, and increased safety.

The core technology in a smart environment is to detect and track the people and recognize their actions and intentions. The task is normally accomplished by analyzing video signals captured by camera sensors. However, one fundamental problem in this area is that human segmentation and tracking algorithms based on RGB images cannot always provide reliable results. This holds particularly when the environment is cluttered or people suddenly change the illumination conditions, both of which occur frequently in a realistic setting.

This chapter intends to address this problem by selectively combining two types of cameras. The feature of our work is that we complementarily use cameras for different algorithmic purposes and exploit their different properties and specific advantages. Basically, our goal is the implementation of a reliable system for person identification and tracking based on a consumer sensor [10] that is well balanced between the system robustness and efficiency. The system is supposed to be used in a smart home environment because the number of people to be tracked is small. The work introduced in this chapter is an improved version of our previous system [8] in the sense that we redesign the algorithms for human detection and reentry identification.

10.2 Related Work

In our system, there are three key technical components: human detection, human tracking, and human re-identification. For the sake of clarity, we will introduce existing works in each filed, respectively.

10.2.1 Human Detection

The research for human detection generally develops in two ways. At the early stage, researchers exploit the shape matching to distinguish the human and other objects [13]. The basic idea is to measure the distance between the shape of extracted person and shapes stored in the dataset. The human shapes in the dataset normally take different viewpoints (frontal or side view) and different scales of the human into account. If one of the computed distances is smaller than a pre-defined threshold, the detected object is assigned to be a person. Apart from the fact that it is difficult to extract the human silhouette (shape) from the image, the matching is less robust but time consumed considering variations in both shape scales and viewpoints. Therefore, such methods are merely used in the constrained situations, where the complete human shape can be always available and the real-time processing is not needed.

Recently, researchers turn their eyes to more realistic situations, in which a complete human silhouette cannot be extracted easily due to the cluttered background and image noises. Local features, such as Harr wavelet feature, histograms of oriented gradients (HOG), and edgelet features, are derived from the original image. Various discriminative classification techniques including support vector machines (SVMs) and boosted ensemble learning are employed to determine an optimal decision boundary between pattern classes in a feature space. The major drawback of this type of methods is that the local feature is variant to the camera view change.

With the advent of affordable RGB-D sensors, depth image-based human detection has attracted attention in the computer vision community. In Xia [19], authors propose a model-based approach, which detects human using a 2D head contour model and a 3D head surface model. In the first step, the algorithm scans across the whole image and gives the possible regions that may contain people. The candidate region is further examined using a 3D head model, which exploits the relational depth information. Afterward, it matches the 3D model against all the detected regions to make the decision. This 3D head model is generated off-line based on many training samples. The work reported in Salas [15] also tries to detect the head–shoulder shape on a depth image. The innovation is a fast descriptor that calculates the histogram of depth differences. Spinello et al. [17] propose a descriptor, called histogram of oriented depths (HOD), which locally encodes the direction of depth changes and relies on an depth-informed scale space search. Moreover, it also designs a probabilistic scheme to combine HOG and HOD so as to obtain more robust detection. For more detailed introduction, we refer to a survey paper [10].

10.2.2 Human Tracking

A lot of publications have been devoted to this area. One type of systems only utilizes a depth camera to detect and track persons. The algorithm [3] starts with a segmentation of the scene between background and foreground (moving) regions using depth information. Tracking is developed based on considering both human motion and depth changes. A better method is proposed by Hansen et al. [9], where a background model is built by fusing information from intensity and depth images. The EM (Expectation Maximization) algorithm is used for tracking moving clustering of pixels significantly different for the background model. The work done in Arif [1] focuses on improving the foreground detection using graph-cut technique. In general, the tracking based on depth data will fail in the situation that persons have similar depths when occlusion occurs. Another drawback is that it is not possible to distinguish people using depth data only.

On the other hand, some systems fuse the depth information with the RGB information of the image. In Crabb [4], authors fuse depth and color data to segment the foreground pixels in a video sequence. The basic idea is to generate a sort of probability map for each pixel based on depth data, where larger probability means this pixel is likely to be a foreground pixel. Pixels that cannot be definitively classified as foreground or background, typically about 1–2 % of the image, are checked again on the color image considering the edge information. Though the algorithm only conducts an object segmentation task, its execution time is already about 10 frames per second on a powerful PC. The work reported by Gould [6] fuses laser range and color data to train a robot vision system. For each pixel in the robot's field of view, it has color/intensity, depth, and surface normal information, which help to extract 3D features. This technique indeed improves the detection accuracy by 10 %, but the speed of the algorithm is far from the real time (a few seconds per image). In Sabeti [14], two separate particle filter trackers, one using color and the other using depth data, are employed to track objects. The approach is not suitable for real time as it involves heavy processing. Generally speaking, the performance of the algorithm fusing color and depth is better than the algorithm using single-type information only. However, the way of fusing data is too straightforward in the sense that data from different channels are treated equally without considering the advantage of sensor. Therefore, most algorithms cannot reach real-time requirement.

10.2.3 Human Re-identification

Basically, our human re-identification algorithm relies on the visual signature extracted from the RGB image. Therefore, the literature study focuses on those publications dedicated to RGB image human re-identification. Existing works have exploited various features, such as color, texture, human shape, and position. Here, we briefly introduce several representatives for each category.

Plain means, histograms, or the mixture of them on different *color* spaces (e.g., RGB, HSV) [12] are widely used in the descriptors. Regarding the texture features, covariance matrices [2], feature-point-based local descriptors [7], and LBP features [11] have been exploited. Popular shape-related features include width/height ratio, body orientation, moment invariants, and contours. Human position in the image is commonly adopted to match people in the setup with overlapping cameras, given the camera transformation matrix. This information is pretty useful when tracing a person across different cameras.

10.3 Algorithm Description

Our system is a typical indoor video surveillance system that detects humans, identifies humans, and then tracks them. Compared to the system we described in Han [8], the functional modules are more or less the same. However, the algorithms, such as human detection and re-identification, are significantly improved. In this chapter, we focus on two enhanced algorithms: human detection and human reentry identification. For the details of other modules, we refer to our previous publication [8].

10.3.1 Detecting Humans

The task of this module is to determine whether or not a newly detected object is a human-like. If affirmative, we will extract human visual signature (based on features) and compare it against a database of recorded visual signatures of previously observed persons.

As we mentioned previously, segmentation algorithm based on the depth can reliably provide the human silhouette in the realistic situations. Therefore, it enables the possibility of using shape cues to deduce the exist of a human. However, it is still difficult to extract the full-body human silhouette from the image due to the occlusions either among individuals or objects in the scene. To be practical, we turn to analyze the shape of the human upper body, which can always be available in our application.

The next problem is to find viewpoint invariant visual features describing the human shape, as it is realistic to assume a fixed angle between a human and the camera in this scenario. In Fig. 10.1a, we show three typical views of human upper body occurring frequently in the ordinary life. They are front/rear view and two side views with different body orientations. Here, we try to investigate the common features shared by the frontal view and two side views. It is noticed that there are three interesting observations that help to describe the human upper-body shape, each being briefly introduced below.

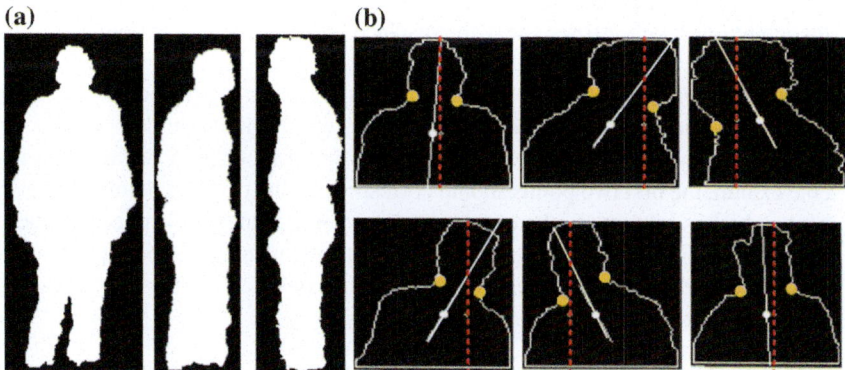

Fig. 10.1 Shape-based human detection. **a** Different views of the human body. **b** Feature extraction from *upper* body of the human with varying postures

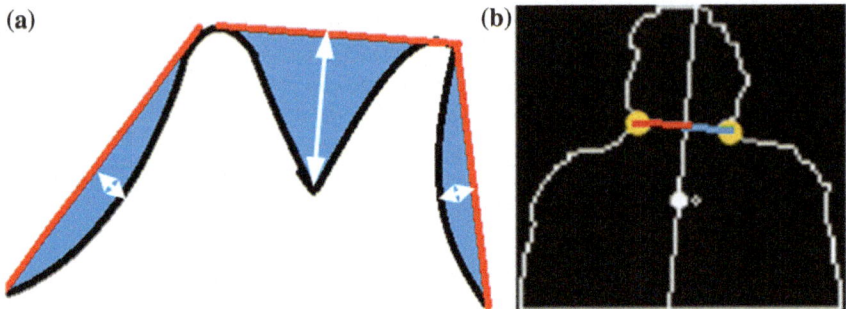

Fig. 10.2 Convex hull example. **a** Convexity defects of a contour. **b** The distance between the farthest point to a convex hull and the human main axis

- *Peak of the projected histogram.* One can see a peak point if we project the human upper-body silhouette to the x-axis. Meanwhile, this peak point is likely to be near the intersection point of the upper-body orientation axis and the head contour, regardless of different postures. This observation can be clearly confirmed by Fig. 10.1b, where the red dash line indicates the x-coordinate of the peak point and the white straight line implies the orientation axis of the human. It can be seen that the distance between two intersection points (the red line with the human contour and the white line with the human contour, respectively) is indeed not large even though the human postures and camera view angles may vary.
- *Convexity defects of the contour.* A useful way of comprehending the shape of an object is to compute a convex hull for the object and then compute its convexity defects. In Fig. 10.2a, we use an intuitive example to show how the convexity defects look like. Here, the black curve is supposed to be the contour of the extracted object; the red line indicates the convex hull around the object; the blue areas refer to the convexity defects in the object contours relative to the convex hull; and the white lines with arrows imply the distance between the farthest point and the convex hull.
- *Symmetry of the defect points.* The defect point here refers to the point having the farthest distance to the convex hull. Normally, we can find one defect point for each convexity defect. If we sort these points in terms of their distances to the convex hull, the first two points should correspond to the two side points of human neck, which is immune to the camera viewing point changes. Symmetry of these two points means that the two points extracted from the human upper body should be located at the different sides of the main axis, and the distances of two points to the main axis should be more or less identical.

Based on the above observations, we are able to generate a feature vector with five dimensions, which is denoted as $\mathbf{vf} = [n_p, d_{pm}, n_d, l_d, d_{dm}]$. In this vector, the first two parameters are related to the projected histogram of human upper-body shape, e.g., n_p refers to the number of peak points extracted from the projected histogram, and d_{pm} represents the distance between the highest peak point and the intersection point of the contour and the body main axis. The other three parameters characterize the convexity defects of the contour. More specifically, n_d means the number of defect points by computing the convex hull based on the contour. The parameter l_d is a binary digit: either 1 or 0. If the first two defect points are located in the different sides of the main axis, l_d equals to 1; otherwise, it is 0. Last, d_{dm} measures the distance different between these two defect points and the main axis. Generating this feature vector for each input silhouette needs to know the main axis of the human upper body as well as the convexity defects. We explain the related techniques in the following sections.

10.3.1.1 Human Upper-Body Main Axis Estimation

Main axis of the human upper-body part implicitly reflects body's tilted degree. Suppose that the human pixel is located in the 2D space (x and y), from the mathematical point of view, this main axis is the direction on which the pixel distribution has the largest variance. Therefore, the well-known *principal component analysis* (PCA) technique is adopted to compute the main axis in our algorithm. Suppose that the location of a pixel belonging to a human silhouette can be represented as (x, y), the covariance matrix Σ based on all human pixels is computed by:

$$\Sigma = \begin{bmatrix} E((x-\mu_x)(x-\mu_x)) & E((x-\mu_x)(y-\mu_y)) \\ E((y-\mu_y)(x-\mu_x)) & E((y-\mu_y)(y-\mu_y)) \end{bmatrix}. \quad (10.1)$$

Here, μ_x and μ_y denote the average value of pixels' positions in x and y directions, respectively. The orientation of the main axis can be obtained by a singular value decomposition (SVD) of the covariance matrix Σ, decomposing Σ into the matrix product $\Sigma = USV'$. The angle of the main axis ϕ is calculated as:

$$\phi = \arctan\left(\frac{V(1,1)}{V(1,2)}\right). \quad (10.2)$$

In Fig. 10.1b, we show a few examples, where the human tilts the body. Seen from the results (white line), our main axis detection technique can indeed follow the change of the posture.

10.3.1.2 Contour Convexity Analysis

The central task of this algorithm is to compute the convexity defects, given the human upper-body silhouette. In the first step, we find the contour of the human silhouette described by a set of boundary points of human body. Here, a border following algorithm [18] designed for digitized binary images is employed. Next, we further reduce the number of unwanted convexity points by approximating the contour with a polygon that has fewer vertices. The algorithm recursively connects a

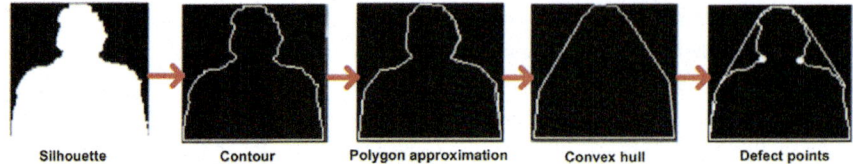

Fig. 10.3 The steps to compute contour convexity

start point and an end point of a line segment by finding the vertex furthest away from the line segment. Later on, we exploit Sklansky's algorithm [16] to find the convex hull of a 2D point set. The output of this step is a sequence containing the hull points. In the last step, we intend to find convexity defects by drawing the convex hull around the contour of the upper body enclosing all points of it. Regions where the contour departs from the convex hull are convexity defects. A defect is characterized by start, end, and depth points. The depth point is called here as the defect point, which has the farthest distance to the convex hull. In Fig. 10.3, we demonstrate each step of our convexity analysis algorithm including contour finding, polygon approximation, convex hull, and defect point detection.

10.3.1.3 Boosted Ensemble Learning for Human Detection

Once we have obtained the visual features for describing the human shape, it is required to deduce whether the input features are related to a human or not. A typical solution is classification algorithms that allow for learning and making decision based on the observations. In this paper, we adopt the popular Adaboosting-based ensemble classifier due to its outstanding capability of handling inhomogeneous multidimensional data.

The basic idea is to combine simple "rules" to form an ensemble so as to boost the performance of the single ensemble. In other words, the single ensemble can be considered as a weak classifier, which is based on a single feature and can provide the results quickly. The final ensemble equals to a strong classifier that combines many weak classifiers. This classification algorithm is suited to the applications that use inhomogeneous features, because the weak classifier can be constructed based on each individual feature without considering the distributions of other features. Mathematically, given a high-dimensional dataset $D = x_1, x_2, ..., x_n$ and their corresponding labels $L = l_1, l_2, ..., l_n$, an ensemble algorithm computes the following: (1) a set of classifiers $f_1, f_2, ..., f_k$, each of which maps data to a class label $f_j(x) = l$ and (2) a combination of classifiers f^* which minimizes generalization error:

$$f^*(x) = \sum_{t=1}^{k} \alpha_t f_t(x), \quad (10.3)$$

where α_t is the wight of the tth weak classifier. In our work, we construct a weak classifier based on a single feature from vector **vf** and use Adaboosting framework to compute optimal weight for each weak classifier. Finally, a trained classifier $f^*(x)$ helps us to decide whether a detected object is a human or not.

10.3.2 Human Reentry Identification Based on Online Learning

As we mentioned previously, two key issues for an online human identification algorithm are as follows: (1) efficient visual features that best discriminate the human appearances and (2) training samples that help the classifier to learn the variation of the human appearances at different positions. A common challenge for these two issues is that we cannot assign the heavy load to the online learning and decision part, because we need immediate result in our application. That is, neither feeding a high-dimensional feature vector into the classifier nor training a classifier with a lot of samples may not be allowed. To solve the first problem, we extract the region-based features from the human appearance, instead of pixel-based visual features that usually generate a high-dimensional feature vector. To deal with the second problem, we take the advantage of the object depth information provided by the depth sensor. The idea is to collect the representatives from the samples at different depth levels. It leads to a better classifier that is able to handle the variation of human appearance at different depth levels where the lighting casted into the human body may be slightly changed.

10.3.2.1 Feature Extraction for Human Identification

In our system, we jointly employ two types of features to distinguish persons. One is the human height, and the other one is the appearance information of the human. Here, the human height actually means the length of the human in the image. It may not be that useful in the RGB image-based algorithms, as this feature is varying dependent on the distance between the human and the camera. However, it can be useful when the depth information is available, because the relationship between the distance to the camera and the object length is linear for small lookdown angles, which is specified by:

$$l(d) = a_1 d + a_2, \tag{10.4}$$

where a_1 and a_2 are two parameters to drive this linear relation. In other words, if a_1 and a_2 are known, we can always compute the human length, given the exact depth of the human. The difference between the computed length and the length measured from the image may help us to distinguish persons. For example, suppose that person A's parameters (a_1 and a_2) are available and are stored in a dataset. Now, an unknown person B is entering into the scene and is detected by our algorithm. Obviously, the length of the person B can be measured from the image, and the depth (distance to the camera) of this person can be obtained from the depth sensor. Using Eq. (10.4), we can estimate the length of the person at the given depth. Afterward, we compare this estimated length with the real length measured from this image. If this difference is too large, person B is definitely not the person A, because the true height of a person is fixed.

Let us now discuss how we implement this idea in our system. Suppose that we have obtained m positive samples and n negative samples for a person at different depth levels in the scene, the a_1 and a_2 in Eq. (10.4) can thus be estimated in the least squares sense based on m positive samples only. Once these two parameters have been available, we can estimate the length for each sample (both positive and negative samples) based on Eq. (10.4), given its depth information. The difference between this estimated length and the length measured from the image is the first element of our feature vector, which indicates the "height" of a given training sample. Ideally, the value of this feature should be around 0 for all positive samples and should be much larger than 0 for all negative samples. Hence, the first element in the feature vector h_d can be formulated as:

$$h_{\text{diff}} = |(l_{\text{img}} - (a'_1 d + a'_2)|, \qquad (10.5)$$

where l_{img} refers to the length of the detected human in the image, and two parameters a'_1 and a'_2 are obtained based on all positive samples. d is the depth of the detected human, which can be directly acquired from the depth sensor.

The second type of our features is related to the appearance of a human. Unlike exiting algorithms that utilize the histogram-based appearance model, we employ here a sort of region-based appearance statistics due to two reasons. First, histogram-based appearance model is normally deployed on the color space, so that it usually has many dimensions. This will impose heavy computational load to our data learning part, which is not preferred. Second, traditional histogram-based appearance model does not take the spacial relation of the human body parts into account. For instance, a person wearing a white shirt and a pair of black pants may have more or less the same appearance model with another person, who wears a black shirt and a pair of white pants. The basic idea of the region-based method is to model the human appearance based on several spatially adjacent regions, where each region may correspond to a human body part. The usage of the region-based method can definitely solve the second problem mentioned above, because it takes the spatial relation of regions into account. As for the first problem, this method can also partially solve it in the sense that the statistics for a few regions will not result in a high-dimensional feature vector. However, it comes with the pain, because normally, region segmentation algorithm is computationally expensive. To reduce the harm, we carry out the segmentation algorithm in the second thread paralleling to the main thread. By doing so, we can ensure that the classifier executing on the main thread can always provide real-time response.

Figure 10.4 depicts our algorithmic architecture. When a new person is entering into the scene, the classifiers will be triggered and will decide whether this new person can be linked to one of existing IDs or not. If he/she appeared before, we

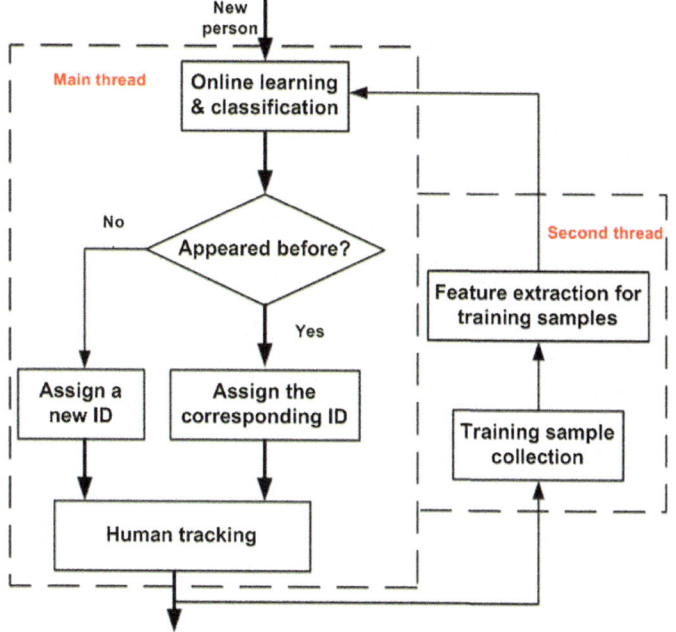

Fig. 10.4 Human reentry identification

assign the same ID to this new person, and his/her locations over the time will be recorded by a tracking algorithm. If it is a new person, we assign a new ID to this person. Meanwhile, the positive training samples as well as the negative ones are collected based on the tracking results. Here, the negative samples are arranged in an *cross-validation* manner, where the positive sample of person A can be used as the negative sample of person B. Once we have obtained the sufficient number of training samples, the extracted feature vectors for both positive samples and the negative samples will be fed into the classifier for an online learning.

Prior to calculating statistics for regions, it is required to segment the human body into several adjacent regions. Here, we exploit a graph-based image segmentation algorithm proposed by Felzenszwalb et al. [5]. We further cluster the regions into two groups: upper-limb part and lower-limb part. The criterion for partitioning is mainly based on the ratio of the human body. More specifically, reusing the contour convexity analysis explained previously can roughly locate the human neck. If the neck positive is available, it is not difficult to compute the length of the human head in the image. According to the human body ratio, it is possible to approximate the bottom boundary of the upper-limb part, from which the lower-limb part starts. It is noted that the upper-limb part we defined in the paper does not include the human head region, because it is less discriminative than other regions when distinguishing persons.

Once we have obtained these two region groups, we can compute a sort of "*entropy*", which is relevant to the number of the region and the size of the region as well. Assume that we have a set of spatial regions $\{R_1, R_2, ..., R_m\}$ within the upper-limb part and the lower-limb part, the entropy H is defined as:

$$H = -\sum_{i=1}^{m} P_i \log_2 P_i, \qquad (10.6)$$

where P_i denotes the probability of the region R_i, and it is:

$$P_i = \frac{\text{size}(R_i)}{\sum_{j=1}^{m} \text{size}(R_j)}, \qquad (10.7)$$

where size $(\cdot)$ counts the number of pixels within the region.

Next, for each group (upper-limb and lower-limb), we select a *dominant* region to be the representative of the group. This procedure can be formulated by:

$$\hat{R} = \arg\max_{R_i} \text{size}(R_i), \qquad R_i \in \Phi. \qquad (10.8)$$

Here, Φ refers to a set of spatial regions within either upper-limb part or lower-limb part. Suppose that $\hat{R}_{ud}$ and $\hat{R}_{ld}$ represent the dominant region of the upper-limb part and the lower-limb part, respectively. We then compute the simple statistics, such as μ and σ, for each of two regions. It is noticed that we calculate the statistics for each color space separately. Therefore, there are 6 parameters for each dominant region. If we use two dominant regions to describe the human appearance, we will have a statistic vector with 12 elements.

In our system, we do not directly use this 12-elements vector to be the feature vector. Instead, we propose to use the maximal distance between regions as the feature. More specifically, suppose that the statistics of $\hat{R}_{ud}$ and $\hat{R}_{ld}$ are $S_u = [\mu_{ur}, \mu_{ug}, \mu_{ub}, \sigma_{ur}, \sigma_{ug}, \sigma_{ub}]$ and $S_l = [\mu_{lr}, \mu_{lg}, \mu_{lb}, \sigma_{lr}, \sigma_{lg}, \sigma_{lb}]$, respectively. We first compute the *average* statistics for these two dominant regions based on all positive samples, which are denoted as $\bar{S}_u = [\bar{\mu}_{ur}, \bar{\mu}_{ug}, \bar{\mu}_{ub}, \bar{\sigma}_{ur}, \bar{\sigma}_{ug}, \bar{\sigma}_{ub}]$ and $\bar{S}_l = [\bar{\mu}_{lr}, \bar{\mu}_{lg}, \bar{\mu}_{lb}, \bar{\sigma}_{lr}, \bar{\sigma}_{lg}, \bar{\sigma}_{lb}]$, respectively. The maximal distance is defined as:

$$D = \max(\text{dist}(S_u, \bar{S}_u), \text{dist}(S_l, \bar{S}_l)), \qquad (10.9)$$

where dist $(\cdot, \cdot)$ measures the Euclidean distance between two vectors. The main purpose is to reduce the dimension of the feature vector, so that the online learning and inference running on the main thread will not have heavy computation. Eventually, the feature vector for describing a person consists of three elements, which are h_diff, H, and D.

Another important issue is the selection of the positive training samples. The real-time response requested by our application does not allow to use a huge number of training samples. In other words, we may have to choose a small number of samples that are able to reflect the variation of the feature. In our application, we noticed that the variation is mainly the color variation of the human appearance. It can be observed that the color of the human appearance may change at different locations, because the lighting in the scene is not uniformly distributed. It is partially determined by the distance to the lighting source and also to the camera position. To solve this problem, we take the advantage of the available depth information again. The basic idea is to choose the training samples in terms of the depth of the human in the scene. More specifically, in our system, we divide the scene into several intervals in terms of the depth (the distance to the camera). We try to choose the same number of samples from each interval. By doing so, we can ensure that we collect the positive training samples that better describe the color variation of the human appearance. This scheme is better than existing solutions, such as randomly choosing samples or selecting representatives using clustering algorithm. Many samples selected randomly may come from the same local region if the person stands still for a long time, while the clustering-based selection method may be computationally expensive. The selection of the negative samples is relatively simple. That is, the positive samples of person A can be used as the negative samples of person B.

Until this stage, we have obtained both positive and negative training samples and have extracted feature vector for each sample; the next step is to train the classifier and infer whether a new detected person appeared before or not. Similar to our human detection algorithm, we use here the boosted ensemble learning method, because the features in the feature vector are inhomogeneous in the sense that they try to discriminate persons from different aspects, e.g., human height and human appearance. We construct a weak classifier based on each feature in the feature vector and use Adbossting algorithm to eventually form a strong classifier.

10.4 Experimental Results

Our system is implemented using C++ on a laptop PC platform (Dual core 2.53 GHz, 4 GB RAM). Our software is based on OpenNI library and OpenCV library, where the former provides the functions to drive the Kinect sensor and implements the object labeling module, while the second library provides basic computer vision algorithms. We have tested the presented system in two difference situations. Each individual algorithm has been evaluated using recorded video sequences while the entire system is tested via a live demonstration in an office environment.

Our object labeling module has been evaluated and compared with a GMM-based foreground pixel detection algorithm. To highlight the difference, we test algorithms in three different situations. First, a person is moving in a room with uniform and stable lighting conditions and his cloth is clearly different with the background. In the second situation, the moving person wares the cloth, which is similar to the background. In the last situation, a person suddenly turns off the light in the room. Obviously, the last two situations are more challenging, but they occur regularly in the realistic environments. Figure 10.5 gives comparison results (the ground truth

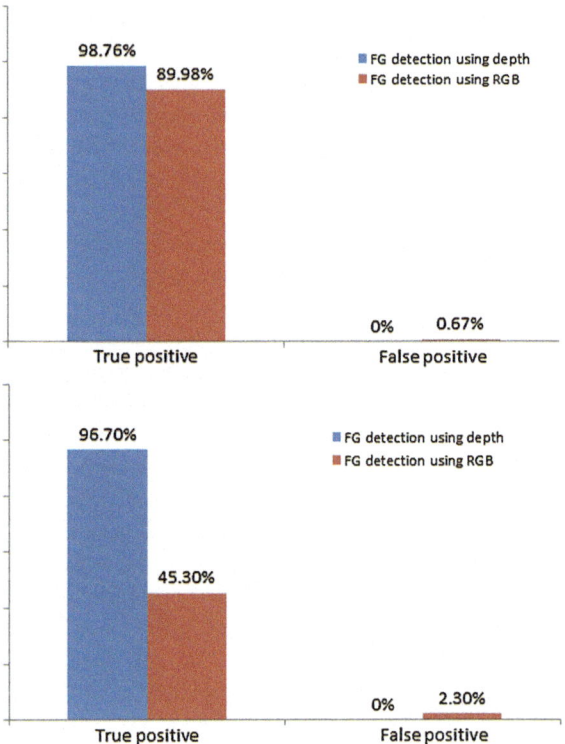

Fig. 10.5 Human segmentation results

is generated manually) [8] for the first situation and the second situation as well. The left bars represent the true positive of the detections, and the right bars indicate the false positive of the detections. It can be noticed from the results that GMM algorithm based on RGB images performs properly in the first situation. However, the performance drops significantly when dealing with the second situation. For the third situation, we do not provide quantitative comparison, because the performance difference is extreme.

Our human detection module has been tested based on several video sequences ($>5k$ frames). The classifier is first trained based on 600 training samples, in which the number of positive and negative samples is equal. The positive samples are binary images obtained from the segmentation module. In Fig. 10.6, we showed some examples for both positive and negative samples. Overall, we have obtained 97 % accuracy rate without generating any false positives. It is noticed that the common failure happens when the player bends the body.

We have also evaluated the human tracking module based on 5 videos (in total 2,600 frames) involving 2 to 3 persons. We have compared it with the mean shift tracker and also a particle filter tracker. The evaluation criterion is that the bounding

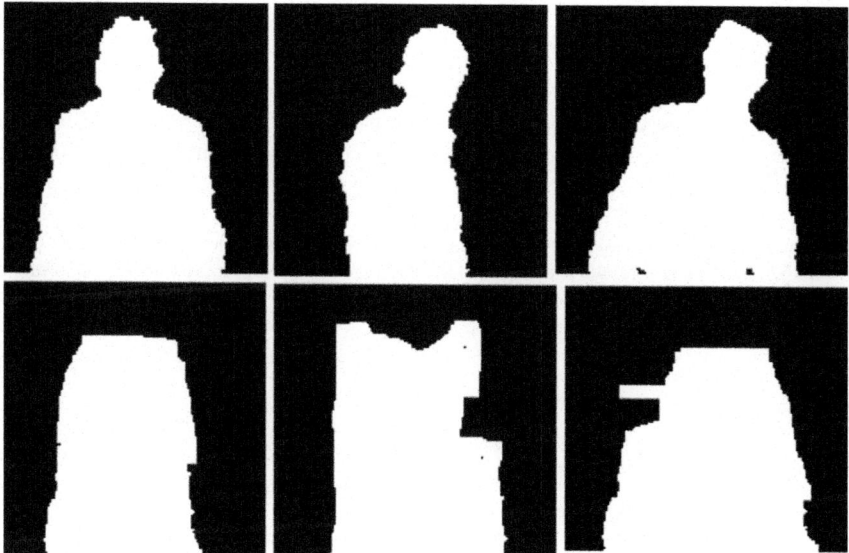

Fig. 10.6 Training samples for human detection. *Top* the positive samples. *Bottom* the negative samples

box should include at least 70 % human body. To test the robustness of our algorithm, we change the illumination of the lighting during one video. The overall accuracy of our tracker is 96.27 %, the accuracy of the particle filter tracker is 83.54 %, and the accuracy of the mean shift tracker is 71.23 %. According to the results, mean shift tracker does not handle occlusion properly, and particle tracker deteriorates on the video where we change the illumination. In contrast to these two algorithms, our tracker fails only once when two person pass by each other (occlusion) after changing the lighting conditions. Our tracker actually works properly even after changing the lighting. The failure reason is that we need to re-identify one person after he was occluded, but the visual signature of this person was generated prior to changing the lighting. This illumination change confuses our re-identification module. We believe that we can solve this problem if we update visual signature of a person regularly.

Eventually, we have set up a demonstration at an office environment and have invited 5 colleagues to test the system. Currently, the system is not possible to track 5 persons simultaneously in real time. Therefore, we limit the number of people within the camera view to 3. The system was running for more than one hour and we did not find any identification errors. In addition, the algorithm can handle one or two persons case properly, but it cannot provide real-time detection when three persons were entering the scene at the same time.

10.5 Conclusion

We have proposed a two-camera system based on the Kinect sensor, which enables human detection, tracking, and re-identification. The system can be the fundamental for a smart environment application. The results obtained by our system can be the input to a human behavior recognition, generating intelligent decisions.

Acknowledgments The major work has been done while Jungong Han was employed by CWI, the Netherlands. Therefore, we would like to thank Dr. Eric Pauwels for granting the opportunity to work on this interesting topic.

References

1. Arif O, Daley W, Vela P, Teizer J, Stewart J (2010) Visual tracking and segmentation using time-of-flight sensor. In: Proceedings of ICIP, pp 2241–2244
2. Bak S, Corvee E, Bremond F, Thonnat M (2010) Person re-identification using spatial covariance regions of human body parts. In: Proceedings of IEEE conference on advanced video and signal-based surveillance, pp 435–440
3. Bevilacqua A, Di L, Azzari S (2006) People tracking using a time-of-flight depth sensor. In: Proceedings of IEEE international conference video and signal based surveillance, pp 89–93
4. Crabb R, Tracey C, Puranik A, Davis J (2008) Real-time foreground segmentation via range and color imaging. In: Proceedings of CVPR workshop on TOF-CV
5. Felzenszwalb P, Huttenlocher D (2004) Efficient graph-based image segmentation. Int J Comp Vis 59(2):167–181
6. Gould S, Baumstarck P, Quigley P, Ng M, Koller A (2008) Integrating visual and range data for robotic object detection. In: Proceedings of ECCV workshop on multi-camera and multimodal sensor fusion
7. Hamdoun O, Moutarde F, Stanciulescu B, Steux B (2008) Person re-identification in multicamera system by signature based on interest point descriptors collected on short video sequences. In: Proceedings of international conference on distributed smart cameras, pp 16
8. Han J, Pauwels E, de Zeeuw P, de With P (2012) Employing a RGB-D sensor for real-time tracking of humans across multiple re-entries in a smart environment. IEEE Trans Consum Electron 58(2):255–263
9. Hansen D, Hansen M, Kirschmeyer M, Larsen R, Silvestre D (2008) Cluster tracking with time-of-flight cameras. In: Proceedings of CVPR workshop on TOF-CV
10. Han J, Shao L, Xu D, Shotton J (2013) Enhanced computer vision with Microsoft Kinect sensor: a review. IEEE T Cybernetics 43(5):1318–1334
11. Hirzer M, Roth M, Kstinger M, Bischof H (2012) Relaxed pairwise learned metric for person re-identification. In: Proceedings of ECCV, Springer, pp 780793.
12. Nakajima C, Pontil M, Heisele B, Poggio T (2003) Full-body person recognition system. Pattern Recogn 36(9):1997–2006
13. Rodriguez M, Shah M (2007) Detecting and segmenting humans in crowded scenes. In: Proceedings of ACM multimedia, pp 353–356
14. Sabeti L, Parvizi E, Wu Q (2008) Visual tracking using color cameras and time-of-flight range imaging sensors. J Multimedia 3(2):28–36. (ACM)
15. Salas J, Tomasi C (2011) People detection using color and depth images. Pattern Recogn, Springer 6718:127–135
16. Sklansky J (1982) Finding the convex hull of a simple polygon. PRL 1:79–83
17. Spinello L, Arras KO (2011) People detection in RGB-D data. In: Proceedings of IROS

18. Suzuki S, Abe K (1985) Topological structural analysis of digitized binary images by border following. CVGIP 30(1):32–46
19. Xia L, Chen C, Aggarwal JK (2011) Human detection using depth information by Kinect. In: Proceedings of computer vision and pattern recognition workshops (CVPRW), pp 15–22

Part IV
Learning-Based Recognition

Chapter 11
Feature Descriptors for Depth-Based Hand Gesture Recognition

Fabio Dominio, Giulio Marin, Mauro Piazza and Pietro Zanuttigh

Abstract Depth data acquired by consumer depth cameras provide a very informative description of the hand pose that can be exploited for accurate gesture recognition. A typical hand gesture recognition pipeline requires to identify the hand, extract some relevant features and exploit a suitable machine learning technique to recognize the performed gesture. This chapter deals with the recognition of static poses. It starts by describing how the hand can be extracted from the scene exploiting depth and color data. Then several different features that can be extracted from the depth data are presented. Finally, a multi-class support vector machines (SVM) classifier is applied to the presented features in order to evaluate the performance of the various descriptors.

11.1 Introduction

Hand gesture recognition is an intriguing problem for which many different approaches exist. Even if gloves and various wearable devices have been used in the past, vision-based methods able to capture the hand gestures without requiring to wear any physical device allow a more natural interaction with computers and many other devices. This problem is currently raising a high interest due to the rapid growth of application fields where it can be efficiently applied, as reported in recent surveys (e.g., [6, 30]). However, hand gesture recognition from images or video data is a very challenging task. The hand and fingers can assume a huge variety of poses and there are often several inter-occlusions between the various fingers. Furthermore, the skin

---

F. Dominio (✉) · G. Marin · M. Piazza · P. Zanuttigh
Department of Information Engineering, Via Gradenigo 6/B, 35131 Padova, Italy
e-mail: dominiof@dei.unipd.it

G. Marin
e-mail: maringiu@dei.unipd.it

M. Piazza
e-mail: mauropia@dei.unipd.it

P. Zanuttigh
e-mail: zanuttigh@dei.unipd.it

© Springer International Publishing Switzerland 2014
L. Shao et al. (eds.), *Computer Vision and Machine Learning with RGB-D Sensors*,
Advances in Computer Vision and Pattern Recognition,
DOI: 10.1007/978-3-319-08651-4_11

has a relatively uniform color that does not help feature extraction and recognition schemes. For all these reasons, it is difficult to recognize complex gestures from the 2D representation given by a single image or from a video.

The introduction of Microsoft's Kinect sensor has made the acquisition of 3D information available to the mass marker, thus paving the way for new solutions for many challenging computer vision problems, including object tracking and recognition, human activity analysis, indoor 3D mapping, and also hand gesture recognition. A complete review of them is presented in [7]. In the computer gaming field, Microsoft's Kinect has already brought gesture interfaces to the mass market, but many new application fields are being considered. These include human-computer interaction, 3D navigation, robotics, gaming, sign-language recognition, vehicle control, and many others. Hand gestures can be used to replace the mouse in computer interfaces and to allow a more natural interaction with mobile devices like smartphones and tablets, but also with newer wearable devices like the Google glasses and other similar tools. Besides controlling standard 2D interfaces, a very interesting field is the interaction with 3D virtual environments, that is much more natural if gestures performed in the 3D space are used. Another key application is automatic sign-language interpretation, that would allow hearing and speech impaired people to interact with computers and other electronic devices. Finally, the healthcare field is another field in which hand gesture recognition can be used for a more natural control of diagnostic data and surgical devices.

Depth data intrinsically contains a very informative three-dimensional description of the hand pose, which can be exploited for gesture recognition. The simplest approaches just use depth data to reliably extract the hand silhouette. This allows us to directly apply many methods derived from color-based hand gesture recognition, but only exploits a limited amount of the information contained in depth data. This chapter shows how several features based on the three-dimensional data in the depth map, representing the hand shape and the finger posture, can be extracted and used to properly recognize complex gestures.

In order to show how depth data can be used in hand gesture recognition, it is assumed that a generic hand gesture recognition scheme encompasses three main steps:

- Hand extraction
- Feature extraction
- Gesture classification

The chapter follows this subdivision and the following sections describe the three main steps. Section 11.3 explains how the hand can be recognized both from depth and color data, by also considering its segmentation into arm, palm and fingers regions. Then the extraction of feature descriptors is analyzed in detail in Sect. 11.4. Several different possible descriptors are presented, including 3D distances from the palm center or from the palm plane, descriptors based on the contour of the hand (e.g., curvature features or approaches based on the perimeter length), convex hull-based features, and other schemes. In order to compare the efficiency of the various features, a classification scheme based on support vector machines (SVM) is presented in Sect. 11.5 and the obtained accuracies from a real dataset are reported in Sect. 11.6. Finally, Sect. 11.7 draws the conclusions.

11.2 Related Work

Hand gesture recognition has been the subject of a large amount of research activity. Until a few years ago, computer vision approaches were only based on the images or videos framing the hand. These methods typically exploit the shape of the hand silhouette, color or motion information to extract relevant features to be used for the gesture recognition. A complete overview of these approaches is out of the scope of this chapter, which focuses on depth information. Complete reviews of this field can be found in [30, 34].

The recent availability of consumer depth cameras based on structured light, like the Kinect or the Asus Xtion, and of matricial Time-Of-Flight sensors, e.g., the Creative SENZ3D or Mesa's Swiss Ranger, has opened the way to a new family of approaches exploiting depth information. Depth data offer an accurate description of the hand pose and compared to images and videos there are several advantages. They include the possibility of capturing the 3D orientation of the hand parts, the availability of metric measures in the 3D space and much simpler options for the hand segmentation.

The basic pipeline of most methods consists in the three steps indicated in Sect. 11.1. Hand segmentation is typically solved by a simple thresholding of the depth data [18, 25]. A common assumption used in this step is that the hand is the closest object to the sensor. After extracting the samples corresponding to the hand only, several different methods may be used for the following steps. A first family of approaches is based on the hand silhouette extracted from the depth data: in [13] silhouette and cell occupancy features are extracted from the depth map and used for building a shape descriptor that is then fed into a classifier based on action graphs. Histograms of the distance of the hand points from its center, extracted from the silhouette, are used in [24, 25]. Other approaches in this family use features based on the convex hull and on the fingertips positions computed from the silhouette, as in [14, 33]. The convex hull is also exploited in the open source library *XKin* [21, 22].

Another possibility is computing descriptors based on the volume occupied by the hand. In [27], 3D volumetric shape descriptors are extracted from the depth map and fed into a SVM classifier. A similar approach is exploited by [32].

Color data can also be used together with the depth data, as in [23], that is based on randomized decision forests (RDFs). RDFs are also used by Keskin et al. [10].

All these approaches are focused on the recognition of static poses, other methods, instead, deal with dynamic gestures. For example, [2] exploits motion information, and in particular the trajectory of the hand centroid in the 3D space, for recognizing dynamic gestures. Depth and color information are used together in [3] to extract the trajectory that is then fed to a dynamic time warping (DTW) algorithm. Finally,

Wan et al. [31] exploit both the convex hull on a single frame and the trajectory of the gesture.

Among the various application of hand gesture recognition, sign-language recognition is one of the most interesting. An approach for sign-language recognition with the Kinect is proposed in [26].

A different but related problem is the extraction of the 3D hand pose, which can then be exploited for gesture recognition. Approaches exploiting depth data for this task are [1, 9, 20].

11.3 Hand Extraction

The first step of the considered gesture recognition pipeline, indicated in Sect. 11.1, consists in segmenting the hand from the rest of the scene, since all the information of the performed gesture is entirely contained in the hand region. The region of the arm is usually discarded, as it does not contain any helpful information about a particular gesture and its shape and size are affected by the presence of sleeves and bracelets. Hand extraction is a crucial step because all the following processing is performed on the segmented region only.

Different methods have been used over the years to tackle this problem, exploiting different clues like appearance, shape, color, depth, context, and tracking. In order to take advantage of both the color and the depth map from the sensor, a joint calibration of color and depth camera [8] is required. Joint calibration, in fact, allows to associate a color and a depth value to each point in the framed scene.

The most common methods based on appearance exploit cascade classifiers based on Haar-like features [29]. However, differently from faces, which have fixed properties related to the position of the mouth, eyes and nose, hands have many degrees of freedom, and so this technique does not produce satisfactory results.

A common scenario is to have users facing the camera with their hand held in front of themselves. This allows to assume that the hand is the closest object to the sensor. In this case, a simple threshold in depth range can be used to isolate the hand. Additional geometric constraints in the hand aspect ratio and size may be used to refine the segmentation, as in [15]. Other approaches exploiting only the depth map, use clustering algorithms such as K-means, iterative seed fill or region growing to separate the hand region from the rest of the scene. In [11], the depth range is fixed and a flood fill algorithm is used to cluster contiguous points with the aim of separate the hand from the body. In [14] instead, the K-means algorithm with two clusters is used in a limited depth range to find the hands.

The assumption that the hand has to be the closest object in the scene can be relaxed by predicting hand depth according to the position of other body parts, such as the face. In addition, since the color image is available as well, skin color segmentation can be used to enforce the hand detection. In [28], skin color segmentation based on both a model trained offline and a further online histogram-based refinement are used to get an initial guess for hand detection. Then, the user face is detected and all the points not belonging to a predefined region in front of the face are rejected. Once the hand is detected, the arm is removed by exploiting the depth and other geometrical constraints.

Color data can be combined with the depth in order to improve the accuracy and better segment the hand from the arm, as in [4]. Other approaches also exploit some physical aids, e.g., in [25], after thresholding the depth map, a black bracelet on the gesturing hand's wrist is recognized in the color image for an accurate hand detection.

More reliable approaches exploit the temporal redundancy to better find and segment the hand, reducing false positive detection. For example, [13] first divide depth map into a number of blobs using a connected-component labeling algorithm, then, for the biggest blob that is assumed to include the body and the hand, compute blob tracking, the blob with the highest track is associated to the hand. Additional geometric constraints are used to identify and remove points of the wrist region.

Once the hand has been extracted, it is also necessary to estimate its position and orientation to ensure that the recognition is rotational and scale invariant. Scale invariance can be easily obtained since, if calibration data are available, depth provide metric measures in the 3D space. The orientation can be computed by detecting the principal direction, e.g., with principal component analysis (PCA) or by fitting a plane on the hand point cloud.

An example of efficient hand segmentation scheme that exploits both color and depth information is presented in [5] and is briefly recalled here. This approach also allows to extract useful information for features extraction that will be exploited in the next section. The acquired depth map $D(u, v)$ is firstly thresholded on the basis of color information. More specifically, the colors associated with the samples are converted into the CIELAB color space and compared with a reference skin color that has been previously acquired, e.g., from the face by using a standard face detector [29]. After the skin color thresholding, the hand region has a higher chance to be the nearest object to the camera.

Let $\mathbf{X}_i = \mathbf{X}_{u,v}$ denote a generic 3D point acquired by the depth camera, that is, the back-projection of the depth sample in position (u, v). A search for the sample with the minimum depth value $D_{\min}$ on the thresholded depth map, avoiding isolated artifact, is performed and the corresponding point $\mathbf{X}_{\min}$ is chosen as the starting point for the hand detection procedure. Points belonging to the hand samples set $\mathscr{H}$ are the ones whose distance from $\mathbf{X}_{\min}$ does not exceed a predefined threshold $T_{\max}$:

$$\mathscr{H} = \{\mathbf{X}_i | \, ||\mathbf{X}_i - \mathbf{X}_{\min}|| < T_{\max}\} \quad (11.1)$$

This algorithm allows to reliably segment the hand samples from the scene objects and from the other body parts. An example of a thresholded depth map obtained with this approach is shown in Fig. 11.1c.

In order to extract some of the feature sets described in Sect. 11.4, it is first necessary to obtain some additional information such as the hand orientation, its centroid, the palm, and fingers regions. A possible approach is to consider the binary mask of the hand samples in the depth image and filter it with a Gaussian kernel obtaining a result similar to the one in Fig. 11.1d. The resulting blurred image represents the hand

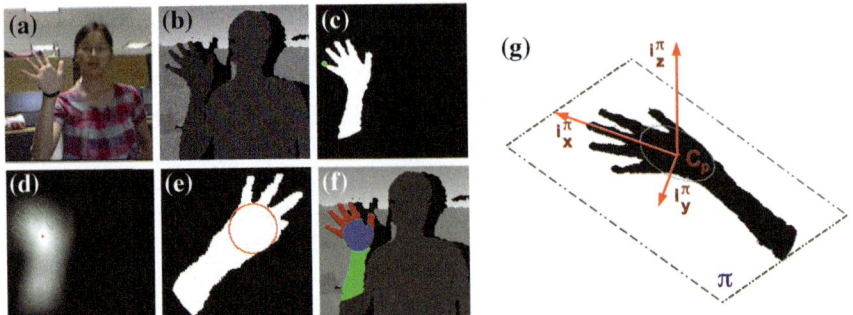

Fig. 11.1 Extraction of the hand and palm samples: **a** acquired color image; **b** acquired depth map; **c** extracted hand samples (the closest sample is depicted in *green*); **d** output of the Gaussian filter applied on the mask corresponding to $\mathcal{H}$ with the maximum in *red*; **e** *Circle* fitted on the sample gesture; **f** palm (*blue*), finger (*red*) and wrist (*green*) regions subdivision; **g** reference system $(\mathbf{i}_x^\pi, \mathbf{i}_y^\pi, \mathbf{i}_z^\pi)$

samples density, where the luminance is directly proportional to the points density, and the point with the maximum intensity (that is, the one representing the maximum density) is chosen as initial value of the palm center. This value can then be refined by fitting a circle or an ellipse [17] whose center and size are updated iteratively by ensuring that most of the points belong to the hand samples. When the process converges, the points of the hand within the fitted shape will give an estimate of the palm region, while the 3D point corresponding to the center of the fitted shape will be the *centroid* **C** of the hand. Note that the *centroid* plays an important role in the features extraction, as most of them strongly depend from the centroid position. At this point, the hand region $\mathcal{H}$ can be segmented into three regions:

- $\mathcal{P}$ containing points corresponding to the hand palm.
- $\mathcal{W}$ containing the points of $\mathcal{H}$ lying on the sub-space below $\mathcal{P}$. Such samples typically belong to the wrist and forearm and are not considered in most gesture recognition schemes.
- $\mathcal{F}$ containing the points of $\mathcal{H} - \mathcal{P} - \mathcal{W}$, which corresponds to the fingers region.

It is useful also to define the set $\mathcal{H}_e = \mathcal{P} + \mathcal{F}$ containing the points of the palm and the fingers, and its projection $\mathcal{B}$ on the binary mask.

Once all the possible palm samples have been detected, a 3D plane π can be fitted on them by using SVD and RANSAC to get its position in 3D space. PCA can be applied, instead, to the 3D points in $\mathcal{H}$ in order to extract the main axis that roughly corresponds to the direction $\mathbf{i}_x$ of the vector going from the wrist to the fingertips.

In order to build a 3D coordinate system centered on the palm centroid projected on π, i.e., $\mathbf{C}^\pi$, the axis $\mathbf{i}_x$ is projected on plane π obtaining $\mathbf{i}_x^\pi$, then $\mathbf{i}_z^\pi$ is the normal to plane π, and the remaining axis $\mathbf{i}_y^\pi$ is obtained by the cross-product of $\mathbf{i}_z^\pi$ and $\mathbf{i}_x^\pi$ thus forming a right-handed reference system $(\mathbf{i}_x^\pi, \mathbf{i}_y^\pi, \mathbf{i}_z^\pi)$, as depicted in Fig. 11.1g.

Finally, the information on the hand orientation and the palm radius can be used to remove all the wrist samples. Let R be the estimated palm radius and

$\mathbf{X}_i^\pi = (x_i^\pi, y_i^\pi, z_i^\pi)$ the coordinates of an hand sample $\mathbf{X}_i$ with respect to the palm 3D coordinate system: it is possible to assume that $\mathbf{X}_i^\pi$ belongs to the wrist whenever $x_i^\pi < -R$ (recall that the x axis points form the palm center to the fingertips as shown in Fig. 11.1g).

11.4 Extraction of the Relevant Features

The next step consists in extracting feature sets from the segmented hand data which will be used for the classification of the performed gestures. Several different types of features have been proposed in the literature, as shown in Sect. 11.2, based on both color and depth data. This section focuses on the information that can be extracted from depth data and presents a set of possible features to be used for reliable gesture recognition. The considered features are:

- **Distance features**: describe the Euclidean 3D distances of the fingertips from the estimated palm center.
- **Elevation features**: account for the Euclidean distances of the fingertips from a plane fitted on the palm samples. Such distances may also be considered as the *elevations* of the fingers with respect to the palm.
- **Contour histogram similarity features**: account for the similarity between the contour points distances in the performed gesture and in the reference acquisitions of the various gestures.
- **Curvature features**: describe the curvature of the contour of the palm and fingers regions.
- **Palm area features**: describe the shape of the palm region and helps to state whether each finger is raised or bent on the palm.
- **Convex hull features**: various feature can be extracted from the convex hull of the hand shape in the depth map. They include the ratios between the area or the perimeter of the hand shape to the one of its convex hull and the number of vertexes in the convex hull.
- **Connected-components features**: they are based on the connected components in the difference between the hand shape and its convex hull. The dimensions and the number of the connected components can be used as features.

11.4.1 Distance Features

The computation of this feature set starts from the construction of an histogram representing the distance of the edge samples in $\mathscr{F}$ from the hand centroid $\mathbf{C}^\pi$. Here, a brief description of the approach of [5] and [4], that in turn extends the scheme of [25], is given.

Let R be the 3D radius of the circle back-projected to the plane π, if the more accurate fitting model with the ellipse is employed, R represents the distance from C^π to the edge of the ellipse and is not a constant value. For each 3D point $\mathbf{X}_i \in \mathcal{F}$, the normalized distance from the centroid $d_{\mathbf{X}_i} = \|\mathbf{X}_i - \mathbf{C}^\pi\| - R$ and the angle $\theta_{\mathbf{X}_i}$ between vector $\mathbf{X}_i^\pi - \mathbf{C}^\pi$ and axis $\mathbf{i}_x^\pi$ on the palm plane π (where $\mathbf{X}_i^\pi$ is the projection of $\mathbf{X}_i$ on π) are computed. Then θ is quantized with a uniform quantization step Δ into a discrete set of values θ_q. Each θ_q thus corresponds to an angular sector $\mathcal{I}(\theta_q) = \theta_q - \frac{\Delta}{2} < \theta \leq \theta_q + \frac{\Delta}{2}$, and the farthest point inside each sector $\mathcal{I}(\theta_q)$ is selected thus producing a histogram $L(\theta)$:

$$L(\theta_q) = \max_{\mathcal{I}(\theta_q)} d_{\mathbf{X}_i} \qquad (11.2)$$

For each gesture in the dataset, a reference histogram $L_g^r(\theta)$ of the type shown in Fig. 11.2 is built. A set of angular regions corresponding to the raised fingers intervals in each gesture (shown in Fig. 11.2) is also defined and will be used for computing the features.

The hand direction estimated by means of the PCA main axes is not very precise and furthermore is affected by several issues, e.g., the number of raised fingers in the performed gesture and the size of the retained wrist region after hand detection. The generated distance histogram, therefore, may not be aligned with the gesture templates, and a direct comparison of the histograms in this case is not possible. In order to compare the performed gesture histogram with each gesture template, they are firstly aligned by looking for the argument maximizing the cross-correlation between the acquired histogram and the translated version of the reference histogram of each gesture.[1] The possibility of flipping the histogram to account for the fact

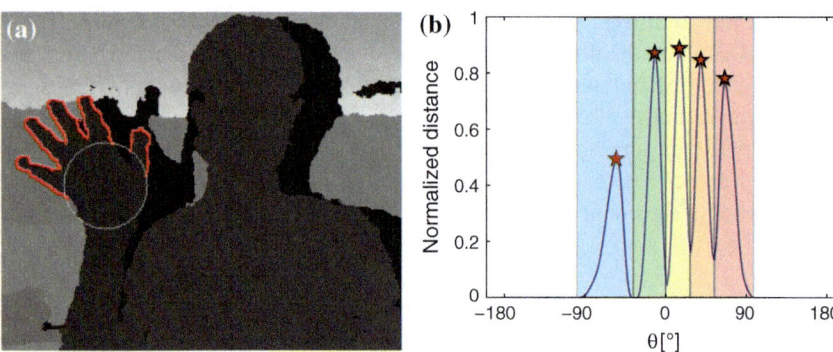

Fig. 11.2 Histogram of the edge distances with the corresponding feature regions: **a** finger edges $\mathcal{F}$; **b** associated histogram $L(\theta)$ with the regions corresponding to the different features $f_{g,j}^l$ (feature points highlighted with *red stars*)

---

[1] In Eqs. (11.3) and (11.4) L is considered as a periodic function with period 2π.

that the hand could have either the palm or the dorsum facing the camera is also considered, by evaluating:

$$\Delta_g = \underset{\Delta}{\operatorname{argmax}} \left(\rho \left(L(\theta), L_g^r(\theta + \Delta) \right) \right)$$
$$\Delta_g^{\text{rev}} = \underset{\Delta}{\operatorname{argmax}} \left(\rho \left(L(-\theta), L_g^r(\theta + \Delta) \right) \right) \quad (11.3)$$

where symbol $\rho(a(\cdot), b(\cdot))$ denotes the value of the cross-correlation between $a(\cdot)$ and $b(\cdot)$. The translational shift Δ that gives the maximum of the correlation of either $L(\theta)$ or $L(-\theta)$ in (11.3) is used to align the acquired histogram with the reference histograms of each gesture. Let $L_g(\theta)$ denote the histogram aligned to the gesture reference histogram $L_g^r(\theta)$. The translational shift to be applied to $L(\theta)$ will be either Δ_g and Δ_g^{rev} depending on the one maximizing the correlation, i.e., $L_g(\theta)$ is defined as:

$$L_g(\theta) = \begin{cases} L(\theta - \Delta_g) & \text{if } \rho\left(L(\theta), L_g^r(\theta + \Delta_g)\right) \geq \rho\left(L(-\theta), L_g^r(\theta + \Delta_g^{\text{rev}})\right) \\ L(-\theta - \Delta_g^{\text{rev}}) & \text{otherwise} \end{cases}$$
(11.4)

Note that there can be a different alignment Δ_g for each gesture, and that different regions can be defined in each gesture reference histogram corresponding to the various features of interest. This approach basically compensates for the limited accuracy of the direction computed by the PCA.

The alignment procedure solves one of the main issues related to the direct application of the approach of [25]. Figure 11.3 shows some examples of the computed histograms for three different gestures. Note that the fingers raised in the various gestures are clearly visible from the plots.

If the database has G different gestures to be recognized, the feature set contains a value for each finger $j \in \{1, \ldots, 5\}$ in each gesture $g \in \{1, \ldots, G\}$. The feature value $f_{g,j}^l$ associated with finger j in gesture g corresponds to the maximum of the aligned histogram within the angular region $\mathscr{I}(\theta_{g,j}) = \theta_{g,j}^{\min} < \theta < \theta_{g,j}^{\max}$ associated with finger j in gesture g (see Fig. 11.2), i.e.,

$$f_{g,j}^l = \frac{\underset{\mathscr{I}(\theta_{g,j})}{\max} L_g(\theta)}{L_{\max}} \quad (11.5)$$

All the features are normalized by the length $L_{\max}$ of the middle finger in order to scale them within range $[0, 1]$ and to account for the fact that hands of different people have different sizes. Note that there can be up to $G \times 5$ features, though their actual number is smaller since not all the fingers are raised in each gesture. The distance features are collected into feature vector $\mathbf{F}^l$.

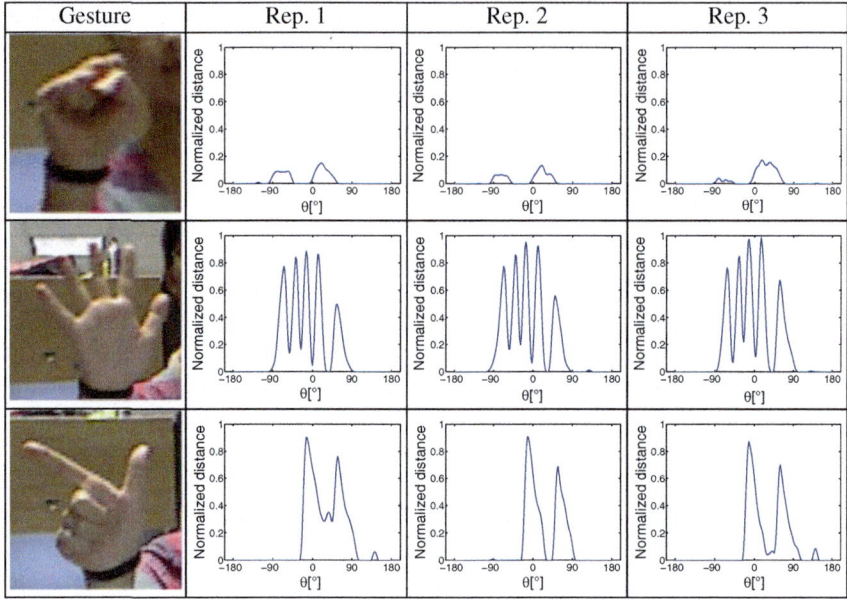

Fig. 11.3 Examples of aligned distance histogram $L_g(\theta)$ for 3 sample frames corresponding to different gestures

11.4.2 Elevation Features

The construction of the elevation features is analogous to the one employed for the distance features of Sect. 11.4.1. The process starts by building an histogram representing the distance of each sample in $\mathscr{F}$ from the palm plane π, namely, for each sample $\mathbf{X}_i$ in $\mathscr{F}$ its distance from plane π is computed:

$$e_{\mathbf{X}_i} = \text{sgn}\left((\mathbf{X}_i - \mathbf{X}_i^\pi) \cdot \mathbf{i}_y^\pi\right) |\mathbf{X}_i - \mathbf{X}_i^\pi| \qquad (11.6)$$

where $\mathbf{X}_i^\pi$ is the projection of $\mathbf{X}_i$ on π. The sign of $e_{\mathbf{X}_i}$ accounts for the fact that $\mathbf{X}_i$ can belong to any of the two semi-spaces defined by π, that is, $\mathbf{X}_i$ can either be on the front or behind π.

Now, as for the distance features, for each angular sector corresponding to a θ_q, the point with greatest absolute distance from the plane is selected, thus producing an histogram:

$$E(\theta_q) = \begin{cases} \max_{\mathscr{I}(\theta_q)} e_{\mathbf{X}_i} & \text{if } \left|\max_{\mathscr{I}(\theta_q)} e_{\mathbf{X}_i}\right| > \left|\min_{\mathscr{I}(\theta_q)} e_{\mathbf{X}_i}\right| \\ \min_{\mathscr{I}(\theta_q)} e_{\mathbf{X}_i} & \text{otherwise} \end{cases} \qquad (11.7)$$

Note that $E(\theta_q)$ uses the same regions computed in Sect. 11.4.1. The histogram $E(\theta)$ corresponding to the performed gesture is then aligned to the various reference gestures in G using the alignment information already computed in Sect. 11.4.1. Let $E^g(\theta)$ be the histogram $E(\theta)$ aligned with the template gesture g. The elevation features are then computed according to:

$$f_{g,j}^e = \begin{cases} \dfrac{1}{L_{\max}} \max_{\mathscr{I}(\theta_{g,j})} E^g(\theta) & \text{if } \left|\max_{\mathscr{I}(\theta_{g,j})} E^g(\theta)\right| > \left|\min_{\mathscr{I}(\theta_{g,j})} E^g(\theta)\right| \\ \dfrac{1}{L_{\max}} \min_{\mathscr{I}(\theta_{g,j})} E^g(\theta) & \text{otherwise} \end{cases} \quad (11.8)$$

Note that the vector $\mathbf{F}^e$ of the elevation features has the same structure and number of elements of the vector $\mathbf{F}^l$ of the distance features.

11.4.3 Contour Histogram Similarity Features

This feature set is based on the similarity between distance histograms of Sect. 11.4.1. For each considered gesture, a reference acquisition is selected and the corresponding distance histogram is computed with the approach of Eq. 11.2, thus obtaining a set of reference histograms $L_g^r(\theta)$, where g is the considered gesture. The distance histogram of the acquired gesture $L(\theta_q)$ is also computed and the maximum of the correlation between the current histogram $L(\theta_q)$ and a shifted version of the reference histogram $L_g^r(\theta)$ is selected:

$$R_g = \max_\Delta \left[\rho\left(L(\theta), L_g^r(\theta + \Delta)\right), \rho\left(L(-\theta), L_g^r(\theta + \Delta)\right) \right] \quad (11.9)$$

where $g = 1, \ldots, G$. Note, how the flipped histogram is also considered for the reasons already outlined in Sect. 11.4.1. The computation is performed for each of the candidate gesture, thus obtaining a set $\mathbf{F}^\rho$ containing a different feature value f_g^ρ for each of them. As expected, ideally the correlation with the correct gesture should have a larger value than the other features.

An important aspect of this feature extraction method is the employed similarity metric, which strongly affects the results. A reasonable high accuracy can be obtained through the zero-mean normalized cross-correlation (ZNCC) between the histograms, since this measure is less affected by the different sizes of different hands. On the other side, this measure is sometimes not able to discriminate two histograms with a similar outline corresponding to different fingers, e.g., an histogram representing a gesture with a raised index only, may have an high correlation value with an histogram representing a gesture with a raised little only. This ambiguity can be often removed by using alternative similarity measurement values in place of or together with the ZNCC. A good alternative is the sum of squared differences (SSD) between the two histograms. The features obtained with this measure will be denoted with $\mathbf{F}^{SSD}$.

11.4.4 Curvature Features

The third proposed descriptor is based on the curvature of the hand shape edges. Since depth data coming from real-time depth cameras are usually rather noisy, a reasonable assumption is to avoid differential operators for curvature description, relying instead on integral invariants [12, 16].

The curvature feature extractor algorithm takes as input the hand edge points $\mathcal{H}_e$ and the binary mask $B(u, v)$. Let $\mathcal{H}_c = \partial \mathcal{H}_e$ be the boundary of $\mathcal{H}_e$, namely the subset of all the points $\mathbf{X}_i \in \mathcal{H}_e$ belonging to the hand contour only. Consider a set of S circular masks $M_s(\mathbf{X}_i)$, $s = 1, \ldots, S$ with radius r_s centered on each edge sample $\mathbf{X}_i \in \mathcal{H}_c$ (reasonable numbers are 25 masks with r_s varying from 0.5 to 5 cm).

Let $V(\mathbf{X}_i, s)$ denote the curvature in $\mathbf{X}_i$, expressed as the ratio of the number of samples of $\mathcal{H}_e$ falling in the mask $M_s(\mathbf{X}_i)$ over $M_s(\mathbf{X}_i)$ size, namely:

$$V(\mathbf{X}_i, s) = \frac{\sum_{\mathbf{X}_i \in M_s(\mathbf{X}_i)} B(\mathbf{X}_i)}{|M_s(\mathbf{X}_i)|} \quad (11.10)$$

where $|M_s(\mathbf{X}_i)|$ denotes the cardinality of $M_s(\mathbf{X}_i)$ and $B(\mathbf{X}_i) = B(u_j, v_j)$, with (u_j, v_j) be the 2D coordinates corresponding to $\mathbf{X}_i$. Note that $V(\mathbf{X}_i, s)$ is computed for each sample $\mathbf{X}_i \in \mathcal{H}_c$. The value s corresponds to the scale level at which feature extraction is performed. Differently from [12] and other approaches, the radius r_s is defined in metrical units and is then converted to the corresponding pixel size on the basis of the distance between the camera and the hand. In this way, the descriptor is invariant with respect to the distance between the hand and the camera.

For faster processing, the circular masks can be replaced with simpler square masks and then integral images can be used for fast computation of the samples in the mask. This approach, even if not perfectly rotation invariant, proved to be significantly faster and the performance loss is negligible.

The values of $V(\mathbf{X}_i, s)$ range from 0 (extremely convex shape) to 1 (extremely concave shape), with $V(\mathbf{X}_i, s) = 0.5$ corresponding to a straight edge. The [0, 1] interval is quantized into N bins of equal size $b_1, \ldots, b_N$. The set $\mathcal{V}_{b,s}$ of the finger edge points $\mathbf{X}_i \in \mathcal{H}_c$ with the corresponding value of $V(\mathbf{X}_i, s)$ falling to bin b for the mask s is expressed as:

$$\mathcal{V}_{b,s} = \left\{ \mathbf{X}_i \mid \frac{(b-1)}{B} < V(\mathbf{X}_i, s) \leq \frac{b}{B} \right\} \quad (11.11)$$

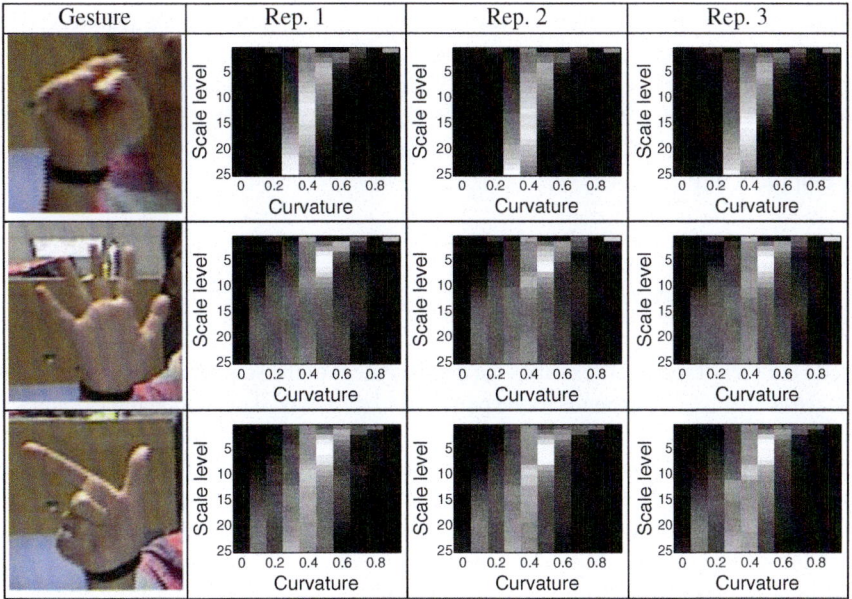

Fig. 11.4 Examples of curvature descriptors for three sample frames from different gestures

Fig. 11.5 Regions corresponding to the various area features shown over a sample gesture

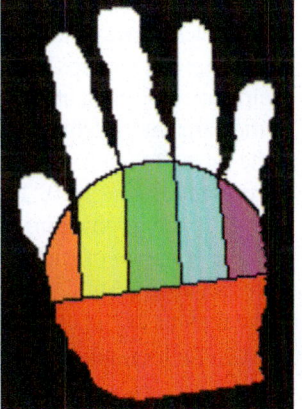

For each radius value s and for each bin b the chosen curvature feature, denoted by $f_{b,s}^c$, is the cardinality of the set $V(\mathbf{X}_i, s)$ normalized by the contour length $|\mathscr{H}_c|$:

$$f_{b,s}^c = \frac{|\mathscr{V}_{b,s}|}{|\mathscr{H}_c|} \qquad (11.12)$$

Note that, because of the normalization, the curvature feature $f_{b,s}^c$ only takes values in $[0, 1]$, which is the same interval shared by both the distances and elevations feature. Finally, all the curvature features $f_{b,s}^c$ are collected within a feature vector $\mathbf{F}^c$ with $B \times S$ entries, ordered by increasing values of indexes $s = 1, 2, \ldots, S$ and $b = 1, 2, \ldots, N$. By resizing $\mathbf{F}^c$ into a matrix with S rows and N columns, and by considering each $f_{b,s}^c$ as the value of the pixel with coordinates (b, s) in a grayscale image, it is possible to graphically visualize the overall curvature descriptor $\mathbf{F}^c$ as exemplified in Fig. 11.4.

11.4.5 Palm Area Features

Palm area set of features describes the displacement of the samples in the palm region $\mathscr{P}$. Note that $\mathscr{P}$ corresponds to the palm area, but it may also include finger samples if some fingers are folded over the palm. The idea is to subdivide the palm region into six different areas, defined over the plane π, as shown in Fig. 11.5. The circle or ellipse defining the palm area is divided into two parts: the lower half is used as a reference for the palm position, and a 3D plane π_p is firstly fitted to this region. The upper half is divided into 5 regions $\mathscr{A}_j$, $j = 1, \ldots, 5$ roughly corresponding to the regions close to the different fingers as shown in Fig. 11.5, that is, each region corresponds to the area that is affected by the position of a finger. Note how the feature values account for the deformation the palm shape undergoes in the corresponding area when the related finger is folded or is moved. In particular, it is worth noting that the samples corresponding to the fingers folded over the palm are associated with $\mathscr{P}$ and are not captured by distance or elevation features, but they are used for the computation of palm area features. The areas positions on the plane strictly depend on the parameters defining the palm area (i.e., the center $\mathbf{C}^\pi$ and the radius R of the circle or the two axes of the ellipse), on the fingers width and on the direction $\mathbf{i}_x^\pi$ corresponding to $\theta = 0$. The alignment of the θ directions can be computed as in Sect. 11.4.1, thus obtaining an alignment for each gesture template. The areas aligned with the template of each gesture will be denoted with $\mathscr{A}_j^g$, where g indicates the corresponding gesture. In this way, the set of points $\mathbf{X}_i$ in $\mathscr{P}$ associated with each of the regions $\mathscr{A}_j^g$ is computed. Then, each area $\mathscr{A}_j^g$ is considered and the distance between each sample $\mathbf{X}_i$ in $\mathscr{A}_j^g$ and π_p is computed. The average of the distances of the samples of the area A_j^g:

$$f_{g,j}^a = \frac{\sum_{\mathbf{X}_i \in \mathscr{A}_j^g} \|\mathbf{X}_i - \mathbf{X}_i^\pi\|}{|A_j^g|} \quad (11.13)$$

is taken as the feature corresponding to the area A_j^g. All the area features are collected within vector $\mathbf{F}^a$, made by $G \times 5$ area features, one for each finger in each possible gesture. The entries of $\mathbf{F}^a$ are finally scaled in order to assume values within range $[0, 1]$, as the other feature vectors.

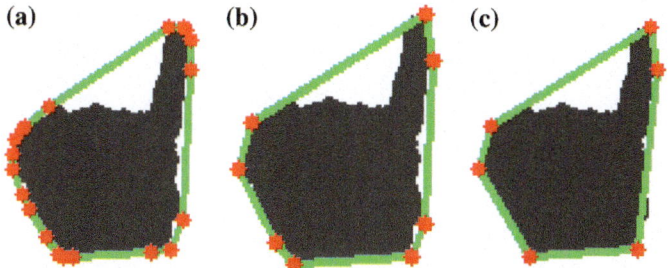

Fig. 11.6 Computation of the vertexes of the convex hull: **a** convex hull of $B(u, v)$; **b** convex hull after the removal of short edges; **c** convex hull after the removal of short edges and of wide angles

11.4.6 Convex Hull Features

The convex hull of the 2D hand shape in the depth map is another source of information that can be exploited for the construction of descriptors of the hand pose [21]. Given the set of points on the hand mask $\mathscr{B}$, the corresponding convex hull is computed. Due to the noise of the sensors, the set of vertexes may contains some artifacts that should be removed before exploiting it for gesture recognition:

1. The hand shape can contain some small holes due to noise that must be removed.
2. There can be close vertexes due to the irregular shape of the acquired hand contour (see Fig. 11.6a). The length of the convex hull edges is computed and in case there were edges shorter than a predefined threshold they must be removed and the corresponding vertexes collapsed into a single point (Fig. 11.6b).
3. Also the presence of angles close to 180° (i.e., two subsequent edges are almost on the same line) is an hint of extra edges due to acquisition artifacts. In this case, the vertex is removed as well and the two edges are combined into a single one, as shown in Fig. 11.6c.

In this way, a simplified convex hull $C_{\text{hull}}(\mathscr{B})$ with vertexes P_{chull} can be built.

11.4.6.1 Convex Hull Vertexes

A first possible feature is the number of vertexes of the convex hull $F^{\text{pch}} = |P_{\text{chull}}|$. This value is an hint of the hand pose and in particular of the number of raised fingers. Note how, ideally, the desired convex hull presents a vertex for each fingertip and a few other vertexes delimiting the palm area. These vertexes, together with the distances histograms computed in Sect. 11.4.1, may also aid the fingertips position estimation: assuming that, for each histogram value, the related 3D point is known, since the histogram local maxima correspond to the hand shape boundary (which contains the fingertips as well), by pairing the convex hull vertexes with them, it is possible to detect which local maxima are likely to be associated with fingertips and which ones, instead, are probably due to noise or associated with the palm edges.

11.4.6.2 Convex Hull Area Ratio

Another good feature is the ratio between the area of the hand shape and the area of the convex hull enclosing it, that is:

$$F^{\text{ch}} = \frac{|\mathcal{B}|}{\text{area}(C_{\text{hull}}(\mathcal{B}))} \qquad (11.14)$$

11.4.6.3 Convex Hull Perimeter Ratio

The ratio between the perimeter of the hand shape and the perimeter of the convex hull:

$$F^{\text{Rp}} = \frac{\text{perimeter}(\mathcal{B})}{\text{perimeter}(C_{\text{hull}}(\mathcal{B}))} \qquad (11.15)$$

is another useful clue. Gestures with bended fingers typically correspond to perimeter ratios close to 1 while when several fingers are pointing out of the hand this ratio is usually smaller. Figure 11.7 shows a couple of examples; note how in the first case, the two perimeters are quite different, while in the single finger gesture of the second row, the two perimeters are more similar.

11.4.7 Connected-Components Features

One of the other relevant clues that can be extracted from the comparison between the convex hull and the hand shape is the shape of the regions within the convex hull region but not belonging to the hand. These typically correspond to the empty regions between the fingers and are a good indicator of the fingers arrangement. Let $S = C_{\text{hull}}(\mathcal{B}) - \mathcal{B}$ be the difference between the convex hull and the hand shape. An example of the region S is shown in Fig. 11.8a. The region S is typically made of a set of connected components. The various connected components S_i are extracted and then the ones that are smaller than a threshold T_{cc} are discarded in order to avoid considering small components due to noise (e.g., the region on the right in the second row of Fig. 11.8). In this way the set $\mathcal{S} = \{S_i : S_i > T_{cc}\}$ is built as shown in Fig. 11.8b.

A first feature that can be extracted from this process is the number of connected components $N_{cc} = |\mathcal{S}|$ bigger than the threshold. Another feature set is, instead, given by the ratio of the areas of the various connected components with the convex hull area, that is:

11 Feature Descriptors for Depth-Based Hand Gesture Recognition

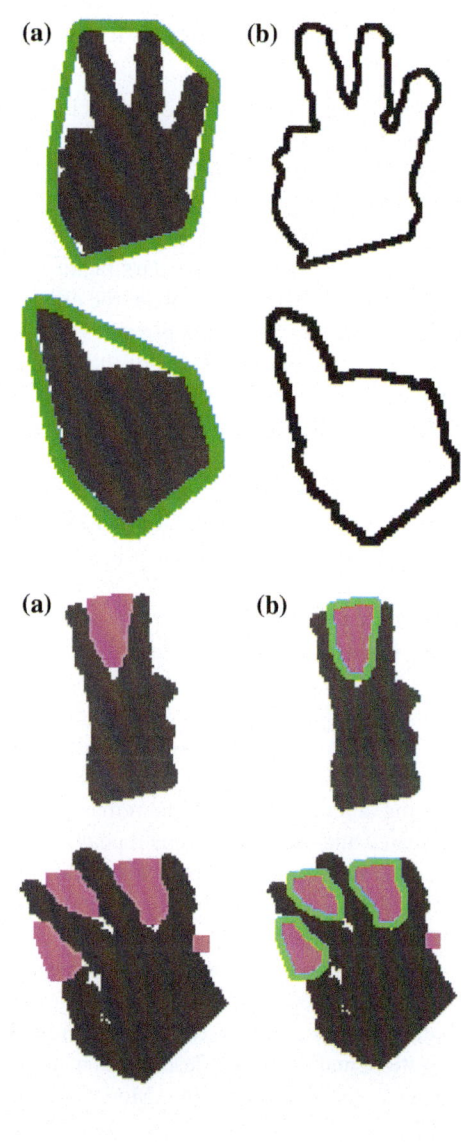

Fig. 11.7 Perimeter of the hand contour and of the convex hull; **a**: convex hull perimeter; **b** hand perimeter

Fig. 11.8 Area of the connected components. **a** Connected components in set S; **b** connected components in set $\mathscr{S}$ highlighted in *green*

$$f_i^{cc} = \frac{\text{area}(S_i | S_i \in \mathscr{S})}{\text{area}(C_{\text{hull}}(\mathscr{B})))} \quad (11.16)$$

where the areas are sorted according to the angle of their centroid with the axes computed by the PCA (i.e., from the thumb to the little).

11.5 Gesture Classification with Support Vector Machines

The third and last step of the Sect. 11.1 pipeline consists in applying an appropriate machine learning technique to classify the features extracted in Sect. 11.4, in order to recognize the performed gestures. Approaches based on SVM, RDF, Neural Networks and many others have been proposed in literature. Presenting the various machine learning methods is beyond the scopes of this chapter that focuses on feature extraction, although the classification with SVM is here briefly recalled only for clarity sake and used to compare the efficiency of the various features.

The feature extraction approaches of Sect. 11.4 provide different feature vectors describing relevant properties of the hand samples. Let $\mathbf{F}$ denote a suitable feature vector describing the performed gesture, e.g., $\mathbf{F} = \mathbf{F}^l$ for distance features. The gesture recognition problem consists in classifying the vectors $\mathbf{F}$ into G different classes corresponding to the considered gestures. A multi-class SVM classifier based on the *one-against-one* approach can be used, and corresponds to a set of $G(G-1)/2$ binary SVM classifiers used to test each class (i.e., gesture) against each other. Each classification output is chosen as a *vote* for a certain gesture and the gesture with the maximum number of votes is the result of the recognition process. Different kernels can be used for the SVM, but the most common choice is the non-linear Gaussian radial basis function (RBF) kernel. In order to set the classifier parameters, a training set containing data from N users is assumed to be available. A naive grid search with cross-validation approach is viable, although not efficient: the space of parameters (C, γ) of the RBF kernel is subdivided with a regular grid and for each couple of parameters, the training set is divided into two parts, one containing $N - 1$ users for training and the other with the remaining user for validation. The performances are evaluated and the procedure is repeated by changing each time the user used for the validation. The couple of parameters that give the best accuracy on average is finally selected. The SVM can then be trained on all the N users of the training set with the optimal parameters.

This approach can also be used to perform the recognition with multiple feature descriptors together. The simplest solution is to concatenate into vector $\mathbf{F}$ the different feature vectors of the descriptors that are going to be used. E.g., to combine distance, elevation, and curvature descriptors a combined feature vector $\mathbf{F} = [\mathbf{F}^l, \mathbf{F}^e, \mathbf{F}^c]$ can be fed to the SVM classifier. More refined combination schemes can be exploited, e.g., as in [19].

11.6 Experimental Results

This chapter analyzes the classification performances of the various feature descriptor described in Sect. 11.4. The experiments were performed on a gesture dataset acquired in the Multimedia Technology and Telecommunications Lab of the University of Padova. Such dataset is a subset of the American manual alphabet, and

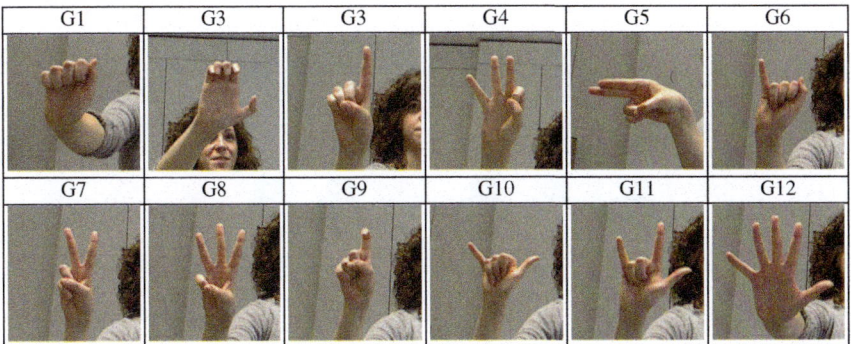

Fig. 11.9 Gestures from the American manual alphabet contained in the experimental dataset

contains ten repetitions of 12 different gestures performed by 14 different people. A representative picture for each gesture is shown in Fig. 11.9 while the complete dataset is made available at the url http://lttm.dei.unipd.it/paper_data/gesture, and provides both the RGB image and the depth map for all the frames.

For each gesture, one of the repetitions in the training set was used for the computation of the reference histogram of Eq. (11.3), required for the extraction of distances, elevations, correlations, and contour histogram similarity features.

The classification model was computed through the SVM implementation provided by the OpenCV library exploiting a variation, tailored for the particular data nature, of the grid-search approach described in Sect. 11.5. Differently from the classic grid-search method, which performs random subsamplings of the feature vectors for splitting the dataset in a train and a test set, or use a *leave-one-out* approach, the method employed for the experiments relies on an extension of the *leave-one-out* which may be named as *leave-one person-out*. Namely, all the feature vectors referred to a specific person belong either to the test or the train set of the current dataset split. Figure 11.10 exemplifies the *leave-one person-out* approach employed for the experiments. The interested reader may find a more detailed discussion on this classification method in [5].

Table 11.1 shows the results obtained from the considered dataset by just using each single feature alone. Distance features (D) alone provide an accuracy of about 68 %. Note that distance descriptors are very good in capturing the fact that the various fingers are folded over the palm or raised, an important element in the recognition of many gestures. Elevation features (E) have lower performance as well (46.0 %); this is due both to the fact that in most gestures in the dataset, the fingers lay very close to the palm plane, and to the varying accuracy in the plane fitting described in Sect. 11.3. Contour histogram similarity features (R) are slightly less performing, since histogram correlations are just a starting point for the distance features extraction and, moreover, due to the zero-mean cross-correlation algorithm exploited, they are not always able to discriminate gestures with the same number of fingers. Sum of squared differences (SSD) provide, instead, poor performances (37.8 %). Such fea-

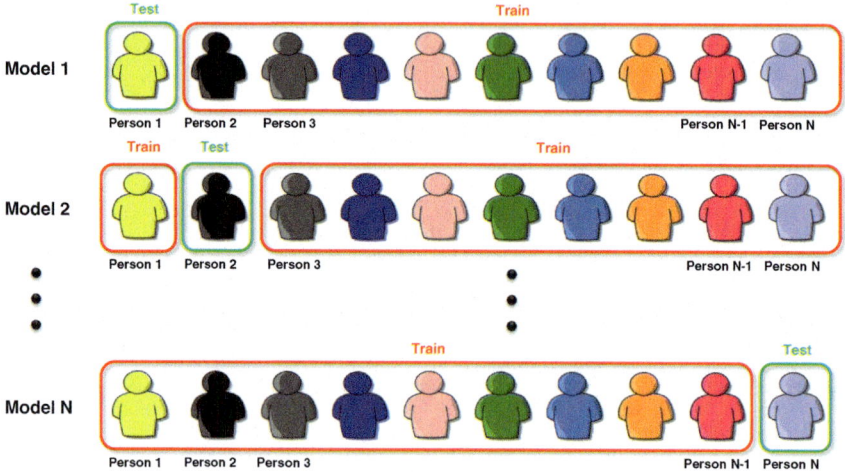

Fig. 11.10 Exemplification of *leave-one person-out* method

tures are anyway helpful when combined with other features as showed in Table 11.2. The curvature-based classifier (C) allows to obtain the best performance (89.5 %), thanks also to the characteristic concavities and convexities of each gesture profile. It is important to note that curvatures do not rely on the computation of the hand orientation or on the positions of the centroid and palm plane. For this reason, curvature-based classifiers are more performing in complex configurations where the estimation of the hand orientation is not always highly accurate. Area-based features (A) allow to obtain, again, a relatively low accuracy (45.4 %), as they are affected by problems similar to the elevations: the different quality in the plane fitting and the fact that in most gestures many fingers lay on the palm plane. Convex hull area (CA) and perimeter ratios (CP) are the least performing features, probably because their vectors are, single scalar numbers, and hence not sufficient to separate a relatively high number of classes. Finally, the convex hull connected-component area (CC) features are ones of the most performing, although their number is sensibly low respect to the curvatures (6 vs. 240 features).

A noteworthy characteristic of the described features is their complementarity, that is, although many of them are not so performing alone, when joined together they are able to increase the overall classification accuracy as one feature type is able to capture properties not detectable by another feature type and vice versa. Table 11.2 shows some examples of the performances that can be obtained combining multiple features. In particular, the distance only classifier is able to recognize some of the gestures that curvatures only can not handle, and their joint usage raises slightly the classification performance (91.4 %). The combination of correlation and sum of squared differences features, instead, leads to a dramatic improvement in accuracy (78.3 % vs. 60.4 and 37.8 %, respectively). Even by combining the convex hull area

Table 11.1 Performance of single features extracted from the considered dataset

Type of features	Accuracy (%)
Distances (D)	68.4
Elevations (E)	46.0
Correlations (R)	60.4
Sum of squared distances (SSD)	37.8
Curvatures (C)	89.5
Areas (A)	45.4
Convex hull area ratio (CA)	29.6
Convex hull perimeter ratio (CP)	37.0
Convex hull connected-component area ratio (CC)	72.0

Table 11.2 Performance of the features combination

Type of features	Accuracy (%)
D + C	91.4
R + SSD	78.3
CA + CP	51.2
D + E + C	93.6
D + A + C	92.0
DA + CP + CC	73.2
D + E + A + C	93.5
R + SSD + CA + CP + CC	86.8

and perimeter ratios, it is possible a significant overall improvement (51.2 % vs. 29.6 and 37.0 % respectively).

The second part of Table 11.2 shows that by combining three feature types a modest overall accuracy improvement can be obtained. This is due to the fact that the accuracy values are already quite high, and not always the added feature carry a sufficient amount of novel information to solve the most critical classification ambiguities. The best accuracy has been obtained by combining four feature types, i.e., distances, elevation, area-based and curvature features. Finally, it is important to be aware that the addition of an increasing number of feature types may not lead to an overall improvement in accuracy and, sometimes, may also lead to overfitting with detrimental effects on the classifier performance.

11.7 Conclusions

In this chapter, effective solutions for the exploitation of depth data in static hand gesture recognition have been presented. The hand recognition and extraction step, a very challenging task with color information, can be effectively solved with simple approaches if depth data is available. Furthermore, depth can be combined with the color data for an even more reliable recognition. Several depth-based feature descriptors have been presented. Depth-based descriptors are typically based on measures in the 3D space and are more robust to issues like the position of the hand, its orientation, lighting, and many others than color-based descriptors. Furthermore, they are able to better capture the pose of the hand and of the various fingers, making the gesture recognitiontask easier. A comparison of the performances of the various features have been presented in Sect. 11.6. Some features, most notably the curvatures, but also distance and correlation features, have better performances and allow alone to obtain a reliable gesture recognition. However, notice how the different features capture relevant complementary properties of the hand gestures. For this reason, the combination of multiple features allows to obtain better performance than each feature alone.

References

1. Ballan L, Taneja A, Gall J, Van Gool L, Pollefeys M (2012) Motion capture of hands in action using discriminative salient points. In: Proceedings of the European conference on computer vision (ECCV), Firenze, October 2012
2. Biswas K, Basu S (2011) Gesture recognition using microsoft kinect. In: 5th international conference on automation, robotics and applications (ICARA), December 2011, pp 100–103
3. Doliotis P, Stefan A, McMurrough C, Eckhard D, Athitsos V (2011) Comparing gesture recognition accuracy using color and depth information. In: Proceedings of the 4th international conference on pervasive technologies related to assistive environments (PETRA'11), pp 20:1–20:7
4. Dominio F, Donadeo M, Marin G, Zanuttigh P, Cortelazzo GM (2013) Hand gesture recognition with depth data. In: Proceedings of the 4th ACM/IEEE international workshop on analysis and retrieval of tracked events and motion in imagery stream, ACM, pp 9–16
5. Dominio F, Donadeo M, Zanuttigh P (2013) Combining multiple depth-based descriptors for hand gesture recognition. Pattern Recognition Lett
6. Garg P, Aggarwal N, Sofat S (2009) Vision based hand gesture recognition. World Acad Sci Eng Technol 49(1):972–977
7. Han J, Shao L, Xu D, Shotton J (2013) Enhanced computer vision with microsoft kinect sensor: a review. IEEE Trans Cybern 43(5):1318–1334
8. Herrera Daniel, Kannala Juho, Heikkilä Janne (2012) Joint depth and color camera calibration with distortion correction. IEEE Trans Pattern Anal Mach Intell 34(10):2058–2064
9. Keskin G, Kirac G, Kara YE, Akarun L (2011) Real time hand pose estimation using depth sensors. In: ICCV Workshops, November 2011, pp 1228–1234
10. Keskin C, Furkan Kıraç, Kara YE, Akarun L (2012) Hand pose estimation and hand shape classification using multi-layered randomized decision forests. In: Proceedings of the European conference on computer vision (ECCV), pp 852–863
11. Eva K, Jochen P, Joachim H, Alexander B (2008) Gesture recognition with a time-of-flight camera. Int J Intell Syst Technol Appl 5(3/4):334–343
12. Kumar N, Belhumeur PN, Biswas A, Jacobs DW, Kress WJ, Lopez I, Soares JVB (2012) Leafsnap: a computer vision system for automatic plant species identification. In Proceedings of the European conference on computer vision (ECCV), October 2012
13. Kurakin A, Zhang Z, Liu Z (2012) A real-time system for dynamic hand gesture recognition with a depth sensor. In: Proceedings of EUSIPCO

14. Li Y (2012) Hand gesture recognition using kinect. In: IEEE 3rd international conference on software engineering and service science (ICSESS), June 2012, pp 196–199
15. Liu X, Fujimura K (2004) Hand gesture recognition using depth data. In: Proceedings sixth IEEE international conference on automatic face and gesture recognition, May 2004, pp 529–534
16. Manay S, Cremers D, Hong B-w, Yezzi AJ, Soatto S (2006) Integral invariants for shape matching. IEEE Trans Pattern Anal Mach Intell 28(10):1602–1618
17. Marin G, Fraccaro M, Donadeo M, Dominio F, Zanuttigh P (2013) Palm area detection for reliable hand gesture recognition. In: Proceedings of MMSP
18. Mo Z, Neumann U (2006) Real-time hand pose recognition using low-resolution depth images. In: Proceedings of IEEE computer society conference on computer vision and pattern recognition, vol 2, pp 1499–1505
19. Nanni L, Lumini A, Dominio F, Donadeo M, Zanuttigh P (2014) Ensemble to improve gesture recognition. Int J Autom Ident Technology (to appear)
20. Oikonomidis I, Kyriazis N, Argyros AA (2011) Efficient model-based 3d tracking of hand articulations using kinect. In: Proceedings of the 22nd British machine vision conference (BMVC 2011)
21. Pedersoli F, Adami N, Benini S, Leonardi R (2012) Xkin—extendable hand pose and gesture recognition library for kinect. In: Proceedings of ACM conference on multimedia 2012—open source competition, Nara, Japan, October 2012
22. Pedersoli F, Benini S, Adami N, Leonardi R (2014) Xkin: an open source framework for hand pose and gesture recognition using kinect. Vis Comput 1–16
23. Pugeault N, Bowden R (2011) Spelling it out: real-time asl fingerspelling recognition. In: Proceedings of the 1st IEEE workshop on consumer depth cameras for computer vision, pp 1114–1119
24. Ren Z, Meng J, Yuan J (2011) Depth camera based hand gesture recognition and its applications in human–computer-interaction. In: Proceedings of International conference on information, communications and signal processing (ICICS), December 2011, pp 1–5
25. Ren Z, Yuan J, Zhang Z (2011) Robust hand gesture recognition based on finger-earth mover's distance with a commodity depth camera. In Proceedings of the 19th ACM international conference on multimedia, MM'11, ACM, NY, USA, 2011, pp 1093–1096
26. Sun C, Zhang T, Bao BK, Xu C, Mei T (2013) Discriminative exemplar coding for sign language recognition with kinect. IEEE Trans Cybern 43(5):1418–1428
27. Suryanarayan P, Subramanian A, Mandalapu D (2010) Dynamic hand pose recognition using depth data. In: Proceedings of international conference on pattern recognition (ICPR), August 2010, pp 3105–3108
28. Van den Bergh M, Van Gool L (2011) Combining rgb and tof cameras for real-time 3d hand gesture interaction. In: IEEE Workshop on applications of computer vision (WACV), January 2011, pp 66–72
29. Viola P, Jones M (2001) Rapid object detection using a boosted cascade of simple features. In: Proceedings of the IEEE computer society conference on computer vision and pattern recognition, CVPR 2001, vol 1, IEEE, pp I–511
30. Wachs JP, Kölsch M, Stern H, Edan Y (2011) Vision-based hand-gesture applications. Commun ACM 54(2):60–71
31. Wan T, Wang Y, Li J (2012) Hand gesture recognition system using depth data. In: Proceedings of 2nd international conference on consumer electronics, communications and networks (CECNet), April 2012, pp 1063–1066
32. Wang J, Liu Z, Chorowski J, Chen Z, Wu Y (2012) Robust 3d action recognition with random occupancy patterns. In: Proceedings of the European conference on computer vision (ECCV)
33. Wen Y, Hu C, Yu G, Wang C (2012) A robust method of detecting hand gestures using depth sensors. In: Proceedings of haptic audio visual environments and games (HAVE), 2012, pp 72–77
34. Zabulis X, Baltzakis H, Argyros A (2009) Vision-based hand gesture recognition for human computer interaction. In: The universal access handbook, human factors and ergonomics, Chap. 34, Lawrence Erlbaum Associates Inc. (LEA), June 2009, pp 34.1–34.30

Chapter 12
Hand Parsing and Gesture Recognition with a Commodity Depth Camera

Hui Liang and Junsong Yuan

Abstract Hand pose tracking and gesture recognition are useful techniques in human–computer interaction (HCI) scenarios, while previous work in this field suffers from the lack of discriminative features to differentiate and track hand parts. In this chapter, we present a robust hand parsing scheme to obtain a high-level and discriminative representation of the hand from raw depth image. A novel distance-adaptive feature selection method is proposed to generate more discriminative depth-context features for hand parsing. The random decision forest is adopted for per-pixel labeling, and it is combined with the temporal prior to form an ensemble of classifiers for enhanced performance. To enforce the spatial smoothness and remove the misclassified isolated regions, we further build a superpixel Markov random field, which is capable to handle the per-pixel labeling error at variable scales. To demonstrate the effectiveness of our proposed method, we have compared it to the benchmark methods. The results show it produces 17.2 % higher accuracy on the synthesized datasets for single-frame parsing. The tests on the real-world sequences show our method is more robust against complex hand poses. In addition, we develop a hand gesture recognition algorithm with the hand parsing results. The experiments show our method achieves good performance compared to state-of-the-art methods.

12.1 Introduction

Vision-based hand pose estimation is an important research topic in human–computer interaction (HCI) which has various applications, such as gesture recognition [35] and animation synthesis. Compared to the intrusive counterparts such as the data

---

H. Liang (✉) · J. Yuan
School of Electrical and Electronics Engineering, Nanyang Technological University,
50 Nanyang Avenue, Singapore 639798, Singapore
e-mail: hliang1@e.ntu.edu.sg

J. Yuan
e-mail: jsyuan@ntu.edu.sg

glove [8] and the optical marker-based methods [1], it can provide more natural interaction experience for the HCI applications at a much lower cost. Though a lot of work has been done in this field [4, 14, 21, 23, 26, 30, 34], robust hand pose tracking and gesture recognition with visual inputs remains a challenging problem and the performance achieved cannot compare to the alternative methods, such as the data glove-based approaches [38].

The performance of vision-based hand pose tracking and gesture recognition systems largely relies on the discriminative power of the input features. Previously, the optical camera is the mainstream to capture the visual inputs [30, 34]. As the hand is quite homogeneous in color, the commonly used features in the RGB images, e.g., edge and silhouette, are sensitive to lighting condition variations and cluttered background and lack the discriminative power for matching [4, 14, 23]. The depth sensors can provide more discriminative features, and various methods have been proposed, e.g., the fast point feature histograms [28], the geodesic distance map [3], and the depth kernel descriptors [6]. Although these low-level features prove effective in rigid object recognition, they are generally inefficient to describe the articulated objects such as the hand. By contrast, the parsed hand parts are very attractive high-level features for both hand pose tracking and gesture recognition tasks. Similar work has been done in full-body tracking [31], and the idea was extended to hand parsing [15, 16]. However, these hand parsing schemes most follow the idea of per-pixel classification of the depth images, and their results are still quite noisy.

This chapter presents a unified framework to enforce both the temporal and spatial constraints for hand parsing, in which we leverage a superpixel Markov random field (MRF) to efficiently remove the misclassified regions produced by per-pixel classification. The pipeline of the proposed hand parsing algorithm and its application to hand gesture recognition is illustrated in Fig. 12.1. The random decision forest (RDF) classifier is used for per-pixel classification based on a depth-context feature. The temporal constraints are enforced by learning the 3D position distribution of the hand parts from the previous frame and combining it with the RDF classifier to form

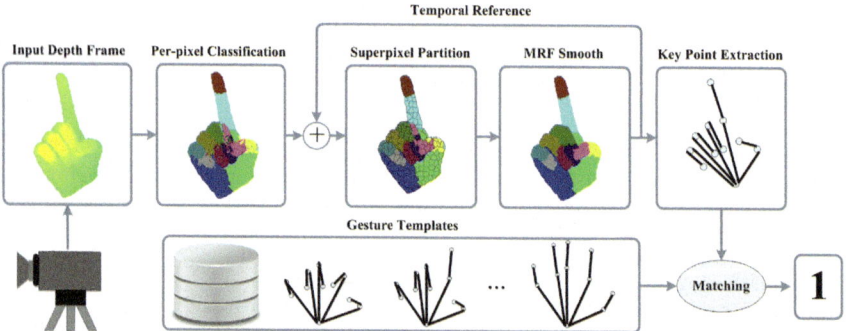

Fig. 12.1 The pipeline of the proposed hand parsing scheme and its application to hand gesture recognition

an ensemble of classifiers. As to the spatial constraints, the neighborhood smoothness of the pixel labels is enforced in the SMRF framework to suppress the per-pixel classification error. Using the superpixel, the misclassified isolated regions can be represented as an atomic element, and the computational complexity of MRF-based smoothing can be largely reduced. Finally, based on the key points extracted from the hand parsing results, we propose a rotation-invariant hand gesture recognition algorithm to recognize digit number gestures.

12.2 Literature Review

The purpose of hand parsing is to refine the raw visual inputs to get a semantic segmentation of the hand region, e.g., the joints, the fingers, and the palm. These hand parts are important features for hand pose estimation and gesture recognition, as they are more efficient and accurate for matching and classification in such tasks. Generally, the methods of hand parsing involve pixel-level hand part detection [15, 36] and inference with the priors of hand part correlations [20, 25]. Although there has been considerable work in the similar field of human body parsing [24, 25], hand parsing has its own challenges. Different from the human body, there are no clear visual boundaries between the hand parts in the color image, and the hand motion is much more flexible. As a result, many part detectors adopted in body parsing, e.g., the HOG templates [9], do not work well for the hand, and the color markers are sometimes placed on the hand to alleviate this problem [36]. Besides, the hand part correlations are also more difficult to model. In the following, we review some of the recent marker-based and markerless methods for both hand and body parsing.

Marker-based methods: The bare hand is homogeneous in color and lacks the boundaries between its different parts. To this end, the color markers are often adopted to parse the hand in RGB inputs, as shown in Fig. 12.2. In [40], twenty reflective markers are placed on the hand joints, and their 3D positions are recovered by the Vicon camera system. Although the identities of the markers are not recovered during runtime, their positions provide strong constraints on the feasible hand pose and

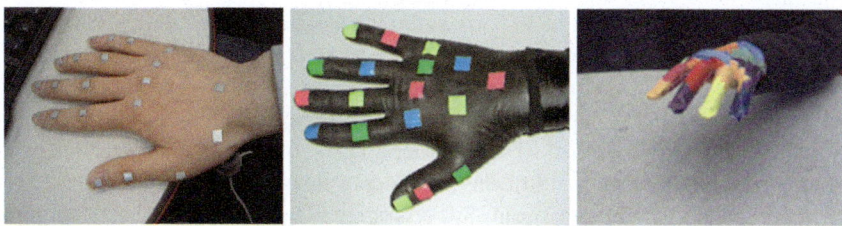

Fig. 12.2 Marker-based methods. *Left* the reflective markers used in [40]. *Middle* the color markers with different colors used in [32]. *Right* the color glove used in [36]

thus largely improve the estimation accuracy. In [32], eighteen markers with four different colors are placed on the hand joints to track the pitcher's hand motion when capturing the baseball. As the number of colors used to label the markers is limited for robust extraction, the markers are distributed to maximize the distance of the markers with the same colors. In this way, the different joints can be better recognized. In [36], a color glove is used to segment each hand part. The glove consists of twenty patches and is labeled with ten fully saturated colors so that the different patches can be robustly segmented. A Hausdorff-like distance metric is used for template matching, and the database is indexed by similarity-sensitive coding to accelerate nearest neighbor search.

Markerless methods: The contour and silhouette are the commonly used features for hand and body parsing in unmarked visual inputs, as they are relatively robust to extract in the controlled environments. Especially, the stretching parts, e.g., the fingers and the limbs, are quite distinct on the contour. Motivated by this observation, some shape analysis techniques have been applied to hand parsing. In [27], the individual fingers and palm are segmented using the convex shape decomposition algorithm, which decomposes the hand contour into separated near-convex polygons. However, this method can only handle the open hand, and the knowledge of the articulated objects is not utilized. To this end, one of the most popular techniques for articulated object parsing has been the deformable pictorial model (DPM) [12], which arranges the different parts of the object in a deformable configuration. A separate detector is trained for each part, and the correlations between the different parts are modeled as a tree structure to allow efficient inference. In the original work of [12], the part detector utilizes only the silhouette, and thus, its capability to handle overlapping parts is quite limited. As the parsing accuracy of the DPM-based methods largely relies on the performance of the part detector, various improvements have been proposed. In [25], an iterative parsing scheme is proposed to parse the body parts in unconstrained color images by finding the optimal body pose. The initial pose is first determined using only the edge feature, and the obtained pose is then used to compute the new appearance model to determine the new parse. This process iterates, and the local features are gradually tuned to detect the individual parts.

The depth cameras are more powerful tools for body and hand parsing compared to the RGB cameras. The occluding parts with similar colors can be separated with their depths, and the pixels can be better described based on the depth value contrast. In [39], a labeled contour model is proposed for gesture recognition. The depth image is first classified into hand parts with the position feature, and the results are then used to label the contour points to provide extra clue for matching. In [31], the feature of the pixel in the input depth image is represented by a set of neighboring point pairs, and the part label of the pixel is determined by classification based on its feature values via a learned RDF classifier. In [15], the randomized decision trees are used to classify each pixel of the input depth image to labeled parts based on the depth feature in [31]. The mean shift algorithm is then used to estimate the joint positions. In [16], the authors further extend the method in [15] with a multilayered random forest framework. The input depth image of the hand is first classified into a predefined gesture set and then parsed into hand parts with expert classifiers specially trained for each gesture set. However, while they achieve good gesture recognition performance, their method is not suitable for hand parsing in full degree of freedom (DOF) hand motion scenarios, given the large variation of hand shape and viewpoint change. In [19], the authors propose to use ICP to build the temporal correspondence between the previous frame and the current frame for hand parsing and extract the hand part edges as additional constraints to refine the parsing results. While this method largely relies on the temporal reference for parsing, it is inherently sensitive to tracking failure due to its assumption of small hand shape deformation between successive frames.

Some of the methods in depth image-based parsing are proven effective in their per-pixel classification performance, while the temporal and spatial constraints are seldom enforced in a unified way to improve the results. This is important since usually the training dataset cannot cover all the possible hand motion due to its high articulation and large viewpoint changes. As a result, a large portion of the input images can be misclassified based on only per-pixel parsing schemes. To address this issue, the spatial and temporal constraints are enforced by a superpixel MRF in [20] to further improve the per-pixel parsing results in depth images.

12.3 System Overview

The proposed superpixel MRF framework enforces both the temporal and spatial correlations of the hand parts to parse the depth image of the bare hand into individual parts. Its input is a sequence of depth images, and we assume that only one hand is visible and the hand is the nearest object to the camera. The output of the hand parsing scheme is the part label images, and key point sets corresponding to the hand parts. These extracted key points are further used for hand gesture recognition. The functions of the key modules are listed as follows:

Hand detection: to extract the hand region from the input depth image and segment it from the forearm.

Per-pixel classification: to assign an initial part label to each pixel by classification with the learned RDF classifier and the temporal position classifier. A distance-adaptive feature selection scheme is combined with a depth-context feature to describe each pixel for classification.

Superpixel partition: to partition the initial hand part segmentation into a set of superpixels to reduce the computational complexity involved in MRF smoothing.

MRF inference: to reassign the hand part labels via superpixel-level inference. The depth discontinuity, superpixel boundary shapes, and hand label co-occurrence are all handled to construct the MRF graph for efficient inference.

Key point extraction: to infer the center of each labeled hand part based on their distributions in 3D space.

Gesture recognition: to recognize static hand gestures from pre-defined sets. Gesture recognition is performed by nearest neighbor search based on the distance between the aligned point sets of the input and templates.

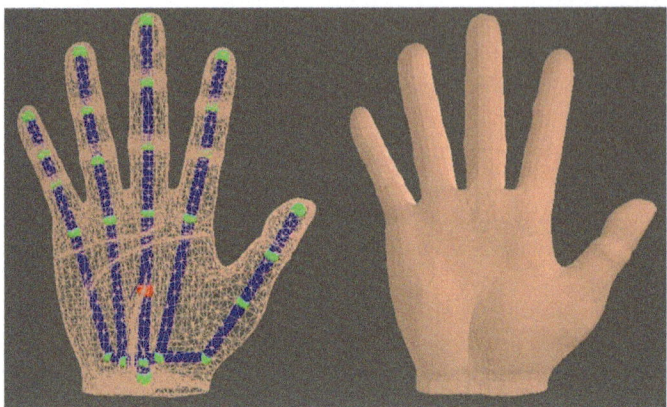

Fig. 12.3 The 3D hand model consisting of the mesh and skeleton

12.4 Hand Modeling

In order to generate the training samples for hand part classification, we build a fully deformable 3D model to simulate the real hand, which consists of a skeleton system and a skin surface mesh. The skeleton has 27 DOF, including 6 DOFs of global motion and 21 DOFs of local motion [10]. It is modeled as a kinematic chain of 20 joints connected by bones in a tree structure with the root at the wrist, as shown in Fig. 12.3. A set of static and dynamic constraints [10, 22] are adopted to limit the parameter space of the hand motion. The skeleton thus has an equivalent of 18 DOF. The skin mesh consists of about 5,000 vertices, which form approximately 7,000 triangles. Each vertex and triangle is assigned a label $l \in L$ to indicate which hand part they belong to. Give a hypothesized hand pose ϕ, the joint positions of the skeleton are first computed using forward kinematics, and the positions of the vertices on the skin mesh are then updated using the skeleton subspace deformation method [18]

We adopt the pinhole camera model [13] to project the hand model onto the image plane to synthesize the depth and label images. This is done by calculating the projection of all the triangles of the skin mesh, as shown in Fig. 12.3. The pixel coordinate $\mathbf{p}_i$ of a 3D point $\mathbf{v}_i = [a_i, b_i, c_i]^T$ is projected by:

$$\mathbf{p}_i = \Psi_P(\mathbf{v}_i) = \frac{F}{c_i} \times \begin{bmatrix} D_x a_i \\ D_y b_i \end{bmatrix} + \begin{bmatrix} a_o \\ b_o \end{bmatrix}, \quad (12.1)$$

where F is the focal length; D_x and D_y are the coefficients to define the metric units to pixels; a_o and b_o are the principal point of the image plane. These parameters are intrinsic parameters of the camera and can be obtained by camera calibration techniques. Based on the projection model, the three vertices of each triangle of the hand mesh are projected onto the image plane to get $(\mathbf{p}_1, \mathbf{p}_2, \mathbf{p}_3)$. The pixels with the projected triangle in the label image are assigned the corresponding label of the triangle (v_1, v_2, v_3). The pixels within the projected triangle in the depth image are filled by linear interpolation of the three vertices. Besides, since the skin mesh is closed, multiple triangles on the mesh can be projected to the same pixel on the depth and label images. In this case, the pixel will take values from the triangle that gives the minimum depth value.

12.5 Hand Detection

The proposed hand detector works on the input depth images and simplifies the problem with several assumptions. First, it assumes the hand is the nearest object to the camera, the in-plane hand rotation is confined within $(-90°, 90°)$, and the out-of-plane rotation is confined within $(-20°, 20°)$. Second, the maximum absolute difference of depth values between the points within forearm region and hand region is confined within a threshold ε, i.e., $\varepsilon = 0.2$ m. Third, based on the morphology of the hand, we assume the palm forms a globally largest blob in the hand and forearm region when the hand rotates within the specified range. The palm region can thus be approximated with a circle $C_p = (p_p, r_p)$, where p_p is the palm center and r_p is the radius.

Based on the above assumptions, the hand region is segmented through three steps: foreground segmentation, palm localization, and hand segmentation. It starts with threshold to the depth image to get the foreground. Here, the foreground consists of the pixels that satisfy $d_z < d_z^* + \varepsilon$, where d_z is the depth value of the pixel, and d_z^* is the minimum depth value in the depth image. This ensures that both the hand and forearm regions are extracted from the depth image. In the second step, the contour of the foreground is approximated by a polygon, and C_p then equals to the largest inscribed circle of this polygon. To reduce the computational complexity of palm localization, the center of C_p can be tracked with a Kalman filter if the temporal information is available. Finally, the hand and forearm regions are separated by a tangent line of C_p which is also perpendicular to the orientation vector of the forearm. We define the orientation vector as the Eigenvector that corresponds to the largest Eigenvalue of the covariance matrix of the contour pixel coordinates of the foreground. An example is shown in Fig. 12.4 to illustrate these three stages during hand detection.

12.6 Per-pixel Classification

The task of hand part classification is to assign a label $l \in L$ to each pixel in the depth image of the hand region. Figure 12.5a shows our hand label partition scheme for classification, and the whole hand is divided into twelve non-overlapping parts. These hand parts are not independent from each other. Rather, the relationship among

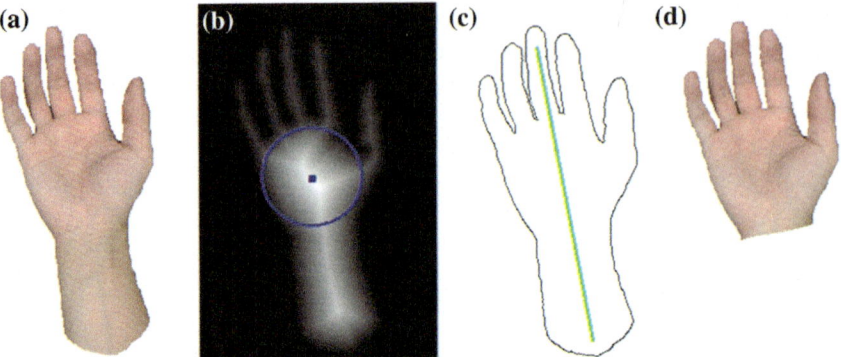

Fig. 12.4 Illustration of hand detection. **a** The foreground region, **b** the palm circle, **c** the orientation vector, and **d** the final segmentation results

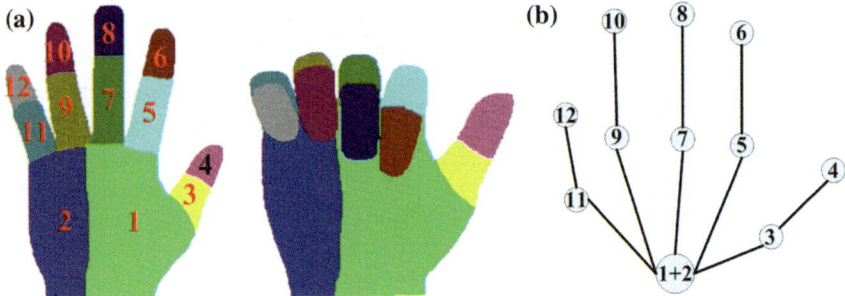

Fig. 12.5 The hand partition scheme. **a** The label distributions for different hand parts. **b** The tree-structured hierarchy of the positions of the labeled hand parts

their positions complies with a tree-structured hierarchy, as shown in Fig. 12.5b. To perform per-pixel classification, a novel depth-context feature is proposed to describe the local depth contrast for each pixel, based on which a trained RDF classifier is used to assign the part labels. In case that the temporal reference is available, the position distribution of each labeled part will also be learned and used in combination with the RDF classifier to form an ensemble of classifiers for per-pixel classification.

12.6.1 Depth-Context Feature

We propose a depth-context feature to describe each pixel in the depth image, which is both depth-invariant and efficient to train the classifier. This feature describes the relative depths between a 3D point and its neighboring points in 3D space, as shown in Fig. 12.6a. The red circle denotes the current point for classification, and the green circles denote the context points to calculate the feature values. Each context point

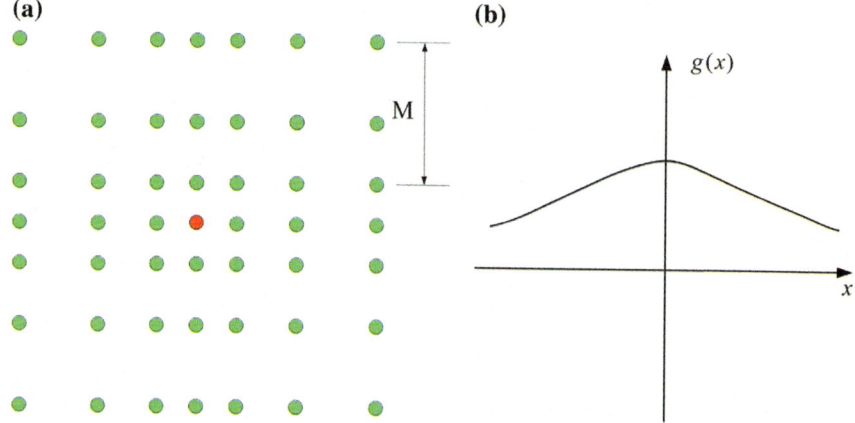

Fig. 12.6 The distance-adaptive scheme for selecting depth image feature candidates, in which the *red circle* indicates the current pixel, and the *green circles* indicate the candidate offset features **a**. The sampling density function along each axis **b**

is represented as a 3D offset $\mathbf{v}_d = [a_d, b_d, 0]^T$. The feature value is defined using the depth difference between the current pixel and the projected pixel of the context point, which is given by:

$$f_F(\mathbf{p}, \mathbf{v}_d) = d_z(\mathbf{p}) - d_z[\Psi_P(\mathbf{v} + \mathbf{v}_d)], \quad (12.2)$$

where $\mathbf{p}$ is the current pixel, $\mathbf{v}$ is the corresponding 3D point, and d_z is the depth value at the given pixel in the depth image. $\Psi_P(\mathbf{v} + \mathbf{v}_d)$ represents the projected pixel coordinates corresponding to the context point $\mathbf{v} + \mathbf{v}_d$ in 3D space. To handle the background variation, all background pixels are assigned with a constant depth value in [31]. However, this introduces inconsistency between the training and testing stages, since the range of the feature values changes as the depth of the hand changes. Instead of assuming constant background, we simply threshold the absolute value of the depth difference by a constant ε_d, which makes the range of the feature values remains relatively stable.

Selection of the context point positions is not well addressed in previous researches [15, 31], in which the context points are randomly generated within certain ranges. However, the nearer points should be more important to describe the context than faraway points, especially for the fingers, as we can see that most of the faraway points lay either on the background or the palm part, both of which are quite homogeneous regions. To this end, we propose a distance-adaptive sampling scheme to generate the context points, as shown in Fig. 12.6a. The points nearer to the current pixel are more densely sampled and vice versa. For simplicity, we focus the discussion on one dimension as the sampling scheme is symmetric. The sampling density function $g(x)$ is adopted to determine the location of each context point. Let the feasible range of the context points be $[-h, h]$. $g(x)$ is a non-increasing function and satisfies

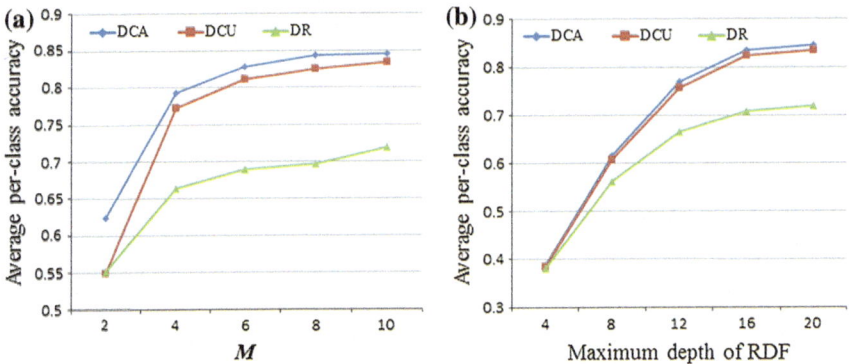

Fig. 12.7 Comparison of the average per-class accuracy of the three depth features. **a** Results with different values of M. **b** Results with different values of the maximum depth of RDF

$\int_0^h g(x)\mathrm{d}x = M$. M is a parameter to determine the grid size. In our implementation, we choose a linear function for $g(x)$. The coordinate of the context point can be obtained by solving the equation $\int_0^{x_d} g(x)\mathrm{d}x = i$ to get x_d for $i = 1, \ldots, M$.

To validate the effectiveness of the depth-context feature as well as the proposed distance-adaptive sampling scheme, we compare the classification accuracy of three candidates: (a) the depth feature in [31] combined with random sampling (DR); (b) the depth-context feature with uniform sampling (DCU), e.g., $g(x)$ is a constant function; and (c) the depth-context feature with distance-adaptive sampling (DCA). The synthesized dataset of about 22.5 k images is used for the experiments with its details given in Sect. 12.9, and 80 % of the dataset is used for training and the rest for testing. Figure 12.7a shows the per-class classification accuracy of the three methods with respect to different number of M, in which the RDF consists of three trees with a depth of 20. Our proposed DCA method outperforms DCU by 2.8 % higher accuracy and outperforms DR by 12.2 %. Especially, the DCA method performs quite well even with a very small value of M, i.e., $M = 2$. This proves the DCA's capability to capture the local context of the pixels in depth image. Figure 12.7b shows the per-class classification accuracy with different depth of the RDF at fixed value of $M = 10$. We can see that the DCA method again provides better classification results for all choices of the tree depths.

12.6.2 RDF Classification

Based on the depth-context feature, we adopt the RDF classifier [7] to label the hand parts by per-pixel classification. The training procedure of the RDF is essentially the same as that in [31]. To generate the training samples, we randomly select ten pixels for each hand part and the background from each training image, and each sample consists of the label of the pixel and the corresponding depth-context feature value.

During the test stage, an input pixel $(\mathbf{p}, \mathbf{v})$ is first processed by each tree in the RDF. For each tree, the posterior probability $P_i(l|\mathbf{v})$ is obtained by starting at the root and recursively assigned to the left or the right child based on the tree node test result until it finally reaches a leaf node. The final posterior probability $P(l|\mathbf{v})$ is obtained by fusing the results of all the trees in the random forest, i.e., $P(l|\mathbf{v}) = \frac{1}{N}\sum_i^N P_i(l|\mathbf{v})$, where N is the number of trees in the RDF. The label of the pixel can be directly determined by MAP estimation: $l^* = \arg\max_l P(l|\mathbf{v})$. However, the final label decision is not made here, and the posterior $P(l|\mathbf{v})$ will be further processed by the superpixel MRF framework to give the refined results.

12.6.3 Key Point Extraction

The key points are a simplified representation of the hand parsing results. Instead of calculating the 3D centroid of each labeled hand part, we calculate the expectation positions of each hand part based on the label distribution given by hand parsing. Let the 3D point set on the input hand be H. Let the label distribution given by the RDF classifier be $P(l|\mathbf{v})$, $\mathbf{v} \in H$. The 3D position distribution of a hand part l can be calculated by:

$$P(\mathbf{v}|l) = \frac{P(l|\mathbf{v})P(\mathbf{v})}{\sum_{\mathbf{v}_i \in H} P(l|\mathbf{v}_i)P(\mathbf{v}_i)} = \frac{P(l|\mathbf{v})}{\sum_{\mathbf{v}_i \in H} P(l|\mathbf{v}_i)}, \quad (12.3)$$

where we assume uniform prior of the 3D positions of the depth points. Thus, the expected position of the hand part l equals to $\mathbf{v}_c^l = \sum_{\mathbf{v}_i \in H} \mathbf{v}_i P(\mathbf{v}_i|l)$. Note for the two hand parts 1 and 2 that belong to the palm in Fig. 12.5a, the 3D points within them and the corresponding label distribution are merged to get the palm position. Let the resulting positions of each hand part be $U_l = \{v_c^l | l = 1, ..., L\}$. These points are further arranged into a tree hierarchy based on their relationship in the hand skeleton, as illustrated in Fig. 12.5b, where the root corresponds to the palm position.

12.6.4 Temporal Constraints

The temporal references are useful when parsing the hands in successive images. Given that the hand parsing result in the previous frame is available, we propose to use it as an auxiliary classifier for the RDF classifier for per-pixel classification in the current frame. This classifier forms an ensemble of classifiers with the RDF classifier. To this end, we first use the 3D Gaussian distribution to approximate the point distribution within each hand part in the previous frame, i.e., $P_T(\mathbf{v}|l) \sim \mathcal{N}(\mu_l, C_l)$, and the parameters μ_l and C_l are learned from the points that belong to each hand part in the previous frame. The temporal classifier is thus given by:

$$P_T(l|\mathbf{v}) \propto P_T(\mathbf{v}|l) P_T(l), \tag{12.4}$$

where $P_T(l)$ is proportional to the number of points within each part. For clarity, we denote the RDF classifier as $P_R(l|\mathbf{v})$. The previous per-pixel classification scheme can thus be accomplished by the ensemble of P_T and P_R to incorporate the temporal reference, that is:

$$P(l|\mathbf{v}) = \eta P_R(l|\mathbf{v}) + (1-\eta) P_T(l|\mathbf{v}). \tag{12.5}$$

Here, η is the coefficient to control the relative weight of the temporal classifier and the RDF classifier. As the variation of hand motion speed is large and the performance of P_T can degrade a lot with fast hand movement, we make P_R outweigh the temporal term P_T so that their combination is robust to tracking failure, i.e., $\eta > 0.5$. In practice, we find a value of 0.5 usually works fine.

12.7 Superpixel MRF Hand Parsing

The hand parsing results produced by the per-pixel classification method in Sect. 12.6 are quite noisy since dependencies between neighboring pixels are not fully utilized. Simply applying the pixel-level filtering techniques, e.g., the median filter, to the labeling results will not work well since many misclassified pixels form small isolated regions surrounded by other parts, as shown in Fig. 12.8. The MRFs [17] can be used to refine the classification results, which can well model the constraints from the neighboring states and the image observations [11]. However, the traditional pixel-based MRF is time consuming for real-time HCI applications. Besides, the isolated misclassified regions are more suitable to be represented as a whole rather than a set of pixels for MRF inference. Therefore, we partition the hand region into superpixels and combine them, and MRF inference to refine the parsed hand parts based on the per-pixel parsing results.

The proposed superpixel MRF framework is built with both the posterior probability $P(l|\mathbf{v})$ given by per-pixel classification and the depth image. The superpixels are constructed with two criteria. First, the depth discontinuity must be conserved when determining the borders of neighboring superpixels. Second, pixels within one superpixel should have similar posterior probability. These principles are incorporated into the SLIC superpixel partition algorithm [29], and the resulting superpixel partition is compact in terms of 3D space distribution and posterior probability. The MRF graph is then constructed for the superpixels similar to [37].

Given the compact representation of the superpixels, they still behave differently from the pixels. Some superpixels have quite irregular shapes in order to conserve the depth discontinuity during superpixel partition. Also, the relative sizes of neighboring superpixels are sometimes uneven, as shown in Fig. 12.8b. This suggests that some superpixels can have larger influence on their neighbors than others. Therefore, in the MRF framework, we model the interaction energies between superpixels based on their common borders and relative sizes and label co-occurrence distribution when determining the pairwise term. That is, if two neighboring superpixels have many common borders, they are quite likely to have the same label. Also, a small superpixel can be more easily smoothed by a big neighbor than opposite. We also take the idea of label co-occurrence from [33] so that the unsmoothness between the neighbors with low co-occurrence rate is high.

12.7.1 Superpixel Partition

Though the per-pixel classification result is somewhat noisy, the labeled parts are mostly locally homogeneous. Besides, a large portion of the wrongly classified pixels form isolated small regions. Therefore, the labeled image is suitable to be represented by a set of super pixels for further processing, which can well model the misclassified regions as well as reduce the computational cost involved in the MRF energy minimization process. To this end, we modify the simple linear iterative clustering (SLIC) algorithm to get the superpixel partition [11]. The original SLIC method is developed for color images, while we need to get the superpixel partition that conforms to both the hand part classification results and the depth discontinuity. To be specific, the criteria for our superpixel partition scheme are as follows:

1. Depth continuity: The depth difference between neighboring pixels within the superpixel is smaller than a threshold d_T.
2. Similar posterior probability: The pixels within a superpixel should have similar $P(l|\mathbf{v})$.

According to these requirements, it is not reasonable to apply the SLIC method directly to the posterior distribution $P(l|\mathbf{v})$, as the Euclidean distance in $P(l|\mathbf{v})$ does not make much sense. Thus, we perform superpixel partition in the space of posterior distributions and adopt the Kullback–Leibler divergence to measure the difference between each pixel and the superpixel cluster center. Let the set of superpixel partition be $S = s_1 \cup s_2 \cup \cdots \cup s_K$. The posterior probability and depth of each superpixel are taken as the average of all the pixels within the partition, that is:

$$d_{s_k} = \frac{1}{|s_k|} \sum_{\mathbf{v}_j \in s_k} c_j \qquad (12.6)$$

$$P(l|s_k) = \frac{1}{|s_k|} \sum_{\mathbf{v}_j \in s_k} P(l|\mathbf{v}_j), \qquad (12.7)$$

where $d_{(s_k)}$ and $P(l|s_k)$ are the depth and posterior probability of the superpixel s_k. For superpixel clustering, we define the distance metric in the posterior probability to measure the difference between the pixels and the superpixel cluster to be:

$$D_{kl}(s_k, \mathbf{p}_j) = \sum_{l=1}^{L} P(l|s_k) \log \frac{P(l|s_k)}{P(l|\mathbf{p}_j)}. \qquad (12.8)$$

Besides, in order to preserve the depth discontinuity in the superpixel partition, the pixel $\mathbf{p}_j$ can be assigned to s_k only if $|c_j - d_{s_k}| \leq d_T$. In the implementation, we set $d_T = 6$ mm. Also, the superpixel should be compact in the 2D image coordinate space, as in the original SLIC method. Therefore, we define the distance metric for superpixel partition as:

$$D = \begin{cases} \sqrt{D_{kl} + \left(\frac{D_S}{M_S}\right)^2 m^2} & \text{if } |c_j - d_{s_k}| \leq d_T \\ \infty & \text{otherwise} \end{cases} \quad (12.9)$$

where M_S is the regular grid step on the image plane to determine the superpixel size; D_S is the pixel distance between $\mathbf{p}_j$ and the superpixel center; m controls the relative importance of the two terms. Based on the distance metric D, the superpixel partition is performed by the clustering scheme in the SLIC method. The posterior probability of these superpixels forms the observation data for the following MRF inference. Note that the sizes of the superpixels are generally quite close, except for some noises, i.e., the wrongly labeled regions are usually small or have irregular shapes, and they are more likely to be neutralized by their neighbors.

12.7.2 Superpixel MRF Inference

Given the set of superpixels $S = \{s_k\}$, the goal for MRF inference is to assign each superpixel a new label $l \in L$. Let the associated labels for the superpixels be $Y = \{y_k\}$. The task for MRF inference of the labels is to get the MAP solution of $Y^* = \arg\max_Y P(Y|S)$, which is equivalent to the minimization of the following energy function:

$$E = E_d + E_S = \sum_{i \in S} \phi_i(y_i) + \sum_{i \in S, j \in N_i} \psi_{i,j}(y_i, y_j). \quad (12.10)$$

Here, E_d is the unary term to measure the discrepancy between the inferred label and the per-pixel classification results, and we set $\phi_i(y_i) = -\log P(y_i|s_i)$.

The pairwise term E_s is used to measure the smoothness between neighboring superpixels, and we utilize the idea of label co-occurrence [33] to define $\psi_{i,j}$. The label co-occurrence represents the conditional probability $P(y_i|y_j)$, which indicates how likely a superpixel with state y_j will have a neighbor with a state y_i. Since some hand parts are more likely to be adjacent than others, e.g., the chances that the part 1 and 2 are adjacent are higher than the part 1 and 6, the label co-occurrence can be useful during inference by punishing the unlikely adjacent states. However, unlike [33] in which a superpixel in the color images is equally affected by all its neighbors, we take the depth discontinuity and the irregular shapes of the superpixels into consideration to model the pairwise interaction energy. First, to handle the depth

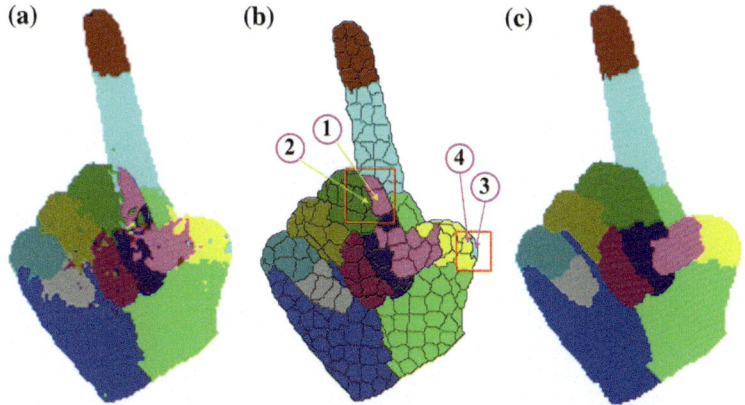

Fig. 12.8 Effectiveness of MRF inference based on superpixel partition and label co-occurrence. **a** Per-pixel classification result. **b** Superpixel partition result. **c** SMRF inference result

discontinuity, we determine the adjacency of a pair of nodes (y_i, y_j) based on the following criteria:

$$\begin{cases} \Omega_i \cap \Omega_j \neq \emptyset \\ |d_{s_i} - d_{s_j}| \leq d_T \end{cases} \quad (12.11)$$

where Ω is the set of border pixels of the superpixel. With these criteria, there is a pairwise energy term between two nodes only if they are neighboring superpixels and have similar depths. In addition, some superpixels can have quite irregular shapes, which make them interact with their neighbors in an uneven way. Specifically, a superpixel is more likely to take the same label with the neighbors that share more borders than others, and small superpixels are more likely to take the same label with its big neighbors than the opposite way. This is especially significant for the wrongly labeled regions, which are usually isolated and small. For two adjacent nodes i and j, the uneven influences resulting from these factors should be reflected in the pairwise energy term, in addition to their state differences (y_i, y_j). Thus, we define a weight coefficient $\alpha_{i,j}$ for the pairwise term of adjacent nodes:

$$\alpha_{i,j} = \frac{|\Omega_i \cap \Omega_j|}{|\Omega_i|} \times \frac{|s_j|}{|s_i|}. \quad (12.12)$$

A big value of $\alpha_{i,j}$ indicates the superpixel, and i is more likely to be affected by its neighbor j.

Figure 12.8 shows an example to illustrate the effectiveness of modeling the pairwise energy based on the superpixel partition results. Figure 12.8b shows the superpixel partition of the per-pixel classification results in Fig. 12.8a. As the pixels within each superpixel are assigned the same state, the small and scattered misclassified points are largely suppressed even without MRF inference. However, the larger misclassified regions still cannot be removed, e.g., the regions labeled with 1 and 3

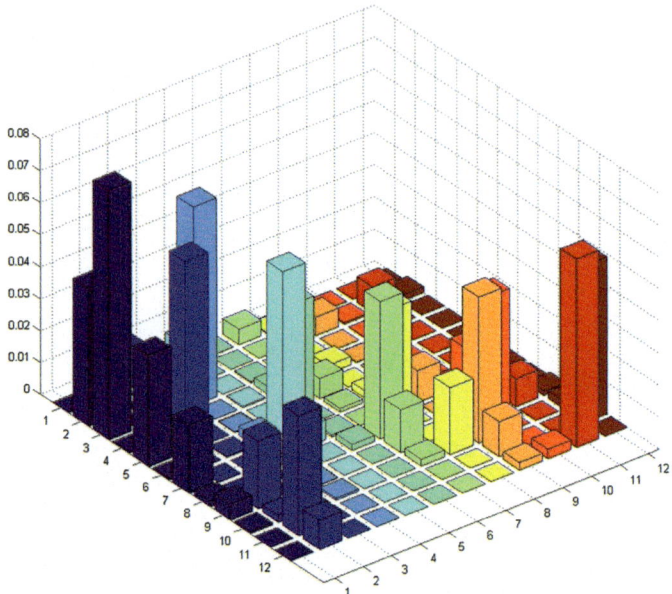

Fig. 12.9 The co-occurrence probability distribution of the labels of the neighboring superpixels for $M_S = 4$

in the red rectangles. Region 1 is misclassified to No. 4 hand part and region 3 is misclassified to No. 5 hand part. According to the co-occurrence probability of different hand parts in Fig. 12.9, both these misclassified regions result in a large pairwise energy. First consider region 3. It is small in relative size compared to its surrounding superpixels, e.g., region 4, thus assigning it with the label of its neighbors will produce a big energy decrease, which is favored during inference. For region 1, note it is only adjacent to the superpixels on the middle finger since depth discontinuity is handled to build the MRF framework, thus it will be influenced by only one misclassified superpixel and multiple correctly classified regions in the middle finger. By comparison, its adjacent region 2, which is correctly classified, has much more correctly classified neighbors. Again, region 1 is more inclined to be neutralized by region 2. Figure 12.8c shows the results given by MRF inference, in which the misclassified regions are successfully removed.

Combing the label co-occurrence, node adjacency and weight coefficient $\alpha_{i,j}$, the pairwise potential function $\psi_{i,j}$ for two adjacent node i and j takes the following form:

$$\psi_{i,j}(y_i, y_j) = -\alpha_{i,j} \times \left[1 - \delta(y_i, y_j)\right] \times \log\left[\frac{P(y_i|y_j) + P(y_j|y_i)}{2}\right] \quad (12.13)$$

where δ is the Kronecker delta function to indicate a zero pairwise energy if the nodes i and j have the same state. $P(y_i|y_j)$ is the conditional probability learned

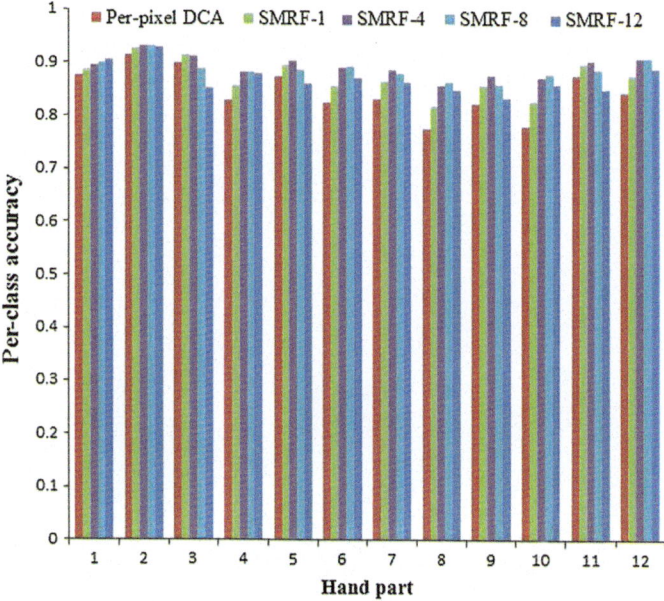

Fig. 12.10 Comparison of classification accuracy between per-pixel classification and SMRF with different superpixel sizes

from the training dataset by counting the co-occurrence of the labels of neighboring superpixels. The co-occurrence distribution of the labels is shown in Fig. 12.9. Note here all the $P(y_i|y_i)$ terms are set to zero as they have no effect on the inference results. By incorporating the co-occurrence probability distribution in SMRF inference, we encode the prior to eliminate the unlikely neighboring labels to smooth the results given by per-pixel classification. Based on the above formulation, we adopt the iterated conditional modes (ICM) algorithm [5] to minimize the energy function to get Y^*, and the initial label for each superpixel is taken to be $y_k = \arg\max_l P(l|s_k)$. The ICM algorithm is a greedy search algorithm and is guaranteed to converge fast.

We have tested the performance of the proposed SMRF framework on the same dataset as in Sect. 12.6, and the results are presented in Fig. 12.10 and Table 12.1. The label "SMRF-#" represents our method running with different superpixel grid step M_S, i.e., we run the SMRF method with $M_S = \#$ based on the per-pixel parsing results with our DCA feature and a feature grid of $M = 10$. Compared to the benchmark method [31], we achieved an overall 17.2 % higher accuracy for the twelve hand part classification for $M_S = 4$. Compared to the per-pixel classification results with our DCA feature, the proposed SMRF framework achieves a 4.7 % higher accuracy with an extra time cost of 216 ms per frame.

The results for the proposed SMRF method with different values of M_S also demonstrate that superpixel is a more appropriate representation to remove the misclassified regions than the pixel. Note that the method "SMRF-1" is equivalent to

Table 12.1 Comparison of overall classification accuracy and extra time costs for SMRF inference with different superpixel sizes

Method	Accuracy (%)	Time cost (ms)
Per-pixel DR [31]	72.0	–
Per-pixel DCA	84.5	–
SMRF-1	87.3	605.4
SMRF-4	89.2	215.9
SMRF-8	88.8	186.5
SMRF-12	87.0	167.0

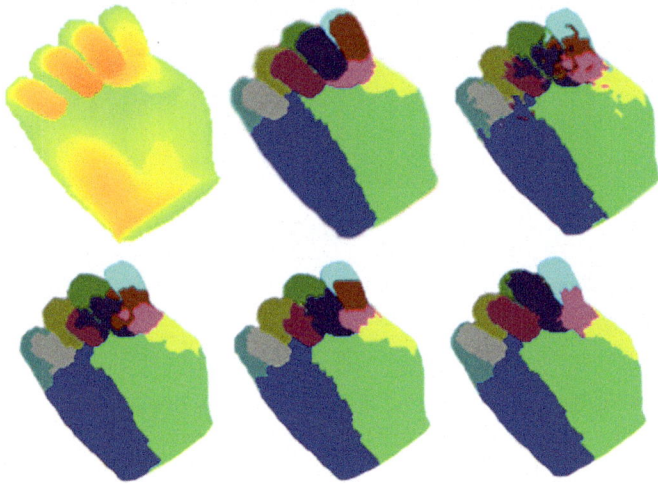

Fig. 12.11 Illustration of SMRF performance with different superpixel sizes. *Upper row* the input depth image (*Left*), the ground truth hand part labels (*Middle*) and per-pixel classification with DCA (*Right*). *Lower row* SMRF results with $M_S = 1$ (*Left*), SMRF with $M_S = 4$ (*Middle*), and SMRF with $M_S = 12$ (*Right*)

per-pixel inference, and the corresponding results are not as good as the superpixel-level counterparts, even at a higher time cost of 605 ms per frame. This is because at the pixel level, a pixel within the isolated misclassified region will be influenced by its surrounding pixels, among which there are always the misclassified pixels. By comparison, at the superpixel level, a well-formed superpixel of the misclassified region is usually surrounded only by the superpixels with the correct labels and thus is more likely to be assigned with the correct label of its neighbors. Besides, according to the results in Table 12.1, the size of the superpixel cannot be too large, as it produces over-smoothing effects. Figure 12.11 shows an example of applying SMRF with different values of M_S. Not the finger regions, we can see the isolated

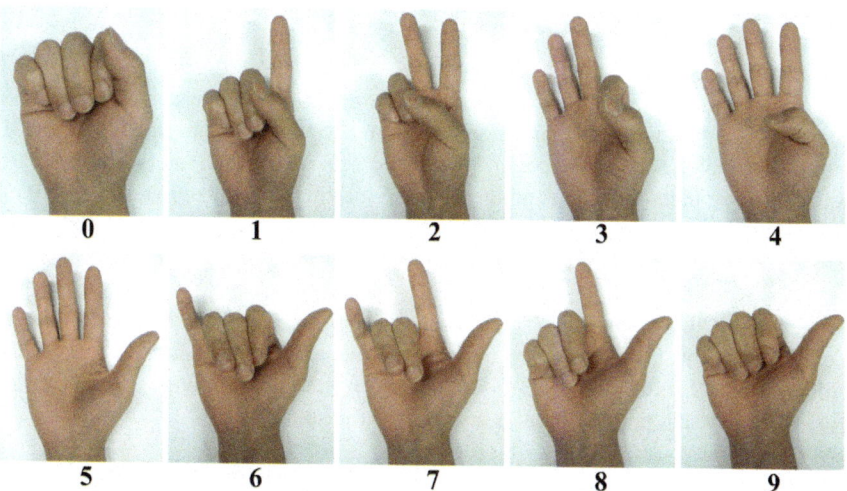

Fig. 12.12 The hand shapes corresponding to the digit gestures

misclassified regions are not well suppressed with $M_S = 1$, while the thumb and index fingers are wrongly smoothed for $M_S = 12$. The size $M_S = 4$ produces the result that best conforms to the ground truth.

12.8 Hand Gesture Recognition

The hand part classification result is utilized for static hand gesture recognition in this section. In some previous researches, the labeled image is directly matched to pre-defined labeled templates via distance transform to recognize the corresponding hand posture [36]. However, this is unsuitable for our framework. The distance transform-based matching is sensitive to both inaccurate hand segmentation and hand rotation, which makes alignment between the input and templates difficult. Besides, the 3D information of the labeled points is not utilized via 2D matching. Therefore, we propose to perform hand gesture recognition based on matching between the extracted 3D key points and the pre-defined templates. The gesture templates are also defined in a tree hierarchy, with different key point positions corresponding to different gestures.

There are totally ten gestures to be recognized. The corresponding hand shapes of the gestures are illustrated in Fig. 12.12, which map to the digit numbers from zero to ten. For the ten gestures, we define a set of key point templates $\{U_t | t = 1, \ldots, 10\}$ for recognition. Given the key point set U_I extracted from the input depth image following the method in Sect. 12.6.3, the input gesture can be recognized by finding the template that best fit U_I. The problem can thus be formulated as:

$$t^* = \arg\min_t D_U(U_I, U_t). \tag{12.14}$$

The key issue in this problem is how to measure the distance D_U against the viewpoint change of the input and the hand size variations. To this end, we propose to use 3D point set matching to evaluate D_U. These two sets are first aligned with the least-squares fitting method in [2], and the distance metric between key point sets is thus defined as:

$$D_U(U_I, U_t) = \|U_t - R_U U_I - T_U\|^2, \tag{12.15}$$

where $R_U = VU^T$ and $\mathrm{Cov}(U_I, U_t) = U\Lambda V^T$ are the SVD decomposition of Cov. T_U is a translation vector to compensate the center difference. To remove the influence of 3D translation, the root positions in the tree-structured hierarchy, i.e., Fig. 12.5b, of each pair of samples are fixed to the same point.

12.9 Experimental Results

In this section, we present the experimental results of the proposed hand parsing scheme on single-frame datasets, continuous hand motion sequences, and real-world hand motion sequences. For quantitative evaluations on the single-frame datasets and continuous motion sequences, we synthesized the depth images with the hand model in Sect. 12.4 based on the hand motion parameters captured by the CyberGlove II [8]. For testing on the real-world sequences, we record the depth images captured by a SoftKinetic DS325 camera. Besides, we also utilize the hand parsing results for gesture recognition and compare its performance with state-of-the-art method.

The whole program was coded in C++ and tested on a PC with Intel i5 750 CPU and 4G RAM. The resolutions of the testing images in all the experiments are 320×240. The size controlling parameter of the feature grid is $M = 10$, the tree depth of the RDF classifier is 20, the weighting parameter to fuse RDF and temporal reference is $\eta = 0.5$, and the superpixel grid size is $M_S = 4$.

12.9.1 Quantitative Evaluation for Single Frames

In order to generate the training data to learn the RDF classifiers, we use the Cyber-Glove II to capture the possible finger articulation parameters that people would make in natural hand motion. To handle the viewpoint variation, the captured finger articulation parameters are combined with 3D global hand rotation in certain ranges. Here, we define the ranges to be $(-20°, 20°)$ for global rotation around the X and Y axes, i.e., the axes parallel to the image plane of the camera, and $(-35°, 35°)$ around the Z axis, i.e., the axis perpendicular to the image plane. A dataset of the depth and label images is synthesized using the 3D hand model with the captured

Fig. 12.13 Examples of the hand configurations in the synthesized dataset

hand motion parameters, which consists of about 22.5 k templates. Some examples of the templates in this dataset are shown in Fig. 12.13. To evaluate the classification accuracy on the synthesized images, we use 80 % of the images in the dataset for learning and the rest 20 % for testing.

The quantitative results on single frames have been presented in Sects. 12.6 and 12.7. The results in Sect. 12.6 show the superiority of the proposed DCA depth feature over our DCU feature and the benchmark DR feature [31]. The results show a 12.2 % increase of the classification accuracy compared to [31]. The results in Sect. 12.7 show the per-pixel classification results can be improved by incorporating spatial constraints and label co-occurrence prior, which gives a further 4.7 % increase in the classification accuracy.

12.9.2 Quantitative Evaluation for Continuous Sequences

To evaluate how the temporal reference can help to improve the hand parsing results, we synthesized two continuous hand motion sequences, both of which are approximately 500 frames long and contain complex combinations of global hand motion and local finger articulations. The first sequence includes the continuous motion of the hand when it is posing digit gestures, including the transition motion to change from one gesture to another. The 3D hand rotation and transition are also included. The second sequence contains different single/multiple finger motions combined with 3D hand rotation. Especially, these two testing sequences contain some clips in

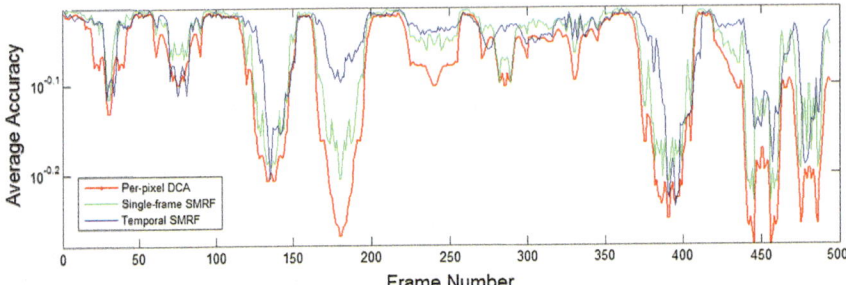

Fig. 12.14 Comparison of the hand parsing results using per-pixel classification with DCA, single-frame SMRF and SMRF with temporal reference on the first synthesized continuous hand motion sequence

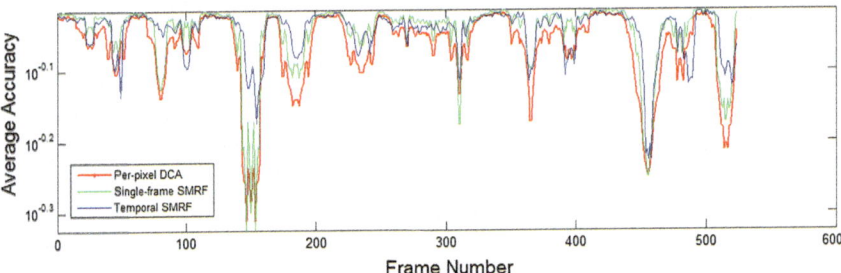

Fig. 12.15 Comparison of the hand parsing results using per-pixel classification with DCA, single-frame SMRF and SMRF with temporal reference on the second synthesized continuous hand motion sequence

which the hand motions are not covered by the training dataset in order to test the robustness of the proposed parsing scheme.

The per-frame accuracy curves are shown in Figs. 12.14 and 12.15, in which we compared three methods: per-pixel classification with the proposed DCA feature and the proposed single-frame SMRF and the temporal SMRF. Note the average accuracy is shown in log-scale for better illustration. The average accuracies on the whole sequences are summarized in Table 12.2, in which the per-pixel classification results with the DR feature [31] are also included. With the temporal reference, our method achieves further 1.5 and 0.7 % increase for the two sequences in addition to the 4.7 and 4.0 % improvement by the SMRF algorithm.

While the improvement given by the temporal reference seems not striking in terms of the average accuracy, it is important to see that it largely increases the overall robustness. Since some parts of the testing sequences are either not covered by the training dataset or are going through complex hand motion and self-occlusion, the performances by per-pixel classification with the pre-trained classifier and the SMRF method that built upon it can suffer from drastic degradation, e.g., frames between 150 and 200 in Seq. 1 and frames between 130 and 160 in Seq. 2. In

Table 12.2 Comparison of the classification results on the two synthesized hand motion sequences

	Per-pixel DR [31] (%)	Per-pixel DCA (%)	Single-frame SMRF (%)	Temporal SMRF (%)
Seq. 1	77.2	82.4	87.1	89.6
Seq. 2	81.7	86.8	90.8	91.5

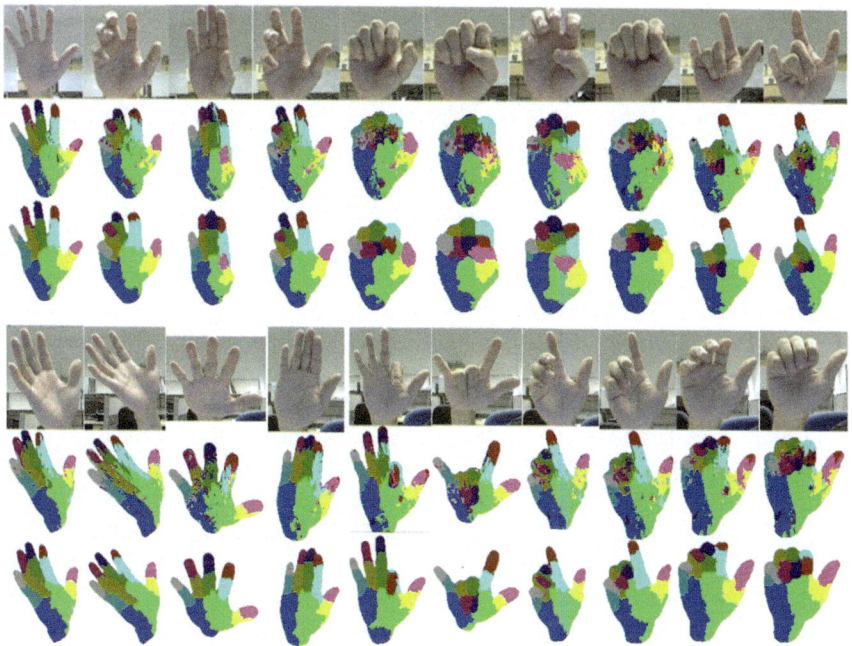

Fig. 12.16 Comparison of the hand parsing results using per-pixel classification with DCA and the RDF classifier (*middle row*) and the proposed Temporal SMRF framework (*lower row*) on real-world hand motion sequences

these parts, we see the system performance is dramatically improved by fusing the temporal information, and thus, the resulting overall classification accuracy remains much more stable than the single-frame-based counterparts.

12.9.3 Qualitative Evaluation

We further test the parsing performance of the SMRF framework on real-world input sequences captured by a SoftKinetic depth camera, which is about 900 frames long, and the result is illustrated in Fig. 12.16. The parsed hand parts are shown with different colors, which is consistent with the labeling scheme in Fig. 12.5a. The results show the effectiveness of the SMRF method. From the figure, we can see that the results of per-pixel parsing are very noisy. In addition, its performance for small finger parts get even worse for the challenging cases such as tightening fingers or when some fingers are occluded. By comparison, the SMRF method produces more meaningful parsing in such cases.

12.9.4 Hand Gesture Recognition

We tested the recognition accuracy of the proposed approach on a hand gesture dataset captured by a SoftKinetic camera, in which the hand can rotate within about $(-30°, 30°)$ around X, Y, Z axis freely. The fingers are also allowed to move in small ranges. The whole test suite contains about 1,000 images, approximately 100 images for each class. Compared to the dataset used in [26], this dataset contains more challenging cases, e.g., the test samples shown in Fig. 12.18. With this dataset, we compare the recognition accuracy of the proposed method and the thresholding decomposition FEMD method in [26]. To simplify the comparison, we ask the users to wear a black belt at the wrist, which is needed for the method in [26]. However, it is worth noting that our proposed method does not need the black belt for accurate segmentation of the hand region, which makes it insensitive to illumination variations. The confusion matrix of the hand gesture recognition results for our method is shown in Fig. 12.17. Our method achieves an average recognition accuracy of 95.4 %. By comparison, the average accuracy of the method in [26] on this dataset is 84.2 %. Especially, our recognition method can handle quite challenging cases, in which the hand contour alone is not discriminative enough to recognize the gesture. Some examples of such gestures are shown in Fig. 12.18, in which the correct finger segments used for EMD-based matching in [26] are difficult to extract, and the

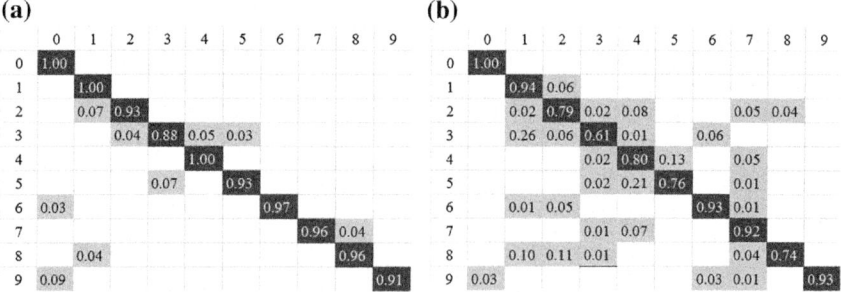

Fig. 12.17 The confusion matrices for digit number recognition with the proposed method (**a**) and the thresholding decomposition FEMD method [26] (**b**)

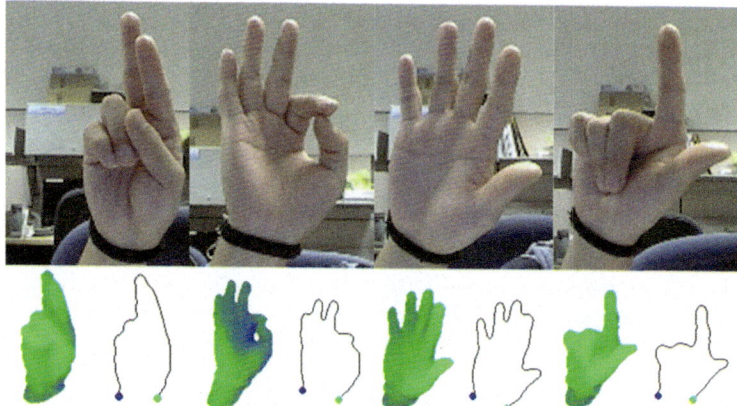

Fig. 12.18 Examples of the gestures that are difficult to be correctly recognized with the hand contour alone. These four gestures correspond to 2, 3, 5, and 8, respectively. The *lower row* shows the corresponding depth image input for the proposed recognition method and the hand contour input for [26]

corresponding results are 1, 2, 4, and 1. In such cases, the key points for our method can still be detected by parsing the hand, and the correct gestures are recognized.

Acknowledgments This work is supported in part by the NTU IMI seed grant M4081078.B40.

References

1. Aristidou A, Lasenby J (2010) Motion capture with constrained inverse kinematics for real-time hand tracking. In: ISCCSP, pp 1–5
2. Arun KS, Huang TS, Blostein SD (1987) Least-squares fitting of two 3D point sets. IEEE Trans PAMI
3. Baak A, Muller M, Bharaj G, Seidel HP, Theobalt C (2011) A data-driven approach for real-time full body pose reconstruction from a depth camera. In: Proceedings of ICCV
4. Belongie S, Malik J, Puzicha J (2002) Shape matching and object recognition using shape contexts. IEEE Trans PAMI
5. Besag J (1986) On the statistical analysis of dirty pictures. J Roy Stat Soc B 48(3):259–302
6. Bo L, Ren X, Fox D (2011) Depth kernel descriptors for object recognition. In: Proceedings of IROS
7. Breiman L (2001) Random forests. Mach Learn 45(1):5–32
8. CyberGlove. www.cyberglovesystems.com
9. Dalal N, Triggs B (2005) Histograms of oriented gradients for human detection. In: Proceedings of CVPR
10. Erol A, Bebis G, Nicolescu M, Boyle RD, Twombly X (2005) A review on vision-based full DOF hand motion estimation. In: Proceedings of CVPR

11. Fauvel M, Chanussot J, Benediktsson JA (2010) SVM- and MRF-based method for accurate classification of hyperspectral images. IEEE Geosci Remote Sens Lett 7(4):736–740
12. Felzenszwalb PF, Huttenlocher DP (2005) Pictorial structures for object recognition. Int J Comput Vis 61(1):55–79
13. Heikkila J (1997) A four-step camera calibration procedure with implicit image correction. In: Proceedings of CVPR, pp 1106–1112
14. Kerdvibulvech C, Saito H (2009) Model-based hand tracking by chamfer distance and adaptive color learning using particle filter. EURASIP J Image Video Process
15. Keskin C, Kirac F, Kara YE, Akarun L (2011) Real-time hand pose estimation using depth sensors. In: Proceedings of ICCV
16. Keskin C, Kirac F, Kara YE, Akarun L (2012) Hand pose estimation and hand shape classification using multi-layered randomized decision forests. In: ECCV 2012
17. Kindermann R, Snell JL (1980) Markov random fields and their applications. The American Mathematical Society
18. Lewis JP, Cordner M, Fong N (2000) Pose space deformation: a unified approach to shape interpolation and skeleton-driven deformation. In: SIGGRAPH
19. Liang H, Yuan J, Thalmann D, Zhang Z (2013) Model-based hand pose estimation via spatial-temporal hand parsing and 3D fingertip localization, in the visual. Comput J 29(6–8):837–848
20. Liang H, Yuan J, Thalmann D (2014) Parsing the hand in depth images. IEEE Trans Multimedia, in Press
21. Li Z, Jarvis R (2009) Real time hand gesture recognition using a range camera. In: Proceedings of ACRA, pp 529–534
22. Lin LJ, Ying W, Huang TS (2000) Modeling the constraints of human hand motion. In: Proceedings of the workshop on human motion, pp 121–126
23. Lu S, Metaxas D, Samaras D, Oliensis J (2003) Using multiple cues for hand tracking and model refinement. In: Proceedings of CVPR, vol 2, pp 443–450
24. Pishchulin L, Andriluka M, Gehler P, Schiele B (2013) Strong appearance and expressive spatial models for human pose estimation. In: Proceedings of ICCV
25. Ramanan D (2007) Learning to parse images of articulated bodies. In: Proceedings of NIPS
26. Ren Z, Yuan J, Meng J, Zhang Z (2013) Robust part-based hand gesture recognition using kinect sensor. IEEE Trans Multimedia 15(5):1110–1120
27. Ren Z, Yuan J, Li C, Liu W (2011) Minimum near-convex decomposition for robust shape representation. In: Proceedings of ICCV
28. Rusu RB, Blodow N, Beetz M (2009) Fast point feature histograms (FPFH) for 3D registration. In: ICRA, Kobe, Japan
29. Shaji A, Smith K, Lucchi A, Fua P, Susstrunk S (2012) SLIC superpixels compared to state-of-the-art superpixel methods. IEEE Trans PAMI 34(11):2274–2282
30. Shen X, Hua G, Williams L, Wu Y (2011) Motion divergence fields for dynamic hand gesture recognition. In: Proceedings of FGR
31. Shotton J, Fitzgibbon A, Cook M, Sharp T, Finocchio M (2011) Real-time human pose recognition in parts from single depth images. In: Proceedings of CVPR
32. Theobalt C, Albrecht I, Haber J, Magnor M, Seidel H (2004) Pitching a baseball—tracking high-speed motion with multi-exposure images. In: SIGGRAPH
33. Tighe J, Lazebnik S (2010) SuperParsing: scalable nonparametric image parsing with superpixels. In: Proceedings of ECCV
34. Van den Bergh M, Koller-Meier E, Bosche F, Van Gool L (2009) Haarlet-based hand gesture recognition for 3D interaction. In: Proceedings of WACV
35. Wachs JP, Kolsch M, Stern H, Edan Y (2011) Vision-based hand-gesture applications. Commun ACM
36. Wang RY, Popovic J (2009) Real-time hand-tracking with a color glove. In: ACM transaction on graphics
37. Wang X (2009) A new localized superpixel Markov random field for image segmentation. In: Proceedings of ICME 2009

38. Wang H, Leu MC, Oz C (2006) American sign language recognition using multi-dimensional hidden Markov models. J Inf Sci Eng, vol 22, no. 5, pp 1109–1123
39. Yao Y, Fu Y (2012) Real-time hand pose estimation from RGB-D sensor. In: Proceedings of ICME
40. Zhao W, Chai J, Xu Y (2012) Combining marker-based mocap and RGB-D camera for acquiring high-fidelity hand motion data. In: Proceedings of the ACM SIGGRAPH/eurographics symposium on computer animation

Chapter 13
Learning Fast Hand Pose Recognition

Eyal Krupka, Alon Vinnikov, Ben Klein, Aharon Bar-Hillel, Daniel Freedman, Simon Stachniak and Cem Keskin

Abstract Practical real-time hand pose recognition requires a classifier of high accuracy, running in a few millisecond speed. We present a novel classifier architecture, the *Discriminative Ferns Ensemble* (*DFE*), for addressing this challenge. The classifier architecture optimizes both classification speed and accuracy when a large training set is available. Speed is obtained using simple binary features and direct indexing into a set of tables, and accuracy by using a large capacity model and careful discriminative optimization. The proposed framework is applied to the problem of hand pose recognition in depth and infrared images, using a very large training set. Both the accuracy and the classification time obtained are considerably superior to relevant competing methods, allowing one to reach accuracy targets with runtime orders of magnitude faster than the competition. We show empirically that using DFE, we can significantly reduce classification time by increasing training sample size for a fixed target accuracy. Finally, scalability to a large number of classes is tested using a synthetically generated data set of 81 classes.

E. Krupka · A. Vinnikov · B. Klein · A. B. Hillel (✉) · D. Freedman
Microsoft Research, Herzelia, Israel
e-mail: aharonb@microsoft.com

E. Krupka
e-mail: eyalk@microsoft.com

A. Vinnikov
e-mail: t-alvinn@microsoft.com

B. Klein
e-mail: t-benk@microsoft.com

D. Freedman
e-mail: danifree@microsoft.com

S. Stachniak
Microsoft Console dev R&D, Redmond WA, USA
e-mail: szimons@microsoft.com

C. Keskin
Microsoft Research Cambridge, Cambridge, UK
e-mail: cemke@microsoft.com

© Springer International Publishing Switzerland 2014
L. Shao et al. (eds.), *Computer Vision and Machine Learning with RGB-D Sensors*,
Advances in Computer Vision and Pattern Recognition,
DOI: 10.1007/978-3-319-08651-4_13

13.1 Introduction

The trade-off of speed versus accuracy is an important topic, widely discussed in the object detection and recognition literature [3, 7, 11, 19, 25]. In applications like Natural User Interface (NUI), algorithms have to obtain high recognition accuracy in real time, on low power platforms. Often accuracy must be obtained with only a small fraction of the available CPU resources, reserving CPU cycles for other operations. The trade-off is natural: high accuracy requires a rich representation, with considerable computational cost at all levels of the system. At the lowest level, this includes using dense sampling of complex local descriptors [21, 27]. Further on, multiple spatial aggregation layers are employed [6, 18], with large dictionaries at higher levels. At the highest level, the best accuracy is often obtained using non-linear kernels [6, 18], requiring kernel computation with many support vectors.

In this section, we attack the problem of hand pose classification using infrared (IR) and depth images from a time of flight depth camera, in the context of a NUI application. There are dual demands for high accuracy and a very low computation budget, the latter a fraction of a millisecond on a low-end CPU. For our problem, standard techniques achieved reasonable enough accuracy for a moderate training set size, but were unable to meet the classification time requirement. One can improve speed by modifying the parameters of such techniques; for example, one may reduce grid density or dictionary size. However, experiments show that this approach is limited, when the target speed is obtained accuracy drops too much.

This calls for a wider consideration of recognition systems based on machine learning. Beyond accuracy and speed, these systems have additional performance characteristics: generalization ability (i.e., ability to learn from a relatively small training set size), training time, and memory consumption. Suppose that it is possible to collect a very large training set, there is no significant limitation on training time, and a moderate amount of memory is available at test time. The question then becomes: for a fixed accuracy target, can we trade training set size for increased speed at test time?

The algorithm proposed here pushes the speed–accuracy envelope at the expense of larger training sets using three steps. First, simple non-invariant features are used, with sharp non-linearity, as they are fast to compute. Using a large enough training set, we can hope that the task-relevant invariance will be learned instead of *a priori* encoded. Second, and most important, an architecture with large capacity and minimal computation is introduced, based on an ensemble of large tables encoding the end results. Such table-based classifiers, termed 'ferns' [6, 19, 24], have high capacity with a VC-dimension higher than 2^K for a single 2^K-entry table, and close to $M2^K$ for a M-tables ensemble.[1] Third, since the classifier form presents a hard learning problem, with high capacity and minimal prior, we develop a discriminative optimization framework for a fern ensemble, which is a departure from the generative formulation used previously for ferns.

---

[1] Assuming that the underlying space is of dimension higher than K and MK, respectively, which are satisfied for the image sizes considered.

Focusing on speed optimization, we use as features spatial aggregates of highly simplistic features, i.e., pixel-pair comparisons; A set (ensemble) of lookup tables (ferns) are then built based on sets of such bit features. Each fern is based on a set of K simple binary features and a large table of 2^K-entries. The binary features are concatenated into an index, and the corresponding index entry in the table contains a weight contribution, summed across the ferns to get the final classification. Each table can be regarded as an efficient codeword dictionary: It maps a patch into one of 2^K words, yet at the cost of K operations. The resulting architecture is highly non-linear, and a feed-forward push of an image through it only requires multiple bit computations and table access operations.

Ferns are traditionally formulated generatively, i.e., conditional class probabilities are stored at the table entries. In contrast, we suggest training the ensemble discriminatively by minimizing the regularized hinge loss, i.e., the loss minimized by Support Vector Machines (SVM). The minimization technique is related to ideas from the Predictive Feature Selection (PFS) algorithm [2]. It is done agglomeratively in a boosting-like framework, promoting complementariness between chosen ferns and between bits in a single fern.

The main technical contribution of this section is in the introduction of a *Discriminative Ferns Ensemble* (*DFE*) approach and empirically demonstrating its ability to considerably shift the speed–accuracy curve. The method is applied to hand pose recognition from IR and depth images, and compared to the best alternatives for this task. In this comparison, the DFE achieves accuracy comparable or better while being one to two orders of magnitude faster. In particular, it is significantly more accurate than a classification based on deep random trees, which have been used for similar tasks [17, 25] and considerably more accurate than a more standard ensemble of random ferns [6, 24]. Several general object recognition methods were also applied to the task, combining fast dense SIFT features, DAISY, random forest dictionaries, and SVM [23, 29, 30]. The best results achieved were slightly less accurate than DFE, but classification time was two orders of magnitude (i.e., 100 times) slower. DFE is also shown to be efficient when the number of classes increases, utilizing ferns sharing between classes and an error-correcting output code (ECOC) classification methodology minimizing the number of classifiers trained.

A second contribution is that we empirically show significant improvements in classification speed—for a given target accuracy—can be achieved by collecting larger training sets. This is done by optimizing K (log of the table size) and M (number of ferns) for a given training set size. In other words, if a DFE classifier is accurate, but not fast enough, collecting larger training set can be used to accelerate classification speed. Note that this trade-off is different from the well-known trade-off between training set size and accuracy.

The approach presented was found practical and was used to train the hand pose recognition in XBox-1, shipped in early 2014.

We discuss related work in Sect. 13.2 and present our approach in Sect. 13.3. In Sect. 13.4, we summarize a set of experiments in which ingredients of the method are tested and the approach is compared with competing techniques. We briefly conclude in Sect. 13.5.

13.2 Relevant Work

With the emergence of cheap $3D$ sensors, and primarily the Kinect sensor, pose estimation and recognition in IR+depth images have been the subjects of increasing study in recent years [1, 5, 10, 15–17, 20, 25, 26]. In contrast to working with RGB images, the depth information enables easier segmentation of body parts, simpler reasoning about occlusion, and usage of simpler features enabling real-time applications. We focus here on techniques that have been applied to hand pose recognition and estimation, as well as more general techniques that bear some similarity to the proposed DFE method.

An important line of work that has influenced our technique uses random forests as the main tool, with the notably successful application of this technique to body pose estimation in the Xbox-360 [25]. In [16], a random forest is trained to classify pixels according to hand part labels. The hand parts positions are then estimated by finding the mode of the posterior part probability using mean shift. In [17], this method is extended to a two-stage method. In a preprocessing stage, the pose space is clustered into 50 clusters, corresponding to global hand shapes. A first random forest is trained to classify pixels as belonging to images from one of the 50 clusters. In the second layer, 50 different random forest 'experts' are trained, one for each of the clusters. Part position estimation is performed by using the chosen expert from the second layer, or by splitting decisions regarding pixels among their most plausible 'experts.' Good empirical results are reported for shape classification (using the first stage) and for pixel part classification.

The pose estimators mentioned above were trained using large datasets of synthetic data, but the random forest-based approach was extended to include a mixture of labeled real data, unlabeled real data, and synthetic data in [26]. The forests trained in this approach included mixed regression and classification trees, and several criteria for node splitting were combined, including a criterion requiring low variance and a criterion requiring that real labeled data and synthetic data with the same label share the same node.

While the random forest approach usually relies on very simple features, another line of work focuses on learning more complex features integrating RGB and depth information. The methods suggested in [1, 5] learn hierarchical descriptors that aggregate RGB and depth information across increasingly larger spatial area. Both show significant improvements in general object recognition using descriptor level fusion of RGB and depth. In [20], an approach is presented, which learns spatio-temporal complex features for a difficult gesture recognition task. Increasingly complex features are created by composition of basic operators like filtering, spatial averaging, and non-linear operations. A genetic algorithm is used to choose the most discriminative features for a linear SVM classifier.

A different traditionally popular approach poses hand pose recognition as a retrieval problem [10, 13]. In [10], a large dataset of synthetic images with known pose parameters was created. The hand is carefully segmented (Kinect depth images are used) and compared to database images using several distance functions: Chamfer distance, L^2 distance between the depth images, and a combination of the two.

Empirical results show that the correct match is often ranked high in the list of retrieved images.

As stated above, fast recognition methods are often based on trees or ferns ensembles [6, 9, 12, 17, 24, 25]. Ferns are often regarded as a special case of trees, in which the condition encoded at all the nodes with the same depth is identical. Boosting of decision trees is a highly popular technique for object detection and classification in RGB [9, 12], but usually shallow trees of depth 1–3 are used, which cannot capture fine-grained partitions. Ferns ensembles were suggested in recent years for RGB image classification [6], keypoint recognition [24], and nearest neighbor finding [19]. In these works, ferns in the ensemble are chosen independently of each other, and bits in a single fern are chosen at random or using an information gain criterion. At the leaves, conditional class posteriors are computed and averaged across ferns [6], or regulated with a prior and multiplied [24].

Among the tree-based methods mentioned above, the works presented in [16, 17, 25] are most related to the DFE, as they also allow fast, real-time classification using simple pixel comparison features and a tree ensemble architecture. However, the DFE departs significantly from the random forest and random ferns tradition in its resort to discriminative optimization. In a DFE, the fern ensemble is regarded as providing the features for a large L_2-SVM problem. Ferns and bits are not chosen at random, nor using a general information criterion, but picked to minimize the loss of this program. In particular, the gradient of the SVM program with respect to adding new features is computed at each round and used to guide choice of the bits in the new fern. Ferns (and bits) are hence grown to be complementary, as in a gradient boosting process [22]. The weights of the fern's table, corresponding to the leaves of a tree, are not conditional probabilities, but rather SVM weights. Due to this optimization, a DFE is more accurate, requires less memory, and less CPU time than approaches presented in [16, 17, 25]. We discuss the differences in Sect. 13.3.2 and compare the methods empirically in Sect. 13.4.

13.3 The Discriminative Ferns Ensemble

We describe the Fern Ensemble classifier in Sect. 13.3.1 and analyze its running time in Sect. 13.3.2. In Sect. 13.3.3, we present the training procedure we use.

13.3.1 The Discriminative Ferns Ensemble Classifier

The ferns ensemble classifier operates on an image patch, which we denote by I, consisting of P pixels. For a pixel p, we denote its neighborhood by $N(p)$, and we denote by $I_{N(p)}$ the subpatch which is comprised of the pixels in p's neighborhood. In what follows, we will consider $I_{N(p)}$ as a vector in $\mathbb{R}^{|N(p)|}$. The ferns ensemble consists of M individual ferns, and its pipeline includes three layers whose structure we now describe.

Bit Vector Computation Let us focus on one particular fern m. For each pixel p, we compute a local descriptor of its neighborhood subpatch $I_{N(p)}$ using computationally light pairwise pixel comparisons of the form

$$I_{q_1} \stackrel{?}{>} I_{q_2} \quad \text{for} \quad q_1, q_2 \in N(p) \tag{13.1}$$

Such a comparison provides a single-bit value of 0 or 1. For convenience of notation, we may rewrite the bit obtained as $\sigma(\beta^T I_{N(p)})$, where β is a $|N(p)|$-dimensional sparse vector, with two nonzero values, one equaling 1, the other equaling -1; and σ is the Heaviside function. For each fern m and pixel p, there are K bits computed, and we denote the kth bit as $b_{p,k}^m = \sigma((\beta_k^m)^T I_{N(p)})$. Collecting all the bits together, the K-dimensional bit vector b_p^m is:

$$b_p^m = \sigma\left(B^m I_{N(p)}\right) \in \{0, 1\}^K \tag{13.2}$$

where the matrix B^m has rows $(\beta_1^m)^T, \ldots, (\beta_K^m)^T$; and now the Heaviside function σ is applied element-wise.

Histogram of Bit Vectors We are interested in some translation invariance, so we take a spatial histogram over codewords. However, as in [24], the bit vectors *themselves* are the codewords; there is no need for an intermediate clustering step. Denote the histogram for the mth fern by $H^m(b)$, where bit vector $b \in \{0, 1\}^K$; then

$$H^m(b) = \sum_{p \in A^m} \delta\left(b_p^m - b\right) \tag{13.3}$$

where δ is a discrete delta function, and $A^m \subset \{1, .., P\}$ is the spatial aggregation region for fern m. Note that H^m is a sparse vector, with at most P nonzero entries.

Histograms concatenation The final decision is made by a linear classifier applied to the concatenation of the M fern histograms.

$$f(I) = W^T H(I) = \sum_{m=1}^{M} \sum_{b \in \{0,1\}^K} w_b^m H^m(b) \tag{13.4}$$

where $H(I) = [H^1(I), \ldots, H^M(I)] \in \mathbb{N}^{M2^K}$ and $W = [W^1, \ldots, W^M] \in \mathbb{R}^{M2^K}$ is a weight vector. Combining Steps 1–3 in the pipeline, we arrive at the discriminative ferns ensemble classifier:

$$f(I; \rho) = \sum_{m=1}^{M} \sum_{b \in \{0,1\}^K} w_b^m \sum_{p \in A^m} \delta\left(\sigma\left(B^m I_{N(p)}\right) - b\right) \tag{13.5}$$

with the parameters $\rho = \{W^m, B^m, A^m\}_{m=1}^{M}$.

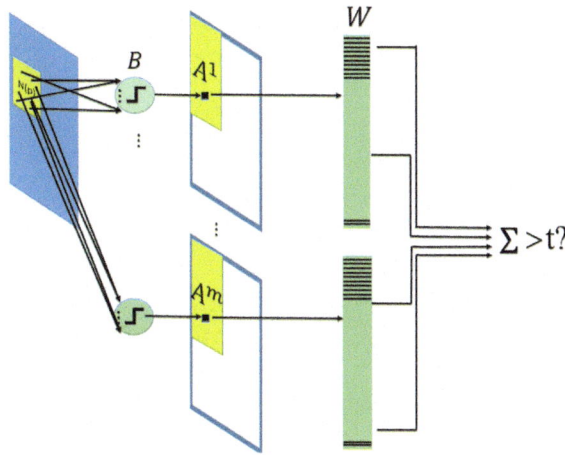

Fig. 13.1 A DFE network. A single fern in a DFE can be viewed as a feed-forward network with one highly non-linear layer and a second spatial summation layer. The DFE is a 3-layer network linearly aggregating the output of M ferns. See text for details

The operation of a DFE is sketched as a three-layered network in Fig. 13.1. Each fern can be conceived as a two-layer network. The first layer extracts a highly non-linear patch descriptor around each pixel p in the aggregation area. The patch descriptor is based on comparison of K pixel pairs, squashed into K bits, and concatenated into an single index. This index is then used to get a weight from the fern table. The operation is repeated for all pixels in the fern spatial aggregation area (the yellow rectangle in the second layer), and the contribution of all the pixels are summed. At a third layer, the contributions of all the ferns are linearly added and compared to a threshold to get the decision.

13.3.2 Classification Speed

Algorithm 1 describes the operation of a DFE classifier at test time. The pipeline is extremely simple. For each fern and each pixel in the fern's aggregation region, we compute the bit vector, considered as a codeword index. The fern table is then accessed with the computed index, and the obtained weight is added to the classification score. The complexity is $O(M\overline{A}K)$ where $\overline{A}$ is the average number of pixels per aggregation region: $\overline{A} = \frac{1}{M}\sum_m |A^m|$.

It is interesting to compare the CPU time of a single fern to a single tree with the depth K. From a pure computational complexity perspective, the number of operations for both is K. Nevertheless, a closer look at their match to common CPU architectures, including cache hierarchies and vector machines, reveals large differences in expected run time. First, a tree needs to store the bit computation parameters for 2^K internal nodes. More importantly, during tree traversal, the working

Algorithm 1 Ferns Ensemble: Classification
___
Input: An image I of size $S_x \times S_y$,
classifier parameters $(B^m, A^m, W^m)_{m=1}^M$, threshold t
$B^m \in \mathbb{R}^{K \times |A^m|}$, $A^m \subset \{1, .., S_x\} \times \{1, .., S_y\}$, $W^m \in \mathbb{R}^{2^K}$
Output: A classifier decision in $\{0, 1\}$
Initialization: Score=0
For all ferns $m = 1, .., M$
    For all pixels $p \in A^m$
        Compute a k-bit index $= \sigma(B^m I_{N(p)})$
        Score=Score+W^m[index]
Return (Score>t)
___

set is accessed K times in an unpredictable manner. A fern's operation requires only a single access to its large working set (W^m), as the index computation is done using a small amount of memory, $O(K)$ in size, which fits in the cache without a problem.

Second, the usage of fixed pixel pairs in a fern enables computation of the K-bit index without indirection and with an unrolled loop. More importantly, ferns are amenable to vectorization using single-instruction multiple data (SIMD) operations, while trees are not. Applying a fern operation to several examples at the same time (i.e., vectorizing the loop over p in Algorithm 1) is straightforward. Doing so for a tree is likely to be extremely inefficient since each example requires a different sequence of memory accesses, and gathering such scattered data cannot be done in parallel in an SIMD framework. In Sect. 13.4.1.4, we further discuss the differences of ferns and random forest, in terms of classification time and memory.

13.3.3 Discriminative Training

The DFE classifier $f(I; \rho)$ is given in Eq. (13.5), and we would like to learn the parameters $\rho = \{W^m, B^m, A^m\}_{m=1}^M$ from a labeled training set $\{(I^i, y^i)\}_{i=1}^N$. Unlike prior work on ferns, e.g., [24], we turn to a discriminative rather than a generative formulation. In particular, we pose the problem as regularized hinge-loss minimization, similar to standard SVM:

$$\min_\rho \frac{1}{2}\|W\|^2 + C \sum_{i=1}^N \left[1 - y^i f\left(I^i; \rho\right)\right]_+ \qquad (13.6)$$

where $[\cdot]_+$ indicates the hinge loss, i.e., $[z]_+ = \max\{z, 0\}$. Rewriting Eq. (13.4) with explicit parameter and image dependence one gets

$$f(I; \rho) = \sum_{m,b} w_b^m H^m\left(b, I\ ; B^m, A^m\right) \qquad (13.7)$$

We can see that f is linear in W, so optimizing (13.6) w.r.t W for fixed $\{B^m, A^m\}_{m=1}^{M}$ is a standard SVM optimization. However, optimizing for the latter parameters is challenging, specifically since they are to be chosen from a large discrete set of possibilities. Hence, we turn to an agglomerative approach in which we greedily add ferns one at the time. As can be seen from Eq. (13.5), adding a single fern amounts to an addition of 2^K new features to the classifier. In order to do that in an sensible manner, we extend known results for the case of a single feature addition [2, 4].

Let $f(I) = \sum_{l=1}^{L-1} w_l x_l(I)$ be a linear classifier optimized with SVM and $L(f, \{I_i, y_i\}_{i=1}^{N})$ the hinge loss obtained for it (Eq. 13.6) over a training set. Assume we add a single feature x^L to this classifier $f^{\text{new}}(I) = f^{\text{old}}(I) + w_L x^L(I)$, with small $|w_L| \leq \varepsilon$. Theorem 1 in [2] gives a linear approximation of the loss under these conditions:

$$L\left(f^{\text{new}}\right) = L\left(f^{\text{old}}\right) - w_L \sum_{i=1}^{N} \alpha_i y_i x_i^L + O\left(w_L^2\right) \quad (13.8)$$

where α_i are the example weights obtained as a solution to the dual SVM problem. The weights $\alpha_i \in [0, C]$ are only nonzero for support vectors. For a candidate feature x_L, the approximated loss (13.8) is best reduced by choosing $w_L = \varepsilon \cdot \text{sign}(\sum_{i=1}^{N} \alpha_i y_i x_i^L)$, and the reduction obtained is $R(x_L) \triangleq |\sum_{i=1}^{N} \alpha_i y_i x_i^L|$. The PFS algorithm [2] is based on training SVM using a small number of features, followed by computing the score $R(x)$ for a large number of unseen features; this allows one to add/replace existing features with promising feature candidates. Note that the score $R(x)$ of a feature column x can be seen as the correlation $R_Z(x) = x \cdot Z$, where $Z = (z_1, \ldots, z_n)$ with $z_i = y_i \alpha_i$ is the vector of signed example weights.

Here, we extend the aforementioned idea to a set of features, as introduced by a single fern. Assume we have trained an SVM classifier over a fern ensemble $f^{M-1}(I)$ with $M-1$ ferns, and we now wish to extend to an additional fern. Assume further that the new weight vector is small with $||w^m||_\infty \leq \varepsilon$. Then, we have

$$f^M(I) = f^{M-1}(I) + \varepsilon \sum_{b \in \{0,1\}^K} w_b^m H^m(b, I) \quad (13.9)$$

with $|w_b^m| \leq 1$ for all b. Treating the new fern contribution as a single feature, we can apply the theorem stated above and get

$$L\left(f^M(I)\right) \approx L\left(f^{M-1}\right) - \varepsilon \sum_{i=1}^{N} \alpha_i y_i \sum_{b \in \{0,1\}^K} w_b^m H^m(b, I_i)$$

$$= L\left(f^{M-1}\right) - \varepsilon \sum_{b \in \{0,1\}^K} w_b^m \sum_{i=1}^{N} \alpha_i y_i H^m(b, I_i) \quad (13.10)$$

Algorithm 2 Ferns Ensemble: Training

Input: A labeled Training set $\{I_i, y_i\}_{i=1}^N$
    Parameters $M, K, C, N_c, \{A^m\}_{m=1}^M$
Output: A classifier $(B^m, A^m, W^m)_{m=1}^M$, threshold t
Initialization: $Z[i] = 1/|\{I_i|y_i = 1\}|$ if $y_i = 1$,
    $Z[i] = -1/|\{I_i|y_i = -1\}|$ if $y_i = -1$
For $m = 1, .., M$
    For $k = 1, .., K$
        For $c = 1, ..N_c$
            Sample a candidate column $\beta_{k,c}^m \in R^{|N(p)|}$
            For $i = 1, .., N$
                Compute $H^m(b, I_i, c) = H^m(b, I_i; B_c^m)$
                with $B_c^m = [\beta_1^m, ..., \beta_{k-1}^m, \beta_{k,c}^m]$
            For $b \in \{0, 1\}^K$
                Compute $R_Z(c) = \sum_{b \in \{0,1\}^K} R_Z(H^m(b; \beta_{k,c}^m))$
            Choose winning candidate $c^* = argmax_c R(c)$,
            and set $\beta_k^m = \beta_{k,c^*}^m$
    Train an SVM with $m2^K$ features $W \cdot [H^1, .., H^m] - t$
    Set $Z[i] = y_i \alpha_i$ for $i = 1, .., N$ with α_i SVM dual variables
Set $\{W^m\}_{m=1}^M$, t based on the last SVM training.
Return $(B^m, A^m, W^m)_{m=1}^M$, threshold t.

---

where the approximation in the first equation is due to omission of $O(\varepsilon^2)$ terms. If we wish to minimize the approximated loss, the optimal choice for w_b^m is $w_b^m = \text{sign}(\sum_{i=1}^N \alpha_i y_i H_t^m(b, I_i))$, in an analogous way to the single feature case. With these w_b^m, we get

$$L\left(f^M(I)\right) \approx L\left(f^{M-1}\right) - \varepsilon \sum_{b \in \{0,1\}^K} R\left(H^m(b)\right) \quad (13.11)$$

This result is an intuitive extension of Theorem 1 in [2] for the case of multiple feature addition.

Our algorithm for fern ensemble growing is based on iterating between SVM training and building the next fern based on Eq. (13.11). This procedure is described more precisely in Algorithm 2. At each fern addition step, we use an SVM classifier trained on the previous ferns to get signed example weights, in a manner similar to boosting. The ensemble score $\sum_{b \in \{0,1\}^K} R_Z(H^m(b))$ is used to grow the fern bit by bit in a greedy fashion. At each bit addition stage, we randomly select N_c candidates for the mask β_k^m, termed $\beta_{k,c}^m$; each candidate is chosen by randomly drawing the two pixels needed for the comparison. The winning bit is chosen as the one producing the highest ensemble score. We currently do not optimize the integration area variables $\{A_m\}_{m=1}^M$, but we experiment with several choices in Sect. 13.4.

The algorithm is presented for a single binary problem, but is easily extended to training of several classes with shared A^m, B^m and separate W^m. In the simplest alternative independent SVMs are trained, one for each class of interest. During optimization, all the SVMs are trained at each fern addition, and $R(c)$ scores of all of them are summed to make the bit choice. Due to the sharing of the same fern-based features, running time scales sublinearly in the number of classes. However, memory and training time are linear in the number of classes. For a large number of classes, error-correcting output codes [8] (ECOC) can be used to decrease the number of SVM classifiers trained, and enable a logarithmic scaling of training time and memory in the number of classes. In Sect. 13.4.2, we present experiments with this approach, showing that it enables economic classifiers with enhanced accuracy.

13.4 Empirical Results

The method described in this paper was developed, tested, and compared to alternatives on a very large data set for hand shape recognition. The task was discrimination between 3 hand state classes, and the resulting classifier was shipped as part of the Microsoft Xbox-1 console in early 2014. We describe these experiments in Sect. 13.4.1. In Sect. 13.4.2, we describe experiments conducted on a synthetically generated data set of 81 hand state classes. Scalability to a large number of classes is obtained by fern sharing and utilizing an error-correcting output codes (ECOC) approach.

13.4.1 Real Data Experiments

We describe the data set used in Sect. 13.4.1.1 and the method's implementation details in Sect. 13.4.1.2. The impact of the main ingredients and parameters of the method is tested in Sect. 13.4.1.3. We compare the accuracy–speed trade-off enabled by the proposed method and various competing techniques in Sect. 13.4.1.4. We conclude by showing the trade-offs between accuracy, classification time, training sample size, and memory in Sect. 13.4.1.5.

13.4.1.1 Data Set

The task we consider is to recognize three different hand shapes and to discriminate between them and other undefined hand states. The recognition results are used as part of a NUI interface. The shapes are termed 'open,' 'closed,' 'lasso,' and 'other,' as shown in Fig. 13.2. The class 'other' includes a large variation in hand poses, including hands holding objects. Hand detection is achieved by tracking the skeleton in a sequence of depth+IR images, using methods based on [25].

The images used for recognition are cropped around the extracted hand position, rotated, and scaled to two 36 × 36 images of the depth and IR channels. A simple preprocessing rejects IR and depth pixels where the depth is clearly far beyond the

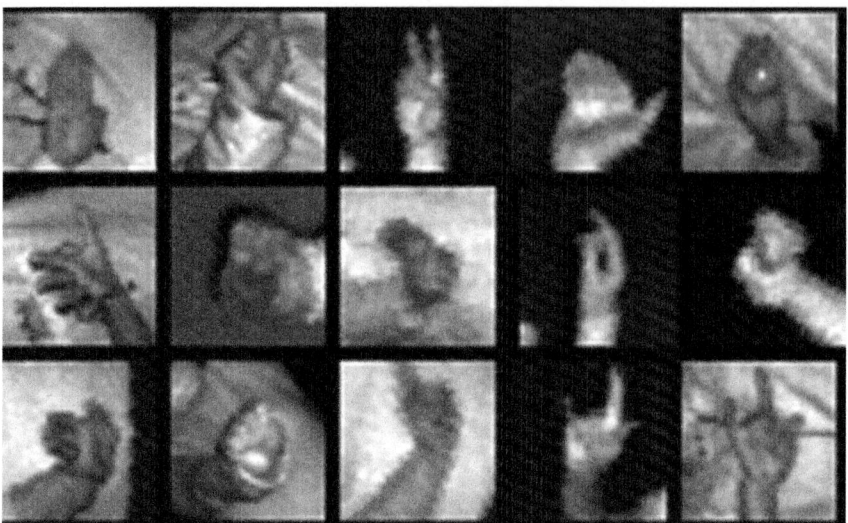

Fig. 13.2 Examples of hand images from our data set. The *left columns* contain examples of 'open,' 'closed,' and 'lasso,' respectively. The two *right columns* contain examples of the complement class 'other'

hand, thereby removing some of the background. The alignment and rotation of the hand are based on estimated wrist position and is sometimes inaccurate, making the recognition task harder.

A dataset of 519,000 images was collected and labeled from video sequences of different people. Images have considerable variability in terms of viewpoints, hand poses, distances, and imaging conditions. The images were taken at distances of up to $\sim$4 m from the camera, where the quality of image drops, and the depth measurement of fingers may be missing. Data were divided into training and test sets with 420,000 and 99,000 images, respectively, such that persons from the training set do not appear in test images and vice versa. The data were collected to give over-representation to hard cases. Given the properties of data, the goal was to achieve 2–5 % false-negative rate, at a false-positive rate of 2 %. Since the test data are hard, the error rate in real usage scenarios is expected to be much lower.

13.4.1.2 Implementation Details

In our experiments, we tested the number of bits per fern K in the range of [3, 18] and the number of ferns M in [6, 768]. At each bit addition step $N_c = 40$, pixel comparison features were randomly generated for evaluation. The spatial aggregation area of the fern A_m was randomly chosen to be one of the 4 standard quadrants of the image patch, and the neighborhood $N(p)$ is 17×17 pixels. We have experimented with limiting the aggregation area A_m further by imposing a virtual checkerboard on the quadrant pixels: for odd bit indices, features are only computed for 'white' pixels, and for even indices, features are computed only for 'black' ones. This policy was found to be useful in terms of accuracy–speed trade-offs.

We have used the LibLinear package [14] for sparse SVM training of our models. The classifier was implemented in C and running times are reported on Intel core i7, 2.6 GHz CPU, using a single thread. Computation time is reported for a single image in milliseconds, without usage of SIMD optimizations. Accuracy of a single binary classifier, i.e., one hand pose versus all, is computed as the false-negative error rate at the working point providing a false-positive (FP) rate of 2 %. Accuracy figures reported here are averaged over the three classes. We selected this approach rather than multi-class error rate, as in each specific NUI usage context, the three classification scores are combined in a different way.

13.4.1.3 Parameters and Variations

Success and failure examples of the DFE classifier can be seen at Fig. 13.3. We now concentrate on understanding the contribution to performance of algorithm components.

Complexity of layers 1: At the first layer, we encode patches into codeword indices, and its complexity is controlled by the number of bits K used for the encoding. In Fig. 13.4 (Left), the classifier accuracy is plotted as a function of K for fixed $M = 50$. Based on this graph, we select the value of $K = 13$ in our subsequent experiments, as it is the minimal value which yet provide close to optimal accuracy.

Complexity of layers 2: At the second, spatial aggregation layer, complexity is controlled by several algorithmic choices. First, we can use multiple aggregation areas, or a single aggregation area containing the whole image for all ferns. Second, we can use or avoid using the checkerboard technique for computational saving. Results are reported in Fig. 13.5 (left). Baseline DFE uses $M = 50$ ferns with

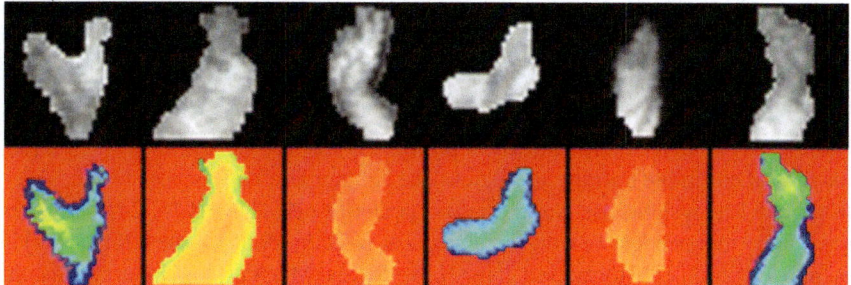

Fig. 13.3 Successes and failures of the DFE classifier: Pairs of depth+IR images are presented, where the *top row* shows the IR images and the *bottom* the depth images in every pair. The three pairs on the *left* show successfully classified pairs for the three hand shape classes considered (open, closed, lasso). The pairs on the *right* show misclassification errors (false negatives)

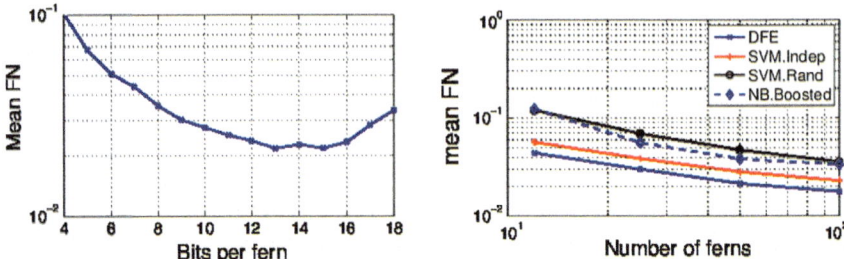

Fig. 13.4 DFE complexity parameters. *Left* False-negative rate of the DFE (at false-positive rate = 0.02 as a function of K, the number of bits. *Right* False-negative rate as a function of M, the number of ferns, for several training procedures. DFE is our baseline variation. For both SVM.Indep and SVM.Rand, SVM is used as final classifier. For SVM.Indep, the bits are selected using $R(c)$ score, but without PFS weight update, i.e., using initial $Z[i]$ for all ferns (see Algorithm 2). For SVM.Rand, bits are randomly selected. NB.Boosted is Naive Bayes with fern boosting and entropy-gain bit choice

Pipe variation	% FN @ FP=2%
Baseline DFE	2.18
Single aggregation area	3.15
No checkerboard sampling	2.42
Naive Bayes + Boosting	3.87
Naive Bayes, MI bits	35.9
Naive Bayes, Rand bits	47.6
Only Depth	4.65
Only IR	5.23

Fig. 13.5 Comparison to alternatives. *Left* Error for several DFE and Ferns algorithm variations. See text for explanation. *Right* Best results of false-negative rate under constraint of classification CPU time for various methods and parameters for each method. For DFE, we modified values of M, K. For random forest [17], the points shown are for one and two trees of depth 21. Fast SIFT can achieve accuracy comparable to DFE, but at cost of more than ×100 classification time

quadrant ferns, checkerboard policy. The number of ferns used in the conditions 'single area' and 'no checkerboard' is reduced by a factor 4 and 2 to get classifiers with approximately the same speed as the baseline. The results show the advantage of baseline DFE over alternatives, hence led to its definition as 'baseline.'

Complexity of layer 3, optimization policy: Figure 13.5 (left) shows the accuracy for several ensemble training strategies. The simpler alternatives uses Naive Bayes, where the leaf weights are based on class posterior probabilities [6, 24]. The ferns are trained independently, with bits chosen at random (Naive Bayes, Rand bits) or by maximization of information gain (Naive Bayes, MI). For these alternatives, the false-negative rate is high.[2] Also, further increasing of the number ferns does not help

---

[2] Note that FN is measured at false-positive rate of 2 %. Hence, FN near 50 % is far better than random. At FP = 10 % the false-negative rates of Naive Bayes MI bits and Rand bits drops to 11 and 18 %, respectively.

as much as in the DFE or boosting framework, as the ferns are learned independently. Another alternative is training complementary ferns by boosting, with bits chosen to maximize the information gain on the boosting-reweighted sample (Naive Bayes + Boosting). This significantly improves accuracy relative to MI and random selection, but is still less accurate than DFE. Figure 13.4 (right) shows the effect of number of ferns, M, on the false-negative rate for selected methods.

From the above results, we can conclude that using discriminative (SVM) approach for both the final classifier and selecting of the fern bits significantly improves accuracy.

The table in Fig. 13.5 also shows that IR and depth are not redundant, and using both of them significantly improves accuracy relative to using only one of them.

13.4.1.4 Speed–Accuracy Trade-Off Comparison

We have compared the fern ensemble method to several alternative architectures, which also have an emphasis on a good speed-accuracy trade-off. The methods compared are:

- Random forest applied to pixel comparisons as suggested by [17]
- A 3-stages pipeline: (a) Fast dense SIFT features computation using the VLFeat library [28]. (b) Encoding into a bag of features using a random forest dictionary [23]. (c) SVM classification with a linear approximation of the histogram intersection kernel, according to [29]. We also tried the same pipeline, but replacing the fast SIFT with dense Daisy features [30].

All the methods were implemented in C/C++, using the original author's code when possible. They were chosen for comparison as each of them was developed with the aim of obtaining a good balance of speed and accuracy. Multiple working points were tested for each of these methods, representing various optimization for speed and accuracy. For the fast SIFT method, shifting between speed and accuracy was done by changing the stride parameter, controlling the density of the SIFT greed. For the Daisy, we also choose the Daisy complexity to optimize speed/accuracy, as recommended in [30].

The CPU time (accuracy) of the best working points obtained by each of the algorithms, including DFE, is plotted together in Fig. 13.6 (left). We see that random forest can achieve similar classification time to that of DFE, but is significantly less accurate (FN = 10.6 % vs. FN = 2 % for DFE, for the same CPU budget). Consistent with [17], we found that the best accuracy is achieved by training on a small number of deep trees, with little improvement when increasing the number of trees. This leaves us with less flexibility on controlling the trade-off between accuracy and classification time. There are several reasons why using 50 ferns DFE is about as fast as using two trees. First, each fern operates on relatively small number of pixels (50), which is only ∼4 % of the image. Second, calculating the ferns bits requires less operations than forest with the same depth, as discussed in Sect. 13.3.2. Third, the number of bit per fern is 13, while the depth of tree is 21. Also, the memory size

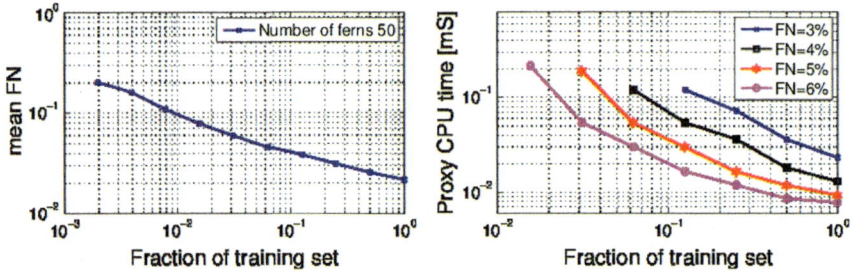

Fig. 13.6 *Middle* Accuracy obtained by DFE as a function of training sample size. X-axis is the fraction of training set size relative to the full set (420,000 images). *Right* The classification CPU time, as a function of training sample size. This is measured for several target false-negative rates (for a fixed FP = 2 %)

of the forest is in order of 80 MB versus 2.5 MB of ferns. Since 80 MB cannot fit into the cache, we pay with more cache misses.

The accuracy of with fast SIFT and Daisy alternatives can approach the accuracy of the DFE. However, their classification time is two order of magnitudes longer. By optimize them for speed, we significantly loose accuracy without getting to the target classification time.

In the next section, we show that in addition to high accuracy and fast classification, DFE approach enables significant flexibility for various trade-offs of speed, accuracy, memory size and generalization from various sizes of training set.

13.4.1.5 Training Sample Size and Memory

As discussed before, the fern ensemble architecture trades speed and accuracy for sample size and memory. For each training set size, constraints on memory, and classification time, we optimize accuracy by tuning M and K. In this section, we show that increasing the training set size enables us not only to improve accuracy, but also to significantly reduce the classification time.

Figure 13.6 (middle) shows the effect of increasing the training set size on FN, for fixed M and K. We modify the training set size we used from ∼0.2 % of the full set (820 images) to the full training set (420,000 images). The subset of training set is selected randomly. As expected, the false-negative rate reduces with increase of training set size.

In our problem, however, even with a training set size of ∼30,000 samples (0.07 in X-axis of Fig. 13.6), the accuracy we got met minimum requirements for the product. However, even after full code optimization, the classification time significantly exceeded the target budget. The question is if we can reduce classification time by increasing the training set size and modifying M and K.

Figure 13.6 (right) shows the classification time as a function of the of training set size, relative to the full set, for various target false-negative rates. We can see that for a fixed target accuracy, the classification time can be reduced by an order of

Table 13.1 Accuracy obtained by DFE under memory limits

LUT entries	Ferns # (M)	Bits # (K)	% FN @ FP = 2 %
768	48	4	10.7
1536	96	4	7.78
3072	96	5	6.07
6144	192	5	5.42
12288	384	5	4.21
24576	384	6	2.97
49152	768	6	2.32

LUT entries is the total number of entries in all the lookup tables (ferns) together, which is $2^K M$. In our implementation, each LUT entry requires 6 bytes—two bytes per class, representing the SVM weights

magnitude, if we increase the training set size by an order of magnitude. In general, as training set size increases, we slightly increase K and significantly reduce M to achieve same target accuracy with lower classification time. This can be explained by the effect of K on the capacity of each fern and hence should be adapted to the training set size. On the other hands, the accuracy can be improved by increasing M, but at a significant cost of classification time. These results are significant for building practical systems. While it is well known that increasing training set size enables improvement in accuracy, here, we show that it can also reduce classification time significantly.

Finally, we show the trade-off between memory and accuracy. Table 13.1 presents false-negative rate versus memory consumption for a fern ensemble. Memory consumption can be reduced by lowering either M or K, and in the table, we chose the optimal M, K parameters for each memory limit point. From the table, we can see adding a memory constraint leads to significant reduction in the number of bits per fern and increasing the number of ferns. The result is very different from the case of optimizing for classification time, where optimal number of bits is high. This is not surprising, as the memory size increases exponentially with number of bits, but classification time increases only linearly. The result classification time is about 5–10 larger when we optimize for memory instead of for speed. Note, however, that in our baseline implementation, with 50 ferns and 13 bits, the memory size is about 2.5 MB, which still fits into the cache.

13.4.2 Class Scalability Experiments

In this section, we show how a DFE can efficiently scale up to a large number of classes, while maintaining its beneficial accuracy and speed characteristics. Experiments are done using a synthetically generated dataset of 81 classes.

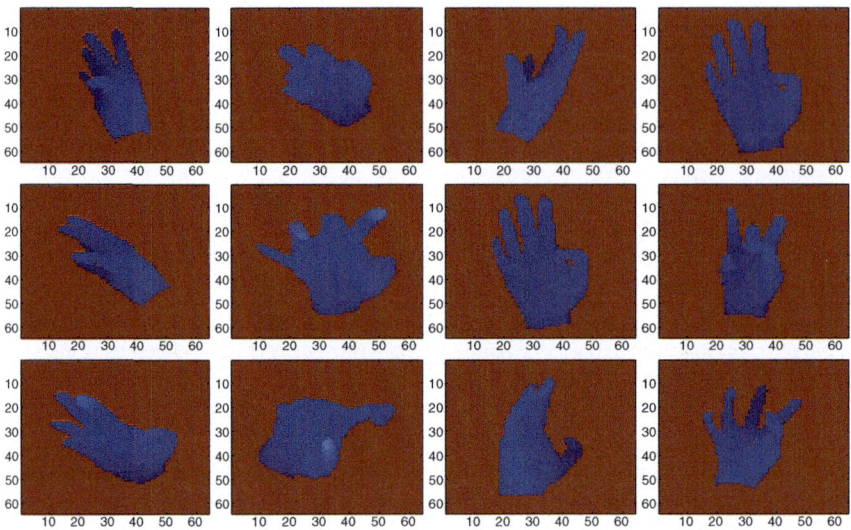

Fig. 13.7 Synthetic data for 81 classes. Hand state classes were generated by varying 4 independent variables: hand bend angle, twist angle, side angle, and pose. *Left Column* The bend angle was sampled uniformly in [−30, 90] degrees, with 0 corresponding to a vertical hand. The range was split into 3 equal partitions to get the bend label of 1, 2 or 3, examples of which are given at rows 1, 2, 3, respectively. *Second column* The twist angle was sampled uniformly in [−60, 60] degrees. Like the bend angle, it was quantized uniformly into 3 classes. *Third column* The side angle was sampled uniformly in [−45, 45] degrees and quantized into 3 classes. *Right Column* 3 basic finger poses were considered: flat (*top*), half open (*middle*), and open (*bottom*). Independent finger noise was added to each finger's open/close parameter. The class label was set as a Cartesian product of the 4 base labels

13.4.2.1 Dataset and Parameters

We used POSER, a commercially available software package, for generating a dataset of hand pose depth images. A dataset of 62,317 examples was generated and randomly split into 37,390 training samples and 24,927 test samples. Data variance was controlled by varying 4 independent parameters of hand generation: the 3 rotation angles and the basic hand pose. Figure 13.7 shows examples from the dataset and explains its 4 dimensions of variability, as well as the labels that were given to the images. The 3 rotation angles (bend, twist and side) were uniformly sampled in ranges covering the viewing sphere of a frontal hand. The pose was generated by choosing a base pose from the set (flat hand, half-open hand, open hand) and adding a small amount of noise to the bend parameter of each finger independently. Each of the 4 dimensions was quantized into 3 different classes, and the final label is the combination of the 4 single-dimension labels.

The data included only depth images, 8 bits per pixel, and no attempt was made to synthesize IR images. In each image, the hand bounding box was found (the tightest box containing all nonzero pixels), and the hand box was rescaled to 64 × 64 pixels images, which are the input of the DFE.

Preliminary experiments were done with 1/4 of the training set in order to choose DFE parameters and configuration. According to these experiments, we chose the pixel neighborhood $N(p)$ to be a large 32 × 32 patch. The integration area A_m was set to the internal 32 × 32 square of the 64 × 64 image. Checkerboard sampling was applied, but the use of quadrant ferns was not found to be superior; thus, we use the same integration area for all the ferns. The optimal number of bits was found to be 14.

13.4.2.2 Experiments

We have experimented with two variants of M-classification. The first is the basic one-vs-all, in which 81 SVMs are trained, one per class. As mentioned in Sect. 13.3.3, fern bits are chosen to optimize the sum of the gradient scores $R(c)$ of all the classes. A second alternative we tried was to solve for each of the label dimensions independently, i.e., we built 4 classifiers predicting the pose, bend angle, twist angle, and side angle of the hand. Each of these 4 classifiers, in turn, is composed of 3 one-vs-all SVMs, trained to separate one cell of the partition from the other 2 cells. Overall, in this approach, only 12 SVMs are trained, and the final label is determined based on the product code of the predicted 4 aspect labels.

Figure 13.8 (right) shows the multi-class accuracy obtained by both methods as a function of the number of ferns used. Both methods go beyond 80 %, which is quite high considering the large number of classes and the lack of margin in the boundaries between classes. Interestingly, the product code DFE, training only 12 classifiers, achieves higher accuracy than the one-versus-all version when the number of ferns is large (>10). Hence, in this domain, this version dominates the one-versus-all version in all respects, as it also provides higher speed in test and training, and requires less memory.

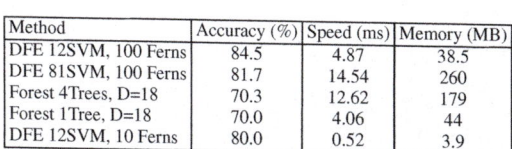

Method	Accuracy (%)	Speed (ms)	Memory (MB)
DFE 12SVM, 100 Ferns	84.5	4.87	38.5
DFE 81SVM, 100 Ferns	81.7	14.54	260
Forest 4Trees, D=18	70.3	12.62	179
Forest 1Tree, D=18	70.0	4.06	44
DFE 12SVM, 10 Ferns	80.0	0.52	3.9

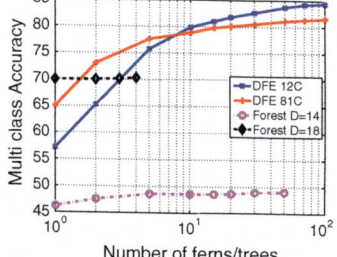

Fig. 13.8 Results for 81 classes. *Left* Multi-class accuracy, classifier speed, and model memory foot print of several hand classifiers. *Right* Accuracy as a function of the number of ferns/trees for DFE and Random forest classifiers

For comparison, we plot the accuracy obtained by a generatively trained forest, using code from [17]. When trees of depth 14 are used (matching our 14-bit ferns), performance is significantly inferior. The forest does better when its depth is not limited, and in this case, its maximal depth, limited by the dataset size, is 18. Forests of depth 18 are able to achieve 70 % accuracy, but their memory footprint is very large and becomes prohibitive for more than a few trees. We have experimented with up to 4 trees in this setting, and it seems that accuracy hardly improve with the number of trees.

In Table 13.1 (left), we compare the results obtained by the two DFE versions to the best results obtained by a classification forest [17] in terms of accuracy, speed, and memory. It can be seen that DFEs provide superior performance in each of the relevant measurements.

13.5 Conclusions and Further Work

We have seen that the *discriminative fern ensemble* framework enables significant push of the accuracy–speed envelope for visual recognition in IR+depth images. Thin, efficient architecture, and discriminative optimization were found important for this purpose. The method was shown to be scalable in the number of classes, thanks to feature sharing among classifiers and an ECOC methodology. In terms of architecture, it would be interesting to extend the table-based approach to deeper models with more table layers. Another interesting direction is to explore the trade-off between classification time and training sample size for other algorithms and analyze this trade-off theoretically.

References

1. Bar-Hillel A, Hanukaev D, Levi D (2011) Fusing visual and range imaging for object class recognition. In: IEEE international conference on computer vision (ICCV) 2011
2. Bar-Hillel A, Levi D, Krupka E, Goldberg C (2010) Part-based feature synthesis for human detection. In: Computer vision-ECCV 2010
3. Benenson R, Mathias M, Timofte R, Gool LJV (2012) Pedestrian detection at 100 frames per second. In: IEEE conference on computer vision and pattern recognition (CVPR) 2012
4. Bi J, Zhang T, Bennett K (2004) Column-generation boosting methods for mixture of kernels. In: Proceedings of the tenth ACM SIGKDD international conference on Knowledge discovery and data mining (KDD) 2004
5. Bo L, Lai K, Ren X, Fox D (2011) Object recognition with hierarchical kernel descriptors, In: IEEE conference on computer vision and pattern recognition (CVPR) 2011
6. Bosch A, Zisserman A, Muñoz X (2007) Image classification using random forests and ferns. In: IEEE international conference on computer vision (ICCV), pp 1–8
7. Dean T, Ruzon M, Segal M, Shlens J, Vijayanarasimhan S, Yagnik J (2013) Fast, accurate detection of 100,000 object classes on a single machine. In: Proceedings of IEEE conference on computer vision and pattern recognition, Washington, DC, USA, 2013

8. Dietterich TG, Bakiri G (1995) Solving multiclass learning problems via error-correcting output codes. J Artif Intell Res 2(1):263–286
9. Dietterich TG, Fisher D (2000) An experimental comparison of three methods for constructing ensembles of decision trees. Mach Learn, 139–157
10. Doliotis P, Athitsos V, Kosmopoulos DI, Perantonis SJ (2012) Hand shape and 3d pose estimation using depth data from a single cluttered frame. In: ISVC 2012
11. Dollár P, Belongie S, Perona P (2010) The fastest pedestrian detector in the west. BMVC, UK
12. Dollár P, Tu Z, Perona P, Belongie S (2009) Integral channel features. BMVC, UK
13. Erol A, Bebis G, Nicolescu M, Boyle RD, Twombly X (2007) Vision-based hand pose estimation: a review. Comput Vis Image Underst 108(1–2):52–73
14. Fan R, Chang K, Hsieh C, Wang X, Lin C (2008) Liblinear: a library for large linear classification. J Mach Learn Res 9:1871–1874
15. Han J, Shao L, Xu D, Shotton J (2013) Enhanced computer vision with microsoft kinect sensor: a review. In: IEEE transactions on cybernetics 2013
16. Keskin C, Kirac F, Kara Y, Akarun L (2011) Real-time hand pose estimation using depth sensors. In: IEEE international conference on computer vision (ICCV) 2011
17. Keskin C, Kirac F, Kara YE, Akarun L (2012) Hand pose estimation and hand shape classification using multi-layered randomized decision forests. In: Computer vision-ECCV 2012
18. Lazebnik S, Schmid C, Ponce J (2006) Beyond bags of features: spatial pyramid matching for recognizing natural scene categories. In: IEEE Computer Society conference on computer vision and pattern recognition (CVPR) 2006
19. Levi D, Silberstein S, Bar-Hillel A (2013) Fast multiple-part based object detection using kd-ferns. In: IEEE Computer Society conference on computer vision and pattern recognition (CVPR)
20. Liu L, Shao L (2013) Learning discriminative representations from RGB-D video data. In: Proceedings of the twenty-third international joint conference on artificial Intelligence (IJCAI) 2013
21. Lowe DG (2004) Distinctive image features from scale-invariant keypoints. Int J Comput Vis 60(2):91–110
22. Mason L, Baxter J, Bartlett P, Frean M (2000) Boosting algorithms as gradient descent. NIPS
23. Moosmann F, Triggs B, Jurie F (2007) Fast discriminative visual codebooks using randomized clustering forests. Adv Neural Inf Process Syst
24. Ozuysal M, Calonder M, Lepetit V, Fua P (2010) Fast keypoint recognition using random ferns. IEEE Trans Pattern Anal Mach Intell 32(3):448–461
25. Shotton J, Sharp T, Kipman A, Fitzgibbon AW, Finocchio M, Blake A, Cook M, Moore R (2013) Real-time human pose recognition in parts from single depth images. Commun ACM 56(1):116–124
26. Tang D, Yu T, Kim T-K (2013) Real-time articulated hand pose estimation using semi-supervised transductive regression forests. In: International conference on computer vision (ICCV) 2013
27. Tola E, Lepetit V, Fua P (2008) A Fast Local Descriptor for Dense Matching. In: IEEE conference on computer vision and pattern recognition (CVPR) 2008
28. Vedaldi A, Fulkerson B (2008) VLFeat: an open and portable library of computer vision algorithms. http://www.vlfeat.org/
29. Vedaldi A, Zisserman A (2011) Efficient additive kernels via explicit feature maps. Pattern Anal Mach Intell 34(3)
30. Winder S, Hua G, Brown M (2009) Picking the best daisy. In: IEEE conference on computer vision and pattern recognition (CVPR)

Chapter 14
Real-Time Hand Gesture Recognition Using RGB-D Sensor

Yuan Yao, Fan Zhang and Yun Fu

Abstract RGB-D sensor-based gesture recognition is one of the most effective techniques for human–computer interaction (HCI). In this chapter, we propose a new hand motion capture procedure for establishing the real gesture data set. A hand partition scheme is designed for color-based semi-automatic labeling. This method is integrated into a vision-based hand gesture recognition framework for developing desktop applications. We use the Kinect sensor to achieve more reliable and accurate tracking in the desktop environment. Moreover, a hand contour model is proposed to simplify the gesture matching process, which can reduce the computational complexity of gesture matching. This framework allows tracking hand gestures in 3D space and matching gestures with simple contour model and thus supports complex real-time interactions. The experimental evaluations and a real-world demo of hand gesture interaction demonstrate the effectiveness of this framework.

Y. Yao (✉)
School of Mechatronic Engineering and Automation, Shanghai University,
408a HD Building, 99 Shangda Road, Shanghai 200444, China
e-mail: yaoyuan@shu.edu.cn

F. Zhang
Department of Information Science and Electrical Engineering,
Institute of Electronic Circuits and Information Systems, Zhejiang University, Room 603,
Administration Building, 38 Zheda Road, Hangzhou 310027, Zhejiang, China
e-mail: fanzhang@zju.edu.cn

Y. Fu
Department of Electrical and Computer Engineering, College of Engineering, Northeastern University, 403 Dana Research Center, 360 Huntington Avenue, Boston, MA 02115, USA
e-mail: yunfu@ece.neu.edu

Y. Fu
College of Computer and Information Science (Affiliated), Northeastern University, 403 Dana Research Center, 360 Huntington Avenue, Boston, MA 02115, USA

© Springer International Publishing Switzerland 2014
L. Shao et al. (eds.), *Computer Vision and Machine Learning with RGB-D Sensors*,
Advances in Computer Vision and Pattern Recognition,
DOI: 10.1007/978-3-319-08651-4_14

14.1 Introduction

Human–computer interaction (HCI) is an important driving force for computer vision and pattern classification fields. With the development of mobile devices and sensors, hand gestures have become a popular way to interact with tablet PC, smart phones, and personal computers. This trend is not only occurring on the two-dimensional screen, but also happens in the 3D world. However, color images cannot provide enough information for tracking hands in three-dimensional space because much of the spatial position information has to be inferred and this leads to multiple 2D–3D mappings. New sensors, such as Kinect, Xtion, and Leap Motion, can provide the ability to monitor 3D motions, thus make it simple to build systems for human computer interaction via 3D hand movements. This technological progress is very important for applications in the domain of the arts [1], computer gaming [2], computer-aided design [3], and remote control for robots [4]. Combining RGB and depth data will reduce the complexity of target tracking in complicated environments. In addition, the depth information can be utilized to avoid ambiguous mappings between images and hand poses, and generate gestures with clear semantics. In the future, we can expect more devices with built-in depth sensors.

Many hand gesture recognition methods are based on the body of work related to body pose estimation [5]. The state of the art of body estimation techniques began to make use of depth sensors to track human body parts [6, 7]. In recent research, simple pixel features [8] and patches [9] were used as input. They use a random decision forest to recognize different body parts and the orientations of a head, respectively. These methods can be used directly in hand gesture recognition. However, classifiers in these methods must be trained on a large dataset because the recognition process is sensitive to appearance variations of the target shape and backgrounds. Such dataset containing large variations is often hard to achieve.

For those applications using finger movements, accuracy is the primary consideration. It requires the hand to move in a constrained desktop environment and be close to the camera. In environments where the hand is close to the background, segmenting that hand becomes difficult as the background features can be mistaken for the hand and vice versa. In addition, the shape of the hand and the possible hand motions are more complex than those found in the rest of the human body. These problems make it difficult to apply the assumptions made by previous research on body pose estimation.

There are two main challenges in developing hand gesture-based systems at present. The first is how to locate the naked hand and reconstruct the hand pose from raw data. There has been much investigation into hand tracking, hand pose estimation, and gesture recognition. Erol et al. [5] summarized the difficulties faced by these efforts. From the perspective of application development, we summarize the hand tracking, hand pose estimation, and gesture recognition into a single challenge of reconstructing the hand pose from raw data. The second is how to represent the hand model, so that the hand gesture database can be efficiently acquired, and corresponding indexing and searching strategies can be designed to satisfy the real-time hand gesture recognition requirements. Hand models are important for training and recognition accuracy. However, collecting the labeled data required for training is difficult.

We propose a new framework to solve the aforementioned problems. Firstly, we segment a hand into different parts and use a 3D contour model to represent the hand pose configuration. Then, a feature fusion technique [10] is used to unify color and depth information for accurate hand localization. We use a pixel classifier to recognize the different parts of a hand. In order to reduce the workload of establishing real training data, we develop a semi-automatic labeling procedure, which uses both RGB data and depth data to label colored hand patches. Finally, we generate the 3D contour model from the classified pixels. Instead of matching between images, the 3D contour model can be coded into strings. Therefore, the correspondence sample gesture can be found by the nearest neighbor method. Using this framework, we develop a hand gesture-controlled desktop application. Experiments show that gesture matching can speed up efficiently to satisfy real-time recognition requirements.

14.2 Related Work

Over the past decades, many hand gesture-based interaction prototyping systems have been developed. Ali et al. [5] reviewed some of this work. From a technical point of view, the methodologies of pose estimation used in these systems can be roughly divided into model-based generative methods [11], regression-based methods [12], classification-based methods, and examplar-based methods [13].

Most of these methods do not focus on detecting hands. Some of them directly use marker-based motion capture devices, such as a glove fixed with LEDs [14], gloves with colored patterns [15], and data glove [16] to capture the motion of palms and fingers. The accuracy of these systems is determined by the hardware, which is less susceptible to interference from the environment. The shortage is that hardware configurations for these systems are often expensive, inconvenient, and uncomfortable, which make them difficult to use outside the laboratory environment.

People are most likely to adapt to tools for HCI that are less cumbersome. There has been a growing interest in the bare-hand-based gesture-controlled system. Different methods have been developed to build the interactive systems. The essential techniques are varying in these works, but the processing steps are similar, which consists of hand detection and pose estimation. Therefore, we organized them into two main categories, hand tracking and hand pose estimation, and are mainly concerned about the methods that use RGB-D sensors.

14.2.1 Hand Localization and Tracking

Segmenting a hand from a cluttered background and tracking it steadily and robustly is a challenging task. The skin color [17] and background subtraction [18] techniques are the preferred methods for detecting the image regions containing hands. These types of methods, however, make a number of assumptions, e.g., hand is the only active object in the camera scene; otherwise, complex classification methods must be used. Low-level features-based classification methods [19], histogram [20, 21], multi-scale model [22], and motion cues [23] are employed to overcome this problem. Guo et al. [24] presented a method that combines the pixel-based hierarchical feature for AdaBoosting, skin color detection, and codebook foreground detection model to track the dynamic or static hand under changing backgrounds.

In order to improve the robustness and reduce the computation time, current methods combine the ability of a depth camera with RGB information to extract hand regions from multiple candidate regions based on volume bounding box [25], scale [20], pixel probability [26], feature probability [10] and the distance to the camera. Paul et al. [27] have given a comparison on depth image-based hand extraction and RGB image-based hand extraction.

In some relatively early research works, depth data are usually used independently to locate hands. David and Zahoor [28] detected local peaks from low-resolution depth images, which are used as potential hand centers, and a palm radius is used to segment the hand from wrist and arm. Paul et al. [29] used a minimum enclosing ellipsoid to extract the major arm axis. In the perpendicular direction, the local minimum of blob width can be used to segment the hand region from an arm. Depth-based methods are fast. However, the segmentation accuracy is dependent on the method of body pose estimation. Therefore, skin color map is computed to determine which regions of the depth image should be selected [30]. In a recent review article, Han et al. [31] gave a more detailed description on this topic, which covered the depth data preprocessing, object tracking and recognition, human activity analysis, and hand gesture analysis.

14.2.2 Hand Pose Estimation

In hand pose estimation, there are a number of methods developed to find a relationship between 2D hand shape and hand posture [32]. What we called the "hand posture" is commonly defined by an articulated model along with joint angles and the orientation of the palm. These parameters can be assigned different values based on the hand shape extracted from image, and therefore, a large number of postures can be generated. Some of them have predefined semantics, which can serve as gestures and can be further used in human–computer interactive applications.

Model-based methods have also been popular because they can easily incorporate constrains on hand shapes. However, they need complex trackers that are computationally expensive. Due to the fast movement of human hand, image database an indexing technique [23] is employed, which makes it possible to recover hand tracking from each frame. Wang and Popović [15] provided a real-time hand pose estimation system based on this technique.

To remove the ambiguity generated in the 2D projection of hand shapes, depth sensors are used. Mo and Neumann [33] used 3D contours to identify fingers based on a low-resolution depth image. Suryanarayan et al. [34] constructed a volume descriptor in depth space and utilized it to recognize six gestures. Ren et al. [35] used a finger-shape-based distance to distinguish different hand gestures. Liu and Shao [36] proposed a adaptive learning methodology to generate discriminative spatio-temporal features from RGB-D data, which can be used for high-level recognition tasks. A dataset called Sheffield KInect Gesture (SKIG) is provided for hand gesture recognition test.

To reconstruct a full degree of freedom hand model, the different parts of a hand must be pre-labeled and recognized. One of the major approaches for dealing with depth image-based body part recognition is to convert the pose estimation task into a per-pixel classification problem [8]. A simple pixel feature can be used to decrease the computational complexity. This technique can be directly used on hand parts recognition if enough labeled training data are provided. Keskin et al. [37] divided the hand into 21 different parts and used this method to train a per-pixel classifier for segmenting each part. Then, a mean shift algorithm is used to estimate the position of joints. Liang et al. [38] presented a novel framework which exploits both spatial features and the temporal constraints to recover a hand model with 27 degrees of freedom from RGB-D video sequences. So far, only small-scale experimental results on hand pose estimation based on such methods are reported. Different properties of hand poses, such as big deformation and fast motion, make it difficult to identify the different parts of a hand from simple pixel features.

14.3 Framework Overview

As shown in Fig. 14.1, our framework consists of three stages: hand parts classification, hand gesture recognition, and application definition. Each stage contains two different workflows. The upper workflow is used for acquiring training data

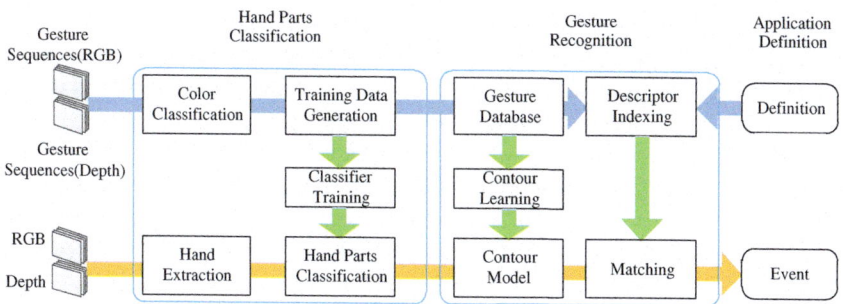

Fig. 14.1 Framework of our hand gesture recognition system

and to define gesture templates; the lower is employed to recognize hand gestures in real-time applications. We decide to use a Kinect camera instead of a dedicated camera as the input sensor for two reasons: (1) the Kinect sensor can provide both RGB and depth information; (2) the accuracy of Kinect is very close to a laser-based devices within a short range [39]. This makes Kinect a good choice for building gesture-driven desktop applications, especially for Augmented Reality applications. In addition, Kinect makes it easier to create a labeled training dataset using a semi-automatic technique that combines the depth and RGB information. Once real hand gestures are captured and labeled in the first stage, we can generate the corresponding contour descriptors in the second stage and provide semantics for them in the third stage. These definitions can then be used in the real applications.

14.3.1 Hand Parts Classification

In hand parts classification stage, we apply the per-pixel technique based on the work by Shotton et al. [8]. To improve the framework's usability in building real HCI applications, we develop a new semi-automatic method for labeling depth pixels containing hand into different classes. A glove with multiple colors is employed to assist the labeling process. The labeling results are fairly noisy and require some manual processing. The output of this procedure is a labeled training dataset. The training set is fed into a classifier based on random decision forest [8]. For real applications, we use a two-step segmentation process: the first step is to segment the hand from the background, which is a binary classification problem; the second is to segment the hand into individual parts based on the per-pixel classifier. Once hands are extracted from a depth image, they are fed into the classifier that roughly partitions them into different parts.

14.3.2 Gesture Recognition

In the second stage, we use an improved 3D contour model based on the model proposed in [10]. The basic idea is that prior knowledge of hand structure can be used to improve the accuracy of classification results. Thus, a contour model is used to recognize both static and dynamic hand gestures.

This stage also contains two workflows. In the upper, training data are converted into contour model-based descriptors and are incorporated into a gesture database. The gesture templates in the database are indexed by a K-d tree structure to speed up the gesture matching procedure. Once the detected hand is segmented into several hand patches, we can generate a 3D hand contour model from it in the lower work flow. This model contains not only gesture descriptors but also the 3D position of the hand. In the demonstration application, we show how they are used for recognizing dynamic gestures.

14.3.3 Application Definition

In order to simplify the process of building real applications, we directly define application-specific gestures in the gesture database. Once a similar hand contour descriptor is matched in the database, an event is triggered to drive the system's response to that gesture.

14.4 Training Data Generation

Training data collection is always a nontrivial task. Inspired by the current research of color-based motion tracking technique [15], we design two configurations of the color glove. As shown in Fig. 14.2, the left pattern includes 9 patches, while the right one includes 14 patches. Both patterns can be used. How to choice depends on requirements of the application. In our previous work [40], the pattern of 14 patches is used. We adopt the one with 9 patches to simplify the recognition in this chapter.

In order to collect the training data in a semi-automatic way, we need to combine both RGB and depth information for labeling. The first task is to calibrate the RGB and depth camera. There are many techniques that can be used to calibrate the two cameras [41–43]. However, in our experiments, we directly obtain the pixels mapping between RGB and depth cameras from the OpenNI Kinect SDK. The second task is to locate the multi-color glove and recognize different color regions. We manually initialize the hand location in the color image and then use mean shift for hand tracking. After the location of the hand is estimated, the different parts of a hand are identified. This is a challenging task because the measured color value can shift from frame to frame due to illumination changes [44], which will result in very noisy signals when depth pixel labeling is performed. In our work, a simple method is employed. The different parts of a hand are initially labeled by using corresponding color mask extracted from the color image. We trained a random forests classifier in the HSV color space and use this classifier to refine the labeling. Finally, we manually finish the labeling work.

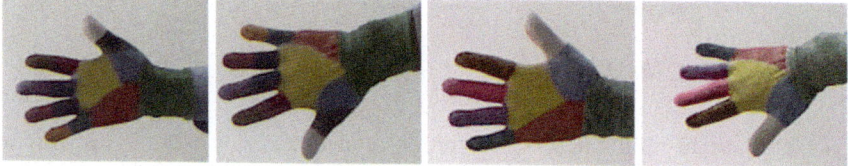

Fig. 14.2 *Color* glove design

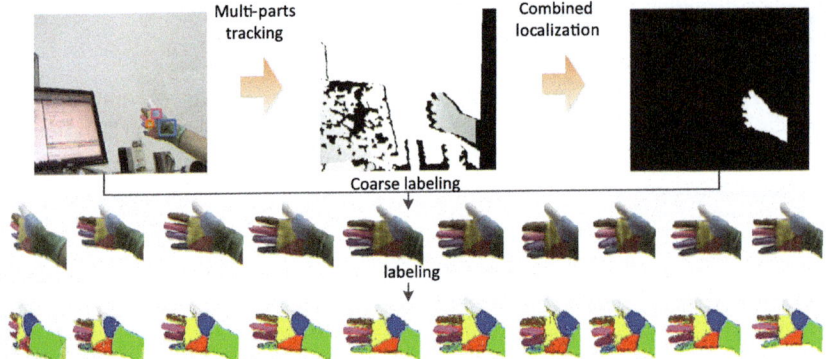

Fig. 14.3 Hand location and labeling

14.4.1 Hand Localization

Depth sensors make segmentation under constrained conditions simpler than ever. However, segmenting the hand from a cluttered background is still a challenging problem, because the shape of the hand is very flexible. In our sample collection stage, both RGB and depth information are used for localization of the hand. Figure 14.3 shows the procedure of recognizing the hand.

First, we ask users manually select several parts within a hand region (top left image in Fig. 14.3). This selection uses a fixed sequence, which usually includes three color regions from the first image of a gesture sequence. Then, a mean shift method is used to track multiple hand parts simultaneously for these gesture sequences. Therefore, the location and direction of the hand can be confirmed during the tracking process.

At the same time, the shapes of foreground targets are segmented from the depth image. We make use of the relationship between RGB and depth image to find where the hand is located. This process generates a hand mask. Each depth pixel in this region can be assigned a RGB color, which will generate a coarsely labeled gesture sequence on depth pixels.

14.4.2 Color Classification

Coarsely labeled results need to be further refined. As shown in the last row of Fig. 14.3, we use a random forests classifier to generate labels depending on pixel colors on the glove. Those colors are converted into HSV space. We trained a random forests classifier based on the 9 groups of manually labeled samples. In the training and classification process, only the component of hue is considered.

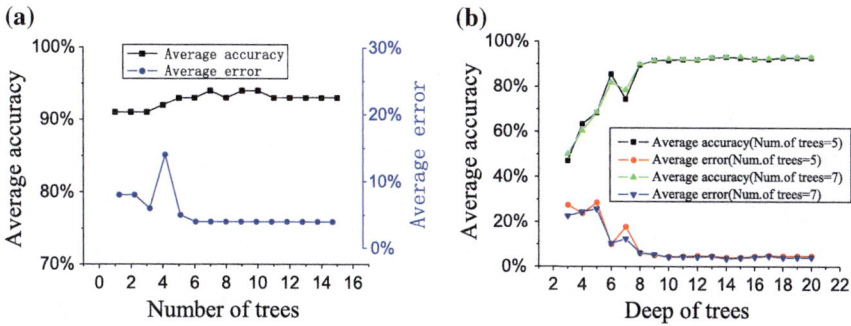

Fig. 14.4 **a** Average accuracy and average error vs Number of trees **b** Average accuracy and average error vs Deep of trees

Figure 14.4 shows the performance of the random forests-based labeling. In the experiments, 50 % manually labeled samples are used as training set, and the other data are used to test. Figure 14.4a reports the trends of average recognition accuracy and average false identification rate with different number of decision trees. Figure 14.4b gives the average recognition accuracy and average false identification rate with different deep of the random forests trees.

The output of the color classification step is used as training data for generating 3D hand contours for the gesture database. During the semi-automatic labeling process, there are many incorrectly labeled pixels. After color classification, manually labeling process is still employed to remove this noise. There are 2,400 labeled frames of hand samples from 6 people in our training database. Five different types of hand gesture sequences are included in the database. By using the classification results, the average labeling time is decreased from 6 min to 30 s for each image in our experiments.

14.5 Hand Patches Segmentation

There are two problems that need to be solved in the hand pose estimating process: hand extraction and hand parts classification. Without strong assumptions about the range of activities, segmenting hands from a cluttered background is difficult, because of the interference of different objects in the scene and other body parts, such as arms, head, and shoulder. Segmenting a deformable and rotatable hand into different parts is also a challenging task. We use a two-step segmentation process in our approach. One is the full hand extraction step, and the other is hand parts segmentation. The former step uses a classification and tracking procedure to distinguish hand objects from other objects. The latter step is to segment hand into parts depending on the feature extracted from depth image.

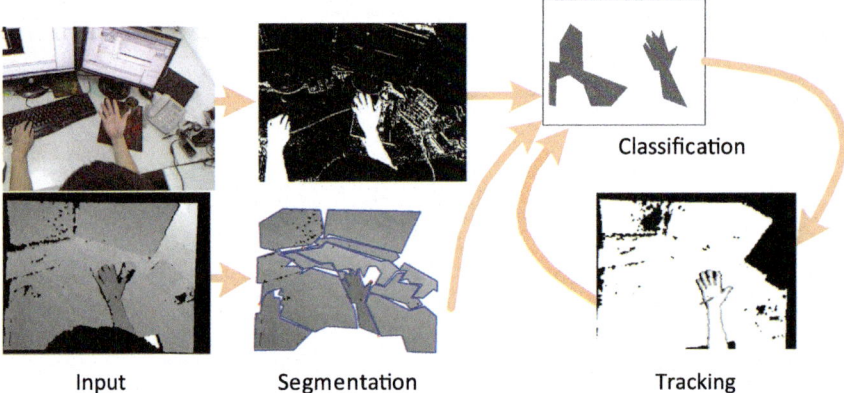

Fig. 14.5 Hands extraction

14.5.1 Hand Extraction

In order to discriminate hand-like objects from other foreground objects, a tracking technique is used. The complete procedure is shown in Fig. 14.5.

For RGB images, the skin color pixels are extracted from RGB image by [45] to generate the skin color mask (as shown in Fig. 14.5 upper middle).

For the depth image, we first assume that hands move within a certain distance range to the camera (distance <1.6 m). Outside this range, part of the depth data is often missing due to multiple reflections and scattering on the surface of the hand. The assumption is also helpful in removing some of the noise. Then, a dynamic threshold segmentation is used to extract multiple targets from the depth data (as shown in Fig. 14.5 bottom middle). In this segmentation process, we convert the depth image into a 8-bit gray image. A histogram with 256 bins is constructed on this image, which is further smoothed by a Gaussian kernel. The local max and min values in the histogram can be found by computing the gaussian derivatives for each bin. Therefore, we can segment the depth image into multiple regions by the depth clusters.

Both depth and RGB images are used to get the initial segmentation. The candidate targets containing enough skin-colored pixels are kept as potential hand locations. In experiments, this percentage is set to a constant value. We found that areas containing 70 % skin-colored pixels perform well during classification. A simple 2D shape feature is used to classify targets into hands and other objects. After this process, the selected targets are fed into a Kalman filter-based tracker to avoid any jitter, noise, occlusions, and large deformations of the hand in the input video. We use a standard Kalman filter described in [17] to track the trajectory of the palm center in 2D space. The segmentation and classification procedure are done for each frame. Even if the hand is lost in a certain frame due to noise or temporary occlusion, it will be recovered in the successive frames.

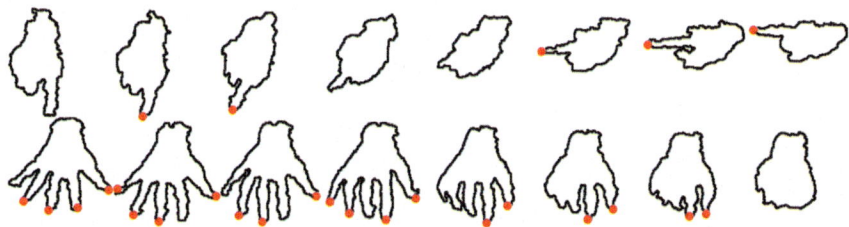

Fig. 14.6 2D shape features defined on hand contour. The *red* points indicate the locations of features

We use a 2D silhouette feature for determining if an object is a hand or not. This feature uses local curvature on the contour to describe the geometry of the fingertips. For each pixel on a contour, the feature is calculated by

$$\mathrm{acos}((x_{i-1}^A - x_i^{A,H}) \cdot (x_{i+1}^A - x_i^{A,H})) < T, \qquad (14.1)$$

where x^A represents the coordinate of a depth pixel on a target contour A. A is an approximated curve computed from the original hand contour extracted from a depth image. $x_i^{A,H}$ is the coordinate of a depth pixel on A's convex hull H. T is an empirical threshold. As shown in Fig. 14.6a, the red points indicate where the features are located. We found that $T = 0.8$ performs well in practice. It is not very robust because the shape feature cannot always be detected from the contour in some frames. In order to segment the hand from other extracted targets, we learn the prior probability of the number of features from a group of training depth images.

Bayes rule is used to compute the posterior probability of an object being a hand. The posterior is represented by $P(h = 1|\mathscr{S})$, which represents the likelihood of observing a hand object when shape features $\mathscr{S}$ are given, we have

$$P(h = 1|\mathscr{S}) = \frac{P(\mathscr{S}|h = 1)P(h = 1)}{P(\mathscr{S})}, \qquad (14.2)$$

where $P(h)$ is the prior probability that measures whether the target is a hand ($h = 1$) or not ($h = 0$) without observing its color. We can estimate the probability density function of $P(\mathscr{S}|h = 1)$ and $P(\mathscr{S}|h = 0)$ from the training database. Here, $P(\mathscr{S}) = P(\mathscr{S}|h = 1)P(h = 1) + P(\mathscr{S}|h = 0)P(h = 0)$. Candidate regions are chosen if their posterior probability is greater than a threshold.

14.5.2 Hand Parts Classification

Depending on a weak spatial prediction, the position feature defined in the depth image [8] is simple and effective. However, it is not rotation invariant. The property of rotation invariance is important for hand pose estimation, especially in the case, the support of the body pose estimation is missing.

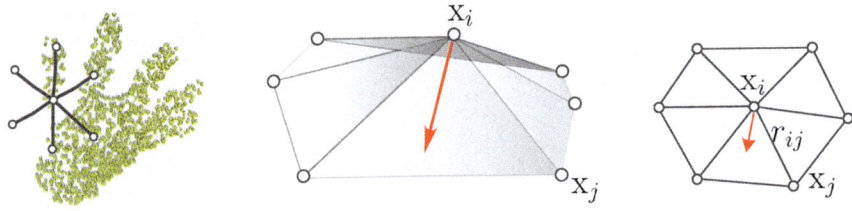

Fig. 14.7 Position feature is a geometrical feature defined on the depth image (*left*), which represents local details. The *red arrow's* direction approximates the normal, and the size approximates the mean curvature (*middle*). In the 2D depth image, this feature can be computed by a neighborhood sampling descriptor (*right*)

In order to overcome this problem, we create a new feature, which is defined over the 3D surface constructed by the depth pixels. The distribution of depth values in a neighborhood of a pixel is considered to identify which part of the hand that pixel belongs to. As shown in Fig. 14.7(left), the relationship of depth pixels in a neighbor domain can be represented as a graph $G = (X, E)$, with pixels X and topology E. Where $X = [x_1, x_2, \ldots, x_n]$, $x_i = \{x_{iu}, y_{iv}, d_I(x_i)\}$ is the depth pixels set. $d_I(x_i)$ is the depth value of pixel x_i. Inspired by [46], we define the position feature for each pixel x_i by

$$f_i(I, x) = \sum_{i,j \in E} \omega_{i,j} (x_j - x_i), \qquad (14.3)$$

where $\sum_{i,j \in E} \omega_{i,j} = 1$.

A graphical description of this position feature is given by Fig. 14.7(middle). The neighbor domain information is introduced by the topology. In Eq. (14.3), the direction of $f_i(I, x)$ approximates the pixel's normal, and the size of $f_i(I, x)$ represents the mean curvature. We only use the size; thus, the position feature is rotation invariant. In order to improve the computational efficiency, we use the pixel's normal and the mean curvature to compute the feature. In the algorithm, the key parameter is the feature scale parameter $r_{i,j}$, which represents the distance between x_i and x_j (Fig. 14.7 right). By using a constant $r_{i,j}$, we can define the position feature on the depth image as

$$\delta_i = L(x_i) = d_I(x_i) - \frac{1}{n} \sum_{j \in E} s_I(x_j), \qquad (14.4)$$

where $s_I(x)$ is the depth value of pixel x, n is a predefined number of sampling points, and

$$s_I(x) = \begin{cases} d_I(x) & x \in \text{hand} \\ b & x \notin \text{hand} \end{cases}. \qquad (14.5)$$

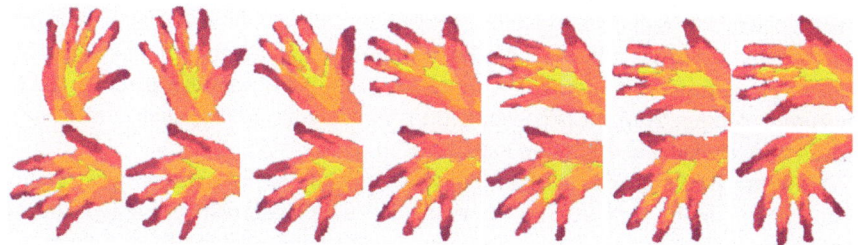

Fig. 14.8 Position feature in a rotated hand

Figure 14.8 shows that examples of the position features are computed on a series of rotated hands. For illustration purposes, feature values are mapped into the RGB color space. As can be seen in Fig. 14.6b, there is no clear boundary between the palm center and hand edge. This means that the signal is weak. To overcome this problem, we use a random decision forest to combine these features in all training data. Since the contour of each hand is already detected, the position feature does not depend on a specific background.

We use the 2D shape feature and the position feature to segment hand patches. The geometry feature that was used in the original framework [10] is removed, because its contribution for improving the accuracy is insignificant. Figure 14.8 shows the result of classifying different parts of a hand using features of different scale extracted from 1906 frames of test data. To improve the accuracy of classification and reduce the false-positive rate, we refine the estimation results with a contour model in the "gesture recognition" stage.

14.6 Gesture Recognition

For many applications, the goal of hand gesture recognition is not to recognize arbitrary 3D hand pose, but to recognize if a gesture is one of a fixed number of hand poses. Therefore, in this work, we use a database indexing technique to implement gesture recognition. A hand contour database is collected by using the training samples. In the following sections, we give the description of the contour model and the similarity measures.

14.6.1 Contour Model

The final output of the estimation process is a labeled 3D contour. There are several advantages of using labeled 3D contours as hand models. First, a contour is a simple structure. It is easier to match two contours with different scales than matching image patches or articulated models. Second, the representation of a contour only needs a small size descriptor, so it is more appropriate for database indexing-based gesture recognition techniques, in which a large number of samples are collected for gesture matching. Third, it is convenient to convert contours to other models, such as articulated model and 3D skin model.

Contour Descriptor. The hand contour model C is represented by a ordered list of points on the contour $\mathbf{c} = \{\mathbf{v}_1^c, \mathbf{v}_2^c, \ldots \mathbf{v}_n^c\}$ with its corresponding label vector $\mathbf{l} = \{l_1, l_2, \ldots l_n\}$. Where v is a vertex on contour c. The value of n is determined by the distance of the hand to the camera and describes the size of a hand contour and is decided by the distance of the hand to the camera. Label vector provides the information about specific hand contour segments belonging to certain hand parts. As a descriptor, both 3D coordinate sequence and labeling index sequence cannot provide a rotation and scale invariance. We add another sequence, $\mathbf{m} = \{m_1, m_2, \ldots m_n\}$, for the contour representation. $\mathbf{m}$ is a normalized length sequence.

$$m_i = \frac{\text{Length}(\{\mathbf{v}_j^c | l_j\})}{\text{Length}(\mathbf{c})}, \quad (14.6)$$

where j represents the continuous indexing. The descriptor of the ith hand contour C^i is represented by the $\{l_1^i m_1^i, l_2^i m_2^i, \ldots l_d^i m_d^i\}$, where d is the dimension of the descriptor. By selecting d, most significant m_i, d can be set to a fixed dimension.

14.6.2 Contour Generation

Given a 3D contour $\mathbf{c}$, a natural method for constructing $\mathbf{l}$ is to directly search the set of labeled points and, for each point v_i, find the class with the maximum probability. We define the probability as

$$P(\mathbf{c}|\mathbf{v}_i^c) = \frac{1}{n} \gamma_i \sum_{j \in N(i)} P_j(\mathbf{c}|\mathbf{v}_j), \quad (14.7)$$

where $N(i)$ represents a vertex set in the neighbor area of $\mathbf{v}_i^c$. $P_j(\mathbf{c}|\mathbf{v}_j)$ can be deduced from $P(\mathbf{c}|\mathbf{x})$. γ_i is a learning parameter defined as

$$\gamma_i = \frac{p_c^i}{M} \sum_{k \in \varsigma} P(\mathbf{c}|\mathbf{v}_k^c), \quad (14.8)$$

which considers the continuity of the 3D contour. Here, ς is a contour segment that consists of some subset of indices of v_i and its neighbor domain. M represents the size of ς. p_c^i is a learning parameter, which defines a connectivity relationship between different contour segments. By using this model, the gesture recognition

Fig. 14.9 Contour descriptor alignment

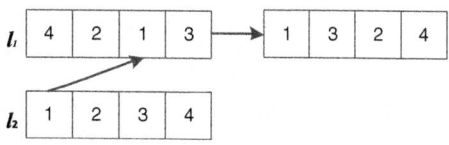

process can be described as a sequence matching problem, which can also be used to recover the 3D hand position.

14.6.3 Contour Matching

In order to measure the similarity of two contours, our task is to find a distance function $D(\cdot)$ for fast matching. Once $D(\cdot)$ is determined, the descriptor can be aligned according to Fig. 14.9. That means given a contour descriptor C^i, the query result from a database should satisfy

$$C^i = \arg\min_{i \in \Psi, j \in \Omega} D(C^i, C^j) w, \qquad (14.9)$$

where Ψ is the test set of contours, Ω represents the template database. w is a weight, which is computed by

$$w = \sum_{k=\{1,\cdots d\}} l_k^i \text{ xor } l_k^j. \qquad (14.10)$$

There are two possible cases where errors arise in generating of hand contours: whole-to-whole matching and whole-to-part matching. We use Smith–Waterman [47] algorithm to deal with both cases. In our application, we select the arm class as the start of the descriptor, because in the data, the arms are typically longer than any other hand parts and are always visible.

14.7 Validation

We evaluated our method on the dataset collected in Sect. 14.4. A total of 2564 frames was captured, each of which includes calibrated depth data, labeled hand parts information, and a mask image of the hand region. All these data are compressed and stored in a SQLite database. In the hand gesture recognition test, we compared our method on a second RGB-D dataset provided in [35].

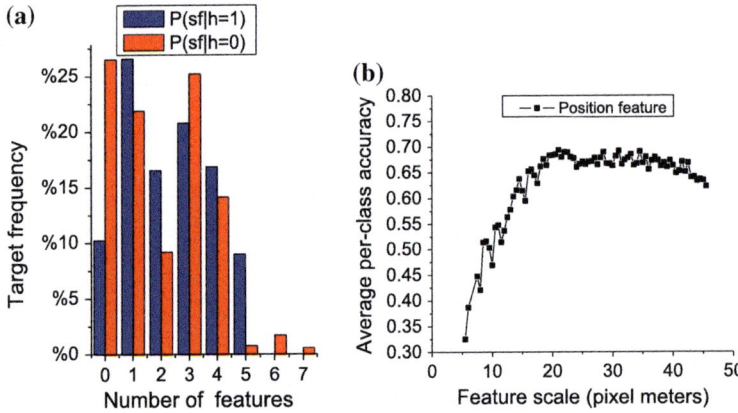

Fig. 14.10 a Prior distribution of shape features. b Feature scale and average per-classes accuracy

14.7.1 Hand Detection

In most indoor bare-hand interaction applications, hands and objects often appear together. So we assume $P(h = 1) = P(h = 0) = 0.5$; thus, Eq. (14.2) can be simplified to

$$P(h = 1|\mathscr{S}) = \frac{P(\mathscr{S}|h = 1)}{P(\mathscr{S}|h = 1) + P(\mathscr{S}|h = 0))}. \quad (14.11)$$

The distribution of $P(\mathscr{S}|h = 1)$ is learned from 600 frames that are randomly chosen from the training database, while other objects of size similar to the hand, such as head, bottles, apples, keyboards, computer mice, and books in the database, are used to estimate $P(\mathscr{S}|h = 0)$. These two distributions are given in Fig. 14.10a, where the blue bars and red bars represent the statistic results on hand and other objects, respectively. With depth information, shape features can be extracted quickly employing a pre-defined threshold. The number of shape features is counted and used to compute Eq. (14.2). This method is tested on the remaining 1,800 images containing a cluttered background. The hand detection procedure achieves 54.5 % accuracy. After using the skin color segmentation described in section V, the accuracy increases to 94.7 %. The classification results are heavily dependent on the environment. In our application, the frame-loss rate is less than 1 % during the tracking procedure. Multiple hands can be processed simultaneously with small amount of additional calculation. The disadvantage is that it will not work in the following scenarios: (1) the scene contains the body; (2) one hand is occluded by another hand; (3) a person is wearing gloves. Body skeletal trackers can be used to solve these problems.

14.7.2 Hand Parts Classification

In hand parts classification experiment, we select 600 frames from 6 subjects for training and use the other frames for testing. The training samples and testing samples are collected from multiple indoor environment and with different backgrounds and camera view angles.

Figure 14.10b shows the relationship between position feature scale and per-part recognition accuracy rate. The mean per-class accuracy is used as a baseline. Instead of using a single shape feature, we use the pixel's normal and the pixel's mean curvature defined in Sect. 14.5 as the position feature. Compared with the per-part recognition accuracy rate in our previous work [10], the classification results show a significant improvement. This curve will change slightly when different topologies are selected for shape feature.

Table 14.1 shows the per-pixel classification results of detecting different hand patches. The experiment is done on 1,800 frames, where "CMC" indicates the region near the root of little finger, and "TM" indicates the region near the root of thumb. The average accuracy of recognition is 58.48 %. However, the misclassification rate is still high. Shotton et al. [8] showed that using more training samples will improve the mean per-class accuracy. However, labeling real data and generating synthetic training data are nontrivial. Combining more features into the position feature will also improve the mean per-class accuracy [10] but too many features might result in the over-fitting problem.

Figure 14.11 shows the per-class accuracy for pixels located on the hand contour (Fig. 14.11 black) and the per-class accuracy by using the contour model (Fig. 14.11 red). Compared with the results provided by the pixel classification, there is a large improvement in contour model-based classification. The average accuracy of hand parts classification is improved from 58.48 % to 77.68 %. The error rate is still large, but hand orientation can be estimated from the contour, which can also be used in gesture matching.

Table 14.1 Per-pixel hand parts classification results

Category	Sample quantity	True positive (%)	False positive (%)
Thumb	1,574,265	51.0	46.30
Index	1,335,410	33.5	3.10
Middle	1,540,891	74.3	80.60
Ring	1,383,038	66.3	57.40
Small	1,085,247	29.6	21.60
CMC	2,756,895	63.0	44.80
Palm	2,587,585	85.1	83.20
TM	1,602,793	29.8	3.94
ARM	9,866,422	93.7	7.96
Average accuracy		58.48	38.78

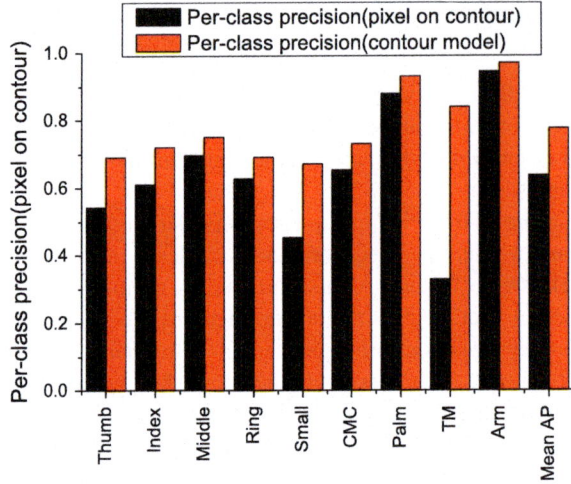

Fig. 14.11 Per-pixel classification accuracy and per-segment classification accuracy with contour model

14.7.3 Gestures Recognition

Our method is tested on the database provided by the authors of [35] without changing any parameters and features. Because these samples do not provide the hand parts segmentation, we capture the same gestures and manually labeled them for each subject. Then, the entire dataset of [35] is used for testing. Figure 14.12 shows the test results in confusion matrix. Compared with the near-convex decomposition-based Finger-Earth Mover's Distance (FEMD) method, our method achieves a similar accuracy by using 40 training samples. Although the recognition rate of some categories has not been significantly improved, the average true-positive rate is better.

We use a desktop computer with an AMD Phenom II X4, 3.0 GHz CPU with 3G RAM to run the test. For each frame, the computation time includes approximately 10 ms for target segmentation, 22 ms for tracking, 17 ms for sampling and features computation, 3 ms for classification, and 32 ms for contour matching. We use a small gesture database that includes 320 hand contour descriptors to test the matching of hand contours. Our C++ implementation processes each frame in 87 ms. GPU acceleration is not used. It is capable to do a real-time gesture recognition on a faster machine. A GPU version is needed when the application contains complex interactions and scene rendering.

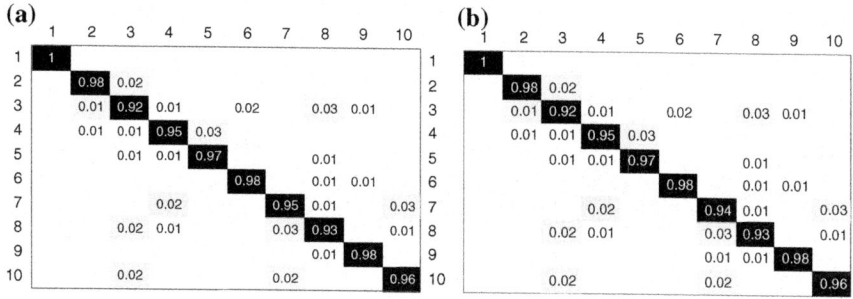

Fig. 14.12 Confusion matrix of gestures recognition results. The gesture categories is ordered by the original database. **a** Near-convex decomposition + FEMD [35]. **b** Hand contour matching

14.8 System Application

In order to evaluate the feasibility and effectiveness of the proposed framework, we perform two case studies.

14.8.1 Augmented Reality Molecular Assembler

The fist application is based on a HCI program named AR Chemical [48], which is an application that utilizes a tangible user interface for organic chemistry education. The interface uses an Augmented Reality (AR) mouse and AR makers to allow users to compose and directly interact with 3D molecular models. All interactions are done on a real desk. The operation includes moving, dragging, positioning, and assembling virtual structures in a 3D space. Therefore, delicate and complex interactive behaviors and hand position information are needed.

We simulate this system and provide three hand gestures to replace the original operation that used with the AR paddle and computer mouse. First, we use keyboard to select atom and then use raising thumbs to simulate the mouse button. The finger pointing action is used for positioning objects.

Once a gesture is detected, we need to record the starting position of the hand and rotate the indicator mark on the 3D molecule, which inserts the atom into the right position pointed to by the finger. Finally, the waving hand with a different orientation is used to assist this assembling process by rotating the assembled molecule on the platform.

The dynamic gesture recognition is realized in the application layer. We set up two gesture buffers in the application: one is for reserving sequential contour with 3D vertices to get hand position; the other is for holding hand contour descriptors to match the hand pose. We define simple interaction action rules on the buffers. This scheme is easy to extend.

Fig. 14.13 Waving gesture for rotation control

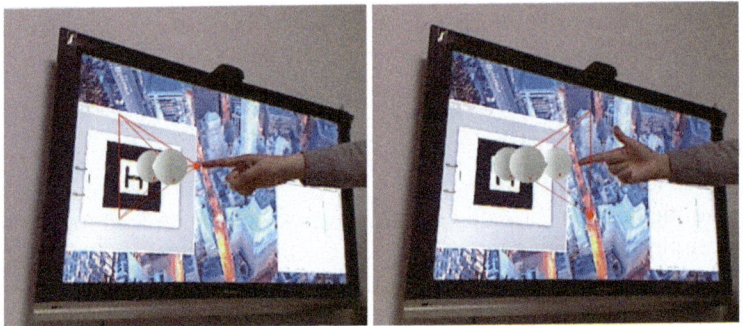

Fig. 14.14 Atom position selection and molecular assembling operation

Figure 14.13 shows the rotation operation. Figure 14.14 is sampled from a procedure of adding an atom into a molecule. This combination of four hand gestures can drive the real-time visual interaction with complex visual feedback. Such type of interactions can increase natural feeling of the operation. The Kinect-based system is able to overcome the problem of illumination changing. We believe that other applications, such as digital sculpture, painting and computer-aided design system could benefit from this framework as well.

14.8.2 Xerrys Intelligent Rehabilitation System

By combining the body pose estimation, we applied our technology to a medical system called Xerrys Intelligent Rehabilitation System for Hospitals, in short XIRSH. XIRSH is a platform of new Kinect-based applications. The major objective of XIRSH is to help patients conduct trainings and practices at the late stage of rehabilitation in hospitals. It can be considered as a comprehensive rehabilitation tool, which provides new methods for occupational and physical therapy and combines the motion control with cognitive and speech rehabilitation. A variant version of XIRSH can be served as a home based application to further extend the tele-rehabilitation process.

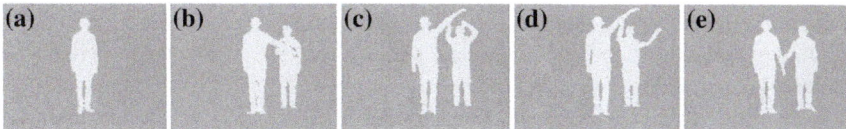

Fig. 14.15 Upper limb training scenario. **a** A patient is captured by the Kinect sensor and given the control. **b** A therapist walks in and helps the patient lift his upper limb. The therapist takes the control of the training game. **c** The therapist waves one of his hands to the *left*. **d** The therapist waves one of his hands to the *right*. **e** The therapist releases the control and the patient finishes the motion

In XIRSH, the gesture control is widely used as an efficient and attracting interaction to motivate the patients. We illustrated two application-level scenarios where the hand gesture recognition results can be directly utilized.

In the first scenario (Fig. 14.15), the patient is asked to lift his upper limb from the body side to conduct the abduction for his shoulder joint. However, this motion might be difficult for an individual patient who just passes level 4 (Brunstrom). Therefore, a physical therapist has to stand by the patient and help the patient's lifting. Two skeletons will be tracked simultaneously through the depth view by the Kinect sensor. The corresponding tracking ID for the patient is not fixed during this process, which causes the incontinence at the application level. As the patient may have the difficulties in motion, a wave hand gesture from the therapist is proposed. Once the waving is detected, the system can identify the situation that there is a therapist who is helping the patient. As a result, the control and focus of the application will be released from the therapist back to the patient. All the corresponding data flows will be correctly led to the patient himself.

In the second scenario (Fig. 14.16), a training is specially designed for exercising the shoulder joint. The patient is immersed into a virtual reality and asked to move the items, such as a clock and a football, into to the correct categories, such as sporting items and living items. During this training, the items are generated at the upper corners of the screen, and the containers are at the bottom corners. The practice is

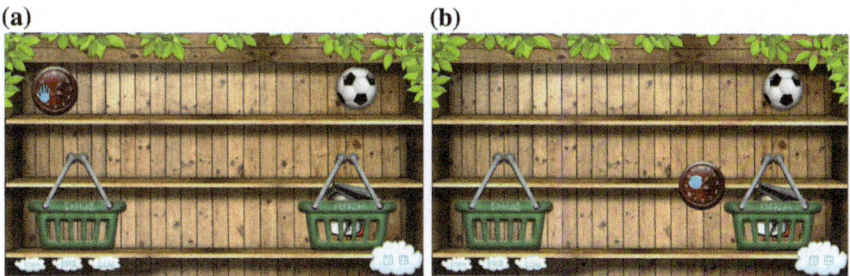

Fig. 14.16 Hand training scenario. **a** A hand over to select the clock (*Basic level*). **b** A grab to pick up the clock and a release to drop it to the living items category (*Advanced level*)

motivating the patient to do some diagonal motions. At the basic level, the patient can move his hand to conduct the mouse cursor movement. A hand over the items for seconds is considered as to select the item. A hand over the corresponding container is to drop the item. The basic training aims to improve the stability and balance. However, some patients with better conditions could be asked to conduct advanced trainings. For example, the hand over gesture is replaced with the hand grab for the picking and the hand release for the dropping. One advantage to motivate the patients to do more practices with fingers and hands.

In both aforementioned scenarios, hand gestures are used to interact with the software programs and provide the biometric feedback such as text prompts or audio reminders. The feedback is very important because it can inform the patients, whether their motions are correct or not. Our experimental results show that the technique proposed the previous section can efficiently recognize the different gestures and send the feedback at a real-time level.

14.9 Summary

We have introduced a novel framework for recognizing hand gestures, which is inspired by the current depth image-based body pose estimation technology. A semi-automatic labeling strategy using a Kinect sensor is described. This procedure is used to generate the samples used for both hand detection, and hand pose estimation. The 3D hand contour with labeled information provides a simplified hand model to facilitate building real-time bare-hand-controlled interface. Our framework can be easily extended to incorporate different desktop applications. We also notice that 3D gesture interaction is not user-friendly enough, because there are still many visual and touch feedbacks needed to improve the realism.

The current work still has several limitations that we plan to focus on in the future work:

(1) Segmenting hand from a long arm or a body is not well handled with the proposed hand extraction and hand parts classification method. Therefore, the form of camera setup is limited.
(2) The accuracy of the contour model is limited by the classification result of hand parts.
(3) To some applications, the classifier needs to be re-trained due to the different application configurations.

Another future research directions include designing new hand partition patterns to improve the recognition accuracy. The contour matching algorithm can be further revised and evaluated to improve the matching accuracy. Moreover, we also would like to develop new hand gesture-controlled applications with the support of this framework and implement a GPU version of the algorithm.

References

1. Riener A (2012) Gestural interaction in vehicular applications. Computer 45(4):42–47
2. Roccetti M, Marfia G, Semeraro A (2012) Playing into the wild: a gesture-based interface for gaming in public spaces. J Vis Commun Image Representat 23(3):426–440
3. Fernandez-Pacheco DG, Albert F, Aleixos N, Conesa J (2012) A new paradigm based on agents applied to free-hand sketch recognition. Exp Syst Appl 39(8):7181–7195
4. Luo C, Chen Y, Krishnan M, Paulik M (2012) The magic glove: a gesture-based remote controller for intelligent mobile robots. In: SPIE on intelligent robots and computer vision: algorithms and techniques, vol 8301, CA, USA, San Francisco
5. Erol A, Bebis G, Nicolescu M, Boyle RD, Twombly X (2007) Vision-based hand pose estimation: a review. CVIU 108(1–2):52–73
6. Zhu Y, Fujimura K (2007) Constrained optimization for human pose estimation from depth sequences. In: Proceedings of the 8th Asian conference on computer vision—volume Part I, November 2007, pp 408–418
7. Siddiqui M, Medioni G (2010) Human pose estimation from a single view point, real-time range sensor. In: IEEE computer society conference on computer vision and pattern recognition workshops (CVPRW), June 2010, pp. 1–8
8. Shotton J, Sharp T, Kipman A, Fitzgibbon A, Finocchio M, Blake A, Cook M, Moore R (2013) Real-time human pose recognition in parts from single depth images. Commun. ACM 56(1):116–124
9. Fanelli G, Gall J, Van Gool L (2011) Real time head pose estimation with random regression forests. In: Proceedings of computer vision and pattern recognition (CVPR), June 2011, pp. 617–624
10. Yao Y, Yao Y, Fu Y (2102) Real-time hand pose estimation from rgb-d sensor. In: IEEE international conference on multimedia and expo (ICME), July 2012, pp 705–710
11. Oikonomidis I, Kyriazis N, Argyros A (2011) Efficient model-based 3d tracking of hand articulations using Kinect. In: BMVC 2011, August. 2011, pp 101.1–101.11
12. de Campos TE, Murray DW (2006) Regression-based hand pose estimation from multiple cameras. In: IEEE computer society conference on computer vision and pattern recognition, June 2006, pp 782–789
13. Xiaohui S, Gang H, Williams L, Ying W (2012) Dynamic hand gesture recognition: an exemplar-based approach from motion divergence fields. Image Vis Comput 30(3):227–235
14. Jun P, Yeo-Lip Y (2006) Led-glove based interactions in multi-modal displays for teleconferencing. In: Proceedings of international conference on artificial reality and telexistence, December 2006, pp 395–399
15. Wang RY, Popović J (2009) Real-time hand-tracking with a color glove. ACM Trans Graph 28:63:1–63:8
16. Sturman DJ, Zeltzer D (1994) A survey of glove-based input. IEEE Comput Graph Appl 14:30–39
17. Mo Z, Lewis JP Neumann U (2005) Smartcanvas: a gesture-driven intelligent drawing desk system. In: Proceedings of international conference on intelligent user interfaces, January 2005, pp 239–243
18. Ogihara A, Matsumoto H, Shiozaki A (2007) Hand region extraction by background subtraction with renewable background for hand gesture recognition. In: international symposium on intelligent signal processing and communications. Japan, Nov, Yonago, pp 227–230
19. Bilal S, Akmeliawati R, El Salami MJ, Shafie AA, and Bouhabba EM (2010) A hybrid method using Haar-like and skin-color algorithm for hand posture detection, recognition and tracking. In: IEEE international conference on mechatronics and automation, August 2010, pp 934–939
20. Chai X, Fang Y, Wang K (2009) Robust hand gesture analysis and application in gallery browsing. In: Proceedings of IEEE ICME, June 2009, pp 938–941
21. Van den Bergh M, Van Gool L (2011) Combining RGB and tof cameras for real-time 3D hand gesture interaction. In: Proceedings IEEE WACV, January 2011, pp 66–72

22. Li H, Greenspan M (2011) Model-based segmentation and recognition of dynamic gestures in continuous video streams. Pattern Recogn 44(8):1614–1628
23. Alon J, Athitsos V, Yuan Q, Sclaroff S (2009) A unified framework for gesture recognition and spatiotemporal gesture segmentation. IEEE Trans PAMI 31(9):1685–1699
24. Guo JM, Liu Y-F, Chang C-H, Nguyen H-S (2012) Improved hand tracking system. IEEE Trans Circ Syst Video Technol. 22(5):693–701
25. Patlolla C, Mahotra S, Kehtarnavaz N (2012) Real-time hand-pair gesture recognition using a stereo webcam. Proceedings IEEE international conference on emerging signal processing applications, pp 135–138
26. Tang M (2011) Recognizing hand gestures with Microsoft's kinect. Tech. Rep. 2011
27. Doliotis P, Stefan A, McMurrough C, Eckhard D, Athitsos V (2011) Comparing gesture recognition accuracy using color and depth information. In: Proceedings of the 4th international conference on PErvasive technologies related to assistive environments, vol 20 May 2011, pp 1–7
28. Minnen D, Zafrulla Z (2011) Towards robust cross-user hand tracking and shape recognition. In: 2011 IEEE international conference on computer vision workshops (ICCV Workshops), November 2011, pp 1235–1241
29. Doliotis P, Athitsos V, Kosmopoulos DI, Perantonis SJ, (2012) Hand shape and 3D pose estimation using depth data from a single cluttered frame. In: Proceedings of international symposium on visual computing (ISVC), vol 7431. April 2012, pp 148–158
30. Oikonomidis I, Kyriazis N, Argyros AA (2012) Tracking the articulated motion of two strongly interacting hands. In: Proceedings of the 2012 IEEE conference on computer vision and pattern recognition (CVPR), June 2012, pp 1862–1869
31. Han J, Shao L, Xu D, Shotton J (2013) Enhanced computer vision with microsoft kinect sensor: a review. IEEE Trans Cybern (T-Cyb), 43(5):1318–1334
32. de La Gorce M, Fleet DJ, Paragios N (2011) Model-based 3d hand pose estimation from monocular video. IEEE Trans PAMI 33:1793–1805
33. Mo Z, Neumann U (2006) Real-time hand pose recognition using low-resolution depth images. In: Proceedings of IEEE CVPR, June 2006, pp 1499–1505
34. Suryanarayan P, Subramanian A, Mandalapu D (2010) Dynamic hand pose recognition using depth data. In: Proceedings IAPR ICPR, December 2010, pp 3105–3108
35. Ren Z, Yuan J, Meng J, Zhang Z (2013) Robust part-based hand gesture recognition using Kinect sensor. IEEE Trans Multimedia 15(5):1110–1120
36. Liu L, Shao L (2013) Learning discriminative representations from RGB-D video data. In: Proceedings of the twenty-third international joint conference on artificial intelligence (IJCAI'13) August 2013, pp 1493–1500
37. Keskin C, Kirac F, Kara YE, Akarun L, (2011) Real time hand pose estimation using depth sensors. In: IEEE workshop on consumer depth cameras for computer vision, November 2011, pp 1228–1234
38. Liang H, Yuan J, Thalmann D, Zhang Z (2013) Model-based hand pose estimation via spatial-temporal hand parsing and 3d fingertip localization. Vis Comput 29(6–8):837–848
39. Stoyanov T, Louloudi A, Andreasson H, Lilienthal AJ (2011) Comparative evaluation of range sensor accuracy in indoor environments. In: Proceedings of the European conference on mobile robots (ECMR), September 2011, pp 19–24
40. Yao Y, and Fu Y (2014) Contour model based hand-gesture recognition using Kinect sensor. IEEE Trans Circ Syst Video Technol, pp 1–1
41. Kramer J, Burrus N, Echtler F, Daniel HC, Parker M (2012) Object modeling and detection. In: Hacking the Kinect, Apress, Berkely
42. Canessa A, Chessa M, Gibaldi A, Sabatini SP, Solari F (2013) Calibrated depth and color cameras for accurate 3d interaction in a stereoscopic augmented reality environment. J Vis Commun Image Represent, 2013, article in Press
43. Herrera DC, Kannala J, Heikkila J (2012) Joint depth and color camera calibration with distortion correction. IEEE Trans Pattern Anal Machine Intell 34(10):2058–2064

44. Wang R, Paris S, Popović J, (2011) Practical color-based motion capture. In: Proceedings of the 2011 ACM SIGGRAPH/Eurographics symposium on computer animation, August 2011, pp 139–146
45. Chai D, Ngan KN (1998) Locating facial region of a head-and-shoulders color image. In: Proceedings of the 3rd international conference on face and gesture recognition, April 1998, pp 124–129
46. Nealen A, Igarashi T, Sorkine O, Alexa M (2006) Laplacian mesh optimization. In: Proceedings of the 4th international conference on computer graphics and interactive techniques in Australasia and Southeast Asia, November 2006, pp 381–389
47. Smiths TF, Waterman MS (1981) Identification of common molecular subsequences. J Mol Biol 147(1):195–197
48. Fjeld M, Fredriksson J, Ejdestig M, Duca F, Boschi K, Voegtli B, Juchli P (2007) Tangible user interface for chemistry education. In: Conference on human factors in computing systems, April 2007, pp 805–808

Index

A
Application, 109–111, 118–121, 123–125, 133, 134

B
Background-oriented Schlieren, 159
Blind, 173–181, 183, 187, 190, 191

C
3D cameras, 9, 11–14, 16, 21, 23, 24
Contour model, 291, 294, 301, 302, 305, 310

D
Data fusion, 99
Depth, 215–219, 221, 229, 233, 236
Depth camera calibration, 49
Depth camera distortion model, 19, 49, 111
Depth map enhancement, 66, 70
Depth sensors, 17, 19
Depth-context feature, 240, 243, 246, 248
Distance transform, 65, 66, 70, 71, 257

E
Energy consumption, 120, 121, 123–125

F
Fast classification, 282
Feature extraction, 216, 225, 226, 232
Flow capturing, 158

G
Gas capturing, 159

Gesture recognition, 215–218, 220, 221, 229, 232, 235, 236, 239–241, 243, 257, 258, 262

H
Hand gesture, 290–294, 301, 303, 308, 310
Hand parsing, 240–243, 249, 250, 258–260
Hand pose recognition, 269, 270
Human action, 126, 127, 134
Human performance capture, 91, 93, 106
Human reentry identification, 195, 199
Human–computer interaction, 290, 291, 307

I
Interference, 28, 31, 34–36, 92, 95, 97, 105

J
Joint bilateral filter, 7, 11, 66

K
Kinect, 27, 28, 31, 34–37, 39–41, 48, 49, 53–56, 61, 92–99, 102–106, 216–218
Kinect datasets, 111, 121, 132

M
Markerless motion capture, 31, 93, 241, 242
Markov random field, 240, 241, 243, 250
Matching of 3D curves, 137
Matching of depth images, 140, 141
Multiple kinects, 94, 105
Multiple RGB-D sensor setups, 31

O

3D object matching, 148
3D object retrieval, 138, 148, 150
Object category recognition, 268–270
Object feature points, 141, 143, 146, 148, 149, 153
Object recognition, 13, 37, 137, 139, 140, 174, 179

R

RGB-D camera, 110, 174, 175, 179–181, 183, 185–187, 189, 191
Random decision forest, 240, 248, 249
Real human reconstruction, 110
Real-time tracking, 205, 209
RGB-D, 92, 94, 96–100
RGB-D sensor, 291

S

Semi-automatic labeling, 291, 297, 310

Signal Processing, 28
Structured light, 3, 6, 10–13, 16, 19, 20, 24
Supervised learning, 268
SVM, 215–217, 232, 233

T

Time of flight, 3, 6, 9, 11–13, 16–18, 20, 22, 24

V

Visual signature, 198, 199, 209
Visually impaired, 173–175, 177, 179–181, 185, 187, 190

W

Wayfinding and navigation, 174, 177, 190, 191

The manufacturer's authorised representative in the EU is Springer Nature Customer Service Centre GmbH, Europaplatz 3, 69115 Heidelberg, Germany. If you have any concerns regarding our products, please contact ProductSafety@springernature.com

Printed and bound by CPI Group (UK) Ltd, Croydon, CR0 4YY

23/03/2026

02076658-0002